THE DAVIDIC DYNASTY TRADITION
IN EARLY JUDAISM

SOCIETY OF BIBLICAL LITERATURE

EARLY JUDAISM AND ITS LITERATURE

Series Editor
William Adler

Number 07

THE DAVIDIC DYNASTY TRADITION IN EARLY JUDAISM
Its History and Significance for Messianism

by
Kenneth E. Pomykala

THE DAVIDIC DYNASTY TRADITION IN EARLY JUDAISM

Its History and Significance for Messianism

by
Kenneth E. Pomykala

Scholars Press
Atlanta, Georgia

THE DAVIDIC DYNASTY TRADITION
IN EARLY JUDAISM
Its History and Significance for Messianism

by
Kenneth E. Pomykala

© 1995
Society of Biblical Literature

Library of Congress Cataloging-in-Publication Data
Pomykala, Kenneth E.
    The Davidic dynasty tradition in early Judaism : its history and
significance for Messianism / by Kenneth E. Pomykala.
        p.   cm. — (Early Judaism and its literature ; no. 07)
    Includes bibliographical references and index.
    ISBN 0-7885-0068-6 (cloth). — ISBN 0-7885-0069-4 (pbk.)
    1. Messiah—Judaism— History of doctrines. 2. Judaism—History—
Post-exilic period, 586 B.C.–210 A.D. 3. David, King of Israel—
Family. 4. Bible. O.T.—Criticism, interpretation, etc. 5. Dead
Sea scrolls—Criticism, interpretation, etc. I. Title.
II. Series.
BM615.P59   1995
296.3'3—dc20   94-41342
                                          CIP

Printed in the United States of America
on acid-free paper

To the memory of my father

and

To my mother

Table of Contents

Preface xi
Abbreviations xiii

CHAPTER 1: Introduction 1
  A. Scope of the Present Study 2
  B. Reasons for the Present Study..3
  C. Purpose and Plan 8

CHAPTER 2: The Biblical Background..11
  A. Introduction 11
  B. Pre-exilic Traditions..12
    1. Texts in the Deuteronomistic History...12
    2. Texts in the Psalms...15
    3. Texts in Prophetic Literature...17
    4. Non-davidic Royal Traditions..22
    5. Summary 24
  C. Exilic Traditions 25
    1. Ezekiel 25
    2. Exilic Traditions in Jeremiah 32
    3. Exilic Edition of the Deuteronomistic History 34
    4. Isaiah 55:3–5..38
    5. Summary 41
  D. Post-exilic Traditions...42
    1. Jeremiah 33:14–26 42
    2. Haggai 2:20–23 45
    3. Zechariah 1–8...53

4. Amos 9:11–15 61
5. Jeremiah 17:19–27 63
6. Summary 66
E. Significance of the Background 67

CHAPTER 3: Texts from the Late Persian Period.....................................69
A. 1–2 Chronicles 69
1. History of the Question...69
2. The Extent and Date of the Chronicler's Work 77
a. Extent 77
b. Date 81
3. Internal Evidence..88
a. The Dynastic Oracle 88
b. Other Narrative Evidence 97
c. 1 Chronicles 3:17–24 104
d. The Function of the Davidic Dynasty Tradition in Chronicles 107
4. Summary and Conclusion 110
B. Zechariah 12:2–13:1 112
1. Introduction...112
2. Analysis of Zechariah 12:2–13:1 113
a. Literary Context, Integrity, and Structure...................................113
b. Interpretation...116
c. The House of David..117
d. Date 123
3. Conclusion 124

CHAPTER 4: Texts From the Hellenistic and Roman Periods: Part I...............127
A. The Septuagint..128
B. The Wisdom of Jesus Ben Sira...131
1. 45:25 132
2. Other Texts in the Hymn in Praise of the Fathers 144
3. Lines 8 and 9 of a Psalm in a Hebrew Edition................................148
4. Summary 150
C. 1 Maccabees 2:57 152
D. Psalms of Solomon 17 159

CHAPTER 5: Texts From the Hellenistic and Roman Periods: Part II.............171
  A. Qumran Literature 171
    1. 4QDibHam^a 1/2 4:6–8 172
    2. 4QpGen^a 5:1–7 180
    3. 4QFlorilegium 1:10–13..191
    4. 4QpIsa^a 8–10:11–24 197
    5. 4QSerek HaMilhamah 5:1–6 203
    6. The Davidic Messiah at Qumran...212
  B. 4 Ezra 12:32 216
  C. Josephus 222

CHAPTER 6: Davidic Figures and Other Royal Messianic Figures 231
  A. Royal Messiahs at Qumran 232
  B. The Messiah of Judah in the Testaments of the Twelve Patriarchs...........246
  C. Other Royal Messiahs and Models of Jewish Kingship 255
    1. Sibylline Oracles 3 256
    2. Popular Messianic Figures in Palestine 258
  D. Conclusion 264

CHAPTER 7: Summary and Conclusion...265

Bibliography..273
Indexes..295

Preface

This book is a moderately revised version of my doctoral dissertation submitted to The Claremont Graduate School in 1992. The most extensive revisions were required in sections dealing with Qumran literature because of newly released texts pertaining to the davidic dynasty tradition. In particular, 4QSerek HaMilhamah and portions of 4QpGen[a] were not available for analysis in my dissertation, but have proven valuable in filling out the picture of how the davidic dynasty tradition functioned at Qumran. Moreover, I have tried to take account of the ever burgeoning secondary literature on the Dead Sea Scrolls. Other significant changes reflected in the present work include a separate section on the Septuagint, rearrangement of some materials, and updated notes and bibliography, not to mention a host of minor alterations.

A number of people have helped bring this study to fruition. Thus, I wish to express my gratitude to my advisor, Professor James A. Sanders (Claremont), who first introduced me to the study of biblical interpretation in early Judaism, and whose help and encouragement I have valued. Thanks also go to Professor Burton L. Mack (Claremont) for his encouragement to pursue this topic and for his many helpful comments during the dissertation stage. I am grateful as well both to Professor William A. Beardslee (Claremont) and to my outside examiner, Professor Lewis M. Barth (Hebrew Union College—Jewish Institute of Religion, Los Angeles), whose careful reading of my dissertation yielded many helpful comments. Furthermore, I want to thank my fellow students at The Claremont Graduate School, who in numerous conversations stimulated and clarified my thinking on the subject considered here, especially in the initial phase of my work. But of course I take full responsibility for the contents of this book.

In addition, I am grateful to Early Judaism and Its Literature for accepting my manuscript into this series. In particular, I wish to thank the series editor, William Adler, for his cordial help and advice in bringing this work to publication. Also, I want to communicate my appreciation to Calvin College for granting me a Calvin Research Fellowship for the summer of 1993, which allowed me to concentrate on making necessary revisions to my manuscript. And I wish to acknowledge the Ancient Biblical Manuscript Center, Claremont, CA, for promptly supplying me with transparencies of Qumran texts not available in published works.

Finally, I want to express my thanks and affection to my family: to my wife, Teresa, for her patience and support in what has become a rather lengthy project; and to my children, Taylor, Kaitlyn, and Logan, whose lives help me remember the relative value of what is contained between these covers.

This book, like the dissertation, is dedicated to the memory of my father, Thaddeus Pomykala, whose interest in history I take to be the source of my own interest in that subject, and to my mother, Ruth Pomykala, whose love and support have never gone unnoticed.

Kenneth Pomykala
Grand Rapids, MI
September 1994

Abbreviations

AB	Anchor Bible
AGJU	Arbeiten zur Geschichte des antiken Judentums und des Urchristentums
ASV	American Standard Version
ATAT	Arbeiten zu Text und Sprache im Alten Testament
ATD	Das Alte Testament Deutsch
BA	*Biblical Archaeologist*
BARev	*Biblical Archaeology Review*
BBB	Bonner biblische beiträge
BDB	Brown, F., S. R. Driver, and C. A. Briggs, ed. *A Hebrew and English Lexicon of the Old Testament*. Oxford: Clarendon, 1907.
BELT	Bibliotheca ephemeridum theologicarum lovaniensium
BHS	*Biblia Hebraica Stuttgartensia*
BHT	Beiträge zur historischen Theologie
Bib	*Biblica*
BibOr	Biblica et orientalia
BIOSCS	*Bulletin for the International Organization for Septuagint and Cognate Studies*
BJS	Brown Judaic Studies
CBC	Cambridge Bible Commentary
CBQ	*Catholic Biblical Quarterly*
CBQMS	Catholic Biblical Quarterly—Monograph Series
CRINT	Compendia Rerum Iudaicarum ad Novum Testamentum
CTM	*Concordia Theological Monthly*
DJD	Discoveries in the Judaean Desert
FRLANT	Forschungen zur Religion und Literatur des Alten und Neuen Testaments
GCS	Griechischen christlichen Schriftsteller
HAT	Handbuch zum Alten Testament
HBT	*Horizons in Biblical Theology*
HDR	Harvard Dissertations in Religion
HSM	Harvard Semitic Monographs
HSS	Harvard Semitic Series
HTR	*Harvard Theological Review*
HTR	Harvard Theological Studies
HUCA	*Hebrew Union College Annual*
ICC	International Critical Commentary
IEJ	*Israel Exploration Journal*

JB	Jerusalem Bible
JBL	*Journal of Biblical Literature*
JJS	*Journal of Jewish Studies*
JSJ	*Journal for the Study of Judaism in the Persian, Hellenistic and Roman Period*
JSNTSup	Journal for the Study of the New Testament—Supplement Series
JSOT	*Journal for the Study of the Old Testament*
JSOTSup	Journal for the Study of the Old Testament—Supplement Series
JSP	*Journal for the Study of the Pseudepigrapha*
JSPSup	Journal for the Study of the Pseudepigrapha—Supplement Series
JTS	*Journal of Theological Studies*
Judaica	*Judaica: Beiträge zum Verständnis …*
KAT	Kommentar zum Alten Testament
KB	Köhler, L. H. and W. Baumgartner. *Lexicon in Veteris Testamenti Libros.* 2 vols. Leiden: Brill 1948–1953.
KJV	King James Version
LCL	Loeb Classical Library
LSL	Liddel, H. G., R. Scott, and H. S. Jones. *A Greek-English Lexicon, with a Supplement.* Oxford: Clarendon, 1968.
LTQ	*Lexington Theological Quarterly*
LXX	Septuagint
MT	Masoretic Text
NCB	New Century Bible
NEB	New English Bible
Neot	*Neotestementica*
NIV	New International Version
NovT	*Novum Testamentum*
NovTSup	Novum Testamentum, Supplements
NTL	New Testament Library
NTS	*New Testament Studies*
OTL	Old Testament Library
OTS	Outestamentische Studiën
PVTG	Pseudepigrapha Veteris Testamenti graece
RB	*Revue biblique*
RevQ	*Revue de Qumran*
RSV	Revised Standard Version
RTP	*Revue de théologie et de philosophie*
SBL	Society of Biblical Literature
SBLDS	Society of Biblical Literature Dissertation Series
SBLMS	Society of Biblical Literature Monograph Series
SBLRBS	Society of Biblical Literature Resources for Biblical Study
SBLSCS	Society of Biblical Literature Septuagint and Cognate Studies
SBT	Studies in Biblical Theology
ScrHier	Scripta hierosolymitana
Sem	*Semitica*
SJ	Studia judaica
SNTSMS	Society for New Testament Studies Monograph Series
SSN	Studia semitica neerlandica
SSS	Semitic Study Series
STDJ	Studies on the Texts of the Desert of Judah
SVTP	Studia in Veteris Testamenti pseudepigrapha

TTZ	*Trierer theologische Zeitschrift*
TynBul	*Tyndale Bulletin*
TZ	*Theologische Zeitschrift*
VT	*Vetus Testamentum*
VTSup	Vetus Testamentum, Supplements
WBC	Word Biblical Commentary
WMANT	Wissenschaftliche Monographien zum Alten und Neuen Testament
WUNT	Wissenschaftliche Untersuchungen des Neuen Testament
ZAW	*Zeitschrift für die alttestamentliche Wissenschaft*

CHAPTER 1
Introduction

It is a commonplace to say that Second Temple Jewish writers regularly drew upon biblical traditions and texts to express their own ideas. That they did is fully evident in early Jewish documents included in the Apocrypha and Pseudepigrapha, as well as in the writings from Qumran, Philo, and Josephus. Moreover, biblical traditions and texts were not merely cited, but interpreted and often transformed in order to meet the demands of new situations and problems entirely different from those originally addressed in the text. When earlier biblical traditions are appropriated within the canonical text, it is usually called intra-biblical exegesis; when biblical texts are appropriated in literature outside the canon, it is often called midrash.[1] In either case, however, the phenomenon is essentially the same: in the imaginative space between the biblical tradition or text and the new historical and social context, authors attempted to express an authoritative message to their contemporary readers.[2] One important biblical tradition is that about the davidic dynasty. The goal of this monograph, therefore, is to examine how the

---

[1]On intra-biblical exegesis, see M. Fishbane, *Biblical Interpretation in Ancient Israel* (Oxford: Clarendon, 1985); on midrash, see R. Bloch, "Midrash," *Approaches to Ancient Judaism: Theory and Practice* (BJS 1; ed. W. S. Green; Missoula, MT: Scholars Press, 1978) 29–50; for further works on midrash, see L. Haas, "Bibliography on Midrash," *The Study of Ancient Judaism I: Mishnah, Midrash, Siddur* (ed. J. Neusner; New York: Ktav, 1981) 93–103.

[2]See especially, J. A. Sanders, "Adaptable for Life: The Nature and Function of Canon," *Magnalia Dei: The Mighty Acts of God* (ed. F. M. Cross, W. E. Lemke, and P. D. Miller, Jr.; Garden City, NY: Doubleday, 1976) 531–560; *Canon and Community* (Philadelphia: Fortress, 1984). Cf. also J. Z. Smith, "Sacred Persistence," *Approaches to Ancient Judaism: Theory and Practice* (BJS 1; ed. W. S. Green; Missoula, MT: Scholars Press, 1978) 11–28; G. Vermes, "Bible and Midrash: Early Old Testament Exegesis," *The Cambridge History of the Bible: Vol I* (ed. P. R. Ackroyd and C. F. Evans; Cambridge: Cambridge University Press, 1970) 199–231; as well as the literature cited in the previous note.

davidic dynasty tradition was interpreted and applied during the period of early Judaism.

A. Scope of the Present Study

It will be helpful at the outset to delineate more fully the two parameters of this study, namely, the davidic dynasty tradition and early Judaism. I mean by the davidic dynasty tradition the complex of ideas and images set forth in biblical texts that speak about a promise or covenant made with David establishing the davidic dynasty, those that describe the nature of the dynasty and its continuance, and those that refer to the future of the davidic line or family or to a future royal figure connected in some way to the davidic promise and dynasty. This definition is thereby meant to exclude from its scope mere references to David, davidic kings, or the davidic kingdom that have no relationship to the davidic promise or dynasty. All plausible references to this davidic dynasty tradition in early Jewish literature will be considered.

As for the meaning of early Judaism, G. W. E. Nickelsburg calls it a "ragged-edged" period for which it is difficult to assign unambiguous chronological lim-its.[3] Indeed, no fixed dates for this era called "early Judaism" exist; therefore, as is true for any so-called historical period, temporal limits must be assigned. In this regard, Nickelsburg makes a plausible case for defining it as the period from 330 BCE to 138 CE, that is, from Alexander the Great's conquest of Palestine-Syria to the Roman Emperor Hadrian.[4] An alternative approach would be to include the entire Second Temple period from ca. 520 BCE to 70 CE. Both of these options are defensible.

Yet one must be willing to accommodate chronological boundaries to the demands of the material under study. Specifically, the book of Chronicles is undoubtedly a rich source for ideas about the interpretation of the davidic dynasty tradition in the late post-exilic period. Below I will argue that its composition is to be dated to ca. 400 BCE. Technically this would place it outside the period of early Judaism as defined by Nickelsburg. But to exclude it from the present study simply because its composition falls outside arbitrary chronological parameters would weaken our understanding of an important stage in the history of the davidic dynasty tradition. On the other hand, to extend the beginning limit of this study to ca. 520 BCE would set before us literature and historical circumstances

---

[3]G. W. E. Nickelsburg with R. A. Kraft, "Introduction: The Modern Study of Early Judaism," *Early Judaism and Its Modern Interpreters* (ed. G. W. E. Nickelsburg and R. A. Kraft; Philadelphia: Fortress/Atlanta: Scholars Press, 1986) 1–2.

[4]Nickelsburg, "Introduction," *Early Judaism*, 2.

quite different from those of the main body of evidence being examined here. Thus, the *terminus a quo* for this study will be ca. 400 BCE.

As for the *terminus ad quem*, a date of 70 CE is reasonable, but it would lop off from our inquiry the writings of Josephus and 4 Ezra. Hence, it seems advisable to set a concluding limit for this study to around the time of the composition of these works, that is, ca. 100 CE. To extend the boundary further would again encroach on literature and circumstances largely distinct from the Judaism before 100 CE. Therefore, in the present work "early Judaism" will refer to the period from ca. 400 BCE to ca. 100 CE.[5]

B. Reasons for the Present Study

One reason for an investigation into the davidic dynasty tradition in early Judaism is the absence of any recent comprehensive treatment of this topic. To be sure, discussion of the present subject is common in works on Second Temple messianism or early Christology. Yet studies like those of Mowinckel and Klausner, though comprehensive, do not focus specifically on davidic messianism and do not take account of Qumran literature.[6] Other studies, such as the chapter on messianism in the revised edition of Schürer,[7] articles by M. de Jonge, E. Lohse, and D. C. Duling,[8] relevant chapters in *Judaisms and Their Messiahs at*

---

[5]Also, I will use Second Temple Judaism as a synonym for this definition of "early Judaism."

[6]S. Mowinckel, *He That Cometh* (Nashville: Abingdon, 1954), Norwegian original published in 1951; J. Klausner, *The Messianic Idea in Israel: From Its Beginning to the Completion of the Mishnah* (New York: Macmillian, 1955), translated from the third Hebrew edition published in 1949. Cf. also J. Liver, *The House of David from the Fall of the Kingdom of Judah to the Fall of the Second Commonwealth and After* [Hebrew, with an English summary] (Jerusalem: Magnes, 1959) 104–148. Although written in Hebrew and not widely accessible, the bulk of Liver's treatment of the early Jewish materials can be found in J. Liver, "The Doctrine of the Two Messiahs in Sectarian Literature in the Time of the Second Commonwealth," *HTR* 52 (1959) 149–185.

[7]E. Schürer, *The History of the Jewish People in the Age of Jesus Christ (175 B.C.–A.D. 135)* (3 vols.; revised English edition; ed. G. Vermes, F. Millar, and M. Black; Edinburgh: T. & T. Clark, 1973–1987) 2:488–554.

[8]M. de Jonge, "The Use of the Word 'Anointed' in the Time of Jesus," *NovT* 8 (1966) 132–148; E. Lohse, "Die König aus Davids Geschlect—Bemerkungen zur messianischen Erwartung der Synagoge," *Abraham unser Vater* (ed. O. Betz, M. Hengel, and P. Schmidt; Leiden: Brill, 1963) 337–345; D. C. Duling, "The Promises to David and Their Entrance into Christianity—Nailing Down a Hypothesis," *NTS* 20 (1973) 55–77, which summarizes Duling's unpublished dissertation, "Traditions of the Promises to David and His Sons in Early Judaism and Primitive Christianity," (Ph.D. dissertation, University of Chicago, 1970). This last work comes closest to representing a comprehensive study, offering a detailed treatment of nearly half of the relevant texts from the early Jewish period.

the *Turn of the Christian Era* and *The Messiah*,[9] as well as "Jewish background" sections in works on Christology,[10] tend to be general in their approach to the data or limited in scope. There is, therefore, a need for a comprehensive and detailed examination of the meaning and function of the davidic dynasty tradition in early Judaism.

A second reason for the present study is that it attempts to depart from some of the assumptions and methodological presuppositions of previous work. Most importantly, discussion of the meaning and function of the davidic dynasty tradition in early Judaism has often taken place within the context of the assumption that Second Temple Judaism was characterized by a widespread, continuous, and dominant expectation for a davidic messiah, the Son of David.[11] No doubt this assumption about what may be called a "traditional" davidic hope derives from the prominence of the title "Son of David" in the New Testament[12] and the presence of davidic messianism in rabbinic Judaism.[13] But of course ideas from

---

[9]*Judaisms and Their Messiahs at the Turn of the Christian Era* (ed. J. Neusner, W. S. Green, and E. S. Frerichs; Cambridge: Cambridge University Press, 1987); *The Messiah* (ed. J. H. Charlesworth; Minneapolis: Fortress, 1992).

[10]F. Hahn, *The Titles of Jesus in Christology* (London: Lutterworth, 1969) 136–148; R. H. Fuller, *The Foundations of New Testament Christology* (New York: Scribner's Sons, 1965) 23–31,33–34,65; O. Cullmann, *The Christology of the New Testament* (NTL; rev. ed.; Philadelphia: Westminster, 1963) 113–117; G. Vermes, *Jesus the Jew* (London: Collins, 1973) 130–134; C. Burger, *Jesus als Davidssohn* (FRLANT 98; Göttingen: Vandenhoeck & Ruprecht, 1970) 16–24.

[11]This view is widely held. Besides the works in the previous note, see, for example, Lohse, "Die König," 337; Mowinckel, *He That Cometh*, 159–162, 286–291; Klausner, *Messianic Idea*, 250; Schürer, *History*, 2:518–519; M. E. Stone, *Scripture, Sects, and Visions* (Philadelphia: Fortress, 1980) 76; L. H. Schiffman, *The Eschatological Community of the Dead Sea Scrolls* (SBLMS 38; Atlanta: Scholars Press, 1989) 1; I. M. Zeitlin, *Jesus and the Judaism of His Time* (Cambridge: Polity, 1988) 39; R. N. Longenecker, *The Christology of Early Jewish Christianity* (SBT 2/17; London: SCM, 1970) 109; J. O'Dell, "The Religious Background of the Psalms of Solomon (Re-evaluated in the Light of the Qumran Texts)," *RevQ* 3 (1961) 249; along with many works cited in the body of this study.

[12]Mark 10:47–48; Matt 1:1–17; 9:27; 15:22; 21:9,15; Luke 1:32; 2:4; 3:23–38; Acts 13:22–23; Rom 1:3–4; Rev 5:5; 22:16.

[13]For references to the messiah as Son of David in the Babylonian Talmud, see G. Dalman, *The Words of Jesus* (Edinburgh: T. & T. Clark, 1909) 317; on the davidic messiah in rabbinic thought, see also J. Neusner, *Messiah in Context* (Philadelphia: Fortress, 1984) 175,187–191; Klausner, *Messianic Idea*, 459–462; on davidic messianism in the Targums, see S. H. Levey, *The Messiah: An Aramaic Interpretation* (Cincinnati: Hebrew Union College Press, 1974), esp. p. 142; for an example of Jewish davidic messianic hopes in the second century CE, see Hippolytus (ca. 170–235 CE), *Ref. omn. haer.* 9.30 (quoted in Schürer, *History*, 2:512–513). There are, however, no references to a davidic messiah in the Mishnah (see J. Neusner, "Mishnah and Messiah," *Judaisms and Their Messiahs at the Turn of the Christian Era* [ed. J.

early Christianity and rabbinic Judaism cannot serve as a barometer for Jewish expectations in the Second Temple period.

Moreover, there are two initial reasons why the assumption of a widespread, continuous, and dominant expectation for a davidic messiah in early Judaism should be called into question. On the one hand, there has been increasing acknowledgment among scholars that early Judaism was much more diverse than previously thought.[14] Moreover, this diversity extended to the types of messianic figures that played a role in Second Temple thought.[15] Consequently, the expectation of a messianic Son of David must be placed without prejudice alongside expectations of other messianic figures whether priestly, prophetic, royal, or angelic.

A second reason against a putative "traditional" davidic hope is the relative infrequency of texts that attest to such a hope in early Jewish literature outside the New Testament.[16] The first explicit expression of hope for a davidic messiah is in *Pss. Sol.* 17, which dates from the middle of the first century BCE. References to the davidic kings or dynasty in Chronicles, Ben Sira, and other works certainly show interest in the davidic dynasty tradition, and are often cited superficially in support of a tradition of davidic messianism, but these passages may not reveal an expectation for a davidic figure. In addition, neither Josephus nor Philo mentions such an expectation. In fact, one finds some six passages in early Jewish literature that clearly attest to an anticipated davidic messiah, four of which come from Qumran literature.[17] The paucity of references suggests, therefore, that a wide-

---

Neusner, W. S. Green, and E. S. Frerichs; Cambridge: Cambridge University Press, 1987] 269–270).

[14]See Stone, *Scripture, Sects, and Visions*, for a illuminating portrait of early Judaism's variegated landscape; also, G. G. Porton, "Diversity in Postbiblical Judaism," *Early Judaism and Its Modern Interpreters* (ed. G. W. E. Nickelsburg and R. A. Kraft; Philadelphia: Fortress/Atlanta: Scholars Press, 1986) 57–80.

[15]Cf. for example, S. Talmon, "Types of Messianic Expectation at the Turn of the Era," *King, Cult and Calendar: Collected Studies* (Jerusalem: Magnes, 1986) 202–224; and the title of the recent collection of essays on early Jewish messianism: *Judaisms and Their Messiahs at the Turn of the Christian Era.*

[16]J. J. Collins, *The Apocalyptic Imagination* (New York: Crossroad, 1984) 113; and M. de Jonge, "The Expectation of the Future in the Psalms of Solomon," *Neotestamentica* 23 (1989) 101, make a similar observation. Furthermore, I am assuming that references to other royal messianic figures should not immediately be taken as references to a davidic figure unless textual evidence supports that identification (see below, chap. 6).

[17]Rabbinic references to a davidic messiah from the second century CE are not particularly common either; for instance, there are none in the Mishnah (see above n. 13).

spread, continuous, and dominant expectation for a davidic messiah should not be presumed from the outset.[18]

In contrast to this assessment, G. Vermes, although quite aware of the pluriform speculation about messianic figures in the Second Temple period and the limited textual evidence for a specifically davidic messiah, nevertheless maintains that hope directed toward a Son of David was the general expectation of Palestinian Jewry.[19] He bases his view on the presence of a Son of David expectation in "the least academic, and at the same time most normative, literary form: prayer."[20] Specifically, he points to *Pss. Sol.* 17 and the Eighteen Benedictions. Moreover, he claims that the *Psalms of Solomon* represent "mainstream Jewish religious ideology."[21]

There are, however, several weaknesses to Vermes' argument. First, his claim that the *Psalms of Solomon* represent mainstream Judaism lacks support.[22] Indeed, it is questionable whether one can speak at all about mainstream Judaism during the first century BCE. Secondly, his contention that prayer embodies the non-academic and most normative religious ideology cannot be used to argue that davidic messianism was the dominant expectation among Palestinian Jews. All that can be asserted is that prayer, based on its popular use, may reflect the non-academic and most normative religious ideology *for people who used those prayers*.[23] How widely the *Psalms of Solomon* were used in the Second Temple period is not known. Furthermore, the didactic prayers in the *Psalms of Solomon* probably reflect more the ideas of learned circles than popular ideology.[24]

---

[18]A. Caquot, "Le messianisme qumrânien," *Qumrân: Sa piété, sa théologie et son milieu* (BETL 46; ed. M. Delcor; Paris: Leuven University Press, 1978) 232, states that belief in a perpetual and exclusive davidic messianism in the early Jewish era is a presupposition that has burdened the study of messianism in this period.

[19]Vermes, *Jesus the Jew*, 130.

[20]Vermes, *Jesus the Jew*, 130.

[21]Vermes, *Jesus the Jew*, 130.

[22]The community associated with the *Psalms of Solomon* is not certain, although a good case can be made for the Pharisees; but Pharisaical ideology cannot be labelled "mainstream Jewish" in the first century BCE.

[23]Similarly, prayers from Qumran often embody ideas particular to the Qumran community; no one would claim that these prayers, simply because they are prayers, reflect "mainstream Jewish ideology."

[24]Cf. D. Flusser, "Psalms, Hymns and Prayers," *Jewish Writings of the Second Temple Period* (CRINT 2:2; Assen: Van Gorcum/Philadelphia: Fortress, 1984) 573, who writes, "It is difficult to assume that they were written for liturgical purposes or later became part of any liturgy." Cf. also R. A. Horsley and J. S. Hanson, *Bandits, Prophets, and Messiahs* (San Francisco: Harper & Row, 1985) 102–106, who attribute *Psalms of Solomon* to learned groups.

Thirdly, whether the lines in the Eighteen Benedictions that speak of a davidic messiah even date from the first century CE cannot be demonstrated.[25] While the number, sequence, and general subject matter of various benedictions may emanate from the end of the first century CE, the precise wording for each benediction remained fluid, even into the Amoraic period; nor can any *Ur-text* be reconstructed.[26] Consequently, since the Eighteen Benedictions cannot be counted as a witness to use of the davidic dynasty tradition within the early Jewish period, they provide a shaky foundation for the assumption of a dominant davidic hope at this time.[27] Finally, other evidence about popular religious sentiment in the early Jewish period, such as one finds in Josephus, makes no mention of a dominant expectation for a davidic messiah.[28]

Yet, it is not my purpose at this point to argue against a "traditional" davidic hope, but only to call into question the assumption of one. A reasoned judgment about the status of davidic messianic expectations in early Judaism can only be offered after a full consideration of the relevant textual and historical data. The point here is that in my analysis of that data I will not presuppose a widespread, continuous, or dominant expectation for a Son of David. When a passage does express hope for a davidic messiah, I will assume that this was not done as a matter of course, because it was traditional, but rather that it was cited with particular intention, because the concept of a davidic messiah would carry with it connotations and overtones that other messianic designations did not. Indeed, what its conceptual content included and what its particular intention was are important interests of this study.

The absence of an assumption of a "traditional" davidic messianic hope is an important departure from previous studies, because this assumption has in effect acted as a lens through which the texts dealing with the davidic dynasty tradition have been viewed—a lens that has, in my judgment, often prejudiced the analysis of these texts. This observation points to two other methodological problems the present study intends to avoid.

First, most discussion of the davidic dynasty tradition in early Judaism has taken place within the framework of the larger subject of messianism—whether

---

[25]For an English translation of the relevant benedictions, see Schürer, *History*, 2:461. In the Palestinian version, see Benediction 14; in the Babylonian, see Benedictions 14 and 15.

[26]J. Heinemann, *Prayer in the Talmud* (SJ 9; Berlin: De Gruyter, 1977) 48–50,219–221.

[27]Note again that mention of a davidic messiah is not present in the Mishnah, the earliest document in rabbinic literature (ca. 200 CE). This seems unusual if the daily prayers of Jews beginning in the Second Temple period included a request for the davidic messiah.

[28]See below, chap. 6.

Jewish or Christian. This tends, however, to limit from the outset one's interpretive options about the possible ways in which the davidic dynasty tradition may have functioned. Specifically, all references to that tradition need not have been oriented toward hope for a messianic figure; reference to the davidic dynasty tradition could serve other functions. By not assuming that the davidic dynasty tradition always functioned "messianically," this study allows for a methodological approach that is open to a diversity of functions for the davidic dynasty tradition in the literature of early Judaism. And as I will argue below, the davidic dynasty tradition was used in very different ways.

Secondly, when considering texts where the davidic dynasty tradition is used in connection with a davidic messianic figure, a number of previous studies have employed a methodological approach that has tended to combine several references to a davidic figure, each with its own particular contours, into a synthetic depiction of this figure which exists in no individual text.[29] Hence, one has spoken of *the* Son of David or *the* davidic hope. This, however, has suggested a uniform portrait of a davidic messiah and obscured both the individual characterizations of davidic figures found in these passages and the specific functions of these characterizations within their literary context. In contrast to this synthetic approach, the present study will investigate each text about a davidic messiah in its own integrity and not assume a uniform expectation for a davidic messianic figure. If connections exist between the various characterizations of a davidic messiah, they will be noted.

Accordingly, this examination of the davidic dynasty tradition in early Judaism is meant to be a detailed and comprehensive treatment of the topic that avoids the methodological problems of previous work.

C. Purpose and Plan

There are two main purposes of the present study. The first is to offer a history of the davidic dynasty tradition in early Judaism. The second is to evaluate whether there existed in this period a widespread, continuous, dominant, or uniform expectation for a davidic messiah. In order to accomplish these purposes, I will first offer a thorough review of the davidic dynasty tradition in the biblical tradition prior to the late Persian period. Then I will investigate each early Jewish text that makes a plausible reference to the davidic dynasty tradition to ascertain its specific content and particular function within its own literary context and socio-historical setting. This investigation will be undertaken in accordance with the

---

[29]See for example Lohse, "Die König," *passim*; Vermes, *Jesus the Jew*, 130–134; Schürer, *History*, 2:518–519; Mowinckel, *He That Cometh*, 286–291.

methodological approach sketched in the previous section. Moreover, for each text special attention will be given to the question of whether it offers evidence for a davidic messianic hope.

This study will pursue the following plan. Chapter 2 will examine the biblical background of the davidic dynasty tradition up to the late Persian period, focusing particularly on exilic and post-exilic texts. Chapter 3 will take up the use of this tradition during the late Persian period in Chronicles and Zechariah. In chapters 4 and 5, the content and function of the davidic dynasty tradition in Jewish texts from the Hellenistic and Roman periods will be investigated. Here passages from the Septuagint, Ben Sira, 1 Maccabees, *Psalms of Solomon*, Qumran literature, 4 Ezra, and Josephus will be studied. Chapter 6 will deal with the question of the relationship between davidic messianic figures and other royal messianic figures known from Second Temple history and literature, such as the Messiah of Israel, mentioned in Qumran texts, and the Messiah of Judah, known from the *Testaments of the Twelve Patriarchs*. Finally, chapter 7 will summarize the evidence and state my conclusions.

CHAPTER 2
The Biblical Background

A. Introduction

The tradition of a divinely ordained ongoing davidic dynasty is attested in many biblical texts. Accordingly, these passages provided the context for reflection for authors in the Second Temple period who sought to appropriate the davidic dynasty tradition to their own historical and social context. It will be helpful, therefore, to survey these texts, since several of them exerted a significant influence upon the language and ideas used by authors of early Jewish texts. The chief goal of this part of our study will be to analyze what conception of the davidic dynasty and davidic figures is presented in the various texts. For this purpose, it is unnecessary—nor is it feasible—to address all the historical-critical problems connected with these passages; they need not be solved for understanding how writers in the Second Temple period appropriated the concepts and language of these texts. Early Jewish interpreters did not analyze these passages according to modern critical methods, but perceived them synchronically as traditional writings within sacred scriptures. In other words, they perceived the Bible as a "flat text."

    A second aim of this survey will be to give special attention to exilic and post-exilic biblical passages. On the one hand, whereas pre-exilic passages about the davidic dynasty would have functioned in some way to legitimate a sitting davidic king, the exilic and early post-exilic passages offer an indication of how some tradents attempted to carry forward or transform the davidic dynasty tradition at a time when there was no davidic king on the throne of Israel. This latter situation parallels that of Jews in the late Persian, Hellenistic, and Roman periods, who would likewise utilize the davidic dynasty tradition in the absence of a davidic king. Moreover, the exilic and early post-exilic texts are the nearest precursors for ideas about davidic figures and the davidic dynasty in the late

11

Persian period and beyond. It will be important, therefore, to observe what understanding of the davidic dynasty tradition existed in the time just prior to the early Jewish period. Thus, exilic and early post-exilic passages will require more detailed examination.

This second purpose, however, requires us to enter into the problem of dating these passages—a problem that could lead us far afield from the basic issues at stake in this survey. In light of this, the following procedure will be pursued. The survey is organized in broadly chronological order according to the pre-exilic, exilic, and post-exilic eras (up to the late Persian period). Since it is often easy to assign a passage within these broad historical categories, establishing the date of each text becomes less of an issue. When texts have special problems regarding their date or setting, the question will be taken up when the passage is reviewed. But even then, I recognize that in light of the often wide spectrum of possible dates put forward by scholars for some texts, any dating arrived at in this review must ultimately remain tentative. Yet, this should pose no difficulty for the results of this chapter, for the goal we are seeking is not a precise history of davidic dynasty tradition in the Hebrew Bible. Rather, our intent is to review the conception of the davidic dynasty and davidic figures in the biblical material in order to illuminate in a general way the language and symbols, as well as interpretive strategies, available to later Jewish writers when they reflected on the davidic dynasty tradition. For this purpose, a general approach to questions of dating will be sufficient. At the end of each subsection, I will summarize the data, and at the conclusion of the chapter, I will discuss its significance for our treatment of the early Jewish material.

B. Pre-exilic Traditions

Beginning then with pre-exilic passages, I will treat these under four rubrics: 1) texts in the Deuteronomistic History; 2) texts in the Psalms; 3) texts in the prophetic literature; 4) texts about non-davidic kingship.

1. Texts in the Deuteronomistic History

Although the final edition of the Deuteronomistic History (Dtr) was composed during the exile, sometime after 560 BCE, almost all the traditions concerning the davidic monarchy incorporated into it are of pre-exilic origin. Thus, they will be dealt with presently. The attitude of the final editors of Dtr toward the davidic dynasty and its continuance will be addressed below in the section treating exilic texts.[1]

---

[1] See F. M. Cross, *Canaanite Myth and Hebrew Epic* (Cambridge, MA: Harvard University

Of primary importance for the davidic dynasty tradition is 2 Sam 7:11b–16, Nathan's oracle to David that the Lord would make for David a house (בית יעשׂה־ לך יהוה) [v. 11b]. Specifically, after David's death, God promised to raise up his seed (הקימתי את־זרעך) after him, one who would build the temple, and establish the throne of his kingdom forever (עד־עולם) [vv. 12–13]. Moreover, the Lord would be a father to him and he a son to the Lord (v. 14), thus establishing a filial relationship between God and davidic kings. When he commits sin, there will be temporal punishment, but God will not take his steadfast love (חסד) from him (vv. 14b–15). "And your house and your kingdom shall be made sure for ever before me; your throne shall be established for ever" (v. 16).[2] Here, then, is the promise of an everlasting davidic dynasty, free of conditions.[3]

Several passages in 1–2 Kings, although not always citing the dynastic promise specifically, appear to presuppose it and assert the ongoing nature of davidic rule. For instance, the prophecy concerning the division of the kingdoms in 1 Kings 11 states that in spite of Solomon's apostasy, the Lord would not take the entire kingdom from Solomon's son, but leave one tribe to him for David's sake (1 Kgs 11:12,13,32,34–36). 1 Kgs 11:34–36 captures the idea:

> Nevertheless I will not take the whole kingdom out of his (Solomon's) hand; but I will make him ruler all the days of his life, for the sake of David my servant (למען דוד עבדי) whom I chose, who kept my commandments and my statutes ... to his son I will give one tribe, that David my servant may always have a lamp before me in Jerusalem, the city where I have chosen to put my name.

Press, 1973) 219–289, for a discussion of the redactional history of Dtr. Although Cross' theory of two editions of Dtr may not capture all the complexity of its redactional history (see P. R. Ackroyd, "The Historical Literature," *The Hebrew Bible and Its Modern Interpreters* [ed. D. A. Knight and G. M. Tucker; Chico, CA: Scholars Press, 1985] 300–305; R. Rendtorff, *The Old Testament: An Introduction* [Philadelphia: Fortress, 1986] 183–187), for the davidic dynasty material his hypothesis comports well with the data. For a different view, see T. Veijola, *Die Ewige Dynastie* (Annale Academiae Scientiarum Fennicae, Ser. B 193; Helsinki: Academia Scientiarum Fennica, 1975), who presupposes Dietrich's redactional hypothesis (W. Dietrich, *Prophetie und Geschichte: Eine redaktionsgeschichtliche Untersuchung zum deuteronomistischen Geschichtswerk* [FRLANT 108; Göttingen: Vandenhoeck & Ruprecht, 1972]). For a critique of Dietrich—and thereby Veijola—see A. D. H. Mayes, *The Story of Israel between Settlement and Exile* (London: SCM, 1983) 113–120.

[2]Ordinarily biblical quotations are taken or adapted from the Revised Standard Version.

[3]It should be noted that it is possible to read the Lord's promise not to withdraw his steadfast love, but only to impose temporal punishment, as applying only to David's son who would build the temple, Solomon. But it just as easily can be read to apply to all future davidic kings, undoubtedly the reading of the Judean royal ideology (see Psalm 89).

This metaphor of leaving a lamp for David in Jerusalem appears in 1 Kgs 15:4 and 2 Kgs 8:19, the latter text specifically alluding to a dynastic promise:

> Yet the Lord would not destroy Judah, for the sake of David his servant, since he promised (אמר) to give a lamp to him and to his sons for ever.

In contrast to this understanding of the davidic dynasty as everlasting without condition, Dtr also contains traditions that impose conditions on the davidic monarchy if it is to continue. For example, in David's charge to Solomon in 1 Kgs 2:1–4, he tells his son to keep the commandments in the law of Moses

> that the Lord may establish his word which he spoke (דבר) concerning me saying, "If your sons take heed to their way, to walk before me in faithfulness with all their heart and with all their soul, there shall not fail you a man on the throne of Israel (v. 4).

Similarly, in Solomon's prayer at the temple dedication, he entreats,

> Now therefore, O Lord, God of Israel, keep with thy servant David my father what thou hast promised (דברת) him, saying, "There shall never fail you a man before me to sit upon the throne of Israel, if only your sons take heed to their way, to walk before me as you have walked before me" (1 Kgs 8:25).

And in the divine response to Solomon's prayer in 1 Kgs 9:3–9, again the perpetuity of the dynasty as promised to David is conditioned upon obedience. What is noteworthy is that in all three of these passages explicit reference is made to the continuing dynasty promised to David, but in each case this promise is understood conditionally, dependent on the obedience of the king.

Finally, in 2 Sam 23:1–7, the last words of David, there is a reference to an everlasting covenant made with David (v. 5).[4] Yet, the nature of this covenant—whether conditional or unconditional—is not elaborated. A conditional understanding may be implied, however, since vv. 3–4 connect just rule (v. 3b) with divine blessings (v. 4).[5] In light of this connection, v. 5 states:

> Yea, does not my house stand so with God? For he has made with me an everlasting covenant (כי ברית עולם שם לי), ordered in all things and secure.

In contrast, vv. 6–7 state that godless men are to be swept away. In any case, the precise terms of the covenant remain ambiguous. Nonetheless, two further features of this text are important. First, the term "covenant" (ברית) is used of the davidic promise only here in Dtr (except for possibly the more general reference

---

[4]See Cross, *Hebrew Epic*, 234–237, for a more detailed treatment of this difficult passage.

[5]Cross, *Hebrew Epic*, 236f.

to God's keeping covenant in 1 Kgs 8:23). Secondly, David is called "the anointed of the God of Jacob" (משיח אלהי יעקב) [v. 1].

2. Texts in the Psalms

Psalm 89 reflects an understanding of the davidic dynasty tradition very similar to that found in 2 Sam 7:11–16, but here, as in 2 Sam 23:5, covenant terminology is used to describe the promise of an everlasting davidic dynasty.[6]

> Thou hast said, "I have made a covenant with my chosen one, I have sworn to David my servant: 'I will establish your descendants (זרעך) for ever (עד־עולם), and build your throne for all generations'" (vv. 4–5).

The central section of the psalm (vv. 20–38) consists of a detailed rehearsal of this promise, given to David in a vision (בחזון) [v. 20]. God commits himself to be with David as his anointed king, securing his victory over enemies (vv. 21–26). Moreover, the relationship between David and the Lord is expressed in filial terms (cf. 2 Sam 7:14):

> He shall cry to me, "Thou art my Father" ... And I will make him the first-born, the highest of the kings of the earth (vv. 27–28).

Further, the future of David's line is based on the Lord's steadfast love for David and secured by covenant (vv. 29–30). The dynastic line, like celestial phenomena, will be everlasting (vv. 30,37–38) because the promise is unconditional; disobedience will be punished, but the royal line continually perpetuated due to God's solemn oath (vv. 31–36) [cf. 2 Sam 7:14b–16]. The final section of the psalm (vv. 39–52) presents an appeal to the Lord to honor his promise to David in the face of some grave crisis in which the davidic king, called the anointed (משיח) [vv. 39,52], has suffered defeat and humiliation.

In contrast to the unconditional dynastic promise in Psalm 89, Psalm 132 reflects an explicitly conditional version of this promise, dependent on the obedience of davidic kings:[7]

---

[6]Older commentators tended to see the crisis mentioned in vv. 39ff as referring to the fall of Jerusalem in 586 BCE and therefore dated this psalm in the exilic or post-exilic period. However, there is no specific allusion to the events of 586 BCE; the crisis probably refers to some earlier defeat (cf. A. Weiser, *The Psalms* [OTL; Philadelphia: Westminster, 1962] 591). The psalm may have been used in a pre-exilic royal coronation liturgy (cf. Cross, *Hebrew Epic*, 252, who also notes the psalm's archaic language [p. 260]) or as a royal lament after a lost battle (cf. S. Mowinckel, *The Psalms in Israel's Worship* [2 vols.; Nashville: Abingdon, 1962] 1:70). On the interpretation of this psalm, see J. L. McKenzie, "Royal Messianism," *CBQ* 19 (1957) 27–31; and N. Sarna, "Psalm 89: A Study in Inner Biblical Exegesis," *Biblical and Other Studies* (ed. A. Altmann; Cambridge: Harvard University Press, 1963) 29–46.

[7]See Cross, *Hebrew Epic*, 232–234, for discussion of vv. 11–12, and Psalm 132 generally.

> The Lord swore to David a sure oath from which he will not turn back: "One of the sons (פרי) of your body I will set on your throne. If your sons keep my covenant and my testimonies which I shall teach them, their sons also for ever shall sit upon your throne" (vv. 11–12).

The terminology used in this psalm deserves attention. The davidic king, as well as David, is called the anointed one (מֹשִׁיח) [vv. 10,17]. Furthermore, it is said that the Lord will make a horn sprout (אצמיח קרן) for David, and prepare a lamp (נר) for him (v. 17). Finally, while the word "covenant" (ברית) occurs (v. 12), it does not refer to the davidic covenant; nor is there any notion of the divine adoption of the king.

On the other hand, in Psalm 2, the filial relationship between the davidic king, designated here "the anointed" (מֹשִׁיח), and the Lord is underlined:

> I will tell of the decree of the Lord: He said to me, "You are my son, today I have begotten you" (ילדתיך) [v. 7].

Although this psalm makes no mention of dynastic continuance, it emphasizes the davidic king's domination over the nations, envisioning universal rule:

> Ask of me, and I will make the nations your heritage, and the ends of the earth your possession. You shall break them with a rod of iron, and dash them in pieces like a potter's vessel (vv. 8–9).

Likewise, Psalm 72 reflects the same hope for world dominion (v. 8), along with other idyllic features that will accompany the reign of a davidic king, such as full justice (vv. 1–4,12–14), peace (v. 7), prosperity (v. 3) and fertility (v. 16).[8] Other psalms express ideas similar to those cited already. Thus, for instance, Ps 18:51 offers thanks:

> Great triumphs he gives to his king, and shows steadfast love to his anointed, to David and his descendants (זרע) forever.

Similarly, Psalm 110 accents the king's victory over enemies and his execution of justice.[9]

---

[8]The ideal vision of earthly davidic kingship in Psalm 72, a psalm undoubtedly part of the pre-exilic royal cult liturgy, should engender suspicion toward any hypothesis that treats ideal pictures of davidic kingship as strictly messianic or eschatological, or characteristic of exilic and post-exilic thinking.

[9]For similar ideas in other royal psalm, see Ps 45:6 and Ps 78:68–72.

3. Texts in Prophetic Literature

Hos 3:4–5 foretells the return of Israel to the Lord their God and David their king after a period in which they would be deprived of political and cultic institutions.[10]

> For the children of Israel shall dwell many days without king or prince, without sacrifice or pillar, without ephod or teraphim. Afterward the children of Israel shall return and seek the Lord their God, and David their king; and they shall come in fear to the Lord and to his goodness in the latter days.

The period of cultic and political deprivation is balanced by a future cultic (seeking the Lord) and political (seeking David their king) restoration. This is the first example of the idea of an ideal Israelite king designated as a type of David (see also Jer 30:9 and Ezek 34:23–24; 37:24–25).[11] Moreover, this return to an ideal king, David, is associated with the reunification of the Northern Kingdom with Judah. A similar conception is present in Hos 2:2 (Eng: 1:11), although this one ruler (ראש) is not specifically designated a davidic king or even a royal figure. In general, then, the future is characterized as life in an ideal (reunited) Israel ruled by an ideal king, like David.

Mic 4:14–5:4a (Eng: 5:1–5a) proclaims that in contrast to the present king now under siege (4:14), a new ruler (מושל) will come forth from Bethlehem Ephrathah (5:1) who will shepherd (רעה) [5:3] Israel.[12] His origins are both

---

[10]The date for this saying is uncertain. Among recent commentators, F. I. Andersen and D. N. Freedman, *Hosea* (AB 24; Garden City, NY: Doubleday, 1980) 307–308; D. K. Stuart, *Hosea-Jonah* (WBC; Waco, TX: Word, 1987) 65–68; and G. I. Emmerson, *Hosea: An Israelite Prophet in Judean Perspective* (JSOTSup 28; Sheffield: JSOT Press, 1984) 102–113, judge this saying to be authentic. H. W. Wolff, *Hosea* (Hermeneia; Philadelphia: Fortress, 1974) 59; J. L. Mays, *Hosea* (OTL; Philadelphia: Westminster, 1969) 60; and G. M. Tucker, "Hosea," *HBC*, 711, consider vv. 4–5 to be authentic with the exception of the phrases "and David their king" and "in the latter days," which are ascribed to a later Judean redactor. G. A. Yee, *Composition and Tradition in the Book of Hosea* (SBLDS 102; Atlanta: Scholars Press, 1987) 57–62, dates 3:1–5 to the exile, but her reasons, such as evidence of a hope for a return of the North under davidic dominion and the presence of Deuteronomic terminology, fit better the period of Hezekiah and Josiah than the exile. Emmerson, *Hosea*, 113,161f, argues that these ideas are from Hosea, who influenced the Deuteronomic position on monarchy in the seventh century BCE under Hezekiah and Josiah. In short, there is no reason to place this saying in the exile, unless all statements of future hope are to be denied to pre-exilic prophets, a view that is no longer credible (see Tucker, "Hosea," 708).

[11]See below in the treatment of Ezekiel 34 and 37 for a more detailed discussion of this davidic typology.

[12]For a pre-exilic date for Mic 4:14–5:4 (often excluding 5:2), see H. W. Wolff, *Micah the Prophet* (Philadelphia: Fortress, 1981) 92–93; D. R. Hillers, *Micah* (Hermeneia; Philadelphia: Fortress, 1984) 65–66; J. L. Mays, *Micah* (OTL; Philadelphia: Westminster, 1976) 113–114; K. Koch, *The Prophets* (2 vols.; Philadelphia: Fortress, 1983) 1:104.

humble—from the small clan in Bethlehem Ephrathah, David's ancestral village—and ancient (5:1). Israel will be given up for a time until this new ruler's
mother gives him birth, at which time his brothers will return to Israel (5:2).[13] He
will rule in the power of the Lord, Israel will be secure, his fame will be universal, and if 5:4a is to be included in the unit, his reign will bring an era of peace. In
short, his reign will coincide with ideal circumstances.

The somewhat mysterious characterization of this future ruler makes his relationship to the davidic dynasty tradition ambiguous. What is clear, however, is
that this new ruler will not emanate from the davidic line currently in power in
Jerusalem.[14] Consequently, some kind of genealogical break with the currently
ruling royal line is envisioned, thus indicating a tradition here that is in opposition
to the dynastic promise found in 2 Sam 7:11–16 and Psalm 89.[15]

Instead the new ruler's origin goes back to the beginning of the davidic dynasty tradition—to Bethlehem Ephrathah and to days of old.[16] The dual reference
to David's birthplace and to "days of old" have led some to see in this text a hope
for the return of David himself, the so-called David *redivivus*.[17] This, however, is
not very plausible.[18] More likely it refers to a figure who is typologically similar
to David—a new David, a conception not unlike that expressed in Hos 3:5; Jer
30:9; and Ezek 34:23f; 37:24f. Here the accent would be on a figure who like
David rose from humble origins to greatness by ruling in God's power. Yet this
typological interpretation alone may not capture the genealogical aspect implied
in the designation of Bethlehem Ephrathah as his place of origin. This ruler seems
to come from the same family soil as David, whether that be understood as from
the stump of Jesse (cf. Isa 11:1) or merely from the tribe of Judah (cf. Gen
49:10). The implication is that the new David need not be from the davidic line,
but only from similar stock. Of course, all these above possibilities would be
available to later interpreters.

Several passages from Isaiah 1–39 are related to the davidic dynasty tradition.[19] First, 8:23–9:6 (Eng: 9:1–7) portrays a situation in which a period of

---

[13]5:2 is considered by many commentators, a later (exilic) addition.

[14]Wolff, *Micah the Prophet*, 93; Mays, *Micah*, 113.

[15]W. Rudolph, *Micha, Nahum, Habakuk, Zephanja* (KAT 13/3; Gütersloh: Gütersloher Verlagshaus Gerd Mohn, 1975) 98; Mays, *Micah*, 115.

[16]This archaic tone is supported by the designation of the ruler as a מושל, a term for leaders in premonarchical Israel (cf. W. Harrelson, "Nonroyal Motifs in the Royal Eschatology," *Israel's Prophetic Heritage* [ed. B. W. Anderson and W. Harrelson; New York: Harper & Brothers, 1962] 155–157.

[17]Hillers, *Micah*, 66; Koch, *Prophets*, 1:104; Rudolph, *Micha*, 98.

[18]See below, p. 27.

[19]In addition to the texts treated below, some scholars have enlisted Isa 16:5 as a witness for

gloom is transformed into light and glory, a time when the lost territories of the Northern Kingdom will be rejoined to Israel (8:23–9:1), a time of joy and freedom from external oppression (9:2–4).[20] This new situation is related to the appearance of a new davidic king:

> For to us a child is born, to us a son is given; and the government will be upon his shoulder, and his name will be called Wonderful Counselor, Mighty God, Everlasting Father, Prince of Peace. Of the increase of his government and of peace there will be no end, upon the throne of David, and over his kingdom, to establish it, and to uphold it with justice and with righteousness from this time forth and for evermore (9:5–6).

First, we should observe that this passage is an enthronement hymn for a davidic king, and accordingly, in this context the mention of birth and sonship is likely a reference to the king's status as God's adopted son such as one finds in Ps 2:7 and 2 Sam 7:14.[21] Secondly, the throne names assigned to this royal figure in 9:5, probably on the model of Egyptian practice,[22] highlight his role as a wise leader (Wonderful Counselor), military hero (Mighty God, translated better as Divine Warrior), protector of the people (Everlasting Father, i.e., the father of his people), and the guarantor of peace and prosperity (Prince of Peace, i.e., שלם or well-being). Moreover, his rule on the throne of David will be characterized by

---

a promised davidic messiah (for example, O. Kaiser, *Isaiah 1–12* [OTL; Philadelphia: Westminster, 1972] 72). The text occurs in an oracle about Moab, in which there is an appeal to accept Moabite refugees. On the one hand, there is no way to ascertain its date (cf. Kaiser, *Isaiah 1–12*, 61–62,65; R. E. Clements, *Isaiah 1–39* [NCB; Grand Rapids, MI: Eerdmans, 1980] 150f) despite speculation, or its orientation, since v. 5 can be interpreted as referring either to the present (cf. J. H. Hayes and S. A. Irvine, *Isaiah the Eighth Century Prophet* [Nashville: Abingdon, 1987] 244) or the future. If taken as a future promise, however, it offers no comfort to the Moabites in their present plight, and thus fits the context poorly. Nevertheless, this passage speaks of a king on the throne in Jerusalem (tent of David) who rules with justice and righteousness. Little more can be said. Further, Isa 33:17 mentions the king in the context of a future age of salvation. Dates for this verse diverge widely from the eighth century BCE to the Hellenistic Age, but more importantly, the reference to the king almost certainly refers to the Lord as king (see J. M. Roberts, "Isaiah 33: An Isaianic Elaboration of the Zion Tradition," *The Word of the Lord Shall Go Forth* [ed. C. L. Meyers and M. O'Connor; Winona Lake, IN: Eisenbrauns, 1983] 15–25; O. Kaiser, *Isaiah 13–39* [OTL; Philadelphia: Westminster, 1974] 347). The verse is therefore not part of the davidic dynasty tradition. For a detailed treatment of so-called messianic passages in Isaiah 1–35, see P. D. Wegner, *An Examination of Kingship and Messianic Expectation in Isaiah 1–35* (Lewiston, NY: Mellen, 1992).

[20]For the pre-exilic date of 8:23–9:6, see Cross, *Hebrew Epic*, 228; Kaiser, *Isaiah 1–12*, 125–130; Clements, *Isaiah 1–39*, 6,103–104; Koch, *Prophets*, 1:132; Hayes and Irvine, *Isaiah*, 170–171.

[21]Cross, *Hebrew Epic*, 257; Clements, *Isaiah 1–39*, 107; Hayes and Irvine, *Isaiah*, 180f.

[22]Hayes and Irvine, *Isaiah*, 181.

greatness and peace—over David's kingdom, including the northern territories—accompanied by justice without end (v. 6a). Finally, this is all ultimately attributed to God (v. 6b).

Isa 10:33–11:10 presents another ideal image of a royal figure.[23] It explains that after the destruction of an enemy (Assyria) or Israelite leaders (10:33–34), a new king will arise:

> There shall come forth a shoot (חטר) from the stump (גרע) of Jesse, and a branch (נצר) shall grow out of his roots (משרשיו) [11:1].

The precise meaning of the imagery is open to interpretation. On the one hand, it may imply that this future king will come from the source of the davidic tradition and not from the current royal line in Jerusalem.[24] This idea of a collateral line stemming from the very beginnings of the davidic house, spawning a new David, would be akin to ideas in Mic 5:1. On the other hand, it could simply reflect the hope that even if the present davidic king is threatened or overthrown, the davidic line itself will continue.[25] In any case, this king will possess superlative spiritual endowments including wisdom, counsel, might, knowledge, and fear of Lord (11:2). His rule will not only be characterized by justice and righteousness (11:3b–5), but by paradisal conditions of peace and harmony extending to the whole earth (11:6–9). The nations will seek him and his rule will be glorious (11:10).[26]

Isa 32:1–8 is a passage that uses the language of the wisdom tradition to characterize an ideal king and his rule:[27] "Behold, a king should[28] reign in right-

---

[23]Kaiser, *Isaiah 1–12*, 159; Koch, *Prophets*, 1:132–134; Hayes and Irvine, *Isaiah*, 207, date this passage to the eighth century BCE, as an authentic oracle of Isaiah; Cross, *Hebrew Epic*, 228, dates it in the sixth century BCE; and Clements, *Isaiah 1–39*, 121–122,125, assigns it a post-exilic date. Yet the grounds offered by Clements for a exilic date or later, namely, that the text assumes the deposition of davidic kings on the throne of Jerusalem, that its position in the book of Isaiah indicates its reapplication of earlier promises, and its more developed character than exilic messianic traditions in Ezekiel 37 and Jeremiah 33, are far from convincing. On the other hand, there are sound reasons for dating this passage sometime during the Assyrian crisis (see first group of scholars cited above).

[24]Kaiser, *Isaiah 1–12*, 157,160; Koch, *Prophets*, 1:136.

[25]Clements, *Isaiah 1–39*, 122; Hayes and Irvine, *Isaiah*, 212–213.

[26]Isa 11:10 and 11:11–16 may be independent oracles appended at a later time (see Clements, *Isaiah 1–39*, 125; for an opposing view, see Hayes and Irvine, *Isaiah*, 206–207). If 11:11–16 is to be included with 10:23–11:10, then the return of the remnant of Israel and the destruction of enemies will take place at this time as well.

[27]See, for example, Kaiser, *Isaiah 13–39*, 320; Hayes and Irvine, *Isaiah*, 354.

[28]The RSV translates the imperfect (ימלך) as a future, rather than a modal, which is here more appropriate to the generalized sense common to the wisdom tradition (see Hayes and Irvine, *Isaiah*, 354).

eousness, and princes rule in justice" (v. 1). This passage, unlike other prophetic statements about future davidic monarchs, lacks a future orientation; there is no indication of hopes for a restoration of a defunct monarchy.[29] Thus, many commentators read it as referring to a sitting monarch, such as Hezekiah[30] or Josiah.[31] Nevertheless, others have seen messianic overtones here and dated these verses to the post-exilic period.[32] Although a pre-exilic date for 32:1–8 appears more likely, the date of this passage is really beside the point, for its character as wisdom literature makes it applicable to any historical context. That a king should concern himself with justice is a common theme in Israelite wisdom literature (Prov 20:8,26,28; 25:5; 29:4,14; 31:4–5; see also 16:10). Accordingly, 32:1–8 is better thought of as a treatise on kingship from the wisdom tradition. And while perhaps this passage was used to counsel sitting davidic kings, it is conceptually quite distinct from the davidic dynasty tradition. So, far from being messianic or davidic, this passage seems to illustrate that the Judean royal ideology was not the only model of kingship known to ancient Israel.[33]

In the book of Jeremiah, there are three passages, likely of pre-exilic date, that pertain to the davidic dynasty tradition. In 22:24–30, Jeremiah denounces Coniah (Jehoiachin) characterizing this king of Judah as a signet ring that the Lord will tear off his finger and hand over to Nebuchadnezzar. But more importantly, in v. 30 he adds, "Write this man down as childless ... for none of his offspring shall succeed in sitting on the throne of David and ruling again in Judah." This rejection of Coniah does not necessarily indicate, however, a wholesale dismissal of the davidic royal line, but possibly only the line through Coniah.[34]

Another passage, Jer 22:1–9, promises the continuance of the davidic dynasty if the king and Israel are obedient: "For if you will indeed obey this word,

---

[29]Clements, *Isaiah 1–39*, 259; cf. Hayes and Irvine, *Isaiah*, 354.

[30]Hayes and Irvine, *Isaiah*, 354.

[31]Clements, *Isaiah 1–39*, 259; G. Stansell, "Isaiah 32: Creative Redaction in the Isaian Tradition," *SBL 1983 Seminar Papers* (ed. K. Richards; Chico, CA: Scholars Press, 1983) 6, both of whom follow H. Barth, *Die Jesaha-Worte in der Josiazeit* (WMANT 48; Neukirchen-Vluyn: Neukirchener Verlag, 1977).

[32]Kaiser, *Isaiah 13–39*, 320–321; see Stansell, "Creative Redaction," 5, for a summary of viewpoints on this issue.

[33]See below for further examples of non-davidic models of kingship.

[34]R. P. Carroll, *Jeremiah* (OTL; Philadelphia: Westminster, 1986) 442, suggests that originally this oracle may have served to legitimate Zedekiah as the lawful king of Judah against the claim that Coniah was king of Judah in exile; yet the injunction against Coniah's offspring would have been valuable to an anti-Zerubbabel movement in the post-exilic period. The latter suggestion, however, is quite speculative.

then there shall enter the gates of this house kings who sit on the throne of David, riding in chariots and on horses ... " (v. 4). On the other hand, disobedience will result in the destruction of the royal house: "But if you do not heed these words, I swear by myself, says the Lord, that this house shall become a desolation" (v. 5). Here, the continuation of davidic kingship is conditioned upon the faithfulness of Israel and the royal house. This notion recalls the conception of the davidic dynasty familiar from Psalm 132 and various texts in Dtr.

The last text from the book of Jeremiah, plausibly related to Jeremiah (or possibly the exilic period), does look for a future ideal davidic king.[35] In Jer 23:5–6, the Lord promises to raise up for David a righteous branch (צמח צדיק). This ideal king will rule wisely, with justice and righteousness, and in his time Israel and Judah will be safe from enemies. His name will be called "The Lord is our righteousness" (יהוה צדקנו). Here, the future expectation is grounded in the davidic dynastic promise ("raise up for David") and looks for a righteous davidic king in contrast to the evil shepherds mentioned in the previous verses (23:1–4).

4. Non-davidic Royal Traditions

Apart from the specifically davidic royal texts we have reviewed above, there exist passages that speak of a ruler or king who is not explicitly davidic. Of course, already in the pre-exilic period these passages may have been viewed as referring to the davidic king—and some would be viewed this way in the early Jewish period, but in themselves they do not bear any specifically davidic characteristics. All the same, since these passages are taken up in varying degrees in early Jewish royal or messianic traditions, their basic content will be outlined.

Deut 17:14–20, the so-called "Law concerning the King," lays down the qualifications, limitations, and obligations of the king that the Israelites will ask for once they enter the land of Canaan. Thus, God permits Israel to set up a king (v. 14), but his qualifications include his being one whom the Lord will choose, with the further stipulation that he be an Israelite, not a foreigner (v. 15). Moreover, this king is prohibited from multiplying horses, or causing the people to return to Egypt for that purpose; nor may he multiply wives, silver, and gold for himself. Finally, the king must possess and read a copy of "this law" (presumably

---

[35]The actual dating of this passage is disputed, ranging from the beginning of the reign of Zedekiah (597 BCE) to the exilic and even post-exilic periods (see the summary of views in J. Unterman, *From Repentance to Redemption* [JSOTSup 54; Sheffield: JSOT Press, 1987] 128). Those commentators viewing it as an authentic saying of Jeremiah tend to see it as referring to Zedekiah, while those holding an exilic date perceive a hope for a future davidic king. Carroll, *Jeremiah*, 446–447, believes both aims are consistent with the passage. McKane, *Jeremiah* (2 vols.; ICC; Edinburgh: T & T Clark, 1986) 1:560–565, suggests an exilic or post-exilic date, the latter with little supporting evidence.

a form of Deuteronomy), so that he may fear the Lord and act obediently. In this way, he and his children will continue long in his kingdom.

In v. 14, monarchy in Israel is a concession to the people's desire to be like the nations around them, a motif familiar from the anti-monarchical texts preserved in Dtr.[36] Accordingly, the king is warned against the extravagances which bedeviled Israelite and Judean kings. Interestingly, the qualifications for kingship are described as being chosen by the Lord and being an Israelite; absent is any requirement of Judean or davidic lineage, and although a dynasty is envisioned in v. 20, its continuance is based on the reigning king's adherence to the commandments in the law. It is strictly conditional. In contrast to the davidic royal ideology that we witnessed above, here is another model of kingship, possibly stemming originally from the era of Saul, David, or the Northern Kingdom, based on charismatic endowment from the Lord and conditioned on the faithfulness of the king. The concept of kingship is not unlike the one in Psalm 132, but here it need not be applied to a davidic figure.

Gen 49:8–12 is Jacob's blessing of his son Judah. In v. 8, it is said that Judah's brothers will praise him and bow down before him, and that Judah will dominate his enemies. Apparently, Judah is to be revered for his heroics against enemies.[37] In v. 9, Judah is compared to a lion, an apparent allusion to Judah's greatness and power. Then the problematic v. 10 reads:

> The scepter shall not depart from Judah, nor the ruler's staff from between his feet, עד כי־יבא שילה and to him (לֹך) shall be the obedience of the peoples.

Clearly, this verse has something to do with Judah's ruling capacity, but its precise meaning is elusive because of the difficulties in v. 10αβ.[38] Without emending the text, it can be read as: 1) until he comes to Shiloh; or 2) until Shiloh comes. Unfortunately, neither of these possibilities makes much sense. More fruitful are the suggestions that see in שילה a reference to a ruler either by emending the text (מֹשְלֹה =his ruler, or שֹלֹה =to whom it belongs [see LXX]) or on the basis of an Akkadian cognate (*selu*=ruler).[39] This hypothesis is supported both by the personal pronoun לֹך, which refers back to the subject of יבא as a person, and the association of this person with dominion over the peoples.

---

[36]Cf. G. von Rad, *Deuteronomy* (OTL; Philadelphia: Westminster, 1966) 119, for fuller discussion of this passage.

[37]See C. Westermann, *Genesis 37–50: A Commentary* (Minneapolis: Augsburg, 1986) 227–228, for a detailed discussion of v. 8; he reads v. 8 as present tense, instead of future.

[38]See Westermann, *Genesis 37–50*, 229–231; G. von Rad, *Genesis* (rev. ed.; OTL; Philadelphia: Westminster, 1972) 425, for a discussion of the possible meanings.

[39]See Westermann, *Genesis 37–50*, 231, for the specific emendations and their grounds.

The point seems to be that Judah's dominance will continue until it reaches new heights in a ruler or king who, beyond the honor of his brothers, would gain the obedience of the peoples. In any case, later interpreters would be free to interpret this ambiguous passage in various ways. Finally, we should note that in v. 11 an era of paradisiacal blessings—marked by fertility (v. 11) and beauty (v. 12)—is associated with the figure mentioned in v. 10.

Num 24:17–19 contains an oracle of the prophet Balaam predicting that a ruler would come out of Israel in the "latter days" (see v. 14b):

> I see him, but not now; I behold him, but not nigh; a star shall come forth out of Jacob, and a scepter shall rise out of Israel (24:17).

It is further stated that this ruler will defeat and subdue Moab and Edom, and give dominion to Jacob. This mysterious figure is compared to a star and a scepter coming out of Israel, images that lend themselves easily to royalty.[40] Whether or not this passage at some point functioned to legitimate the rise of David,[41] its application would not be limited to the davidic tradition. Moreover, its frequent use in the Second Temple period is no doubt related to the mysterious characterization of this ruler figure and his connection with the latter days.

5. Summary

Perhaps the most striking feature in the preceding overview is the diversity present in the pre-exilic davidic dynasty tradition. In a few texts, dynastic continuance is understood as guaranteed by an unconditional promise,[42] while in others it is conditioned on the king's faithfulness to the Torah.[43] In only two texts—2 Sam 23:5 and Psalm 89—is the davidic dynastic promise conceived of in terms of a covenant.[44] Three times the relationship between God and the davidic king is construed in terms of a filial relationship.[45] In the prophetic literature, a conception of a future "new David" appears.[46] Nevertheless, monarchy in Israel could be spoken of apart from direct reference to the davidic dynasty

---

[40]See J. Milgrom, *Numbers* (Jewish Publication Society Torah Commentaries; Philadelphia: Jewish Publication Society, 1990) 207–208.

[41]Cf. M. Noth, *Numbers* (OTL; Philadelphia: Westminster, 1968) 192–193.

[42]2 Sam 7:11b–16; 1 Kgs 11:12–36; 15:4; 2 Kgs 8:19; Psalm 89.

[43]1 Kgs 2:1–4; 8:25; 9:3–9; Psalm 132; Jer 22:1–9; and probably 2 Sam 23:5; Jer 22:24–30 (cf. also Deut 17:14–20).

[44]See J. D. Levenson, "The Davidic Covenant and Its Modern Interpreters," *CBQ* 41 (1979) 216–217.

[45]2 Sam 7:11b–16; Psalm 89; Psalm 2; and possibly Isa 9:5–6.

[46]Hos 3:4–5; probably Mic 5:1ff; possibly Isa 11:1.

tradition, such as in Deut 17:14–20, Gen 49:8–12, Num 24:17–19, and Isa 32:1–8.

Davidic figures are described with a variety of terms and images. Plant imagery is common, including such terms as fruit, seed, sprout, branch, stump, and root, but other metaphors like lamp, horn, signet ring, and shepherd also appear. In the Psalms and in 2 Sam 23:5, likewise a hymnic passage, the davidic king is called מָשִׁיחַ (the anointed one).[47] In addition, frequently the rule of davidic figures is associated with ideal conditions in Israel where a united Israel defeats its enemies, ushering in an era of peace and universal Israelite rule. This time will be accompanied by fertility and prosperity, as well as justice and righteousness in Israel.

Thus, in the pre-exilic period the davidic dynasty tradition is well attested, yet quite diverse. In light of this diversity, perhaps scholarly terminology should begin to speak of davidic dynasty *traditions*—in the plural rather than the singular—to represent the lack of uniformity and even contradictory conceptions that are in evidence. In subsequent periods of Israelite literature, when no davidic king reigned, we will see even more diverse expressions of the davidic dynasty tradition.

C. Exilic Traditions

1. Ezekiel

The book of Ezekiel contains four passages which bear on the issue of the davidic dynasty tradition in the exilic period.[48] The first one, in 17:22–24, which emanates from Ezekiel himself or his school during the exile,[49] follows the allegory of the eagles (17:1–21), which speaks of the fortunes of Judah's last two kings, Jehoiachin and Zedekiah.[50] The first eagle came to Lebanon, broke off the topmost twig of the cedar, and took it away to a land of trade (vv. 1–4). Then it planted a new seed which sprouted and became a vine (vv. 4–6). This refers to Nebuchadnezzar's deportation of Jehoiachin to Babylon and his appointment of

---

[47]For example, Psalms 2; 89; 132; 15:51. David is called the anointed one in 1–2 Samuel, and the king is called the anointed in Lam 4:20 (perhaps also in Hab 3:13).

[48]Ezek 21:30–32 should not be considered a "messianic" prophecy based on Genesis 49:10 or a reference to Jehoiachin. See especially W. L. Moran, "Gn 49,10 and its Use in Ez 21,32," *Bib* 39 (1958) 405–425; cf. also J. D. Levenson, *Theology of the Program of Restoration of Ezekiel 40–48* (HSM 10; Atlanta: Scholars Press, 1976) 75–77; W. Zimmerli, *Ezekiel 1* (Hermeneia; Philadelphia: Fortress, 1979) 447–448.

[49]See Levenson, *Ezekiel 40–48*, 79–80; Zimmerli, *Ezekiel 1*, 368.

[50]The structure of the chapter is easily laid out: vv. 1–10: allegory of eagles; vv. 11–21: interpretation of allegory; vv. 22–24: allegory of the cedar.

Zedekiah as king of Judah (cf. vv. 11–13). But the new vine bent toward another eagle and because of this will be uprooted (vv. 7–10). This alludes to Zedekiah's alliance with Egypt, and predicts his downfall, because he broke his covenant with Nebuchadnezzar (vv. 15–21). Finally, in vv. 22–24, there is a supplement to the allegory; part of it reads:

> Thus says the Lord God: "I myself will take a sprig from the lofty top of the cedar, and will set it out; I will break off from the topmost of its young twigs a tender one, and I myself will plant it upon a high and lofty mountain, on a mountain height of Israel will I plant it, that it may bring forth boughs and bear fruit, and become a noble cedar ... " (vv. 22–23).

This undoubtedly is a promise that God will raise up a new king in Judah. Moreover, since the language of v. 22 is very similar to that in v. 3, it is reasonable to assume that the person represented by the sprig taken by the Lord will be from the house of David.[51] Further, the high and lofty mountain, explained as the mountain height of Israel, refers to Zion—though Zion, as elsewhere in Ezekiel, is elevated to mythic and paradisal proportions.[52] Finally, the future fecundity and stature of the new davidic planting is assured (v. 23), in contrast to the former tree (v. 24).

Several items in Ezekiel's conception of a future davidic monarch should be noted. First, as in Isaiah and Jeremiah, plant or tree metaphors are used for the davidic royal figure (here ראש ינקותיו; "top of its branches"). In addition, a universal scope is suggested by the references to "every sort of bird" (v. 23) and "all the trees of the field" (v. 24). Lastly, the new king's status as a vassal of the Lord is implied in the emphasis on the Lord's actions in breaking off the sprig and planting it, the stress on his sovereign control over which trees flourish (v. 24), and the parallel between God's actions and Nebuchadnezzar's detailed in the allegory of the eagles. On this last point, Levenson has pointed out that just as Nebuchadnezzar is both king and king-maker in the allegory, appointing kings who rule only inasmuch as they maintain their covenant faithfulness to him, God takes that role in the supplement. Implicit then is a subordinate role for this future Israelite king who must rule as a vassal in accordance with the terms of a covenant, which in Ezekiel is the Sinai covenant: " ... the messianic figure whom he (God) establishes is the visible token to the world of YHWH's sovereignty."[53]

---

[51]Zimmerli, *Ezekiel 1*, 366; or if not, at least from the root of Jesse (see above the discussion of Mic 4:14–5:3 and Isa 11:1).

[52]W. Eichrodt, *Ezekiel* (OTL; Philadelphia: Westminster, 1970) 288; Levenson, *Ezekiel 40–48*, 80.

[53]Levenson, *Ezekiel 40–48*, 80–81, esp. p. 80.

The next relevant text is Ezek 34:23–24, a passage attributed to Ezekiel or his school in the exile.[54] These verses are preceded by two units: an oracle offering a word of judgment for the irresponsible shepherds of Israel, promising that in the future the Lord himself will be Israel's shepherd (34:1–16), and an oracle declaring the Lord's judgment between the oppressive and oppressed sheep (34:17–22). Then it reads:

> And I will set up over them one shepherd, my servant David, and he shall feed them: he shall feed them and be their shepherd. And I, the Lord, will be their God, and my servant David shall be prince among them; I, the Lord have spoken (34:23–24).

This then is followed by a promise of an idyllic future in which there is deliverance from oppression, peace, prosperity, and knowledge of the Lord.

Of interest in determining the conception of kingship present in this passage are some of the terms used to describe this future Israelite monarch. First, the future leader will be "one shepherd," who will feed the flock, in contrast to the irresponsible shepherds, like Jehoiachin and Zedekiah. In addition, the reference to "one" implies a united Israel, both north and south under one king.[55]

Secondly, and most striking, is the designation "my servant David."[56] Theories about Ezekiel's hope for a resurrected David are very implausible.[57] Instead, this designation asserts that the future king will be typologically like David, the ideal king who ruled over a united Israel as the Lord's faithful servant. Moreover, almost all commentators understand this typological relationship to entail a genealogical relationship as well, and thus maintain that the new ideal king will come from the davidic line.[58] This of course is not an unreasonable assumption; yet not a necessary one. For instance, few would take Malachi's proclamation of a coming Elijah to mean that the typological fulfillment of this prophecy would entail that the person also be genealogically related to Elijah (cf. Mal 3:23). The key difference, however, between Elijah and David would be that David was promised a continuing dynasty, while Elijah was not. Thus, if one assumes that Ezekiel and his school held fast to that davidic promise, then certainly the davidic typology would entail a davidic genealogy for the future king. But the question

---

[54]Zimmerli, *Ezekiel 2* (Hermeneia; Philadelphia: Fortress, 1983) 220; Levenson, *Ezekiel 40–48*, 87.

[55]This idea is explicit in Ezek 37:24–25.

[56]Hos 3:5 and Jer 30:9 are two other biblical passages that speak of a future David.

[57]Cf. the discussion in Zimmerli, *Ezekiel 2*, 219; Eichrodt, *Ezekiel*, 476.

[58]Zimmerli, *Ezekiel 2*, 219; Eichrodt, *Ezekiel*, 476; Levenson, *Ezekiel 40–48*, 87. See above the discussion of Mic 4:14–5:3, where it appears a new king will not be from the ruling davidic line.

that interests us is whether Ezekiel and his school did in fact expect the revival of the davidic dynasty. Consequently, Ezekiel's use of David as an ideal type of Israelite king cannot demonstrate that he did, for to do so begs the question.[59] In any case, use of this David typology emphasizes the servanthood and ideal character of the future king.

Thirdly, this future leader is not explicitly called מלך ("king"), but נשיא ("prince"). The precise connotation of this terminology is debated, some seeing it as a synonym for מלך and not inappropriate for a davidic figure, others viewing it as an indication of a significant change in Ezekiel's view of leadership in Israel.[60] Actually, there is an element of truth in both positions. On the one hand, נשיא is used of Israelite kings both in Ezekiel and elsewhere in the Hebrew Bible,[61] and therefore does not preclude the idea of monarchy, nor of davidic status. On the other hand, the use of נשיא does seem to imply a more limited view of kingship for Ezekiel. For one, in Ezekiel נשיא is used for vassal kings; the term מלך, with few exceptions, is reserved for Babylonian or Egyptian suzerains.[62] Moreover, as the title for pre-monarchical tribal heads,[63] נשיא may connote authority of a more limited kind known from Israel's archaic period prior to the development of a royal ideology and the abuses associated with Judean kings. In a similar vein, Levenson has drawn attention to 1 Kgs 11:34, where Ahijah the prophet declares that although the Lord would take the ten northern tribes from Solomon, he would make him a נשיא for the sake of David.[64] Here Solomon, although stripped of great political power, would as נשיא continue to represent the fulfillment of the dynastic promise.[65] Altogether, this suggests that the term נשיא designates a king whose power is dependent upon and limited by a superior king, in this case the Lord.[66]

Furthermore, this understanding of נשיא comports well with the notion that the Lord himself will be Israel's shepherd (34:15), while at the same time raising up "my servant, David" as shepherd. This same conception of God's sovereignty in relationship to the נשיא is reflected in Ezek 34:24: "And I, the Lord will be

---

[59]Ezek 17:22–24 is the only evidence that Ezekiel may have held to a davidic hope.

[60]See Levenson, *Ezekiel 40–48*, 57–62, for a brief history of the problem.

[61]See Ezek 7:27; 12:10,12; 19:1; 21:30; 37:24; 1 Kgs 11:34 (used of Solomon).

[62]Zimmerli, *Ezekiel 1*, 209.

[63]Zimmerli, *Ezekiel 1*, 209.

[64]Levenson, *Ezekiel 40–48*, 63f.

[65]Levenson, *Ezekiel 40–48*, 63–64.

[66]K.-M. Beyse, *Serubbabel und die Königserwartungen der Propheten Haggai und Sacharja* (Stuttgart: Calwer, 1972) 61; Zimmerli, *Ezekiel 2*, 219; Levenson, *Ezekiel 40–48*, 90–91.

their God, and my servant David shall be prince among them." In addition, the above interpretation of נשיא fits with the view of limited kingship identified in chap. 17, and as we will see, a similar perspective in following passages. Lastly, while the designation נשיא is consistent with a genealogically davidic figure, it does not require it.

A passage closely related to 34:23–24 is Ezek 37:24–25, again verses attributed to Ezekiel or his school:.[67]

> My servant David shall be king over them; and they shall all have one shepherd
> ... and David my servant shall be their prince for ever.

The similarities with 34:23–24 will allow us to deal with the present text more briefly. We may begin by observing one point of contrast with 34:23–24, namely, the context. Ezek 37:15–20 relates Ezekiel's sign-action of putting together two sticks. This symbolizes the reunification of Israel and Judah as one nation with one king, living faithfully as the Lord's people with the Lord's sanctuary in their midst (37:21–28). Accordingly, the emphasis in v. 24 falls on the expression "one shepherd." Levenson has suggested that this emphasis is in conscious opposition to the Judean royal ideology's exclusion of the Northern Kingdom from divine blessing as expressed in Ps 78:67–72.[68] In any case, this one shepherd reigns over a united Israel.

In vv. 24–25, the future monarch is called "my servant David" and נשיא. In addition, however, he is also specified as מלך. Thus, as stated earlier, the vassal-like status of the future monarch is not inconsistent with the title of king. Finally, the presence of one shepherd in a united Israel is but one aspect of the ideal future time envisioned here. It will be a time of faithfulness to the Lord (v. 24b), as Israel lives forever in the land of their fathers (v. 25) in an everlasting covenant of peace with the Lord, a covenant in which the Lord blesses Israel and sets his sanctuary among them (vv. 26,28b), dwelling with them (v. 27a). The point to observe here is that the prophecy of a new David is only a component part of Ezekiel's vision of an ideal future for Israel, where the emphasis is on the Lord's relationship with his people and the presence of his sanctuary among them. To be sure, within this theocratic ideal the new David is given a role, but any specification of his activity is absent. Zimmerli is certainly on the right track when he remarks that on the holy mountain of Israel,

---

[67]Levenson, *Ezekiel 40–48*, 94; Zimmerli, *Ezekiel 2*, 94–95.

[68]Levenson, *Ezekiel 40–48*, 92–93.

> it is not in the long run the prince of Israel who is the decisive factor, but the
> sanctuary in it ... In 37:24b–28 it is further underlined by placing the David
> promise before the clearly emphasized promise of God's holy dwelling place.[69]

The final passage that merits our attention is Ezekiel 40–48, where the role
of a נשׂיא is spelled out.[70] In Ezekiel's program of restoration, the temple, along
with priests and cultic matters, is at the center of attention. Yet within this hiero-
centric theocracy, the figure of the נשׂיא is assigned certain privileges, obligations, and limitations. His privileges include rights of special access to temple
areas (44:3; 46:2,8,10) and an allotment of personal land (45:7; 48:21–22). The
single obligation of the נשׂיא is to furnish offerings for sacrifice (45:16–17,22;
46:4,12–15); in other words, he is a patron of the cult.[71] But in addition to privileges and duties, the prerogatives of the נשׂיא are limited. Although he is to
possess private holdings of land, he is not to infringe on the land rights of any
Israelites: he is forbidden to evict people from their land (45:8–9), particularly not
so as to enrich the inheritance of his sons (46:18). Furthermore, gifts of inheritance may only be passed to his sons; gifts to servants revert back to the נשׂיא in
the year of release. This last provision, according to Levenson, would prevent the
נשׂיא from building up a loyal bureaucracy.[72]

Yet none is really necessary, because the נשׂיא appears to have no administrative duties.[73] Thus it is not surprising that royal administrative units have given
way to an idealized schema of tribal allotments in the theocracy. Moreover,
instructional and judicial responsibilities will reside with the priests (44:23–24).
Actually, in Ezekiel's program of restoration, mention of a political role for the
נשׂיא is absent. For that matter, besides a few privileges, the נשׂיא has only a
limited role in the cult. As Levenson remarks, "Clearly the *nāśî* is here a figure of
great honor, however impotent."[74] This impotence is all the more striking in
contrast to the power exercised by kings in pre-exilic Judean monarchy. In
Ezekiel 40–48, the role and status of the נשׂיא is both pared down and strictly
regulated.

---

[69]See Zimmerli, *Ezekiel 2*, 279,

[70]Both H. Gese, *Der Verfassungsentwurf des Ezechiel* (BHT 25; Tübingen: Mohr, 1957)
85–87; and Zimmerli, *Ezekiel 2*, 552f, hold that the texts about the נשׂיא are a later stratum in
chaps. 40–48, yet still exilic.

[71]Levenson, *Ezekiel 40–48*, 114, alludes to the role of the נשׂיא as the maintainer of standard weights and measures, but this appears to be the responsibility of more persons than just
the political leader (cf. Zimmerli, *Ezekiel 2*, 479).

[72]Levenson, *Ezekiel 40–48*, 114.

[73]Levenson, *Ezekiel 40–48*, 113–114.

[74]Levenson, *Ezekiel 40–48*, 113.

Having outlined the role of the נשיא in Ezekiel 40–48, we must proceed to the question of his identity. Levenson has reviewed the history of the question, and we may summarize the two positions he has outlined.[75] One viewpoint identifies the figure of the נשיא in chaps. 40–48 with the נשיא mentioned in the messianic oracles in chaps. 1–37, and therefore sees him as a davidic king, admitting, however, that his authority is somewhat limited to prevent the kind of abuses that brought down the Judean monarchy. The second position emphasizes the discontinuity between the image of the נשיא in chaps. 40–48 and that in chaps. 1–37, relating the נשיא of chaps. 40–48 to the נשיא mentioned in documents associated with Priestly literature. This view attributes to the authors of chaps. 40–48 no interest in monarchy, believing that they had broken with the davidic hope present in chaps. 1–37. Levenson himself, who argues that a more limited form of davidic kingship is expressed in chaps. 1–37, sees the נשיא of chaps. 40–48 as an example of this limited understanding.[76]

In my opinion, the נשיא mentioned in chaps. 40–48 does stand in some continuity with the limited view of future kingship present in the messianic oracles in 34:23–24, 37:24–25, and even 17:22–24. In this regard, Levenson is correct. But there are some points of discontinuity that should not be ignored. Gone is the explicit David typology, the promises of fruitfulness, any allusion to the shepherding or feeding of Israel, and any other image or title, including king, beyond that of נשיא. Accordingly, if the role of the נשיא was limited in chaps. 1–37, it is further diminished and circumscribed in chaps. 40–48. Likewise, if the portrait of the נשיא in chaps. 1–37 was undeveloped, in chaps. 40–48 it has become an even more colorless figure, possessing some privilege but little power.[77]

Finally, we may ask whether the נשיא of chaps. 40–48 is a davidic figure. Those scholars connecting him with the נשיא or royal figure in chaps. 1–37 think so,[78] but mostly because of their assumption that the David typology in 34:23–24 and 37:24–25 implies a davidic genealogy. But beyond this, there is nothing that connects the נשיא in chaps. 40–48 to the davidic dynasty tradition. On the basis of 46:16ff—the restrictions regarding gifts of inheritance to the sons of the נשיא—Gese has claimed that the office of נשיא was hereditary, and thus asks, "An welches andere Geschlecht aber kann man dabei denken als an das

---

[75]Levenson, *Ezekiel 40–48*, 57–62; cf. also S. S. Tuell, *The Law of the Temple in Ezekiel 40–48* (HSM 49; Atlanta: Scholars Press, 1992) 105–112.

[76]Levenson, *Ezekiel 40–48*, 62–69.

[77]See Zimmerli, *Ezekiel 2*, 278–279, who makes essentially the same point about the role of the נשיא in the restoration: "The 'prince' stands as a servant figure on the fringe of this event."

[78]Levenson, *Ezekiel 40–48*, 57,66.

davidische?"[79] Yet, 46:16ff hardly entails a hereditary office. Gese goes on to explain how his view confirms the much debated davidic status of Sheshbazzar, the first leader of the returning exiles in 538 BCE, who in Ezra 1:8 is called נשׂיא of Judah.[80] On the other hand, if Gese is right, that Sheshbazzar indeed represents the נשׂיא of the restoration program in chaps. 40–48, then his argument for the davidic status of the נשׂיא in chaps. 40–48 collapses. For, as P.-R. Berger has shown, attempts to identify Sheshbazzar (שׁשׁבצר) with the Shenazzar (שׁנאצר) listed as one of the sons of Jehoiachin in 1 Chr 3:18 are faulty.[81] Hence, the only post-exilic נשׂיא mentioned—Sheshbazzar—is non-davidic.[82] In sum, then, the davidic status of the נשׂיא in Ezekiel 40–48 is possible, but by no means necessary or even highly likely. On the other hand, if this נשׂיא is to be viewed as the continuation of the davidic dynasty, then his davidic status is not only downplayed, but his role is a far cry from that of the pre-exilic monarchy.

2. Exilic Traditions in Jeremiah

Several passages from the book of Jeremiah concerning the davidic dynasty appear to be exilic. The narratives in chap. 52 represent a strand of tradition favorably inclined toward Jeconiah as the last legitimate king of Judah, presumably over against Zedekiah. Thus, on the one hand, we have a report that Zedekiah's sons were executed and Zedekiah himself died in prison in Babylon (vv. 10–11); hence, no royal line would come through him. On the other hand, it is reported that Jehoiachin was released from prison (vv. 31–34; cf. 2 Kgs 25:27–30). Some have interpreted this as an indication of a continued dynastic hope focused on this former king. Yet below, I will suggest that this interpretation, as it is offered for a parallel passage in 2 Kgs 25:27–30, is untenable. We might simply observe here that if this were the point of chap. 50, it would stand in stark contrast to Jer 22:24–30, where Jehoiachin and his offspring are vehemently denounced.

In another portion of the Jeremiah tradition (chaps. 40–41), one finds an anti-monarchical, and thus, anti-davidic tendency. Judah under Gedaliah's rule is viewed in a positive light: Jeremiah supports him, the land produces abundantly,

---

[79]Gese, *Der Verfassungsentwurf*, 118.

[80]Gese, *Der Verfassungsentwurf*, 118.

[81]P.-R. Berger, "Zu den Namen שׁשׁבצר und שׁנאצר," *ZAW* 83 (1971) 98–100; cf. also H. G. M. Williamson, *1 and 2 Chronicles* (NCB; Grand Rapids, MI: Eerdmans, 1982) 57.

[82]To consider Zerubbabel a נשׂיא, as Gese does (*Der Verfassungsentwurf*, 119), on the basis of his title "governor," which he shared with Sheshbazzar, is to stretch the evidence to the breaking point.

and scattered refugees return.[83] According to Jeremiah 39–41, the rulership of Gedaliah is legitimate.[84] Moreover, Gedaliah's assassin, Ishmael, whose membership in the davidic royal family is explicitly stated (41:1), is portrayed in the worst possible terms,[85] and his attempt to reinstate davidic leadership was rejected by the remnant of the Judean military and populace.[86] This account therefore betrays an anti-monarchical attitude,[87] and seems to assume the end of the davidic dynasty.[88]

Another passage in the book of Jeremiah that may be exilic has a positive expectation for an ideal davidic king or a restoration of the davidic dynasty.[89] Jer 30:8–9 proclaims:

> And it shall come to pass in that day, says the Lord of hosts, that I will break the yoke from off their neck, and I will burst their bonds, and strangers shall no more make servants of them. But they shall serve the Lord their God and David their king, whom I will raise up for them.

Here there exists a clear hope for an ideal king as a type of David, similar to what we have seen in Hos 3:4–5 and Ezek 34:23f; 37:24f. Motifs connected with God's raising up of this new king are liberation from foreign rule and Israel's service to

---

[83]J. M. Miller and J. H. Hayes, *A History of Ancient Israel and Judah* (Philadelphia: Westminster, 1986) 421–422, argue that Gedaliah was in fact appointed king of Judah, not governor, as many translations state. They suggest that the authors of Dtr suppressed this information so as not to reveal that a non-davidic king ruled Judah.

[84]K. Baltzer, "Das Ende des Staates Juda und die Messias-Frage," *Studien zur Theologie der alttestamentlichen Überlieferungen* (ed. R. Rendtorff and K. Koch; Neukirchen: Neukirchener Verlag, 1961) 36.

[85]Baltzer, "Das Ende," 35.

[86]Miller and Hayes, *History*, 424.

[87]Baltzer, "Das Ende," 35–36; Beyse, *Serubbabel*, 60.

[88]Beyse, *Serubbabel*, 60, states that these reports show that Jeremiah assumed the davidic dynasty was at an end, but we cannot so easily leap from the view of this account in the book of Jeremiah to the view of the prophet himself. E. W. Nicholson, *Preaching to Exiles* (Oxford: Basil Blackwell, 1970) 90, writes "in the earlier stages of its development the Jeremianic tradition held out no hope for the survival and restoration of the house of David."

[89]The setting for 30:8–9 is very difficult to ascertain. Nicholson, *Preaching*, 88f, dates it in the exilic period due to its Deuteronomistic themes; Carroll, *Jeremiah*, 576, opts for after 587 BCE; W. L. Holladay, *Jeremiah 2* (Hermeneia; Philadelphia: Fortress, 1989) 166, suggests as a "guess" the last decades of the sixth century BCE. Since v. 9 may assume there is no king ("whom I will raise up") a date after 586 BCE seems likely, but this is not assured. The point could be that God will raise up an ideal king, like David, in contrast to the flawed davidic kings known to have reigned during Jeremiah's ministry prior to 586 BCE. Jer 30:9 is almost identical to Hos 3:5, a text of uncertain date, and its theme of an ideal David is reminiscent of Ezek 34:23; 37:24, an exilic text. An exilic date is therefore probable, but there is little certainty about this assigned date.

the Lord their God. On the whole, then, the book of Jeremiah points to a variety of viewpoints concerning the fate of the davidic royal house prior to and after the fall of the Jerusalem in 586 BCE.

3. Exilic Edition of the Deuteronomistic History

In the previous section concerning pre-exilic traditions, I surveyed the material relevant to the davidic dynasty that was incorporated into Dtr. The composition of Dtr (or at least its final edition), however, can date from no earlier than 560 BCE (cf. 2 Kgs 25:27–30), and is thus properly addressed in this section on exilic texts. The question is this: what view of the davidic dynasty and its continuance does one find in this final edition of Dtr. Unfortunately, answering this question with any kind of certainty has proved exceedingly difficult. The contradictory conceptions of the davidic dynasty embodied in Dtr,[90] along with questions about the redactional history of Dtr have complicated matters.[91] Moreover, the interpretation of 2 Kgs 25:27–30—a key text because it is clearly exilic—is debated. Thus, it may be helpful to offer a brief sketch of the debate before proposing my own view.

M. Noth saw no davidic expectation in Dtr—indeed, no future expectation at all. In his view, Dtr's story of Judah was one of unmitigated disaster. 2 Kgs 25:27–30 was no indication of hope, merely a report of information.[92] In contrast, G. von Rad emphasized the abiding significance of the dynastic promise set forth in 2 Sam 7:11–16 and alluded to several times in 1–2 Kings. Consequently, he saw in 2 Kgs 25:27–30 a glimmer of hope for the future of the dynasty.[93] H. W. Wolff, like Noth, saw no future hope for the davidic dynasty, but pointed to passages in Dtr that made restoration of the people dependent on repentance and obedience.[94] What these first three scholars did agree on, however, was that a single edition of Dtr was composed during the exile.

F. M. Cross, while agreeing with Wolff, wanted also to account for the emphasis on the davidic dynasty within Dtr, which had been observed by von Rad. Thus, he argued that in a primary edition of Dtr (Dtr¹), composed at the time of Josiah, the eternal promise to David was stressed, while in a second edition (Dtr²), written during the exile, expectation for a continuing davidic dynasty was

---

[90]See Cross, *Hebrew Epic*, 288. See also the above summary of passages.

[91]Ackroyd, "Historical Literature," 303–305.

[92]M. Noth, *The Deuteronomistic History* (JSOTSup 15; Sheffield: JSOT Press, 1981) 98.

[93]G. von Rad, "The Deuteronomic Theology of History in *I and II Kings*," *The Problem of the Hexateuch and other essays* (London: Oliver & Boyd, 1966) 219–221.

[94]H. W. Wolff, "Das Kerygma des deuteronomistischen Geschichtswerks," *ZAW* 73 (1961) 171–186, esp. 174.

given up.[95] Subsequent views have either endorsed or modified one of the above viewpoints.[96] One modification that must be mentioned presently is that proposed by J. D. Levenson, who presupposed the correctness of Cross' hypothesis of two editions of Dtr, but on the basis of his analysis of 1 Kings 8 assigned 1 Kgs 8:25 with its conditional understanding of davidic kingship to Dtr[2].[97] Then, in a subsequent article, he attempted to show that this conditional conception of davidic kingship in Dtr[2] not only had retrospective significance, as an explanation of the disaster of 586 BCE, but when linked with a proper interpretation of 2 Kgs 25:27–30, also possessed prospective significance, setting forth the nature of a future davidic kingship.[98]

Accordingly, the four basic opinions regarding the view of the davidic dynasty in the final edition of Dtr can be summarized as follows: 1) there is no future expectation for the davidic dynasty or Israel (Noth); 2) there is no future expectation for the davidic dynasty, only for Israel as a people (Wolff; Cross); 3) there is a future for the davidic dynasty based on the unconditional promise of an eternal dynasty (von Rad); 4) there is a future for the davidic dynasty based on the conditional promise, dependent on royal adherence to the Torah (Levenson). Now, to assist in adjudicating between these options, I will first examine 2 Kgs 25:27–30, and secondly, review passages that portray the nature of future restoration for a penitent Israel. All the passages are clearly exilic on any redactional theory of Dtr and therefore should offer a good indication of the view of the davidic dynasty and its continuance found in the final edition of Dtr.

2 Kgs 25:27–30 reads as follows:

> And in the thirty-seventh year of the exile of Jehoiachin king of Judah, in the twelfth month, on the twenty-seventh day of the month, Evil-merodach king of Babylon, in the year that he began to reign, graciously freed Jehoiachin king of Judah from prison; and he spoke kindly to him (וידבר אתו טבות), and gave him

---

[95]Cross, *Hebrew Epic*, 274–288.

[96]See the review in C. T. Begg, "The Significance of Jehoiachin's Release: A New Proposal," *JSOT* 36 (1986) 50; see also Baltzer, "Das Ende," 37–39; and R. Friedman, *The Exile and Biblical Narrative* (HSM; Chico, CA: Scholars Press, 1981) 33.

[97]J. D. Levenson, "From Temple to Synagogue: 1 Kings 8," *Traditions in Transformation* (ed. B. Halpern and J. D. Levenson; Winona Lake, IN: Eisenbrauns, 1981) 143–166. Cross, *Hebrew Epic*, 281–285, had assigned both the conditional and unconditional dynastic promises to Dtr[1].

[98]J. D. Levenson, "The Last Four Verses in Kings," *JBL* 103 (1984) 353–361. Levenson's view is not unlike that of Veijola, *Die Ewige Dynastie*, 127–142, who would differ in dating the first edition of Dtr (DtrG) shortly after 586 BCE, which held to an unconditional davidic promise; a second edition early in the exile (DtrP), in which davidic expectations were absent, and a third edition shortly after Jehoiachin's release (DtrN), which set forth a conditional understanding of the davidic promise.

a seat (כסאו) above the seats of the kings (כסא המלכים) who were with him in Babylon. So Jehoiachin put off his prison garments. And every day of his life he dined regularly at the king's table; and for his allowance, a regular allowance was given him by the king, every day a portion, as long as he lived.

C. T. Begg's recent analysis of these verses forms the basis of much of the subsequent discussion.[99] Begg points out that one is immediately struck by what is not present in these concluding verses of Dtr. For instance, God is not mentioned, and Jehoiachin's release is in no way attributed to him. Neither is there any allusion to the dynastic promise in 2 Sam 7:11–16, a particularly striking omission given Dtr's penchant for noting prophetic fulfillment.[100] I would add to Begg's observations that this is also in contrast to Dtr's practice of specifically relating the continuation of the dynasty, in spite of disobedient kings, to the Lord's goodness to David (cf. 1 Kgs 11:12–36; 15:4; 2 Kgs 8:19). Begg further explains that although Jehoiachin is specifically noted as an evil king (2 Kgs 24:9), his release is not preceded by any gesture of repentance, a situation at odds with other passages in Dtr which link future restoration to repentance (1 Kgs 8:33–34,46–53; cf. Deut 4:29–31; 30:1–10).[101] Nor is there any suggestion that Evil-merodach's goodwill implied permission for Jehoiachin to return to Judah.[102] Lacking too is any indication that benefits bestowed on Jehoiachin extended to his sons, an omission problematic for any dynastic interpretation of this text, especially since 2 Kgs 25:27–30 presupposes that Jehoiachin has already died ("as long as he lived").[103] Accordingly, the release of Jehoiachin in 2 Kgs 25:27–30, while certainly a positive note, in no way suggests the beginning of the restoration of the davidic dynasty based on an eternal promise.

Levenson, in support of his attempt to see in 2 Kgs 25:27–30 a continuation of the davidic dynasty, now on conditional terms, saw more significance in the terminology. On the one hand, he interpreted כסא (v. 28) to mean "throne," rather than "seat."[104] On the other, he claimed that, on the basis of cognate Semitic parallels, וידבר אתו טבות (v. 28) should be understood as "established a covenant," rather than merely "spoke kindly."[105] Thus, he translates v. 28 as: "He established a covenant with him and set his throne above the thrones of the other

---

[99]Begg, "Jehoiachin's Release."

[100]Begg, "Jehoiachin's Release," 50–51; Wolff, "Das Kerygma," 174, notes that in contrast the destruction of Jerusalem is explained as the fulfillment of prophecy (2 Kgs 24:2).

[101]Begg, "Jehoiachin's Release," 51.

[102]Begg, "Jehoiachin's Release," 52.

[103]Begg, "Jehoiachin's Release," 52,53.

[104]Levenson, "Last Four Verses," 356f.

[105]Levenson, "Last Four Verses," 357.

kings who were with him in Babylon." Accordingly, 2 Kgs 25:27–30 reflects a statement that the davidic dynasty continued even in exile, albeit in the conditional form articulated in 1 Kgs 8:25—a modification required by historical reality.[106]

Yet both of Levenson's points based on terminology are questionable. While כסא can mean "throne," it also simply means "seat." This latter sense of כסא is supported by the context of eating bread before the king, presumably at a table with seats. Moreover, the point is not that Jehoiachin received a כסא, but that his כסא was set above the כסא of the other kings with him in Babylon. The understanding of כסא as "seat" means that Jehoiachin received an honorable place at the king's table.[107] With respect to the phrase וידבר אתו טבות, again while it is possible for this phrase to mean "establish a covenant," it can also mean "speak kindly," as in Jer 12:6.[108] In addition, where וידבר אתו טבות does mean "establish a covenant," the context clearly implies this, and here the context fails to support such a reading, particularly in the absence of any mention of Jehoiachin's sons.[109] Finally, even if Evil-merodach did conclude a treaty with Jehoiachin, this would not in and of itself entail a continuation of the davidic dynasty. Consequently, Levenson's attempt to find evidence for an ongoing davidic monarchy in 2 Kgs 25:27–30 must be judged unsuccessful.

We can conclude this section by considering what positive function 2 Kgs 25:27–30 served, if it does not witness to a dynastic hope. Noth's view that it is merely information must be judged unsatisfactory. More helpful is the suggestion that vv. 27–30 reflect Dtr's attempt to endorse life in exile under Babylonian rule.[110] Moreover, this would indicate the same pro-babylonian outlook characteristic of the last chapters of 2 Kings, illustrated most vividly in Gedaliah's words in the immediately preceding pericope: "Do not be afraid because of the Chaldean officials; dwell in the land, and serve the king of Babylon, and it shall be well with you" (2 Kgs 25:24).[111] While 2 Kgs 25:25–26 shows how this hope was transformed into fear by Ishmael's murder of Gedaliah, vv. 27–30 demonstrate the positive benefits of life under Babylonian rule.[112] Therefore, the last four verses

---

[106]Levenson, "Last Four Verses," 358

[107]If כסא is interpreted as "throne," it is not clear what it would mean that Jehoiachin had a throne above the throne of other kings.

[108]Begg, "Jehoiachin's Release," 52f.

[109]Begg, "Jehoiachin's Release," 52,53.

[110]See B. O. Long, "2 Kings," *Harper's Bible Commentary* (ed. J. L. Mays; San Francisco: Harper & Row, 1988) 341.

[111]Begg, "Jehoiachin's Release," 53–54.

[112]Begg, "Jehoiachin's Release," 54.

of 2 Kings close Dtr on a positive note, which cautiously looks for a "good life" for Israel under exilic conditions. Hope for the restoration of the davidic dynasty is absent in this passage.

A second indication of the absence of hope for the renewal of davidic kingship in the final edition of Dtr comes from Deuteronomistic texts that speak of an opportunity for restoration. Three of these texts that are clearly of exilic provenance are Deut 4:25–31; 30:1–10; and 1 Kgs 8:46–53,[113] and none of them implies that the monarchy—davidic or otherwise—is to be restored. Deut 4:31 promises that God will not destroy Israel and will remember the covenant with their fathers; Deut 30:3–7 expects restoration of Israel's fortunes, compassion, the gathering of the peoples from all places, possession of ancestral lands, prosperity and fruitfulness, circumcised hearts insuring obedience, and a curse upon their enemies; and 1 Kgs 8:46ff on the basis of the Sinai covenant requests forgiveness, compassion from God, and compassion from their captors. It is noteworthy too that in this last passage, only the city and temple are called "chosen" (v. 48). The omission of any reference to the monarchy in these portraits of restoration strongly suggests that for the final edition of Dtr davidic rule had no place in Israel's future.

Thus, it appears that of the four options summarized above, the one put forward by Wolff and modified by Cross (view #2) fits the evidence best. While Dtr maintained a hope for the restoration of Israel as the people of God, there is no future expectation for the davidic dynasty. The passages in Dtr which do speak of a promise to David for a permanent dynasty—and they are quite few[114]—must be assigned to the first edition of Dtr. In this I agree with Cross' assessment:

> In the retouching of the original work by an Exilic hand, the original theme of hope is overwritten and contradicted, namely the expectation of the restoration of the state under a righteous Davidid to the remembered greatness of the golden age of David.[115]

4. Isaiah 55:3–5

Isa 55:3–5 is a brief but important text indicating one way in which the davidic promise functioned in the exilic period. The passage reads as follows:

---

[113]See for example, Cross, *Hebrew Epic*, 252 n. 141. Wolff, "Das Kerygma," 175–183, treated a number of passages that seem to promise restoration for a repentant and obedient Israel, but not all of these can be definitively identified as exilic (see Cross, *Hebrew Epic*, 277–278).

[114]2 Sam 7:11–16; 1 Kgs 11:12–36; 15:4; 2 Kgs 8:19.

[115]Cross, *Hebrew Epic*, 288. See below in the discussion of Chronicles why the characterization of the promise as עד־עולם is not an argument against this conclusion.

Incline your ear, and come to me; hear, that your soul may live; and I will make with you an everlasting covenant, my steadfast, sure love for David. Behold, I made him a witness to the peoples, a leader and commander for the peoples. Behold, you shall call nations that you know not, and nations that knew you not shall run to you, because of the Lord your God, and of the Holy One of Israel, for he has glorified you.

We may begin by observing that 55:3b makes a clear reference to the davidic promise known from texts like 2 Sam 7:11–16, 23:5, and Psalm 89, by mentioning an everlasting covenant (ברית עולם) and the Lord's steadfast sure love for David (חסדי דוד הנאמנים).[116] Some older interpreters had taken this passage as a reference to the davidic messiah.[117] But O. Eissfeldt argued persuasively that in Isa 55:3–5 the promises to David are transferred to the people of Israel as a whole, and his conclusions have been widely received.[118] The following discussion will rely on this interpretation as put forward by Eissfeldt and others.

First, in light of the plural verbs in v. 3a and plural pronoun in v. 3b (לכם), those addressed are clearly the people. Consequently, it is with the people Israel, now languishing in exile, that the Lord will make an everlasting covenant based on his sure steadfast love for David. Verse 4 then harks back to the past,[119] describing the fulfillment of this covenant in terms of David being a witness to and leader of peoples. Here we should observe that the significance of the covenant with David has been limited to David's role as witness and leader of peoples. Furthermore, we should assume that David's witness consisted of his testimony, through his victories, of the presence and greatness of the Lord in the world (cf. Ps 18:44–50).[120] Accordingly, v. 5 describes how this promise will be fulfilled

---

[116]Cf. 2 Sam 23:5 (ברית עולם); Ps 89:2–5,20–38; esp. v. 25 (ואמונתי וחסדי עמו); 2 Sam 7:15 (חסדי) and 7:16 (נאמן). O. Eissfeldt, "The Promises of Grace to David in Isaiah 55:1–5," *Israel's Prophetic Heritage* (ed. B. W. Anderson and W. Harrelson; London: Harper & Brothers, 1962) 197–201, has noted especially close connections between 55:3–5 and Psalm 89.

[117]See the summary of views in J. Muilenburg, "The Book of Isaiah, 40–66," *The Interpreter's Bible, Vol. 5* (ed. G. A. Buttrick; Nashville: Abingdon, 1956) 645.

[118]Eissfeldt, "Promises," 206–207; cf. also C. Westermann, *Isaiah 40–66* (OTL; Philadelphia: Westminster, 1969) 283–286; Cross, *Hebrew Epic*, 265; Beyse, *Serubbabel*, 62; D. L. Petersen, *Late Israelite Prophecy* (SBLMS 23; Missoula, MT: Scholars Press, 1977) 21; See already P. Volz, *Jesaia II* (KAT 9; Leipzig: A. Deichert, 1932) 139–143; Muilenburg, "Isaiah," 645; G. von Rad, *Old Testament Theology* (2 vols.; New York: Harper & Row, 1965) 2:240.

[119]Westermann, *Isaiah 40–66*, 284–285.

[120]Eissfeldt, "Promises," 202; Westermann, *Isaiah 40–66*, 285. Cf. Ps 18:44–50; esp. vv. 44–45,50: "Thou didst deliver me from strife with the peoples; thou didst make me the head of the nations; people whom I had not known served me. As soon as they heard of me they obeyed me; foreigners came cringing to me ... Great triumphs he gives to his king, and shows steadfast love to his anointed, to David and his descendants for ever."

through Israel:[121] they will be the Lord's witness to the world, calling nations they do not yet know (v. 5a), as well as receiving unknown nations.[122] In this way, the Lord will glorify Israel (v. 5b).[123] Thus, Israel as a whole, in their role as witness to the nations, along with the glory which will accrue to them, is heir to the davidic promise.

This interpretation of Isa 55:3–5 is confirmed by other data from Isaiah 40–55 which indicate the democratization of Israel's royal traditions. For one, this role assigned to Israel as witness to the nations is the same one appointed for them elsewhere in Deutero-Isaiah (cf. 43:10; 44:8).[124] Moreover, "War Oracles," a genre typically addressed to kings, are now directed to the exiles in Isaiah 40–55.[125] In addition, and most importantly, when the term "messiah" is used, it is applied to Cyrus, the Persian king (45:1). It is also said of Cyrus: "He is my shepherd" (44:28). Indeed, the word "king" is never applied to an Israelite.[126]

In this light, then, it is not surprising that an expectation for a future davidic messiah is absent in 55:3–5 and throughout Isaiah 40–55. Eissfeldt writes:

> In Isa 55:1–5, as elsewhere in Second Isaiah, there is no reference whatever to that which, for the author of Ps 89, is the particular content of the promise of God to David: that a Davidic representative should always sit upon the Jerusalem throne and rule over the other nations. This is hardly accidental, for our Exilic prophet does not count the Davidic kingdom among the blessings hoped for in the coming Day of Salvation ... [127]

Rather the davidic dynastic promise is transferred to the people and will be embodied in their role as a the Lord's servants in the world.[128] Henceforth, the

---

[121]Eissfeldt, "Promises," 202; Westermann, *Isaiah 40–66*, 284–285.

[122]Note the close connection with Ps 18:44; in a sense, the ideas represented in this verse have become the interpretive key for understanding how the davidic covenant now applies to the people in exile.

[123]The idea of authority over the peoples seems to have been dropped (cf. Eissfeldt, "Promises," 202); Westermann, *Isaiah 40–66*, 285, calls it a radical transformation of the promise of victory over nations.

[124]Eissfeldt, "Promises," 202f; Muilenburg, "Isaiah," 645.

[125]E. W. Conrad, "The Community as King in Second Isaiah," *Understanding the Word* (JSOTSup 37; ed. J. T. Butler, E. W. Conrad, and B. C. Ollenburger; Sheffield: JSOT Press, 1986) 99–112.

[126]Eissfeldt, "Promises," 203f.

[127]Eissfeldt, "Promises," 203; he adds that it is uncertain whether this implies a complete renunciation or merely a temporary one.

[128]Levenson, *Ezekiel 40–48*, 99, sees the democratization of the davidic promise in Isa 55:3–5 as a further development from what occurs in Ezekiel where the royal office is depoliticized, in contrast to Zimmerli, *Ezekiel 2*, 279, who sees strong similarities between the prince in Ezekiel 40–48 and resignification of the davidic promise in Isa 55:3–5.

everlasting covenant with David will be fulfilled in the witness and glorification of Israel. Here, hope for an individual davidic king or messiah has been abandoned.

5. Summary

In the exilic period, the davidic dynasty traditions known from the pre-exilic period were carried on, transformed, or abandoned. Ezek 17:22–24 witnesses to the expectation that the monarchy would be reestablished, and appears to imply that it will be davidic in character. Ezek 34:23f; 37:24f, and Jer 30:9 reflect hope for a "new David," an ideal king typologically like David, perhaps of davidic lineage. On the other hand, in Ezekiel 40–48, the ideal theocracy included a ruler called the נשׂיא, whose characterization is not specifically davidic. In quite a different move, Isa 55:3b transferred the eternal covenant promise given to David to the people as a whole, thereby abandoning a desire to see the davidic monarchy reinstated. Finally, Jeremiah 40–41 and the exilic edition of Dtr (cf. 2 Kgs 25:27–30; see also Jeremiah 52) reveal no hope for the restoration of the davidic dynasty.

What is somewhat surprising in all this is the infrequency of direct reference to any form of pre-exilic royal ideology. Noteworthy also may be the observation that the passages usually dated toward the end of the exile, such as Ezekiel 40–48, Isa 55:3b, and 2 Kgs 25:27–30, lack any expectation for the literal continuation of the dynasty. In any case, in the exile the conception of the meaning of the davidic dynasty is again marked by diversity.

This diversity applies to the characterization of davidic figures as well, whether genealogically or typologically conceived. In Ezek 17:22–24 plant imagery is used again. Names employed consist of נשׂיא ("prince"), מלך ("king"), and רעה ("shepherd"). Moreover, as in pre-exilic passages, ideas associated with davidic figures envision an idyllic state of affairs, including deliverance from oppression, peace, universal rule, prosperity, a united Israel, knowledge of and faithfulness to the Lord. Yet another feature, while not entirely new, comes in for renewed emphasis—the notion of Israel as a theocracy, in which the Lord lives and rules in the midst of his people with the king or prince as his vassal. This trend, especially noticeable in Ezekiel, seems to reflect an attempt to limit the power of the civil ruler, an attempt doubtless borne out of abuses common among pre-exilic monarchs. In any event, the result was a vision of Israelite kingship more circumscribed than in the pre-exilic period—a vision of kingship reduced to a component part of the theocracy.

D. Post-Exilic Traditions

1. Jeremiah 33:14–26

An important passage concerning the davidic dynasty is found in Jer 33:14–26. Unfortunately, determining the date of this oracle is difficult. Proposed dates range from the pre-exilic ministry of Jeremiah to the end of the fifth century BCE.[129] I have grouped it here with post-exilic texts because, in my judgment, it dates from no later than the early post-exilic period. Accordingly, what follows is a brief digression intended to provide a rationale for this dating.

First, 33:14–26 is missing from the LXX of Jeremiah, and as widely recognized, the LXX of Jeremiah is based on a Hebrew edition different from the MT. Moreover, while the edition behind the LXX is dated to the time of the exile, the edition reflected in the MT derives from the early post-exilic period.[130] Accordingly, the oracles in 33:14–26 have been viewed as a redactional addition in the later edition of Jeremiah.[131] Yet, the inclusion of these oracles in a post-exilic edition of Jeremiah does not preclude the possibility that the oracles themselves come from an earlier period, since the editor of the post-exilic edition included authentic Jeremiah material not found in the exilic version witnessed to in the LXX.[132] In other words, the inclusion of this passage in a post-exilic edition of Jeremiah does not imply that it was composed at that time. In any case, its presence in a post-exilic edition of Jeremiah at least establishes this time as the *terminus ad quem* for 33:14–26.

On the other hand, arguments offered in support of the post-exilic *composition* of this passage are not persuasive. For example, in Jer 23:6, a passage paralleling 33:15–16, it is said that Judah and Israel will dwell securely, while in a paraphrase of this verse in 33:16, Judah and *Jerusalem* will be safe. In addition, the name "The Lord is our righteousness" is not applied to the king, but to the city. This focus on Jerusalem is said to reflect the post-exilic period, when Jerusalem was the center of restoration efforts from 538 BCE on. Further, it is

---

[129]Verse 18 reflects a time when the Levites were disenfranchised, a situation that no longer existed at the time of the Chronicler (cf. Carroll, *Jeremiah*, 638), which in this study is dated ca. 400 BCE.

[130]On the two Hebrew editions of Jeremiah and their dates, see E. Tov, "Some Aspects of the Textual and Literary History of the Book of Jeremiah," *Le Livre de Jérémie* (BETL 54; ed. P.-M. Bogaert; Leuven: University Press, 1981) 145–167. The second edition is dated to the early part of the post-exilic period because the editor is probably from the Deuteronomistic School (see below).

[131]Carroll, *Jeremiah*, 637.

[132]Tov, "Literary and Textual History," 151. Tov, himself, thinks 33:14–26 is an example of authentic Jeremiah sayings (p. 154). Cf. also Untermann, *Repentance*, 142.

asserted that the demotion of the Levites to sub-priestly status implied in 33:18 fits the program found in Ezek 44:6–31 and writings associated with the Priestly authors, materials plausibly dated to the post-exilic period.[133] Nevertheless, while these points allow for a post-exilic date, they do not require it. For one, a specific interest in Jerusalem as the place of restoration is equally suitable to the exilic period, as we see in Deutero-Isaiah, or even earlier. And whether attempts to relegate the Levites to a lower status began during the exile is unknown; thus, the material in Ezekiel 44 and the Priestly writings could easily reflect earlier trends.[134]

Another potential indicator for determining the date of 33:14–26 is the fact that its language, style, and themes appear to reflect the work of the Deuterono-mistic school. The phrase in 33:17, "David shall never lack a man to sit on the throne of the house of Israel," occurs in 1 Kgs 2:4; 8:25; 9:5. The term Levitical priests (כהנים הלוים) [v. 18] is also typical of Deuteronomistic literature,[135] as is the special interest in their status.[136] In addition, the phrase "in those days and in that time" (33:15), the hiphil of קום, and the idea of establishing his (God's) word (והקמתי את-הדבר) [v. 14] are all characteristically Deuteronomistic.[137] Finally, 33:14–26 may be a prose reworking of an earlier oracle, Jer 23:5–6, a stylistic feature typical of the Deuteronomistic editor of Jeremiah.[138] The problem here of course is assigning a date to the Deuteronomistic author of this text. Nicholson holds that this author is the same as the Deuteronomistic editor of Jeremiah, who worked either in the early post-exilic or perhaps the late exilic period.[139] On the

---

[133]Holladay, *Jeremiah 2*, 229.

[134]Other supposed indicators for dating are less helpful. For example, arguments that its style and anthological nature imply a late date (Holladay, *Jeremiah 2*, 228) are too vague; the question is how late. Likewise, attempts to associate 33:14–26 with known post-exilic phenomena such as Zechariah 12 (Holladay, *Jeremiah 2*, 229f), hardships under Zerubbabel or Nehemiah, themes in Trito-Isaiah, Haggai, Zechariah, and Malachi (G. P. Coutier, "Jeremiah," *The New Jerome Bible Commentary* [ed. R. E. Brown, J. A. Fitzmyer, and R. E. Murphy; Englewood Cliffs, NJ: Prentice-Hall, 1990], 291), sources in the Persian period (Carroll, *Jeremiah*, 638) are too subjective. So too, the attempt to connect 33:14–26 with known exilic events, such as the release of Jehoiachin in 560 BCE (Coutier, "Jeremiah," 291), is equally subjective.

[135]Nicholson, *Preaching*, 91; Carroll, *Jeremiah*, 637.

[136]T. W. Overholt, "Jeremiah," *Harper's Bible Commentary* (ed. J. L. Mays; San Francisco: Harper & Row, 1988) 638.

[137]Nicholson, *Preaching*, 89f.

[138]Nicholson, *Preaching*, 89.

[139]Nicholson, *Preaching*, 91. Cf. Tov, "Literary and Textual History," 154–155, who suggests that the editor of the early post-exilic edition of Jeremiah behind the MT "may have been

other hand, 33:14–26 need not come from the hand of the editor of Jeremiah; it could reflect the work of the Deuteronomistic school from an earlier period.

Consequently, this leads us to consider one more possibility, namely, that the passage could be pre-exilic, whether from Jeremiah or some representative of the Deuteronomistic school. In this regard, while the text could be understood to presume the absence of a davidic king on the throne in Jerusalem, thereby implying a time after 586 BCE, it is possible that it assumes only that the davidic king is under a dire threat, though still on the throne, perhaps under foreign domination. In fact, this hypothesis finds supported in v. 17, which says that David "will never lack a man to sit on the throne," and v. 21, which implies that the absence of a davidic ruler on the throne is impossible. If the oracles in 33:14–26 were composed after 586 BCE, these assurances make less sense.[140] Further, Cross posits a pre-exilic date arguing that the phrase "Levitic priests" disappears during the exile.[141] Thus, even a pre-exilic date for 33:14–26 is plausible.

Hence, we must conclude that Jer 33:14–26 could date anywhere from between the end of the pre-exilic period to the beginning of the post-exilic era. As noted above, the *terminus ad quem* here is based on the text's inclusion in the early post-exilic edition of Jeremiah, which underlies the MT, supported as well by the Deuteronomistic style of the passage. Moreover, in light of the argument in the previous section, that the exilic edition of Dtr did not assert hope for the restoration of the davidic monarchy, it would be difficult to ascribe 33:14–26 to a Deuteronomistic editor during the exile. Beyond this, it could be argued that regardless of when they were composed, the oracles in 33:14–26 were added to the post-exilic edition of Jeremiah and therefore reflect the ideology of the redactor. But even this does not necessarily follow, for the MT version of Jeremiah incorporates materials that attest to a variety of different views toward the davidic monarchy and its future.[142] Thus, the redactor apparently included some sayings because they were received from the tradition, not because they expressed his own view. Nevertheless, because 33:14–26 could emanate from the post-exilic

---

one of the last members of that ill-defined 'deuteronomistic school', or he else imitated its style."

[140]In addition, Unterman, *Repentance*, 144, claims 33:14–26 is authentic because of stylistic similarities to Jer 31:35–37, which in his view is authentic. This point is less convincing since: 1) 31:35–37 may not be authentic; and 2) even if it were, the similarity between 31:35–37 and 33:14–26 could easily be the work of a later redactor.

[141]Cross, *Hebrew Epic*, 259.

[142]See above, p. 34

period, I will consider it as relevant to that time. The previous discussion, however, should indicate why this dating must remain tentative.

Turning to the content of the passage, we note a strong statement about the
permanence of the davidic dynasty and the coming of an ideal davidic king.
Verses 14–16, a paraphrase of Jer 23:5–6, look to the future for the fulfillment of
God's word to Israel and Judah, when he will cause a righteous branch to sprout
for David (אצמיח לדוד צמח צדקה). This ideal davidic king will bring justice
and security to Judah and Jerusalem. The name "The Lord is our righteousness,"
as mentioned above, is no longer applied to the king, but to the city of Jerusalem.
Nevertheless, there exists a close connection between the future davidic king and
the city of Jerusalem.

In vv. 17–18, we see a clear appeal to the dynastic promise as expressed in
1 Kgs 2:4; 8:25; 9:5.[143] Thus, not only the enthronement of an ideal figure, but
the restoration of the davidic dynasty is envisioned. This reaffirmation of the
dynastic promise is emphasized in vv. 19–26, where the permanence of the
covenant made with David is compared to the permanence of the cosmic order
(cf. Jer 31:35–37; Ps 89:38) and the multiplication of davidic descendants is
declared. Here the covenant promise for a continuing davidic dynasty is unconditional. Hence, the Lord will not reject the descendants of David, but in mercy
restore their fortunes (v. 26). Accordingly, this passages asserts in the strongest
terms the continuing validity of the davidic covenant. We should note, however,
that it does so in the face of claims that the Lord has rejected the davidic family.[144] Clearly, this passage witnesses to conflicting opinions regarding the continuing relevance of the davidic covenant.

2. Haggai 2:20–23

In one oracle, Haggai speaks of a potential royal role for Zerubbabel, and this has
been widely thought to offer evidence for a post-exilic messianic hope focused on
a davidic descendant.[145] The question we must consider is whether this is indeed
true, and if so, what conception of the davidic descendant or dynasty is implied.

Hag 2:20–23 reads as follows:

> The word of the Lord came a second time to Haggai on the twenty-fourth day
> of the month, "Speak to Zerubbabel, governor of Judah, saying, 'I am about to
> shake the heavens and the earth, and to overthrow the throne of kingdoms; I am

---

[143]Unlike the promises in 1–2 Kings, which are conditioned on the obedience of the king, in
Jer 33:17, the conditional clause is absent.

[144]Carroll, *Jeremiah*, 638, suggests that this view may stem from circles who agreed with
the critique of the davidic monarchy found in Jeremiah 2–20.

[145]Cf. the literature mentioned below.

> about to destroy the strength of the kingdoms of the nations, and overthrow the chariots and their riders; and the horses and their riders shall go down, every one by the sword of his fellow. On that day,' says the Lord of hosts, 'I will take you, O Zerubbabel my servant, the son of Shealtiel,' says the Lord, 'and make you like a signet ring; for I have chosen you,' says the Lord of hosts."

The view claiming that this text represents an expectation of an imminent re-establishment of the davidic dynasty is based on two assertions: first, that Zerubbabel is a davidic descendant; and secondly, that Haggai predicts Zerubbabel's imminent kingship in the language of the davidic dynasty tradition. Each point, however, is questionable. I will consider each claim separately.

Zerubbabel's status as a davidic descendant rests on very fragile grounds. First of all, in the book of Haggai, as well as in the books of Zechariah, Ezra, and Nehemiah, Zerubbabel's davidic descent is never mentioned. In these books, he is either referred to by name only or as the son of Shealtiel. Miller and Hayes write, "If Zerubbabel had been a member of the Davidic family line, it seems almost unbelievable that neither Ezra, Nehemiah, Haggai, nor Zechariah noted this."[146] The only passage that does link Zerubbabel to the line of David is 1 Chr 3:16–19, where he is listed as a grandson of Jeconiah (i.e., Jehoiachin), the second to last king of Judah. But even here, the connection is not without difficulty, for while in Haggai, Ezra, and Nehemiah, Zerubbabel is called the son of Shealtiel,[147] in 1 Chr 3:19, he is listed as a grandson of Jehoiachin through his son Pedaiah, not Shealtiel. It may be that the Chronicler has secondarily grafted Zerubbabel, a non-davidic post-exilic leader, into the davidic family tree to emphasize the continuity between the post-exilic temple built by Zerubbabel and pre-exilic traditions.[148] Finally, it is questionable whether Darius, given the unstable condition of his kingdom between 522–520 BCE, would have placed a member of the Jewish royal line in authority in Judah.[149] In sum, Zerubbabel's status as a davidic descendant is uncertain.

A second consideration is whether Haggai is drawing on the promise of an ongoing davidic dynasty in vv. 21b–23. Several features of the text have been cited as a positive indication of this. For one, the language in vv. 21b–22 has been related to concepts connected with theophany and holy war.[150] Accordingly, it is

---

[146]Miller and Hayes, *History*, 456.

[147]Hag 1:1,12,14; 2:2,23; Ezra 3:2,8; 5:2; Neh 12:1.

[148]Miller and Hayes, *History*, 456.

[149]S. E. McEvenue, "The Political Structure in Judah from Cyrus to Nehemiah," *CBQ* 43 (1981) 357 n. 13; for the opposite view, see P. R. Ackroyd, *Exile and Restoration* (OTL; Philadelphia: Westminster, 1968) 165.

[150]G. Sauer, "Serubbabel in der Sicht Haggais und Sacharjas," *Das Ferne und Nahe Wort*

observed that these verses reflect ideas similar to those in Pss. 2:9,12 and 110:3,5f, royal psalms celebrating the enthronement of the davidic king as the Lord's anointed.[151] Hence, it is argued that vv. 21b–22 provide the context for asserting the establishment of Zerubbabel as a new davidic monarch.

Moreover, various terms in v. 23—חותם, עבד, בחר, לקח—are construed as related to the davidic dynasty tradition. לקח ("to take") is said to point to the unconditionality of God's selection of Zerubbabel.[152] בחר ("to choose") is used in reference to the choosing of David as king[153] and is held by Petersen to be a *terminus technicus* for davidic election.[154] The term עבד ("servant") is common as an epithet for David, especially in 2 Samuel 7,[155] and, according to Petersen, is used as a royal title.[156] And חותם ("signet") is associated with Jer 22:24, where Coniah (Jehoiachin) is compared to a "signet" that God will tear off his hand. Haggai's reference to Zerubbabel as the Lord's signet would then imply a reversal of Jeremiah's prophecy, portraying Zerubbabel as the soon to be appointed davidic monarch.[157]

Yet none of these points is convincing evidence for a specifically davidic expectation concerning Zerubbabel. First of all, while it is true that vv. 21b–22 reflect the language of theophany and holy war, this terminology is by no means limited to contexts associated with davidic monarchs.[158] It is connected to the presence and power of the Lord. Accordingly, the key issue in the use of this language is God's kingship. That in a few passages, like Psalm 2 and Psalm 110, God's kingship is viewed as being exercised through a davidic monarch does not imply that it could not be implemented through a non-davidic leader. Thus, there

---

(ed. F. Maass; Berlin: Töpelmann, 1967) 200–202; K. Seybold, "Die Königserwartung bei den Propheten Haggai und Sacharja," *Judaica* 28 (1972) 70–71; Beyse, *Serubbabel*, 53–56.

[151] Sauer, "Serubbabel," 202–203.

[152] Sauer, "Serubbabel," 203.

[153] Beyse, *Serubbabel*, 58f (see 1 Sam 16:8–10; 2 Sam 6:21; 1 Kgs 8:16; Ps 78:70; 1 Chr 28:4).

[154] D. L. Petersen, *Haggai and Zechariah 1–8* (OTL; Philadelphia: Westminster, 1984) 103,104f.

[155] Beyse, *Serubbabel*, 59.

[156] Petersen, *Hag, Zech 1–8*, 103.

[157] Beyse, *Serubbabel*, 56f; Sauer, "Serubbabel," 204; Seybold, "Königserwartung," 71f; Ackroyd, *Exile and Restoration*, 164; Petersen, *Hag, Zech 1–8*, 104, who refrains from designating Zerubbabel as king, but only earthly representative of God.

[158] Cf. Ps 46:9–10; Ps 48:2–9; Ps 50:1–6; Mic 4:1–3; Deut 33:2; Judg 5:4–5; Isa 2:2–4; Isa 40:3–5; 43:14–17; 45:1–2.

is no necessary link between vv. 21b–22 and the davidic dynasty tradition, only an expression of divine sovereignty.

Neither is the terminology in v. 23 specific to the davidic dynasty tradition; all of it is used more widely. Thus, לקח is so common a term in the Hebrew Bible that only a prior assumption about Zerubbabel's davidic status makes it noteworthy.[159]

Further, בחר is not limited to designating the choosing of David, but refers to any important divine selection, including the choice of Saul (1 Sam 10:24), Solomon (1 Chr 28:5,6,10), Aaron (1 Sam 2:28), Zion (Ps 132:13), Jacob (Ps 135:4), the servant of the Lord (Isa 49:7), and an unnamed ruler of Edom or Babylon (Jer 49:19; 50:44).[160] It is significant too that no kings of the line of David are said to have been "chosen" with the exception of Solomon, and he only in Chronicles, a later text, where he is the one chosen to build the temple. The continuation of the davidic line was secure, because God chose David, not because he chose the reigning davidic monarch (cf. 1 Kgs 11:34; Ps 89:19–51). Thus, if Haggai were invoking the davidic dynastic promise, we would expect to find Zerubbabel's status as a davidic king based on God's having chosen David, not on his having chosen Zerubbabel. In fact, all the people or places "chosen" by God in the above list appear to represent new beginnings of a sort. Thus, the explicit choosing of Zerubbabel is more suggestive of a new era in the rulership of Judah, although the possibility that it implies a new start for the davidic dynasty cannot be excluded.[161]

Moreover, the term עבד, while often applied to David, is rarely used in connection with a member of the davidic line (only of Solomon in the prayers in 1 Kgs 11:32,36 and of Hezekiah in 2 Chr 32:16, which is later than Haggai). As Meyers and Meyers comment, "Clearly 'servant' is not a normal designation for an incumbent king of Israel or Judah."[162] On the other hand, עבד is employed in Jer 25:9 and 27:6 to designated Nebuchadnezzar, the king of Babylon. In addition, עבד is used in the servant songs of Deutero-Isaiah for a non-davidic and non-royal figure. In fact, as Beyse observes, עבד is so general a term, it is difficult to understand it as a specific designation for a king.[163] Thus, while עבד

---

[159]Cf. Petersen, *Hag, Zech 1–8*, 103, "its (לקח) use achieves a special effect when it has as its object a member of the Davidic line."

[160]Cf. also Jer 33:24, where the Lord chose the family of David and Jacob.

[161]See C. L. Meyers and E. M. Meyers, *Haggai, Zechariah 1–8* (AB 25B; Garden City, NY: Doubleday, 1987) 70.

[162]Meyers and Meyers, *Hag, Zech 1–8*, 68.

[163]Beyse, *Serubbabel*, 58.

indicates Zerubbabel's role as an instrument of God, it cannot be cited as evidence for his davidic royal status.

Finally, חותם is used to designate a davidic king only in Jer 22:24. On the other hand, it is an image applied to the king of Tyre in Ezek 28:12,[164] which suggests that its connotation may simply be royal, not specifically davidic.[165]

All in all, Haggai's language in v. 23, although sometimes associated with David, is, on the one hand, not typically applied to succeeding davidic kings, and on the other, used quite widely to designate all kinds of divine agents. If one considers how Haggai's language would have differed if Zerubbabel had clearly not been of davidic stock, it is evident that his present terminology would be equally suitable. In other words, there is nothing exclusively davidic about it.

In light of this, we must note several reasons which argue against associating 2:20–23 with the tradition of a continuing davidic dynasty. First, there is no explicit reference to a dynastic promise, to David, or to the davidic dynasty tradition generally in these verse or elsewhere in the book of Haggai. When sacred tradition is cited in Haggai, it is the Exodus story (2:5). Secondly, as noted above, Zerubbabel is never labeled a Davidide in the book of Haggai. Lastly, and most importantly, the underlying conception of Zerubbabel's role as the Lord's signet is at odds with the tradition of an ongoing davidic royal line rooted in a dynastic promise. As Beyse has shown, according to Haggai the day of Zerubbabel's elevation as the Lord's signet is the day of the Lord's theophany (2:21b–22). At this time, the Lord will appear in his glory in the completed temple (1:8b) and the nations will bring their treasures to enhance its splendor (2:6–8).[166] In other words, the benefits of the Lord's presence in the temple, the temple's splendor, the overthrow of the nations, and Zerubbabel's role as signet all depend on the completion of the temple,[167] which of course is Haggai's central aim. In this sense, Zerubbabel's status as "signet" is conditional, based on the people's ability to finish the temple. This is very different from the conception of a perpetual dynasty rooted in a promise—whether unconditional or conditional—offered to David and realized in his descendants as we find articulated in 2 Sam 7:11–16, Psalm 89, and various passages in 1–2 Kings. In that view of things, dynastic continuity is based on God's faithfulness to David, not to Judah's faithfulness in building the second temple.[168] Appeals to the davidic promise as we find it in

---

[164]On the textual problem, the majority of commentators opt for a reading of חותם (see esp. Zimmerli, *Ezekiel 2*, 81, for further discussion.)

[165]Cf. also 1 Macc 6:15, where the signet is a symbol of royalty.

[166]Beyse, *Serubbabel*, 53–57

[167]Beyse, *Serubbabel*, 57–58.

[168]Ironically, in 2 Sam 7:11–16, the dynastic promise is given in the specific context of

2 Sam 7:11–16 as the basis for Haggai's prophecy about Zerubbabel in 2:20–23[169] fail to recognize the very different conceptions of legitimization for royal rule that lie behind each text.

It is possible, however, as Beyse has suggested, that Zerubbabel is to be understood as a new David, along the lines of Ezek 34:23–24; 37:24–28.[170] Admittedly, this cannot be ruled out, especially since the language in v. 23 is more appropriate to David than to the kings of his line. Yet, if this was Haggai's point, he expressed it in a most oblique manner, never mentioning Zerubbabel's connection to David. Attempts to account for only an indirect expression of davidic messianic or royalist hopes on the basis of Haggai's reluctance to alert Persian suspicions fails to explain why Haggai would offer any prophecy which could be viewed as predicting Jewish autonomy. Presumably, the Persian government would be equally concerned about sedition regardless of whether it was led by a davidic or non-davidic figure. If Haggai's motive was to avoid Persian suspicion, we would expect him to be oblique and indirect about his claim that God would overthrow the nations and rule through Zerubbabel, not merely oblique and indirect about this new ruler's typological relationship to the ideal Israelite king, David. Further, since Zerubbabel was a Persian appointee, the Persians obviously would have known about his davidic lineage, if he had one, thus giving Haggai no reason to speak about it covertly.

To summarize, the case for an expression of davidic royalist or messianic hopes in Hag 2:20–23 rests mainly on the unsure foundation of the Chronicler's identification of Zerubbabel as a member of the davidic line (1 Chr 3:16–19). Modern scholars have largely assumed the trustworthiness of the Chronicler's identification and interpreted Hag 2:20–23 in this light. On the other hand, if we interpret the Chronicler's view of Zerubbabel as ideological rather than historical, then the weight of evidence from Haggai's oracle argues against seeing it as a witness to a davidic hope in Judah in ca. 520 BCE. Nevertheless, 1 Chr 3:16–19, along with 1 Esdr 5:5 (probably first century BCE), represents the view of a later age in which Zerubbabel was clearly seen as a davidic descendant. Therefore, we should outline the conception of his role in the book of Haggai, in order to clarify what ideas would have been available to later interpreters who may have viewed him as davidic.

To do this, it will be important to recognize a distinction in the book of Haggai between the oracles of the prophet and the editorial framework, the latter

---

instructions not to build the first temple.

[169]Beyse, *Serubbabel*, 59; Seybold, "Königserwartung," 73.

[170]Beyse, *Serubbabel*, 63–64; similarly, Meyers and Meyers, *Hag, Zech 1–8*, 83.

consisting of Hag 1:1,3,12,13a,14,15; 2:1,2,10,20, and probably 2:4.[171] In the oracles, which date from August to December 520 BCE, Zerubbabel is only mentioned once, and that is in 2:21–23. The oracle consists of an introduction (v. 21a), a saying concerning the overthrow of the nations (vv. 21b–22), and a saying concerning Zerubbabel (v. 23).

First, we must observe that the proclamation of an impending divine intervention—shaking the heavens and earth and overthrowing nations (vv. 21b–22)—and the introductory phrase "in that day" (v. 23a) provide an eschatological context for Haggai's words about Zerubbabel.[172] (Here we mean by eschatological only the idea that at some future date God would act decisively to crush the power of oppressive nations, liberate his people, and rule all the nations from Jerusalem in an ideal era of justice, peace, and prosperity.) Inherent in this idealized future is the notion of theocratic rule in which God is present in the temple on Zion (1:8b) and takes on military tasks (2:22).[173] The theocratic theme is reinforced by the language of theophany and holy war present in vv. 21b–22, the primary connotation of which is the Lord's kingship.

Within this theocratic context, v. 23 designates Zerubbabel as God's chosen vice-regent. The terms "servant" and "signet," together with Zerubbabel's passive role in the subjugation of the nations, underline his subordination to God's sovereignty.[174] Yet, beyond this notion of Zerubbabel's delegated authority, little else of his actual role is specified in the oracle.[175] In fact, Haggai's main interest is not focused on the civil leadership of the Jewish community, but on temple and cult.[176] Moreover, as noted earlier, Zerubbabel's designation as "signet" is conditioned on the completion of the temple. In this regard, in the oracles of Haggai,

---

[171]R. A. Mason, "The Purpose of the 'Editorial Framework' of the Book of Haggai," *VT* 27 (1977) 414; "Prophets of the Restoration," *Israel's Prophetic Tradition* (ed. R. J. Coggins, A. Phillips, and M. Knibb; Cambridge: Cambridge University Press, 1982) 144–145; W. A. M. Beuken, *Haggai-Sacharja* (SSN; Assen: Van Gorcum, 1967) 54.

[172]Meyers and Meyers, *Hag, Zech 1–8*, 66f; Beyse, *Serubbabel*, 57f.

[173]Meyers and Meyers, *Hag, Zech 1–8*, 83, write, "The overwhelming imagery of the oracle is not only eschatological, it is also theocratic;" cf. also Beyse, *Serubbabel*, 55.

[174]Meyers and Meyers, *Hag, Zech 1–8*, 66–67,83; Beyse, *Serubbabel*, 65.

[175]Thus, interpreters have perceived Zerubbabel's role differently, some speaking of a royal position, though circumscribed in a theocratic context (Meyers and Meyers, *Hag, Zech 1–8*, 83; Beyse, *Serubbabel*, 65), others referring merely to civil leadership, without explicitly connecting it to monarchy (Petersen, *Hag, Zech 1–8*, 105f; R. Coggins, *Haggai, Zechariah, Malachi* [Old Testament Guides; Sheffield: JSOT Press, 1987] 35–36). The issue seems to involve how one understands the metaphor of a "signet," whether it suggests kingship, or whether it implies only delegated authority. What can be said with some certainty is that Haggai's description of Zerubbabel's actual status and role is vague and colorless.

[176]Mason, "Prophets of the Restoration," 140.

cultic concerns seem to take precedence over the issue of civil leadership. As we will now see, this is a trend that is even more pronounced in the editorial framework.

In the editorial framework, Zerubbabel is portrayed differently than in the oracles. First of all, he is mentioned more often. But as Mason points out, in the framework,

> the sole function of Zerubbabel, for all that he is termed 'governor', is the building of the temple. Unlike the last oracle (ii 21–23) no political significance is given to his office whatever ... [177]

In addition, Zerubbabel now stands alongside another leader, Joshua the high priest, who appears only in the editorial framework, suggesting that at the time of the composition of the framework, the priesthood had gained greater prominence.[178]

The precise date of the editorial framework is difficult to ascertain, but a time not too long after Haggai himself may be in order.[179] The identity of the editors is more problematic. Beuken suggested a "Chronistic milieu," while Mason posited "theocratic circles" with affinities to the Priestly work and Chronicles.[180] Whatever the precise identity of the editors, one must nevertheless recognize an important distinction between the oracles of Haggai the prophet, and the ideas and interests of the editors.[181] Further, their idea of Zerubbabel as temple builder alongside Joshua the high priest is similar to the portrayal of Zerubbabel in Zechariah 1–8 and Ezra-Nehemiah. In addition, it may have affinities with the understanding of the davidic dynasty tradition found in Chronicles,[182] as well as later traditions about Zerubbabel in 1 Esdras 3–7 and Ben Sira 49:11–12. Thus, the editorial framework of Haggai is the first indication of a broad tradition emphasizing Zerubbabel as the builder of the second temple alongside the high priest, with his role as a civil ruler being eclipsed. Thus, later tradition, which

[177]Mason, "Editorial Framework," 417.

[178]R. A. Mason, *The Books of Haggai, Zechariah, and Malachi* (CBC; Cambridge: Cambridge University Press, 1977) 25.

[179]Mason, "Editorial Framework," 417.

[180]Beuken, *Haggai-Sacharja*, 27–83; Mason, "Editorial Framework," 415,419; "Prophets of the Restoration," 145.

[181]Contra O. Eissfeldt, *The Old Testament: An Introduction* (New York: Harper & Row, 1965) 428–429.

[182]Mason, "Editorial Framework," 417, if, following P. R. Ackroyd ("History and Theology in the Writings of the Chronicler," *CTM* 38 [1967] 501–507), the Chronicler sees the davidic hope as now embodied in the second temple. Note too that this contention strengthens the possibility that the Chronicler grafted Zerubbabel into the davidic family line.

understood Zerubbabel as a davidic descendant, would honor him as the builder
of the second temple and not as a symbol of a continuing davidic hope.

3. Zechariah 1–8

Most scholars believe that Zechariah both perpetuated and modified the davidic
dynasty tradition, since he proclaimed the coming of a davidic figure—whether
Zerubbabel or some future individual—who would, however, rule alongside a
priestly leader. Accordingly, the issue here is very similar to that faced in our
consideration of Haggai: did Zechariah prophesy the coming rule of some davidic
figure, and if so, what conception of the davidic descendant or dynasty does he
set forth. Moreover, as in the case of Haggai, the basis for understanding
Zechariah as a tradent of the davidic dynasty tradition is his reference to Zerubbabel, who is assumed to be a Davidide, and his use of terminology related to the
davidic dynasty tradition. Yet, in my view, the connection between Zechariah's
prophecies and the davidic dynasty tradition is more tenuous than often presumed.

First, as discussed above, Zerubbabel's davidic status is very doubtful. I
might only reiterate that Zechariah never claims that Zerubbabel is of davidic
lineage, and unlike Haggai, he does not even use Zerubbabel's patronymic, "son
of Shealtiel." Secondly, Zechariah's alleged use of terminology from the davidic
dynasty tradition is limited to עבדי ("my servant") [3:8] and צמח ("branch") [3:8;
6:12]. Again, in the discussion of Hag 2:20–23, we saw that עבדי was not an
indication of one's davidic royal status. On the other hand, צמח is a word used in
the davidic dynasty tradition, so its significance must be probed in more detail.

In Zechariah, the term צמח is used for a figure whom the Lord is bringing:

> Hear now, O Joshua the high priest, you and your friends who sit before you,
> for they are men of good omen: behold, I am bringing (RSV: will bring) my
> servant Branch (צמח) [3:8].

> and say to him (Joshua), "Thus says the Lord of hosts, 'Behold, the man whose
> name is Branch (צמח): for he shall grow up (יצמח) in his place, and he shall
> build the temple of the Lord'" (6:12).

In favor of the davidic connotations for the noun צמח is its use in Jer 23:5 and
33:15, where it refers to a future davidic king.[183] Since צמח is also used of a
coming figure in Zech 3:8 and 6:12 (clearly a ruler in 6:12), most critics reason

---

[183]The verb צמח also appears in texts associated with the davidic dynasty tradition (Jer
33:15; Ps 132:7; cf. also 2 Sam 23:5 and Ezek 17:6, where it is not directly related to any
davidic figure).

that here too it designates a davidic figure. To be sure, this is a plausible inference.

Yet there are several reasons for doubting such an easy association. For one, in the context of future restoration, צמח is not limited to designating a davidic descendant. It is employed more broadly as in Isa 4:2, where in the expression "branch of the Lord," צמח refers to the growth the Lord will bring in the age of salvation.[184] Here the basic meaning of צמח as "sprout," "bud," or "branch," which denotes some new growth that springs up, is used to portray how future restoration will appear from a fruitless setting. The key concept in צמח is therefore that of a sprouting, a new growth. In this sense, although it could be applied to a new start for the davidic dynasty, it did not necessarily have davidic connotations.[185] Whether צמח in Zech 3:8 and 6:12 indicates use of the davidic dynasty tradition depends on whether one connects it with Jer 23:5 and 33:15 or with the more general meaning of any new start. To decide between these two options, we must investigate the precise relationship between the use of צמח in Zech 3:8 and 6:12, and Jer 23:5 and 33:15.

Jer 23:5 reads והקמתי לדוד צמח צדיק ("I will raise up for David a righteous/legitimate branch"); Jer 33:15 is similar: אצמיח לדוד צמח צדקה ("I will cause to sprout for David a righteous/legitimate branch"). In both passages, the bringing forth of the "branch" is "for David" and צמח is paired with an adjective meaning righteous or legitimate, forming a phrase that is a kind of technical term for a legitimate heir.[186] We may now compare these texts with Zech 3:8, הנני מביא את־עבדי צמח ("Behold, I am bringing my servant, Branch"), and 6:12, הנה־איש צמח שמו ומתחתיו יצמח ובנה את־היכל יהוה ("Behold, a man, Branch is his name, and/for he will sprout up from his place and build the temple of the Lord"). We may observe first that neither text in Zechariah uses צמח in conjunction with an adjective form of צדק, and thus does not appear to be employing צמח in the manner of technical terminology as in Jeremiah. Secondly, in Jer 23:5 and 33:15 the stated purpose of the Lord's raising up of the צמח—"for

---

[184]See Clements, *Isaiah 1–39*, 54; Kaiser, *Isaiah 1–12*, 54; H. G. Mitchell, *et al, Haggai, Zechariah, Malachi, and Jonah* (ICC; New York: Charles Scribner's Sons, 1912) 186; this meaning is clear from the parallel expression in v. 2 "fruit of the land." J. G. Baldwin, "*semah* as a Technical Term in the Prophets," *VT* 14 (1964) 93, argues that in Isa 4:2, צמח refers to the messiah; yet she fails to produce compelling evidence. Later, the Targum would put forward such an interpretation.

[185]The common English translation for צמח as branch is therefore biased toward its association with the davidic dynasty tradition in that one imagines a new limb from the davidic trunk rather than a new sprout from virgin soil.

[186]See the discussion of this phrase as a technical term in W. L. Holladay, *Jeremiah 1* (Hermeneia; Philadelphia: Fortress, 1986) 618.

David"—is lacking in Zech 3:8 and 6:12. In fact, in Zech 6:12, the reason for the name צמח is explained not by appeal to the davidic dynasty tradition, but because this figure "will sprout up from his place,"[187] and if Zerubbabel is the person referred to here, it may well be a play on his name.[188] Yet, the very marks that associate צמח with the davidic dynasty tradition in Jeremiah are missing when צמח is used in Zechariah. This observation, therefore, weakens the putative link between Zechariah's use of צמח and the davidic dynasty tradition. One could, of course, assert that in Zechariah's day, the term צמח was so firmly connected to the davidic dynasty tradition and so familiar as a term for a davidic messiah that overt reference or even allusion to the davidic dynasty tradition was unnecessary.[189] This is possible, but merely an assumption without proof. Furthermore, the opposite is equally possible: Zechariah's use of צמח could be drawing on its general meaning of a new beginning, thus designating the person named צמח the Lord's new ruler in the restoration.[190] Consequently, the results of our inquiry must remain uncertain, for צמח in Zechariah can plausibly be related to the davidic dynasty tradition as many interpreters maintain, but this connection is not as obvious and assured as it may appear on the surface.

Other features of Zechariah 1–8 do not support so clear of a connection to the davidic dynasty tradition. First, in Zechariah 1–8 there is nowhere an appeal to the davidic dynastic promise. Secondly, portraits of an ideal future, while including a vision of a restored Jerusalem and Zion (1:14–17; 2:4–5,7,10–12; 8:2–8,15), make no mention of a reestablished davidic monarchy. Finally, the high priest Joshua is given symbols and privileges associated with the monarchy of the pre-exilic period. In 3:5, Joshua receives a clean turban (צניף), a headdress indicative of royalty.[191] In 3:7 he is charged with executing judgment (תדין), a duty formerly possessed by Judean kings,[192] and given access to the heavenly

---

[187]While the verb צמח is also used in the davidic dynasty tradition in Ps 132:17 for a scion of David sprouting up, it is also used more broadly as in Ezek 29:21, where a horn for Israel will sprout up.

[188]See J. C. VanderKam, "Joshua the High Priest and the Interpretation of Zechariah 3," *CBQ* 53 (1991) 561.

[189]W. Rudolph, *Haggai, Sacharja 1–8, Sacharja 9–14, Maleachi* (KAT 13/4; Gütersloh: Gütersloher Verlagshaus Gerd Mohn, 1976) 100.

[190]If we are correct that Zerubbabel was not of the davidic house and he is the one referred to in 6:12–13, as many think, then צמח is being used of a non-Davidide.

[191]Meyers and Meyers, *Hag, Zech 1–8*, 351; Coggins, *Hag, Zech, Mal*, 45f. Rudolph, *Hag, Sach 1–8, 9–14, Mal*, 97, notes too that this is the head covering of the high priest in the Priestly documents.

[192]Mason, "Prophets of the Restoration," 147; Meyers and Meyers, *Hag, Zech 1–8*, 195; Rudolph, *Hag, Sach 1–8, 9–14, Mal*, 97; VanderKam, "Joshua," 559.

council, making him the mediator between God and Israel, again a function formerly exercised by kings.[193] In 6:11, Joshua gets a crown (עטרות) in terminology appropriate to royal, not priestly, power.[194]

Altogether, Zerubbabel's doubtful davidic lineage, the ambiguity present in Zechariah's use of צמח, the absence of direct reference to the davidic dynasty tradition, and the royal prerogatives assigned to the high priest call into question the assertion that Zechariah proclaimed the coming of a davidic messiah. The data is not sufficient to rule out such a hypothesis, but neither does it unequivocally support this often assumed contention. If Zechariah was a tradent of a davidic messianic hope, his specific reference to the davidic dynasty tradition is decidedly muted. Nevertheless, since a connection with the davidic dynasty tradition in Zechariah is possible, and later tradition would view Zerubbabel as a Davidide (see above), material in Zechariah potentially relevant to the davidic dynasty tradition in early Judaism should be reviewed.

Unlike Haggai, in Zechariah it is more difficult to distinguish between sayings of the prophet and editorial work.[195] Yet a helpful form-critical distinction can be made between vision reports, contained in 1:7–6:15, and oracles, which both frame the vision reports (1:1–6 and 7:1–8:23) and are inserted within (or attached to) several of the vision reports (1:14b–17; 2:10–17; 3:8–10; 4:6b–10a; 6:9–15). Moreover, it should be noted that the material usually associated with the davidic dynasty tradition is found in the oracles inserted in or appended to the vision reports (with the possible exception of 4:14, depending on whether one of the "sons of oil" mentioned there is to be identified with Zerubbabel or a later messianic figure).

We may begin by examining what is said about Zerubbabel. He is specifically mentioned only in 4:6b–10a, a group of oracles inserted into the vision of the lampstand:

> Then he said to me, "This is the word of the Lord to Zerubbabel: Not by might, nor by power, but by my Spirit, says the Lord of hosts. What are you, O great mountain? Before Zerubbabel you shall become a plain; and he shall bring forward the top stone amid shouts of 'Grace, grace to it!'" Moreover, the word of the Lord came to me, saying, "The hands of Zerubbabel have laid the foundation of this house; his hands shall also complete it. Then you will know that the Lord of hosts has sent me to you. For whoever has despised the day of small things shall rejoice, and shall see the plummet in the hand of Zerubbabel.

---

[193]Mason, "Prophets of the Restoration," 147. The function of mediator is also related to the role of a prophet (see VanderKam, "Joshua," 559–560).

[194]Meyers and Meyers, *Hag, Zech 1–8*, 351.

[195]Mason, "Prophets of the Restoration," 146.

Two observations are pertinent: one, Zerubbabel's success is not grounded in his own power, but in the power of the Lord's spirit, thus underlining Zerubbabel's dependence on God; two, his sole task is to build the temple.[196] Interestingly, the latter point corresponds to the conception of Zerubbabel found in the editorial framework of Haggai.[197]

Some interpreters have perceived royal or davidic connotations in these verses. Petersen has argued that this passage highlights Zerubbabel's royal pre-rogative as temple-builder over against the competing claims of Joshua the high priest.[198] He then infers, "As Davidic prince, he was proleptic king."[199] His inter-pretation founders, however, on his claim that the "great mountain" before Zerub-babel refers to Joshua and his need to emend לָהּ to לֹה (v. 7), so that Zerubbabel, rather than the headstone of the temple, is acclaimed. Similarly to be rejected as speculation is the suggestion by Meyers and Meyers that "His (Zerubbabel's) direct involvement in the ceremony of refoundation perhaps assuages fears that no Davidide would be present at the momentous event."[200] From what we know about the period, the people seemed to have had little interest in building the temple at all, let alone hesitation based on their fear that a Davidide would not be involved. According to 4:6b–10a, Zerubbabel is not the messianic king, but the Lord's spiritually endowed agent for rebuilding the temple.

Whether more can be claimed for Zerubbabel depends on one's interpreta-tion of a most difficult passage—6:9–14:

> And the word of the Lord came to me: "Take from the exiles Heldai, Tobijah, and Jedaiah, who have arrived from Babylon; and go the same day to the house of Josiah, the son of Zephaniah. Take from them silver and gold, and make a crown (עטרות), and set it upon the head of Joshua, the son of Jehozadak, the high priest; and say to him, 'Thus says the Lord of hosts, "Behold, the man; his name is the Branch, and/for he shall grow up in his place, and he shall build the temple of the Lord. It is he who shall build the temple of the Lord, and shall bear majesty (RSV: royal honor), and shall sit and rule upon his throne. And there shall be a priest by/on his throne, and peaceful understanding shall be be-tween them both.'" And the crown shall be (והעטרת תהיה) in the temple of the Lord as a reminder to Helem, Tobijah, Jedaiah, and Hen the son of Zephaniah."

---

[196]Although there are questions about the precise meaning of some of the terminology and how his role in building of the temple is described, it is clear that the entire passage is focused on rebuilding the temple.

[197]Mason, "Prophets of the Restoration," 148.

[198]Petersen, *Hag, Zech 1–8,* 239–241; D. L. Petersen, "Zerubbabel and Jerusalem Temple Reconstruction," *CBQ* 36 (1974) 366–372.

[199]Petersen, *Hag, Zech 1–8,* 240.

[200]Meyers and Meyers, *Hag, Zech 1–8,* 267.

Several problems must be addressed. The first has to do with the number of crowns involved. עטרות is plural in form, and thus, some commentators have spoken of two crowns.[201] Yet, in Job 31:36 this identical plural form clearly refers to only one crown.[202] Likewise, here in 6:11–14, there is only one crown, as the singular form of the verb in v. 14 (תהיה) confirms. A second question concerns who is crowned. The present text indicates Joshua the high priest, but some scholars suspect Zerubbabel was the original referent,[203] while others believe that both names were originally present.[204] Since I have rejected the presence of two crowns above, the last option must be rejected as well. Further, there is absolutely no textual evidence to support the substitution of Zerubbabel for Joshua, and the text is quite intelligible apart from such an emendation.[205] Hence, if one reads the text as it stands, one crown is placed on Joshua's head (v. 11).

A further issue surrounds the identity of the man named צמח. One possibility is Zerubbabel.[206] Although he is not named, it is stated that the צמח will build the temple of the Lord (vv. 12b–13a), and according to 4:6b–10a, Zerubbabel is the temple builder.[207] Yet some scholars argue that a future messianic figure is envisioned, since Zerubbabel is not named and the figure's coming is cast into the future.[208] But this view is then forced to understand the temple to be built by the צמח metaphorically or in some other less than literal sense.[209] K. Koch believes that צמח refers both to Zerubbabel and to a future messiah, since in Hebrew

[201]Meyers and Meyers, *Hag, Zech 1–8*, 349–350; Beyse, *Serubbabel*, 78; Ackroyd, *Exile and Restoration*, 194; Petersen, *Hag, Zech 1–8*, 275.

[202]Mason, "Prophets of the Restoration," 148; Rudolph, *Hag, Sach 1–8, 9–14, Mal*, 128.

[203]See Coggins, *Hag, Zech, Mal*, 47; see suggested emendation in *BHS*.

[204]Beyse, *Serubbabel*, 77–78; cf. Ackroyd, *Exile and Restoration*, 196.

[205]Ackroyd, *Exile and Restoration*, 196, points out that the theory which claims Zerubbabel's name was edited out is inconsistent with 4:6b–10a where it was left in. Of course, if Zerubbabel was the original referent, this means that his excision from v. 11 would signal the rising importance of the high priesthood shortly after the prophet Zechariah (cf. Coggins, *Hag, Zech, Mal*, 47; Ackroyd, *Exile and Restoration*, 196)

[206]Ackroyd, *Exile and Restoration*, 195; Petersen, *Hag, Zech 1–8*, 276; Mitchell, *Hag, Zech, Mal, and Jonah*, 187; Beyse, *Serubbabel*, 81.

[207]Ackroyd, *Exile and Restoration*, 195–196,197–198; Mitchell, *Hag, Zech, Mal, and Jonah*, 187. Also, this interpretation agrees with the view in Hag 2:20–23.

[208]Mason, "Prophets of the Restoration," 147f; Meyers and Meyers, *Hag, Zech 1–8*, 355–356; Rudolph, *Hag, Sach 1–8, 9–14, Mal*, 130, who sees it as referring to one of Zerubbabel's sons born in Judah, i.e., one who would sprout up "in his place," meaning Judah.

[209]Mason, "Prophets of the Restoration," 148; Meyers and Meyers, *Hag, Zech 1–8*, 355–356.

thought the use of a proper name implied a trend to be fulfilled by that type of person.[210]

In any case, the צמח is described as one who will build the temple of the Lord, possesses majesty, and sit and rule (משל) on his throne. Oddly, however, he is not crowned and his rule is not described with the word מלך ("reign"). It seems full monarchical rule is denied this figure.[211] This more limited conception of a civil ruler nevertheless comports with the idea of a priestly figure alongside the צמח (v. 13b). Whether this priest is conceived of on his own throne or by the throne of the צמח is debated, the former more probable.[212] Further, it is also unclear whether Joshua or some future priestly figure is meant by the simple designation כהן ("priest"). Interpreters who identify the צמח with Zerubbabel tend to see Joshua here, while those who judge the צמח a future davidic figure perceive a future priestly messiah. Nonetheless, amid all the uncertainty about the precise interpretation of these verses, one aspect is clear: a dyarchic leadership is envisioned. There will be two figures at the head of Israel, a priestly figure and the צמח, whether understood as Zerubbabel or a future royal messiah.

This dyarchical formulation of Jewish leadership likewise appears in Zech 3:8, within a group of oracles inserted into a vision of the purification of Joshua.[213] After Joshua is charged with rule of the Lord's house and given rights of access, it says:

> Hear now, O Joshua the high priest, you and your friends who sit before you, for they are men of good omen: behold, I will bring my servant the Branch (צמח).

As in 6:12 opinions differ on whether the צמח is Zerubbabel[214] or a future messiah,[215] but in either case, the צמח is introduced alongside the high priest, again implying a type of dyarchic leadership. The stated status and role of the צמח, however, is quite vague compared to that of Joshua's (cf. 3:4–7). Moreover, it is important to observe that, since the oracles regarding the צמח (6:12f and 3:8)

---

[210]Koch, *Prophets*, 2:155–156

[211]The fact that the צמח is not crowned has led to the proliferation of multiple crown theories which were rejected above.

[212]LXX reads "by his throne." For various views, see Meyers and Meyers, *Hag, Zech 1–8*, 361; Petersen, *Hag, Zech 1–8*, 273; Rudolph, *Hag, Sach 1–8, 9–14, Mal*, 127; Beyse, *Serubbabel*, 77. As Meyers and Meyers point out, על־כסאו is the exact same phrase used for the צמח earlier in v. 13. For the whole problem see B. A. Mastin, "A Note on Zechariah VI 13," *VT* 26 (1976) 113–116.

[213]Ackroyd, *Exile and Restoration*, 189–190; Meyers and Meyers, *Hag, Zech 1–8*, 223.

[214]Ackroyd, *Exile and Restoration*, 190; Petersen, *Hag, Zech 1–8*, 210–211.

[215]Meyers and Meyers, *Hag, Zech 1–8*, 360; Mason, "Prophets of the Restoration," 147.

have been inserted into material dealing with Joshua the high priest,[216] this pairing of the צמח and a priestly figure reflects the intentional design of the editors of Zechariah. Further, it will be recalled that a similar pairing of Joshua and Zerubbabel was present in the editorial framework of Haggai, supporting the view that the same ideology (and editorial hand) stands behind both prophetic books.[217]

Yet, this dyarchic conception of leadership may not be limited to the editorial framework; it appears to be present in the vision of the lampstand in 4:1–6a,10b–14.[218] In the vision, a golden lampstand is flanked by two olive trees on the right and the left (4:2–3). The lampstand represents the Lord, whereas the olive trees are explained in the following way:

> These are the two sons of oil (בני־היצהר) who stand by the Lord of the whole earth (v. 14).

The common understanding of these figures as "anointed ones," i.e., messiahs, cannot be maintained.[219] Oil (יצהר) here is a symbol of blessing and prosperity, not the oil of anointing. Nevertheless, the image of the Lord flanked by two figures linked to the blessing and prosperity of Israel fits the dyarchic conception of leadership found elsewhere in Zechariah.

To sum up this survey of Zechariah 1–8, I believe that the evidence does not substantiate the claim that Zechariah 1–8 sets forth hope for a davidic messiah. Yet, if one were to understand Zerubbabel or the צמח as a davidic figure, then in Zechariah 1–8 one sees a radical transformation of davidic kingship, a transformation probably due to the reality of post-exilic life. The main task of this davidic figure would be to build the temple (4:6b–10a and 6:12–13), a task accomplished by the empowering of the Lord's spirit. Secondly, he would stand and rule alongside a priestly figure (3:8; 4:14; 6:12–13). Moreover, while Joshua the high priest would possess royal symbols and privilege, beyond building the temple, this davidic figure would only bear majesty and rule on a throne (6:13). Consequently, Zechariah 1–8 would represent a new understanding of the status and role of davidic kingship. And while this viewpoint in Zechariah 1–8 is closely related to the understanding one finds in the editorial framework of Haggai, it does not appear to have earlier biblical precursors.

---

[216]Petersen, *Hag, Zech 1–8*, 121.

[217]Mason, "Prophets of the Restoration," 148; Beuken, *Haggai-Sacharja, passim*; cf. Petersen, *Hag, Zech 1–8*, 125. The similar date formula supports this conclusion also.

[218]Meyers, 239, 276; Ackroyd, *Exile and Restoration*, 193; Mason, *Hag, Zech, Mal*, 48; Petersen, *Hag, Zech 1–8*, 233.

[219]See the detailed discussion in Petersen, *Hag, Zech 1–8*, 229–231, where he concludes, "... there is little warrant for understanding the phrase 'sons of oil' to designate them as anointed." Similarly, Meyers and Meyers, *Hag, Zech 1–8*, 258f, 276.

3. *Amos 9:11–15*

Amos 9:11–15 proclaims that at some future time God will raise up the fallen booth of David. This passage has often been construed as an interpretation of the davidic dynasty promise that reflects hope for the restoration of the davidic dynasty. Yet, in my judgment, this is not an oracle about the restoration of the davidic dynasty, but about the restoration of Jerusalem.

Accordingly, to assess the meaning of this oracle, the first issue that must be resolved is the matter of its date, a subject of some dispute. The majority of scholars hold that 9:11–15 constitutes a later addition to the book of Amos,[220] but whether it should be dated to the Deuteronomistic redaction of Amos during the exile or to the post-exilic period is uncertain.[221] In general, then, with some confidence this passage can be dated somewhere between the fall of Jerusalem in 586 BCE and the rebuilding of the walls of Jerusalem by Nehemiah in ca. 445 BCE. Attempts to be more specific must remain tentative, but parallels between 9:11–12 and Isa 58:12 and Mal 3:21 [MT], as well as its similarity to other post-exilic redactional endings of prophetic collections, do suggest a post-exilic date.[222]

In terms of form, 9:11–15 consists of two related oracles, which probably stem from the same hand.[223] The first oracle in vv. 11–12 is of chief importance. It reads:

> In that day, I will raise the fallen booth of David, and wall up their breaches and their ruins I will raise, and I will build it as in days of old, that they may possess the remnant of Edom and all the nations over which my name has been called says the Lord who does this.

---

[220] H. W. Wolff, *Joel and Amos* (Hermeneia; Philadelphia: Fortress, 1977) 352; J. L. Mays, *Amos* (OTL; Philadelphia: Westminster, 1969) 163; G. Fohrer, *Introduction to the Old Testament* (Nashville: Abingdon, 1968) 436–437; Eissfeldt, *The Old Testament*, 400–401; B. S. Childs, *Introduction to the Old Testament as Scripture* (Philadelphia: Fortress, 1979) 405–406; J. Blenkinsopp, *A History of Prophecy in Israel* (Philadelphia: Westminster, 1983) 92, are among recent commentators who view these verses as secondary. See especially Wolff for reasons based on both content and form for why 9:11–15 is secondary; in addition, its position at the end of the book, which serves to form an *inclusio* with the opening hymnic fragment that also refers to Jerusalem, suggests that both the opening and the ending of the book are the work of redactors. Koch, *Prophets*, 1:69f; and J. H. Hayes, *Amos, the Eighth Century Prophet: His Times and Preaching* (Nashville: Abingdon, 1988) 223–224, are among recent commentators who argue that the verses are from Amos.

[221] See the discussion in Wolff, *Amos*, 352–353.

[222] For the parallel to Mal 3:21 and similarities with other post-exilic redactional endings, see Wolff, *Amos*, 353.

[223] Wolff, *Amos*, 351,354.

The vast majority of commentators take the "booth of David" to be a metaphor for the davidic kingdom or the davidic dynasty, and thus see the oracle as promising the restoration of the davidic kingdom.[224] Possible support for this view is found in the phrase "I will build it (ובניתיה) as in days of old," which may hark back to the promise spoken by Nathan in 2 Sam 7:11–16 to build David a house. Further, the restoration of the davidic kingdom will be part of a new era of fertility, prosperity, and peace, as described in vv. 13–15. If this interpretation is correct, then Amos 9:11–12 testifies to an exilic or post-exilic hope for the reemergence of the davidic kingdom and davidic kings.

Yet this reading is not without difficulties. The problem revolves around the interpretation of the unusual phrase "booth of David," which appears only here in the Hebrew Bible. In my judgment, there is little reason to see it as referring to the davidic dynasty or kingdom; rather it refers to Jerusalem.[225] First, the term "booth" (סכה) is never used in the Hebrew Bible for a kingdom or dynasty, but is used in Isa 1:8 for Jerusalem ("And the daughter of Zion is left like a booth [סכה] in a cucumber field"). A similar phrase in Isa 16:5, "the tent (אהל) of David," also appears to refer to the place where davidic kings sit, that is, Jerusalem, and not to their kingdom or dynasty.[226] Secondly, raising up of the booth of David will involve walling up breaches and raising up ruins, images that apply directly to a fallen city like Jerusalem, rather than metaphorically to a kingdom or dynasty. In fact, similar images and several identical words are used in Isa 58:12 to describe what is clearly the rebuilding of cities.[227]

Thirdly, it is more difficult to make sense of the variation between third person singular and third person plural pronouns if the dynasty or kingdom is the referent for the phrase "booth of David." On the other hand, if the city of Jerusalem is in view, the plural pronouns may refer to the people of the city and the singular pronoun to the city itself. Fourthly, the oracle in vv. 13–15 also speaks of the rebuilding of cities and may in part account for the juxtaposition of these two oracles of salvation. Finally, if 9:11–15 forms an *inclusio* with the opening hymnic fragment in 1:2, which mentions Zion and Jerusalem, it suggests that the referent in 9:11 is Jerusalem as well.

---

[224]For example, Wolff, *Amos*, 353; Mays, *Amos*, 163–164; Hayes, *Amos*, 224; Childs, *Introduction*, 407; Blenkinsopp, *Prophecy*, 92; Koch, *Prophets*, 1:69f.

[225]Wolff, *Amos*, 353, considers this option, but without explicitly rejecting it goes on to talk about the dominant idea of davidic imperium.

[226]Booth (סכה) and tent (אהל) not only have a semantic overlap, but in 2 Sam 11:11, סכה is used as a synonym for tent.

[227]Overlap of vocabulary includes בנה ("build"), עולם ("ancient," "of old"), קום ("raise"), גדר פרץ ("wall up a breach"). Also, if the post-exilic dating of Amos 9:11–15 is correct, Isa 58:12 would stem from the same era.

At the very least, therefore, Amos 9:11–15 does not unambiguously testify to a exilic or post-exilic hope for the restoration of the davidic dynasty. Even Hayes has to concede that these words about the davidic dynasty are "subdued and restrained when compared to other claims for the house of David," noting that reference to special promises to David are absent.[228] Admittedly, the rebuilding and restoration of Jerusalem mentioned here implies the independence of Jerusalem and doubtless along with it Judah, since "they" will possess the remnant of Edom. But hope for the restoration and independence of Jerusalem and Judah does not in itself entail a corresponding hope for a davidic ruler, for there are many eschatological promises regarding Jerusalem and Judah that do not so much as hint about a hope for a return to davidic rule.[229]

Thus, Amos 9:11–15 does not testify to a davidic hope in the exilic or post-exilic period, at least not unambiguously. As a footnote it might be mentioned that if Jerusalem is indeed the correct referent for the "booth of David," then this passage's thematic relation to Isa 58:12 and the comment that it will be built as in "days of old," a turn of phrase that implies more than a few years, offer further evidence for a post-exilic dating of the oracle.

4. Jeremiah 17:19–27

Since some commentators have cited Jer 17:19–27 as reflecting post-exilic davidic hopes,[230] we should at least offer some remarks about it, although its usefulness is limited due to the problems of dating and interpretation. Jer 17:19–27 is a sermon addressed to "the kings of Judah, and all Judah, and all the inhabitants of Jerusalem." It begins with an accusation that they have violated the Sabbath commandment (vv. 19–23), then proceeds to offer blessings if the Sabbath command is followed (vv. 24–26) and destruction if it is not (v. 27). Among the benefits of keeping the Sabbath would be:

> then there shall enter by the gates of this city kings who sit on the throne of David, riding in chariots and on horses, they and their princes, the men of Judah and the inhabitants of Jerusalem; and this city shall be inhabited forever (v. 25).

The language of this sermon is not foreign to Jeremiah,[231] but the style is typically Deuteronomistic.[232] Thus many commentators have ascribed these

---

[228]Hayes, *Amos*, 227.

[229]Cf. for example in Isaiah 40–66, Joel, Obad 17–21.

[230]For example, McKane, *Jeremiah*, 1:418–419; Holladay, *Jeremiah 1*, 510.

[231]Overholt, "Jeremiah," 623.

[232]Carroll, *Jeremiah*, 367.

verses either to Jeremiah or to an exilic Deuteronomistic redactors.[233] On the other hand, the subject matter of this passage—Sabbath observance—has led others to date it in the last half of the fifth century BCE, because of the increased importance of the Sabbath in post-exilic times. More specifically, the similarity between Jer 17:19–27 and the concerns in Neh 13:15–22 suggests a common setting for both passages.[234] Yet, while it is true that Jeremiah shows no specific concern for the Sabbath elsewhere in his speeches,[235] the Sabbath was a living institution in pre-exilic times (cf. Ex. 20:8–11; Deut 5:12–15; 2 Kgs 4:23; Isa 1:13; Amos 8:5), and Jeremiah demonstrates marked respect for the provisions of the Deuteronomic law, which of course included Sabbath observance (Deut 5:12–15). In this regard, Fishbane points out how Jer 17:21–22 is an interpretive expansion of Deut 5:12–14.[236] Thus, the problem of dating can hardly be definitively resolved on either stylist or topical grounds; Jer 17:19–27 can plausibly be dated anywhere from Jeremiah's ministry to the late fifth century.

But even if a date in the late fifth century could be sustained, in my judgment, this passage does not indicate a davidic or messianic hope. Whether composed by Jeremiah or in the late fifth century, within its literary context, the sermon is represented as the words of Jeremiah to his contemporaries, and is therefore set in an appropriately pre-exilic context with its mention of the kings of Judah.[237] For readers in the fifth century, the point would be that the people of Jeremiah's time had a choice to keep the Sabbath commandment and experience the blessings detailed in vv. 25–26, including the entrance of kings who would sit on the throne of David, or to violate the Sabbath commandment and receive the destruction promised in v. 27. They of course violated the command and received destruction. In this way, the experience of pre-exilic Israel stands as a testimony that life does indeed depend on Sabbath observance, the very point made at the beginning of the sermon in v. 21 ("Take heed for the sake of your lives, and do not bear a burden on the Sabbath day ... ").[238]

---

[233]See the summary of views in McKane, *Jeremiah*, 1:416–418; Holladay, *Jeremiah 1*, 509. Some commentators, like J. Bright, *Jeremiah* (AB 21; Garden City, NY: Doubleday, 1965) 120, see a exilic redactor updating actual words of Jeremiah.

[234]Carroll, *Jeremiah*, 368; McKane, *Jeremiah*, 1:417; Holladay, *Jeremiah 1*, 509; Overholt, "Jeremiah," 623; Coutier, "Jeremiah," 281.

[235]Holladay, *Jeremiah 1*, 509.

[236]Fishbane, *Biblical Interpretation*, 131–134. Also, Fishbane, takes Neh 13:15–16 as a further use of Jer 17:20–21 (pp. 131–132).

[237]McKane, *Jeremiah*, 417; see also Courtier, "Jeremiah," 281, who claims the mention of kings indicates that an authentic oracle of Jeremiah stands behind this sermon.

[238]Carroll, *Jeremiah*, 368; Overholt, "Jeremiah," 623.

McKane recognizes the points made in the previous paragraph, yet says it is a "reasonable assumption" that the promises in vv. 25–26 are forward looking as well. By this he means that, "More allowance should be made for the splendor of an eschatological consummation (a Messianic Age) in v. 25 ... "[239] He asserts that this future age has a "Davidic ingredient," since the kings of the house of David will preside over this consummation.

McKane's hypothesis labors under great difficulties, however. For one, the promise about kings coming in the gates of the city in v. 25 depends completely on the trappings of the pre-exilic setting in vv. 19–20. Thus, the reference to davidic kings in v. 25 makes perfect sense apart from any assumption that the post-exilic community hoped in its own time for the restoration of the davidic dynasty. Secondly, McKane's theory would imply that the threat in v. 27, announcing that the palaces in Jerusalem will be devoured by fire, should also be forward looking. But this makes no sense in Nehemiah's Jerusalem. Moreover, would McKane think that this passage is threatening the actual destruction of Jerusalem in the late fifth century? Such would be the implications of attempting to apply promised benefits and threats from a pre-exilic context directly to the late fifth century. Finally, and perhaps most damaging to McKane's thesis, Neh 13:15–18, the parallel passage used by McKane and others to date Jer 17:19–27 to the late fifth century BCE, cites the disobedience of the fathers as the reason for their destruction (Neh 13:18). In other words, while Jer 17:19–26 assumes that destruction is a conditional threat, Neh 13:18 takes it as realized,[240] a point against any forward looking aspect in Jer 17:19–26. Moreover, in Neh 13:15–18 there is no suggestion that blessings of the sort mentioned in Jer 17:25 will follow compliance with Sabbath observance.

In fact, if Jer 17:19–26 is of post-exilic provenance, it not only explains why Sabbath observance is so important, but may actually offer an account for why no monarchy exists in post-exilic Israel. Overholt writes:

> The passage thus appears to be a rather late priestly attempt to defend current religious and political practice by linking failure to observe the Sabbath to the national catastrophe of 587 B.C. and by justifying the absence of a king in postexilic Israel.[241]

In this sense, the passage presupposes the conditional nature of davidic dynastic continuance, and since it was well known that the stated conditions were not met

---

[239]McKane, *Jeremiah*, 419; likewise, Holladay, *Jeremiah 1*, 509–510, speaks of "dreams of the restoration of the monarchy" and the "yearnings of this period."

[240]Fishbane, *Biblical Interpretation*, 131f.

[241]Overholt, "Jeremiah," 623.

by pre-exilic Israel, the davidic monarchy did not continue. Thus, we may conclude by saying that the claim for a davidic hope in Jer 17:25 turns out to be
merely an assumption, yet not a reasonable one as McKane asserted, since it is
unnecessary and introduces added difficulties to the meaning of the text.

5. Summary

The preceding treatment of post-exilic texts has called into question the putative
interpretation of some passages as expressing hope for a davidic messiah. If we
are correct in dating Jer 33:14–26 to the early post-exilic period, it alone sets
forth hope for the re-establishment of the davidic dynasty. We should note,
however, that it does so in the face of challenges to the ongoing validity of the
davidic dynasty (cf. Jer 33:23–24). Some, therefore, in the early post-exilic
period had clearly abandoned hope for the restoration of davidic leadership, a
viewpoint similar to that found in Jeremiah 40–41. On the other hand, while
Haggai and Zechariah do look to Zerubbabel for leadership, possibly even kingship, reference to his davidic status and to the davidic dynasty tradition is myste-
riously absent in the words of these prophets. If Zerubbabel is considered a
Davidide, his role consists of being the temple-builder and his rule is exercised
alongside a priestly figure, Joshua. In general, cultic and priestly concerns come
to the forefront in Haggai and Zechariah. Moreover, Amos 9:11–15 and Jer
17:19–27 have even less to do with post-exilic davidic messianic hopes. In fact,
late Israelite prophecy on the whole lacks any reference to a coming davidic
figure.[242]

On the other hand, it is common in biblical scholarship to speak of a post-
exilic expectation for renewal of the davidic monarchy or hope for a davidic
messiah. For the most part, however, this view hangs by a very thin thread: the
presence of Zerubbabel in the davidic genealogy in 1 Chr 3:19. From this it is
inferred that since both Haggai and Zechariah proclaimed Zerubbabel as a leader,
they likewise maintained a hope for the re-establishment of the davidic monarchy.
In turn, having established this post-exilic davidic expectation, many other passages within prophetic literature that indicate a desire for the renewal of the
davidic monarchy—passages considered in earlier portions of this survey—are
assigned dates in the post-exilic period because their contents fit the davidic
expectations of the period.[243] In addition, the interpretation of passages like

---

[242]Petersen's list of late Israelite prophetic texts (see *Late Israelite Prophecy*, 13–19) includes Isaiah 40–55, Isaiah 56–66, Isaiah 24–27, Malachi, Joel 3–4, Ezekiel 38–39, Jer
23:33–40, and Zechariah 9–14. None of these witnesses to a davidic messianic hope. (On the
absence of davidic messianism in Zechariah 12, see below, chap. 3).

[243]See for instance Hos 3:5; Isa 10:33–11:10; Jer 23:5–6.

Amos 9:11–15 and Jer 17:19–27 is assimilated to the now widespread post-exilic davidic messianic hope. Yet to quote a rabbinic proverb, it is like a mountain hanging by a thread. Texts that can be firmly dated to the post-exilic period either lack any mention of the davidic dynasty tradition or do not unambiguously attest to it.

Even if the thread were sound and Zerubbabel indeed was a member of the davidic royal house, the post-exilic expectation for the restoration of the davidic dynasty seems to end with Haggai and Zechariah. Whether it is taken up again by the Chronicler and the author of Zech 12:2–13:1 is the subject of the next chapter.

E. Significance of the Background

Having completed this extensive survey of biblical passages connected with the davidic dynasty tradition, we may state its implications for the following examination of early Jewish texts. First, to assume that every early Jewish text that speaks of David, the davidic dynasty or covenant, or Israelite kingship entails an expectation for the re-establishment of the davidic monarchy or hope for a davidic messiah is a faulty approach. In the biblical tradition, non-davidic models of kingship were available, and in passages from the exilic and post-exilic periods, the davidic dynasty tradition proved adaptable and expendable. Indeed, it is my contention that there is little evidence from the early post-exilic period for an expectation of the re-establishment of a specifically davidic monarchy or hope for a specifically davidic messiah. Thus, at the dawn of the early Jewish period, there existed no dominant and widespread expectation for a davidic messiah that early Jewish authors would inherit and carry on.

Yet, even in the Hebrew Bible as a whole, the davidic dynasty tradition, and more specifically, the tradition of a davidic covenant, may not have been as dominant as often assumed.[244] In this regard, J. Levenson's comments are apt:

> Even in the religious consciousness of an Israelite for whom kingship was of central importance, the entitlement of the House of David could remain peripheral. That is why, despite the presence of a great quantity of material bearing on royal theology, the specific covenant with David is expounded in clear form so very rarely. Not all royal theology was Davidic, and not all Davidic theology was covenantal.[245]

I suspect that biblical scholars have emphasized the frequency and importance of the davidic dynasty tradition in the biblical material—especially late biblical lit-

---

[244]Levenson, " Davidic Covenant," 217, writes, "I consider it a fundamental mistake to see the Davidic Covenant lurking behind all the material relevant to the Judean monarchy."

[245]Levenson, "Davidic Covenant," 217. Cf. also Cross, *Hebrew Epic*, 219–273.

erature—because of the importance of davidic messianism in both Christian and later Jewish thinking.[246] In any case, writers in the early Jewish period would be under no obligation to make use of davidic dynasty tradition, or to use it in service of monarchical or messianic ideologies. They would be free to use it or ignore it, and if they used it, to employ and adapt it for whatever purpose the author chose.

Secondly, our survey indicated that great diversity exists in the biblical traditions about davidic figures and the davidic dynasty. In light of this diversity, when early Jewish texts do make clear reference to the davidic dynasty tradition, one must ask which tradition or what aspect of the tradition is being utilized. This should make one wary of attempts to see every reference to the davidic dynasty in early Jewish literature as an allusion to 2 Sam 7:11–16 with its unconditional covenantal promise. Much more was available. Early Jewish writers who took up the davidic dynasty tradition possessed a rich fund of concepts, images, and terms from which to draw.

This observation leads to the third, and perhaps most important, point: one must ask *how* early Jewish writers employed and adapted the biblical traditions about davidic figures and the davidic dynasty. In essence, this biblical tradition provided early Jewish interpreters with a vast array of raw materials for their reflection. But the particular selection, interpretation, and application of these traditions would be a function of the intention of the individual writers in the Second Temple period. Needless to say, the understanding and application of the davidic dynasty tradition in the Second Temple period would be different, and it is to these we now turn.

---

[246]Cf. Levenson, "Davidic Covenant," 217f; see also R. P. Carroll, *From Chaos to Covenant* (London: SCM, 1981) 317 n. 23, for a similar sentiment.

CHAPTER 3
Texts From the Late Persian Period

A. 1–2 Chronicles

Ascertaining how the Chronicler used the davidic dynasty tradition, especially whether he provides evidence of an expectation for a davidic descendant ascending the throne of Israel in his own or some future time, is of fundamental importance for this study. Yet, the discussion of this issue, begun in the early part of the twentieth century, has produced a number of contradictory positions. Therefore, in an effort to sort out the array of opinions and clarify the nature of the problem, I will offer a brief summary and analysis of the debate. Following this, I will set forth my own thesis concerning the issue at hand.

1. History of the Question

In 1927, Rothstein and Hänel initiated the modern debate when in their treatment of the theology of the Chronicler they suggested that the coming of an eschatological David was a fervent wish of the Chronicler.[1] This same position was developed in some detail several years later by von Rad.[2] Although von Rad insisted that the place of the Levites in the post-exilic community was the central concern of the Chronicler, he nevertheless asserted that the author of Chronicles maintained a messianic hope. He based this claim on the Chronicler's intense interest in the davidic covenant, his sanitized portraits of David and Solomon, his repetition of the dynastic promises even in passages independent of his source,

---

[1] J. W. Rothstein and J. Hänel, *Das erste Buch der Chronik* (KAT 17; Leipzig: Deichertsche, 1927) XLIII. This according to A. Caquot, "Peut-on parler de messianisme dans l'oeuvre du Chroniste?" *RTP* 99 (1966) 113.

[2] G. von Rad, *Das Geschichtsbild des chronistischen Werkes* (Stuttgart: Kohlhammer, 1930) 119–131.

and his affinity with messianic ideas in the larger context. And since the Chronicler betrayed this interest in the davidic covenant at a time when there was no empirical king (400–300 BCE), von Rad concluded that it was an expression of an eschatological expectation—a messianic expectation.[3]

The influence of von Rad's view would be evident in M. Noth's assessment of this issue.[4] Noth, citing the same texts as von Rad, held that the Chronicler hoped for the renewal of the davidic dynasty, though he admitted that the Chronicler "did not speak about it openly."[5] Noth, however, differed from von Rad in that he spoke of the Chronicler's hope for the historical restoration of the davidic dynasty. In this sense, his ideology was not eschatological or messianic, but what may better be termed royalist.[6]

Still, a major problem had not been addressed by those advocating a messianic expectation in Chronicles, namely, that Ezra-Nehemiah, which at the time was almost universally believed to be a part of the Chronicler's work, appeared to lack any interest in the davidic covenant. This problem was taken up by A. Noordtzij in 1940, who argued that, while Chronicles showed the failure of Israel to establish the theocracy during the monarchy, Ezra-Nehemiah likewise demonstrated their failure to establish the theocracy in the restoration period. Accordingly, the net intention of the Chronicler's work was to point to the one whom the prophets spoke of, the one who would institute the true theocracy of God—to Christ.[7]

Yet von Rad's messianic interpretation of Chronicles was not enthusiastically embraced by some critics. A. C. Welch noted that for the Chronicler the davidic dynasty owed its origin to the divine will and its continuance to divine

---

[3]Von Rad, *Geschichtsbild*, 126.

[4]M. Noth, *The Chronicler's History* (JSOTSup 50; Sheffield: JSOT, 1987) 105.

[5]Noth, *Chronicler's History*, 105.

[6]This is the termed coined by H. G. M. Williamson, "Eschatology in Chronicles," *TynBul* 28 (1979) 154. The distinction being suggested here is often not made by interpreters, whose views lump royalist and messianic categories. Nevertheless it is a helpful distinction. But it is, at any rate, not altogether adequate in that, at least for Zerubbabel, the royalist claims made for him by Haggai and Zechariah are connected with the dawning of a new age (cf. Haggai 2:6–9,21–22), which might be termed eschatological. The distinguishing point, however, is that von Rad's messianism points to an ideal figure not associated with a known historical context, whereas the royalism of Noth and others we will treat is connected with an actual historical event. The whole issue of "Eschatology" in the Hebrew Bible is a matter of some confusion. S. Talmon, "Eschatologie und Geschichte im biblischen Judentum," *Zukunft: Zur Eschatologie bei Juden und Christen* (Schriften der Katholischen Akademie in Bayern 98; ed. R. Schnackenburg; Düsseldorf: Patmos, 1980) 13–50, has provided a helpful discussion of this subject. He argues that the Hebrew Bible's future hope is always historical in character.

[7]A. Noordtzij, "Les Intentions du Chroniste," *RB* 49 (1940) 161–168.

care.[8] However, the Chronicler was well aware of the conditional nature of the institution and the apostasy of later kings of Judah. Thus, Welch backed away from von Rad's thesis saying:

> It would be legitimate to say that the Chronicler's attitude on the subject might well give rise to the view that Messiah, when He came, must be of the house and lineage of David and must be endowed with royal attributes; but it would be an exaggeration to say more.[9]

Another evaluation of the Chronicler's eschatological perspective, in stark contrast to von Rad's, was put forward by W. Rudolph in 1954.[10] Rudolph claimed that the Chronicler believed that the Jewish community of the restoration period had fully realized the theocracy and hence possessed no eschatological hope. He writes,

> The failure of the Davidic dynasty could be borne, so long as the second pillar of the theocracy, the Jerusalem Temple, stood firm ... The significance of the house of David for salvation was then limited to the fact that David and Solomon had created for the Temple those ordinances upon which the acceptable worship of the present community depended.[11]

Of course, Rudolph's argument stands or falls with the unity of Chronicles and Ezra-Nehemiah, a unity that has been severely challenged in recent years. Nevertheless, Rudolph offered a well-articulated alternative to von Rad's position, thus establishing the opposite pole of the debate.

Rudolph's interpretation of the eschatology of Chronicles was taken up by O. Plöger in his study of two opposing ideologies present in the post-exilic Jewish community.[12] He held that the Chronicler's non-eschatological perspective "represented the official line of the theocracy," in conscious opposition to prophetic/apocalyptic eschatological expectations.[13]

Next, A.-M. Brunet, dissatisfied with the views of both Noordtzij and Rudolph, attempted a new explanation of the apparent discrepancy between the Chronicler's view of the davidic dynasty in Chronicles and his view of it in Ezra-

---

[8]A. C. Welch, *Post-Exilic Judaism* (Edinburgh: Blackwood & Sons, 1935) 193.

[9]Welch, *Post-Exilic Judaism*, 193f.

[10]W. Rudolph, *Chronikerbücher* (HAT 21; Tübingen: Mohr, 1955); Rudolph's main theses about Chronicles are summarized in W. Rudolph, "Problems of the Books of Chronicles," *VT* 4 (1954) 401–409, see esp. p. 408f.

[11]Rudolph, "Problems of the Books of Chronicles," 409.

[12]O. Plöger, *Theocracy and Eschatology* (Richmond: John Knox, 1968) 40.

[13]Plöger, *Theocracy and Eschatology*, 111.

Nehemiah.[14] While admitting that Ezra-Nehemiah gave no overt evidence of a messianic hope, it did indicate a hope for national liberation as in Neh 9:34–37. Thus, since Chronicles certainly testified to a messianic hope, Brunet concluded that, while the Chronicler viewed the restoration under Ezra and Nehemiah as a positive development, he also perceived it as incomplete, awaiting its consummation in national liberation and the re-establishment of the davidic monarchy.

A completely different approach to the problem was offered by D. N. Freedman in 1961.[15] Freedman was convinced that:

> the purpose of the writing (Chronicles) was to establish and defend the legitimate claims of the house of David to pre-eminence in Israel, and in particular its authoritative relationship to the temple and its cult.[16]

He then went on to conclude that there had existed a first edition of the Chronicler's work that lacked 1 Chronicles 1–9 and ended at Ezra 3, and this work was to be associated with the rebuilding of the temple under Zerubbabel ca. 515 BCE, functioning, so to speak, as the historiographic analog to the prophecies of Haggai and Zechariah. Thus, by questioning the unity of Chronicles and Ezra-Nehemiah—indeed, of Chronicles itself—Freedman was able to date Chronicles much earlier than hitherto supposed, thereby associating it with a historical context that coincided with Freedman's understanding of its purpose. In this way, in contrast to the messianism of Chronicles proposed by von Rad and others, which was directed to an ideal eschatological figure, Freedman pointed to the Chronicler's hope for the actual resumption of the davidic monarchy in a specific historical context. As we have said, this conception is properly termed royalist, rather than messianic.

The influence of Freedman's article would not be immediate, and advocates for the messianic view of von Rad and the non-messianic view of Rudolph would continue to dominate the discussion. On the one hand, W. F. Stinespring, noting the many eschatological features in Chronicles, tried to explain its messianism in terms of the "David of history" and the "David of faith," the former being the Chronicler's description of David during the monarchy, the latter being the eschatological figure he expected.[17] Similarly, R. North argued for an "archaizing

---

[14]A.-M. Brunet, "La Théologie du Chroniste: Théocratie et Messianisme," *Sacra Pagina: Miscellanea Biblica Congressus Internationalis Catholici de Re Biblica* (2 vols.; BETL 12–13; ed. J. Coppens, A. Descamps, É. Massaux; Gembloux: Duculot, 1959) 1:384–397.

[15]D. N. Freedman, "The Chronicler's Purpose," *CBQ* 23 (1961) 436–442.

[16]Freedman, "Purpose," 440–441.

[17]W. F. Stinespring, "Eschatology in Chronicles," *JBL* 80 (1961) 209–219.

royal messianism" in Chronicles, since the Chronicler depicted the awaited eschatological figure in terms of an idealized davidic monarch.[18]

On the other hand, K. Baltzer supported Rudolph's theory.[19] By comparing the presentation of the end of the state of Judah in 2 Kings, Jeremiah, and 2 Chronicles, Baltzer observed that, although the Chronicler, in contrast to 2 Kings, viewed the exiles as the only successors of the people of Israel, he omitted any mention of the favor bestowed on Jehoiachin in exile. Instead, one finds a recognition that God had given all the kingdoms of the earth to Cyrus. Accordingly, if Chronicles is taken to reflect a messianic outlook, the messiah would be Cyrus, much as one finds in Isa 45:1.

A few years later, A. Caquot also supported Rudolph's view.[20] He attempted to account for the Chronicler's emphasis on and idealizing of David and Solomon, and to offer an alternate interpretation of the Chronicler's citation of the dynastic promise, items which for von Rad and others had been the chief indicators of the Chronicler's davidic messianism. Caquot concluded, "Il n'y a pas de messianisme dans les *Chroniques*. David et Salomon plus encore sont mis très haut parce qu'ils ont été les agents de YHWH pour la construction du Temple."[21]

In a similar vein, P. R. Ackroyd, while seeing eschatological elements in the Chronicler's idealization of the davidic monarchy, held that the Chronicler did not understand it in terms of a future for the monarchy.[22] He wrote,

> It is rather the embodiment of the David/Jerusalem theme no longer in political but in theological terms, in relation to the life and worship of the little Judean community of his own time.[23]

For the Chronicler, the enduring value of the davidic monarchy was enshrined in the temple and cultus ordained by David.

Likewise, J. M. Myers acknowledged the Chronicler's interest in the davidic dynasty, but held that by ca. 400 BCE there was no hope for its re-establishment.[24] He allows, however, that an earlier edition of Chronicles may have reflected a messianic interest. In this way, he was close to Freedman.

---

[18]R. North, "The Theology of the Chronicler," *JBL* 82 (1963) 379–381.

[19]Baltzer, "Das Ende," 39–41.

[20]Caquot, "Peut-on parler."

[21]Caquot, "Peut-on parler," 120.

[22]Ackroyd, "History and Theology," 512–515.

[23]Ackroyd, "History and Theology," 512.

[24]J. M. Myers, *I Chronicles* (AB 12; Garden City, NY: Doubleday, 1965) lxxx–lxxxv.

R. Mosis offered yet another interpretation of the Chronicler's eschatological expectation.[25] He agreed with those who rejected the presence of davidic messianism in Chronicles, but he continued to see a future dimension to the Chronicler's message.[26] For him, the Chronicler's future hope was not fixed on a new David or Solomon, but on the re-establishment of the ideal situation illustrated in the Chronicler's portrait of the Solomonic Epoch.[27] Thus, Chronicles was oriented to a future hope, and in this sense, eschatological in character; it was not, however, messianic or royalist.

In 1975, Freedman's thesis received new impetus independently from F. M. Cross and J. D. Newsome.[28] Cross' main purpose was to offer a revised picture of the Judean restoration. Nevertheless, his hypothesis posited a three stage compositional history of the Chronicler's work: Chr_1, including 1 Chronicles 10–2 Chronicles 36, dated ca. 520 BCE, reflected messianic aspirations for Zerubbabel; Chr_2, consisting of 1 Chronicles 10–2 Chronicles 34 plus the *Vorlage* of 1 Esdras, dated ca. 450 BCE, continued to hope for the re-emergence of the monarchy; and Chr_3, consisting of the present Chronicles and Ezra-Nehemiah, dated ca. 400 BCE, in which the messianic features were eclipsed by other interests.[29] Cross' Chr_1 was practically identical with Freedman's first edition of the Chronicler's work.

Newsome's primary aim was to re-evaluate the scope and purpose of the Chronicler's work on thematic grounds. Arguing that the central concerns of the Chronicler were "kingdom, prophecy, and cult," he claimed that the most suitable *Sitz im Leben* for this "cluster of concerns" was the reconstruction of the temple in ca. 520 BCE. Specifically with respect to messianism, Newsome noted the Chronicler's proclamation of the perpetual viability of the davidic dynasty and concluded that it belied no vague eschatological hope, but furnished an ideological buttress for royalist hopes fixed on Zerubbabel.[30]

In the same year, P. D. Hanson in his work on early apocalyptic ideas associated Chronicles with the hierocratic party and referred to the "absence of real messianic interest" and the "absence of an eschatological dimension" in Chron-

---

[25]R. Mosis, *Untersuchungen zur Theologie des chronistischen Geschichtswerkes* (Freiburger Theologische Studien 92; Freiburg: Herder, 1973).

[26]Mosis, *Untersuchungen*, 15–16.

[27]Mosis, *Untersuchungen*, 93–94; see also, 162.

[28]F. M. Cross, "A Reconstruction of the Judaean Restoration," *JBL* 94 (1975) 4–18; J. D. Newsome, "Toward a New Understanding of the Chronicler's Purpose," *JBL* 94 (1975) 201–217.

[29]Cross, "Reconstruction," 11–14.

[30]Newsome, "New Understanding," 209–210.

icles.[31] Here the influence of Rudolph and Plöger was evident. Yet, Hanson suggested that the Chronicler was genuinely interested in the post-exilic davidic house and that the hierocratic program, of which Chronicles was a reflection, had not given up on a dyarchic structure for Jewish life, with the "Davidic figure prominently beside the high priest."[32] What Hanson means is not altogether clear, but he appears to feel that the Chronicler harbored royalist hopes for the davidic house at ca. 400 BCE, or at the very least, intended to legitimate the Davidides in some other way, possibly as governors.

Also in 1975, R. Braun, based largely on his examination of the Chronicler's treatment of Solomon, concluded: "that the dynastic emphasis remains undeveloped suggests that the promise to David has been fulfilled in the temple ... "[33]

H. G. M. Williamson in his 1977 Tyndale Old Testament Lecture, published in 1979, attempted a thorough examination of the whole question.[34] He rejected both the views of Rudolph and his followers as well as those of Freedman and his supporters, and found the arguments of those advocating a messianic interpretation too general and subjective.[35] He himself went on to argue for a royalist interpretation of the Chronicler's davidic hope, suggesting that the Chronicler "inherited and passed on the tradition of hope centered on the Davidic family."[36] Williamson speculates that this royalist hope may have been connected with Judah's involvement with the abortive revolt against Persian domination led by Tennes the Sidonian in the mid-fourth century BCE.[37] Since Williamson provides the most recent and thorough treatment of the subject, we will have occasion to return to the specifics of his position in some detail below.

Since Williamson, there has been no specific treatment of the subject, although scholars have continued to ally themselves with one of the views previously argued: M. A. Throntveit has supported the position of Freedman, Cross, and Newsome;[38] M. Saebo and J. W. Wright have suggested a royalist interpre-

---

[31]P. D. Hanson, *The Dawn of Apocalyptic* (rev. ed.; Philadelphia: Fortress, 1979) 271,276f.

[32]Hanson, *Dawn*, 349.

[33]R. Braun, "Solomonic Apologetic in Chronicles," *JBL* 92 (1975) 515; see also his "Solomon, the Chosen Temple Builder: The Significance of 1 Chronicles 22, 28, and 29 for the Theology of Chronicles," *JBL* 95 (1976) 581–590; *1 Chronicles* (WBC; Waco, TX: Word, 1986) 26–35.

[34]Williamson, "Eschatology in Chronicles," 115–154.

[35]Williamson, "Eschatology in Chronicles," 153,120–130,132.

[36]Williamson, "Eschatology in Chronicles," 154.

[37]Williamson, *1 and 2 Chronicles*, 16.

[38]M. A. Throntveit, *When Kings Speak: Royal Speech and Royal Prayer in Chronicles* (SBLDS 93; Atlanta: Scholars, 1987) 106–107.

tation;[39] S. Japhet and S. J. De Vries see no role for a davidic descendant in the post-exilic community;[40] and R. Mason and W. Riley view the davidic material as legitimating the post-exilic theocracy.[41]

Admittedly, this survey does not do justice to the nuance present in each interpreter's position, but the main contours of the debate have been covered. Accordingly, four different views have emerged on whether Chronicles gives evidence for an expectation of a davidic descendant ascending the throne of Israel in his own or some future time.

First, there is the messianic view represented by Rothstein-Hänel, von Rad, Noordtzij, Brunet, Stinespring, and North.[42] Even though all these interpreters view Chronicles and Ezra-Nehemiah as the work of one author, they found the internal evidence within Chronicles for an expectation of a davidic figure decisive. Moreover, since these interpreters dated the Chronicler's work sometime after 400 BCE, at a time when davidic rule had ceased for 200 years or more, they tended to speak of an expectation of an ideal figure or an eschatological figure not immediately connected with a concrete historical context, what may be called a davidic messiah.

Secondly, the view held by Freedman, Cross (Chr₁), Newsome, and Throntveit may be termed royalist focused on Zerubbabel. This interpretation rests on two grounds: 1) internal evidence within Chronicles that defends the claims of the davidic house, thereby revealing hope for the re-establishment of the dynasty; and 2) a postulated early edition of the Chronicler's work dated to ca. 520 BCE. Above, this view was termed "royalist," because it has in view the actual restoration of the monarchy in a concrete historical context.

Thirdly, and somewhat close to this second view, is the argument that the Chronicler had royalist hopes, though not focused on Zerubbabel. This view is represented by Noth, who sees Chronicles tied to the Samaritan schism, by Williamson and Wright, who date Chronicles to ca. 350 BCE, Cross' Chr₂, and to

---

[39]M. Saebo, "Messianism in Chronicles?" *HBT* 2 (1980) 85–109; J. W. Wright, "The Origin and Function of 1 Chronicles 23–27" (Ph.D. dissertation, University of Notre Dame, 1989) 252–256, links the davidic hope with the Judean revolt against Persia in the mid-fourth century; but see J. W. Betlyon, "The Provincial Government of Persian Period Judea and the Yehud Coins," *JBL* 105 (1986) 633–642.

[40]S. Japhet, *The Ideology of Chronicles and Its Place in Biblical Thought* (Beiträge zur Erforschung des Alten Testaments und des Antiken Judentums; Frankfurt am Main: Peter Lang, 1989) 493–504. S. J. De Vries, "Moses and David as Cult Founders in Chronicles," *JBL* 107 (1988) 636–639.

[41]R. Mason, *Preaching the Tradition* (Cambridge: Cambridge University Press, 1990) 123–124; W. Riley, *King and Cultus in Chronicles* (JSOTSup 160; JSOT Press, 1993) 169–185.

[42]Brunet may be classed as easily with the royalist interpretation.

some extent by Hanson, who places Chronicles at ca. 400 BCE. These critics too find the internal evidence for a davidic hope in Chronicles compelling, but for various reasons settle on a date for Chronicles other than 520 BCE. At least for Williamson, Wright, and Hanson the royalism of Chronicles is associated with actual, though somewhat vague, political contexts.

Finally, the non-messianic/non-royalist viewpoint held by Welch, Rudolph, Plöger, Baltzer, Caquot, Myers, Ackroyd, Braun, Japhet, De Vries, Mason, and Riley argues that the Chronicler, since he was content with the priestly theocracy centered on temple and cult, did not embrace any davidic hope, at least in political terms. Many of these scholars count Chronicles and Ezra-Nehemiah as a united work or at least very closely related, and tend to date this united composition sometime after 400 BCE. Braun, who understands Chronicles as a composition distinct from Ezra-Nehemiah, rejects a messianic or royalist position on the internal evidence of Chronicles alone.[43]

It should be apparent from the above analysis that an interpreter's decision regarding the Chronicler's view of the continuation of the davidic dynasty is the result of both differing interpretations of internal signals within the text, and, often more importantly, prior judgments about the extent and date of the Chronicler's work. Nor are these last two matters separate problems, since a decision on the extent of the Chronicler's work is decisive for questions of dating. Therefore, due to their importance for our topic, I will begin by treating in some detail the questions concerning the extent and date of the Chronicler's work. Following this, I will undertake a careful examination of the internal evidence of Chronicles, arguing that the Chronicler neither hoped for the re-establishment of the davidic monarchy, nor expected a davidic messiah at some indeterminate future time.

2. The Extent and Date of the Chronicler's Work

a. Extent

The issue of the extent of the Chronicler's work involves essentially the question of whether Ezra-Nehemiah or some portion of it was part of the original composition of Chronicles.[44] The hypothesis that the two works were originally one continuous composition, the work of a single author, was until recently a matter of scholarly consensus.[45] This hypothesis was based on the following four

---

[43]Mosis, too, rejects any messianic or royalist interpretation of Chronicles, but his view is so different from those listed above, it would be misleading to group him with them.

[44]A second issue related to the extent of Chronicles will be dealt with briefly below.

[45]S. Japhet, "The Supposed Common Authorship of Chronicles and Ezra-Nehemiah Investi-

arguments: 1) the presence of the same verses at the end of Chronicles and the beginning of Ezra; 2) the book of 1 Esdras, which begins at 2 Chronicles 35 and continues into Ezra; 3) linguistic similarity evident in a common vocabulary, syntax, and style; and 4) similarity of themes and theological conceptions.[46] But in her 1968 article, S. Japhet, while not denying some linguistic similarity, successfully highlighted significant linguistic and stylistic differences, even oppositions, between Chronicles and Ezra-Nehemiah. She concluded that although Chronicles and Ezra-Nehemiah may have emanated from the same general linguistic milieu, that of Late Biblical Hebrew, identity of authorship was not supported by the evidence.[47]

Williamson went on to show in detail that the alleged linguistic similarities did not support the hypothesis of common authorship.[48] R. M. Polzin, on the other hand, in his attempt to work out a typology of Late Biblical Hebrew, found striking similarities between the non-synoptic portions of Chronicles, Ezra, and the non-memoir sections of Nehemiah.[49] Polzin claimed these linguistic contacts formed "an extremely strong case for similarity of authorship of Chr and Ezra," which in turn were both remarkably close to the non-memoir portions of Nehemiah.[50] Throntveit, however, has argued that Polzin's work only demonstrated similarity of language for Chronicles and Ezra-Nehemiah, not similarity of authorship.[51] Accordingly, after acknowledging that Japhet and Williamson had weakened the case for common authorship on linguistic grounds, Throntveit rightly suggested that the issue of common authorship must ultimately be settled on grounds other than linguistic.[52]

With regard to the remaining grounds mentioned above, Williamson showed that arguments for unity based on the presence of the same verses in 2 Chr

---

gated Anew," *VT* 18 (1968) 330–371; for the origin and dominance of this presupposition, see pp. 330–331.

[46]Japhet, "Supposed Common Authorship," 331–332.

[47]Japhet, "Supposed Common Authorship," 332.

[48]H. G. M. Williamson, *Israel in the Books of Chronicles* (Cambridge: Cambridge University Press, 1977) 37–59.

[49]R. M. Polzin, *Late Biblical Hebrew: Toward an Historical Typology of Biblical Hebrew Prose* (HSM 12; Missoula, MT: Scholars, 1976) 69–75.

[50]Polzin, *Late Biblical Hebrew*, 71–72.

[51]M. A. Throntveit, "Linguistic Analysis and the Question of Authorship in Chronicles, Ezra and Nehemiah," *VT* 32 (1982) 215.

[52]Throntveit, "Linguistic," 215; for the inconclusive nature of linguistic analysis, see also Ackroyd, "Historical Literature," 306.

36:22–23 and Ezra 1:1–3a were unfounded;[53] nor could the Greek versions, in particular 1 Esdras, be used to support the hypothesis of a single composition.[54] Moreover, a number of critics were pointing to thematic and theological differences existing between Chronicles and Ezra-Nehemiah. These included their respective interest in or treatment of the davidic tradition,[55] the early traditions of Israel,[56] prophecy,[57] foreigners—in particular, the people of the Northern Kingdom,[58] the so-called doctrine of retribution,[59] the manner of God's intervention in human affairs,[60] the Levitical sermon genre,[61] and a few other minor divergences.[62] We may add to this list their dissimilar view of Solomon, whose entanglement with foreign wives and consequent fall into idolatry is omitted in Chronicles in an effort to portray Solomon as a completely faithful king, but used in Neh 13:26 as an example of why marriage to foreigners is a great evil.[63]

The cumulative effect of these thematic differences, in light of the inconclusive character of arguments for linguistic identity, is significant and, in my judgment, makes the hypothesis of common authorship untenable.[64] On the other

---

[53]Williamson, *Israel*, 7–11; see already P. R. Ackroyd, "Chronicles, I and II," *The Interpreter's Dictionary of the Bible, Supplementary Volume* (ed. K. Crim; Nashville: Abingdon, 1976) 156f.

[54]Williamson, *Israel*, 36.

[55]Freedman, "Purpose," 440. The davidic tradition, so prominent in Chronicles, is absent in Ezra-Nehemiah; Zerubbabel's davidic connection is not mentioned in Ezra-Nehemiah. Instead one finds reference to the Exodus-Wandering-Conquest story (cf. Neh 9:6–37); see also Newsome, "New Understanding," 207f; R. Braun, "Chronicles, Ezra, and Nehemiah: Theology and Literary History," *Studies in the Historical Books of the Old Testament* (VTSup 30; Leiden: Brill, 1979) 59–62. Further, it is important to observe that whether or not Chronicles and Ezra-Nehemiah are different with respect to messianism, as the authors cited above would hold, they nevertheless treat the tradition of a davidic monarchy itself differently.

[56]Williamson, *Israel*, 61–66.

[57]Freedman, "Purpose," 440; Newsome, "New Understanding," 212; Williamson, *Israel*, 68.

[58]Newsome, "New Understanding," 205–207; Braun, "A Reconsideration of the Chronicler's Attitude toward the North," *JBL* 96 (1977) 359–362; Williamson, *Israel*, 60–61, with respect to mixed marriages, and 66–67, in regard to the fall of the Northern Kingdom.

[59]Braun, "Theology and Literary History," 53–56; Williamson, *Israel*, 67–68.

[60]Newsome, "New Understanding," 207–208.

[61]Newsome, "New Understanding," 210–212.

[62]See Williamson, *Israel*, 69.

[63]Noted in passing by Braun, *1 Chronicles*, xx. That 13:26 comes from a source, the Nehemiah memoir, is no argument against this as an example of differences between Chronicles and Ezra-Nehemiah, for if in Chronicles the author was not averse to deleting from his source, material about this negative aspect of Solomon's conduct, one would not expect the same author to balk at deleting the same negative aspect from the Nehemiah memoir.

[64]Ackroyd, "Historical Literature," 309f, however, remains cautious about such thematic

hand, well-known thematic contacts such as an interest in genealogies, the Levites, Torah, the temple, and the fate of the temple objects, as well as a general linguistic similarity cannot be overlooked.[65] Consequently, I concur with those who speak of a Chronistic "tradition" or "school," as a way of accounting for both the similarities and differences between Chronicles and Ezra-Nehemiah.[66] Nevertheless, although I think it most probable that Chronicles is a product of a school tradition that sometime later produced Ezra-Nehemiah, for heuristic purposes, in evaluating the view of the davidic dynasty tradition in Chronicles, I will treat it as a completely independent work.[67] In other words, my case against Chronicles having any messianic or royalist intentions will be made on the basis of a detailed analysis of Chronicles alone.

A second issue related to the extent of Chronicles involves the possibility of redactional additions in the present version of the book. Various suggestions have been made for small redactional additions in the text of Chronicles, and I will treat relevant instances in the context of my examination of particular passages below. However, one proposed redactional addition, namely, 1 Chronicles 1–9, is worthy of a brief preliminary comment.[68]

The chief reason for seeing 1 Chronicles 1–9 as an original and integral part of Chronicles is the presence of contacts between the interest and theology of the

---

difference; see also, J. Blenkinsopp, *Ezra-Nehemiah* (OTL; Philadelphia: Westminster, 1988) 47–54, for a recent attempt to argue for unity of authorship.

[65]Blenkinsopp, *Ezra-Nehemiah*, 53.

[66]See Ackroyd, "Historical Literature," 307; J. R. Porter, "Old Testament Historiography," *Tradition and Interpretation* (ed. G. W. Anderson; Oxford: Oxford University Press, 1979) 154; cf. also Braun, *1 Chronicles*, xxi.

[67]There is some debate about whether the original composition of Chronicles extended into the first several chapters of Ezra (Freedman, "Purpose," 439–440; Cross, "Reconstruction," 11–14; and Braun, *1 Chronicles*, xx, [more tentatively], all favor this hypothesis; Williamson, *Israel*, 70; and Newsome, "New Understanding," 215, oppose it). The view of Freedman and Cross, however, is based on the dubious evidence of 1 Esdras. In any case, even if Chronicles originally extended into the first chapters of Ezra, it would only provide additional evidence for my thesis. Likewise, if all of Ezra-Nehemiah was part of the original Chronistic work, then any case for the Chronicler's positive attitude toward the davidic dynasty is only weakened, since Ezra-Nehemiah betrays no interest in the continuation of a davidic monarchy. If, on the other hand, Chronicles is part of a tradition which later produced Ezra-Nehemiah, then, even if Chronicles reflected a positive attitude about the continuation of the davidic dynasty on the part of the Chronistic "school", then certainly this positive disposition was abandoned by the time Ezra-Nehemiah was composed (cf. for instance how Zerubbabel's davidic lineage is ignored in Ezra-Nehemiah).

[68]See Ackroyd, "Historical Literature," 306–307, for a sample of those advocating this positions; cf. also Williamson, *Israel*, 71f, for a summary of approaches to these chapters.

genealogies and that of the narrative sections of Chronicles.[69] On the other hand, Williamson's careful refutation of the arguments of Noth and Rudolph, who held 1 Chronicles 1–9 to be a later addition, must be judged successful.[70] Moreover, the view of Freedman, Cross, and Newsome, who relegate 1 Chronicles 1–9 to the realm of later additions, do so solely because a portion of it—1 Chr 3:17–24—contradicts their desire to date a first edition of Chronicles to the late sixth century BCE. This, of course, is merely circular reasoning.[71] We conclude, therefore, that 1 Chronicles 1–9, except for a few minor redactional glosses, was an original part of the work of the Chronicler.

b. Date

While it is important to establish a date for the composition of Chronicles, this task is made problematic by the lack of clear indicators for dating in the text. Consequently, proposed dates for its composition have varied widely, extending from 520 BCE to 165 BCE.[72] Nevertheless, in my judgment, there are adequate reasons for positing a date sometime within the last half of the Persian period. Below, I will summarize the evidence for this position, and attempt to augment it with an additional argument.

It is worth noting at the outset that one can no longer date Chronicles after ca. 420 BCE based on the assumption that Chronicles must have been written after the careers of Ezra and Nehemiah, since this view relied on the hypothesis

---

[69]M. D. Johnson, *The Purpose of Biblical Genealogies* (SNTSMS 8; Cambridge: Cambridge University Press, 1969) 44–55; Williamson, *Israel*, 71–82, who builds on the work of Johnson; see also his summary in *1 and 2 Chronicles*, 39–40. Most importantly, both the genealogies and the narrative portions of Chronicles reflect an interest in all twelve tribes—all Israel, yet testify to a somewhat paradoxical attitude toward the Northern Kingdom. Other links include a similar doctrine of retribution, scant mention of Moses and the Exodus, the use of common military terminology, and similar treatment of Jacob.

[70]Williamson, *Israel*, 72–82; cf. also the comment of Ackroyd, "Historical Literature," 307.

[71]Noted by Williamson, *1 and 2 Chronicles*, 40. It can be added that Freedman's deletion of 1 Chronicles 1–9 from his hypothetical early version of Chronicles, ironically also deletes the only biblical reference to Zerubbabel's davidic connections, about which Freedman asserts "there is no doubt whatever" ("Purpose," 439). But without 1 Chr 3:17–24, there is no evidence for Zerubbabel's davidic status, and therefore no evidence for Freedman's attempt to associate the davidism of Chronicles with Zerubbabel. It is true that Haggai and Zechariah speak of Zerubbabel in messianic tones, but neither they, nor Ezra-Nehemiah, ever specifically designate him as a Davidide. Thus, Zerubbabel's status as a Davidide is in great doubt (cf. Miller and Hayes, *History*, 456; see above, chap. 2). Moreover, Throntveit's attempt to justify a sixth century BCE date for Chronicles fails to deal with the crucial objection to this theory posed by 1 Chr 3:17ff (see *Kings Speak*, 97–107).

[72]See Throntveit, *Kings Speak*, 97, for a list of proposed dates; we can add to his list the proposals of Williamson (ca. 350 BCE), Throntveit (ca. 520 BCE), and Wright (ca. 350 BCE).

that Chronicles and Ezra-Nehemiah originally formed a single composition—a hypothesis rejected above. Likewise, a date for Chronicles after Jaddua, mentioned in Neh 12:11, and according to Josephus, the high priest at the time of Alexander the Great, depended on that same hypothesis. Yet, Chronicles' relationship to Ezra-Nehemiah may still provide some evidence of a later rather than earlier date for Chronicles. For, although the linguistic similarity between Chronicles and Ezra-Nehemiah was rejected earlier as a basis for proving identity of authorship, it did point to the same linguistic milieu for the two works.[73] Accordingly, if Ezra-Nehemiah must be dated at the very earliest sometime after 420 BCE, but more likely significantly later,[74] a date for Chronicles in the late sixth century, as Freedman and others suggest, or even early fifth, is less plausible.[75]

Other evidence suggests that Chronicles should be dated in the late Persian period. For one, the ending of Chronicles, which cites Cyrus' decree, may indicate that the author's perspective did not extend beyond the Persian period; likewise, no hint of Hellenistic influence is present in the work.[76] Moreover, anachronisms, such as a reference to Persian darics in 1 Chr 29:7, minted under Darius I, and the use of Persian administration terminology in 2 Chr 8:3f, are said to require a date in the late Persian period, since sufficient time would have to elapse for these anachronisms to go unrecognized by the authors.[77] This evidence, however, is disputed.[78] Further, the citation of Zech 4:10 as an authoritative statement in 2 Chr 16:9 may indicate a time for the composition of Chronicles that is sufficiently later than Zechariah 1–8, since time would be needed for Zechariah's words to acquire such weight.[79] However, the convergence of this evidence, although important, is hardly definitive.[80]

---

[73]See above p. 78

[74]See standard commentaries on Ezra-Nehemiah.

[75]See the chart in Polzin, *Late Biblical Hebrew*, 112, which places Chronicles at some linguistic distance from Dtr.

[76]Williamson, *Israel*, 83; P. R. Ackroyd, *The Age of the Chronicler* (Aukland: Colloquiem, Australian and New Zealand Theological Review, 1970) 7f. Also, the association of Chronicles with the Samaritan schism, a once popular way of dating the Chronicler's work to the early Hellenistic period, has been weaken both by the recognition of a fairly positive attitude toward the North on the part of the Chronicler, and a much later date for that schism—second century BCE—than previously thought (see Braun, "Solomonic Apologetic," 516). See Williamson, *Israel*, 85–86, for a response to suggestions that Greek military and building terms require a third century BCE date.

[77]Williamson, *Israel*, 84; "Eschatology," 123–125.

[78]The reading "daric" is questioned, and Throntveit, *Kings Speak*, 99, claims it occurs in a redactional passage.

[79]Williamson, *1 and 2 Chronicles*, 16.

[80]Less reliable are attempts to relate Chronicles to the rebellion against Persian hegemony

On the other hand, another major reason for dating Chronicles to ca. 400 BCE or afterward is the presence of Jeconiah's genealogy in 1 Chr 3:17–24, which many believe extends to ca. 400 BCE, or even ca. 300 BCE. Freedman, Cross, and Newsome had, of course, rejected this indicator, because they rejected all of 1 Chronicles 1–9 as part of the original version of Chronicles. Earlier, however, the deletion of 1 Chronicles 1–9 from the work of the Chronicler was held to be erroneous, and likewise any theory of dating based on it would be ill-founded. Nevertheless, even if 1 Chr 3:17–24 is viewed as an original part of Chronicles, it is a passage riddled with textual and interpretive difficulties that make its use for dating problematic.[81] Nevertheless, properly interpreted, this text does offer helpful information for the dating of Chronicles. Hence, a careful examination of the passage is in order.

It will be useful to begin by treating the relevant textual problems in the passage. First, let me deal with the simpler textual problem involving the phrase "and the sons of Shemaiah" (וּבְנֵי שְׁמַעְיָה) in v. 22b. For one, after listing five sons of Shemaiah, the verse ends by summing them up as "six." Besides this, v. 22 starts with the phrase "the sons of Shecaniah," but then only lists one person—Shemaiah. Both difficulties can be eliminated by deleting "and the sons of Shemaiah" as a result of dittography or a gloss, thus making Shemaiah the first of Shecaniah's six sons.[82]

With respect to the more complex problem in v. 21b, there are four options for the text: 1) With the MT, reading בְּנֵי four times in v. 21b, v. 21 reads: "And the son(s) of Hananiah: Pelatiah and Jeshaiah; the sons of Rephaiah, the sons of Arnan, the sons of Obadiah, the sons of Shecaniah." The result in v. 21b is a list of four families named after a father—but families with no explicit connection to Hananiah or his sons, that is, with those who precede them in the genealogy. 2) With the LXX, reading בְּנוֹ for MT's בְּנֵי four times and adding בְּנוֹ after Shecaniah in v. 21b, v. 21 reads: "And the son(s) of Hananiah: Pelatiah, and Jeshaiah his son, Rephaiah his son, Arnan his son, Obadiah his son, Shecaniah his son."

---

connected with Tennes of Sidon, mentioned by Williamson, *1 and 2 Chronicles*, 16; also, suggested by Wright, "Origin," 253f.

[81]Throntveit, *Kings Speak*, 98–99, rejects using it for dating purposes because of these problems; Williamson, "Eschatology," 121, uses it only up to 3:21a due to the problems present in v. 21bff.

[82]So D. Barthélemy, *Critique textuelle de l'ancien Testament* (Fribourg: Éditions Universitaires/Göttingen: Vandenhoeck & Ruprecht, 1982) 434, who calls it "une excellente solution;" likewise, Williamson, *1 and 2 Chronicles*, 58; Rudolph, *Chronikerbücher*, 31; E. L. Curtis and A. A. Madsen, *A Critical and Exegetical Commentary on the Books of Chronicles* (ICC; Edinburgh: T. & T. Clark, 1910) 102; Rothstein and Hänel, *Das erste Buch der Chronik*, 43.

Here one finds the typical form of a linear genealogy tracing six generations after Hananiah, as for example in 3:10–14.[83] 3) With the RSV and NEB, amending the four instances of בְּנֵי in v. 21b of the MT to בְּנוֹ, but without the additional בְּנוֹ after Shecaniah, v. 21 reads: "And the son(s) of Hananiah: Pelatiah and Jeshaiah; his son Rephaiah, his son Arnan, his son Obadiah, his son Shecaniah." Here are registered two sons of Hananiah, and then four generations of linear descent after Jeshaiah. 4) Amending the text by replacing the four instances of בְּנֵי in v. 21b with ו's, v. 21 reads: "And the son(s) of Hananiah: Pelatiah and Jeshaiah and Rephaiah and Arnan and Obadiah and Shecaniah." In this case, the text list the six sons of Hananiah.

By way of evaluation, the case for option four is very weak in that it is simply a conjecture with no textual support.[84] Option three can be eliminated, since this emendation, based on a hybrid of the MT and LXX texts, results in בְּנוֹ preceding the name it is in apposition to, a genealogical form unattested elsewhere in 1 Chronicles 1–9.

Option two has both versional support (LXX) and conforms to the typical pattern of a linear genealogy in 1 Chronicles 1–9. Yet there are several reasons against accepting this reading. First, this reading probably originated in an attempt to alleviate the difficulty present in the MT and under the influence of 3:10–14.[85] Moreover, the additional υἱὸς αὐτοῦ (בְּנוֹ) after Shecaniah, while bringing the genealogy into proper form, lacks any textual support in the MT, pointing again to the secondary character of the LXX reading. In contrast, it is hard to understand how the reading of the MT could have been derived from the LXX reading.[86] Thus, option one is to be preferred as the *lectio dificilior*.

Secondly, if option two is interpreted as listing six succeeding generations after Hananiah, then it produces a conflict with v. 22, for it means that Hattush must be dated at least seven generations after Zerubbabel.[87] Assuming 25 years to a generation and a date for Zerubbabel's activity of 520–515 BCE, then the time of Hattush's activity must be ca. 345 BCE. Yet, this Davidide, Hattush, son of Shecaniah, is almost certainly to be identified with the Davidide, Hattush, men-

---

[83]If, on the other hand, the antecedent of "his" refers repeatedly back to the first named father, Hananiah (as appears to be the case in 3:16, although this is exceptional), all six persons named would be sons of Hananiah. While this is possible, it is unlikely.

[84]Rudolph, *Chronikerbücher*, 28, follows Rothstein and suggests that בני was originally a marginal gloss for בן in v. 21a, which later was mechanically added before the names in v. 21b.

[85]Williamson, *1 and 2 Chronicles*, 58.

[86]See Barthélemy, *Critique textuelle*, 434.

[87]Cf. Rudolph, *Chronikerbücher*, 31.

tioned in Ezra 8:2b, who returned to Judah with Ezra.[88] This identification is made virtually certain if Ezra 8:2b–3a is interpreted as a continuous phrase—across the *sop pasuq*—meaning "Hattush, of the sons of Shecaniah."[89] This, in fact, is the way 1 Esdr 8:29 interpreted the text of Ezra 8:2b–3a, translating simply Αττους ὁ Σεχενιου.[90] Now, if this Hattush, son of Shecaniah, was a contemporary of Ezra, the dates for whose activity, though disputed, range from 458 BCE to 398 BCE,[91] Hattush's activity cannot be placed at ca. 345 BCE, as the LXX reading would require. Thus, again, the reading of the MT is to be favored.[92] The resulting genealogy may be schematized and, where possible, given approximate dates (BCE) as in Figure 1 (p. 86).

Read in this way, what implications does 3:17–24 have for the dating of Chronicles? Often, it is asserted that Chronicles was written about the time, or at least sometime after, the last generation listed. In turn, this last generation is dated by counting down generations from Zerubbabel, who was active ca. 520–515 BCE, allowing 25 years per generation.[93] But this method of dating is flawed due to the absence of any explicit connection between the generations listed

---

[88]Suggested by Barthélemy, *Critique textuelle*, 434; Rudolph, *Chronikerbücher*, 31.

[89]See Barthélemy, *Critique textuelle*, 434f.

[90]Amending the MT of Ezra 8:2b–3a as *BHS* suggests is unnecessary. It should be noted that Williamson, *1 and 2 Chronicles*, 58, has questioned this identification, citing the textual difficulties of Ezra 8:2, the problems of dating Ezra, the uncertainty of the date of the genealogy due to v. 21, and the fact that Hattush was a common name citing Neh. 3:10; 10:4; 12:2. In response it can be said that the difficulty in Ezra 8:2b–3a is primarily a matter of punctuation and interpretation, not a matter of textual variation. Secondly, even though dating Ezra is a problem, it does not affect the conclusion that Hattush and Ezra were contemporaries. Thirdly, the uncertainty of dating the genealogy up to v. 22 is irrelevant to the dating of the sons of Shecaniah, since there is no necessary chronological connection between v. 21a and v. 22. Finally, while it is true that the name Hattush is used of individuals mentioned in Neh 3:10; 10:4; and 12:2, the name Hattush in 10:4 is unqualified, and may not represent an additional person named Hattush. So too, there is nothing to preclude that the Hattush mentioned in 3:10 is not the same person referred to in 12:2, since both names refer to persons contemporary with Nehemiah (although, neither of these can be identified with the Davidide Hattush). Thus, while the texts cited by Williamson could give evidence for three other persons named Hattush, they may only testify to one other person by that name. Nevertheless, regardless of how common the name Hattush was, there is no evidence that there was more than one Davidide named "Hattush, son of Shecaniah."

[91]It is theoretically possible that Ezra is to be dated in the seventh year of Artexerxes III, 352/1 BCE, but this is very unlikely. See the discussion in Miller and Hayes, *History*, 468–469; see also, J. Bright, *A History of Israel* (3rd ed.; Philadelphia: Westminster, 1981) 391.

[92]This reading is favored by Barthélemy, *Critique textuelle*, 434–435; C. F. Keil, *The Books of Chronicles* (Edinburgh: T. & T. Clark, 1872) 83; Williamson, *1 and 2 Chronicles*, 58; Braun, *1 Chronicles*, 50.

[93]Cf. Myers, *1 Chronicles*, lxxxix.

```
                b. ca. 595⁹⁴
                a. ca. 545
                            b. ca. 570      b. ca. 545
Jeconiah --- Shealtiel      a. ca. 520      a. ca. 495      b. ca. 520
             Malchiram                                      a. ca. 470
             Pedaiah ----------- Zerubbabel -------- Meshuallam
             Shenazzar      Shimei           Hananiah ---------- Pelatiah
             Jekamiah                        Shelomith(f.)      Jeshaiah//
             Hoshama                         Hashubah
             Nedabiah                        Ohel
                                             Berechiah
                                             Hasadiah
a. ca. Ezra                                  Jushab-Hesed=5


Sons of Rephaiah
Sons of Arnan           a. ca. Ezra
Sons of Obadiah
Sons of Shecaniah ------- Shemaiah
                         Hattush
                         Igal         a. ca. Ezra      a. ca. Ezra
                         Bariah       +25 years        +50 years
                         Neariah ------------ Elioenai -------------- Hodaviah
                         Shaphat=6    Hizkiah           Eliashib
                                      Azrikam=3         Pelaiah
                                                        Akkub
                                                        Johanan
                                                        Delaiah
                                                        Anani=7
```

Figure 1

in vv. 17–21a (from Jeconiah to Jeshaiah) and the generations in vv. 22–24 (from Shecaniah to Anani), because of the families listed in v. 21b.⁹⁵

Recognizing the break in continuity of the genealogy, others have claimed that an early version of the genealogy stopped with Zerubbabel's grandsons,

---

⁹⁴b. = born; a. = active; f. = female; // = break in genealogy; this chart assumes 25 years per generation.

⁹⁵See Keil, *Chronicles*, 84.

Pelatiah and Jeshaiah (v. 21a).[96] But this conclusion is, in my judgment, unwarranted, since, except for v. 21b, the specific form of the genealogy is the same throughout vv. 19–24, particularly with respect to the characteristic enumeration of the sons at the end of a generation in vv. 20–24. On the other hand, it is at least theoretically possible that the listing of the four families in v. 21b is a later insertion. But whether it is original or a later insertion, the chronological break in the genealogy after Pelatiah and Jeshaiah remains, thus making judgments about the originality of v. 21b irrelevant for dating the last portion of the genealogy (vv. 22–24).[97]

The crucial question is whether the last portion of the genealogy (vv. 22–24) can be dated at all. But as already argued above, I believe a date can be assigned to Hattush, son of Shecaniah, mentioned in v. 22, since he can with near certainty be identified with Hattush, son of Shecaniah, who came to Jerusalem with Ezra (Ezra 8:2b–3a).[98] Of course, the obvious problem here is that the date of Ezra's activity is disputed. Yet, this does at least establish some limits. Accordingly, if the span of possible dates for Ezra's activity is from 458 BCE to 398 BCE,[99] then the span for the activity of Hattush, son of Shecaniah, is the same. Counting 25 years per generation from Hattush, the last named generation, the sons of Elioenai (v. 24), would have been active ca. 50 years after Hattush. Thus, if the early date for Ezra is preferred, then the last named generation would have been active ca. 408 BCE; if, on the other hand, one opts for the later date for Ezra, then this generation's activity should be set at ca. 348 BCE.[100]

---

[96]Cf. Williamson, "Eschatology," 121.

[97]The suggestion that v. 21b is a later addition appears to rest on the assumption that the seemingly anomalous inclusion of four families must be the work of a later hand, who inserted them into an originally continuous genealogy from the hand of the Chronicler. However, it is not clear why the seemingly anomalous inclusion of the families could not just as well be the work of the Chronicler. One cannot assume that the Chronicler included only smooth continuous genealogies. Furthermore, later in this section, I will address the question concerning why this list of families may have been included in the genealogy in its present position, and, further, why it was included at all.

[98]See above, p. 84.

[99]See Miller and Hayes, *History*, 468–469; Bright, *History*, 391–402.

[100]Furthermore, there is some, though admittedly not definitive, evidence for preferring the earliest date. First, it is possible that the last named person in the genealogy, Anani (v. 24), is the same person referred to in the Aramaic letter from Elephantine, dated 407 BCE (see *Ancient Near Eastern Texts Relating to the Old Testament* [ed. J. B. Pritchard; 2nd ed.; Princeton: Princeton University Press, 1955] 492; Anani does not appear to be a common name, occurring only here in the Bible, although Ananiah occurs in Neh. 3:23 and 11:32). This circumstance would only fit an earlier date. Secondly, because names similar to those mentioned in the genealogy appear common in documents for the fifth century and earlier, Myers suggests

Finally, if the activity of the last generation named in the genealogy is to be dated between 408 BCE and 348 BCE, then Chronicles may have been written about the same time as this generation's activity, or if written before this generation had children of their own worthy of mention, some twenty-five years or so earlier. Thus, a *terminus a quo* of ca. 435 BCE and a *terminus ad quem* of ca. 348 BCE for the composition of Chronicles would be appropriate. Of course, if one rejects the assumption that Chronicles would have been written about the time of the last mentioned generation, then no *terminus ad quem* can be established.

Even though the above interpretation of 1 Chr 3:17–24 for the dating of Chronicles is, in my view, probable, it should still be recognized that it rests on particular text-critical judgments, the identification of Hattush in 1 Chr 2:22 with Hattush in Ezra 8:2b, and, for establishing a *terminus ad quem*, both the assumption that the genealogy from Hattush to the last named generation in v. 24 has not omitted any generations and that Chronicles was composed about the time of that last generation. Just the same, the results here comport well with the other criteria mentioned above that point to the late Persian period. Thus, a date between ca. 435 BCE and ca. 348 BCE is to be accepted.

3. Internal Evidence

Having established a working hypothesis for the extent and date of Chronicles, we may now proceed to an analysis of internal textual evidence relevant to our subject. This analysis will treat the following three topics with respect to their significance for the author's view of the davidic dynasty tradition: a) the dynastic oracle; b) other narrative texts relevant to the continuity of the dynasty; and c) 1 Chr 3:17–24. In each case, it will be shown that the evidence does not support a messianic or royalist interpretation. Finally, the positive role and function of the centrality and idealization of the davidic dynasty in Chronicles will be explained.

a. The Dynastic Oracle

The Chronicler's version of the dynastic oracle spoken by the prophet Nathan to David is found in 1 Chr 17:10b–14. The text follows 2 Sam 7:11b–16 fairly closely, but not without some important alterations. The first important difference involves the change from "I will raise up your offspring after you, *who shall come forth from your body*" (2 Sam 7:12) to "I will raise up your offspring after you,

---

that the genealogy does not come from a period after the fourth century BCE (Myers, *I Chronicles*, 21).

one of your own sons" (1 Chr 17:12).[101] Further, 2 Sam 7:14b, which predicts discipline for the king in the case of disobedience, is omitted in Chronicles. And lastly, whereas 2 Sam 7:16 reads, "And *your house* and *your kingdom* shall be made sure for ever before me; *your throne* shall be established for ever," the Chronicler's version goes, "But I will confirm *him in my house* and *my kingdom* for ever and *his throne* shall be established for ever." Thus, the establishment of "your [David's] house and your kingdom," and "your throne" in 2 Samuel, become the establishment of "him [Solomon] in my [God's] house and my king-dom," and "his throne," in 1 Chronicles. Together, these changes tend to make Solomon the focus of the dynastic promise and avoid any reference to his poten-tial disobedience. In addition, the accent falls on the temple ("my house") and God's kingdom, rather than David's kingdom. But these changes aside, the key statements about the permanence of the dynasty are present in v. 12 and v. 14.

This data has been interpreted in opposite ways. Those favoring a messianic or royalist interpretation of Chronicles argue that the author's repetition of the oracle, in particular, his retention of the phrase עד־עולם, reflects his conception of the dynastic promise as eternally valid.[102] In contrast, those disavowing a messianic reading point to the oracle's new focus on Solomon, claiming that although the phrases with עד־עולם are still included from his source, the em-phasis has shifted from the eternity of the dynasty to Solomon as the builder of the temple.[103]

Subsequent repetition of the dynastic oracle later in Chronicles reveals the same ambiguity. In his charge to Solomon to build the temple, David cites the dynastic oracle (1 Chr 22:8–10). On the one hand, this reference to the oracle, both in terms of context and content, is clearly centered on Solomon and his role as the temple-builder. On the other hand, in v. 10 one again reads, " ... and I will establish his royal throne in Israel forever (עד־עולם)." More importantly, sup-porters of the messianic interpretation of Chronicles point out that David's speech, including this reference to the eternal character of the dynasty, is the Chronicler's own composition, having no parallel in Dtr.[104] So too, in 1 Chr

---

[101]For the attempt at an alternate translation of 1 Chr 17:12, as in von Rad, *Geschichtsbild*, 124, see the remarks in Williamson, "Eschatology," 134; and Mosis, *Untersuchungen*, 93.

[102]For example, von Rad, *Geschichtsbild*, 123–124; Brunet, "La Théologie du Chroniste," 388; Newsome, "New Understanding," 208–209; Williamson, "Eschatology," 133.

[103]See Caquot, "Peut-on parler," 116–117; Braun, "Solomonic Apologetic," 507,510–511, 515; "The Message of Chronicles: Rally 'Round the Temple," *CTM* 42 (1971) 508; Mosis, *Untersuchungen*, 89–94.

[104]For example, von Rad, *Geschichtsbild*, 125; Newsome, "New Understanding," 209. It should be noted, however, that although this speech of David has no parallel in the Chronicler's

28:1–10—another composition of the Chronicler—where David speaks to the assembly concerning the temple, the dynastic oracle is directed exclusively at Solomon as the temple-builder (esp. vv. 5–6), but again includes a promise of the permanence of the kingdom (v. 7). In sum, due to this ambiguity, the dynastic oracle and its repetition do not in themselves offer sufficient evidence for a firm decision concerning the Chronicler's overall attitude toward the continuation of the dynasty in the post-exilic situation.

Another important question concerning the dynastic promise is whether it is expressed in unconditional or conditional terms. For instance, in the account of the dynastic oracle (17:10b–14) and the first citation of it (22:6–16), it is unconditional.[105] In other passages, however, the promise is couched in terms that make it conditional upon the obedience of the king. The second repetition of the dynastic oracle, mentioned above, reads as follows:

> I will establish his kingdom for ever if he continues resolute in keeping my commandments and my ordinances, as he is today (1 Chr 28:7).

Similarly, in other references to the permanent character of the davidic dynasty conditions are attached. In his prayer at the dedication of the temple, Solomon refers to God's promise to David that:

> There shall never fail you a man before me to sit upon the throne of Israel, if only your sons take heed to their way, to walk in my law as you have walked before me (2 Chr 6:16).

And in the divine response to this prayer, the passage reads:

> And as for you, if you walk before me, as David your father walked, doing according to all that I have commanded you and keeping my statutes and ordinances, then I will establish your royal throne, as I covenanted with David your father, saying, "There shall not fail you a man to rule Israel" (2 Chr 7:17–18).

Thus, unconditional and conditional forms of the dynastic promise appear in Chronicles.

Freedman had recognized this problem, which is also present in references to the dynastic promise in Dtr, and offered this solution:

> The conclusion to be drawn is that both historians acknowledged the undoubted frailty of reigning kings and the disastrous consequences of dereliction of duty

---

source, the reference to עד־עולם itself is taken directly from the dynastic oracle, which is paralleled in 2 Samuel 7.

[105]22:13 makes only prosperity, not the dynasty, conditional on obedience. Correctly observed by Williamson, "Eschatology," 138.

toward God both to the royal house and the nation; at the same time they must
have retained confidence in the overruling grace of God and the ultimate fulfillment of his words, that the day would come when the kingdom would be
restored with a descendant of David upon the throne.[106]

Freedman maintained that the Chronicler's view of the dynastic promise was
similar to the view found in prophets like Hosea, Isaiah, Micah, Jeremiah, and
Ezekiel. Furthermore, he observed that this hope for the reemergence of the
davidic dynasty spanned the exile, being present in the historical records preserved in Ezra and in the prophets Haggai and Zechariah.[107]

Freedman's explanation, however, lacks the support of specific evidence.
One must ask why it would be that, as Freedman says, the Chronicler "must have
retained confidence in the overruling grace of God" to restore the davidic dynasty? It may be that the pre-exilic prophets cited by Freedman did retain such
confidence, but this, of course, in no way entails that the Chronicler shared such
confidence. Freedman sees the same confidence in the historical records of Ezra,
and in the prophets Haggai and Zechariah. On the one hand, it should be observed that the historical records in Ezra indicate no such confidence in the
restoration of the davidic dynasty—in fact, the dynasty is ignored, and while
Haggai and Zechariah do pin hopes of monarchy on Zerubbabel, neither Zerubbabel's davidic qualifications nor the dynastic promise is ever specifically mentioned by either prophet.[108]

But more to the point, Freedman's basic thesis contends that Chronicles
should be associated with the early restoration period because it is ideologically
similar to Haggai and Zechariah with respect to a hope for the restoration of the
monarchy. But here, he identifies this very ideology of the Chronicler by associating it with the viewpoint of Haggai and Zechariah, not on any kind of internal
evidence within Chronicles.[109] This is blatantly circular. Consequently, Freedman's preference for the unconditional examples of the dynastic promise over the
conditional instances cannot be sustained.

In fact, it is mistaken to set up the problem in the manner in which Freedman
has, as if there are two dynastic promises mentioned in Chronicles, one unconditional and the other conditional. There is only one. The question is whether the
Chronicler conceives of this one dynastic promise as being conditioned on the
obedience of the king. Clearly he does, otherwise he would never have stated the

---

[106]Freedman, "The Chronicler's Purpose," 438–439.

[107]Freedman, "The Chronicler's Purpose," 439.

[108]See above, p. 46.

[109]Above, a late sixth century BCE date for Chronicles was rejected, further weakening the
alleged connection between Chronicles and the royalist hopes of Haggai and Zechariah.

dynastic promise in conditional terms. Simply because the conditions are not specified every time the dynastic promise is mentioned does not imply that the Chronicler harbored some underlying sense that ultimately the promise was really unconditional.

Williamson, who believes the Chronicler had royalist hopes, recognized this problem and attempted an ingenious solution.[110] He acknowledged the conditional nature of the dynastic oracle in Chronicles and conceded, unlike most proponents of the messianic interpretation of Chronicles, that although the eternal character of dynastic promise is present, the oracle and subsequent repetitions of it are indeed focused on Solomon. Then, however, he explains:

> Just as the dynastic oracle, as delivered originally to David, is concentrated upon the person of his son Solomon, so too the conditions of obedience, whose fulfillment will lead to the establishment of an eternal dynasty, are focused upon him (1 Chr 28:7). This at once, of course, has the effect of making Solomon's role a foundation for the future of the dynasty equal with David's for upon Solomon's obedience the whole of the that future will depend. The establishment of an eternal dynasty thus rests on two indispensable elements: the promise of God to David, and the carrying out of God's conditions by Solomon.[111]

The conditions that Solomon must meet are both the building of the temple and obedience to the law. Williamson goes on to conclude:

> What is more, it is well known that the Chronicler's account of Solomon's reign presents him as one who did in fact keep both these conditions, and that in as positive a way as it is possible to conceive ... Our contention, then, is that with the completion of the period of Davidic-Solomonic rule, the Chronicler intends his readers to understand that the dynasty has been eternally established.[112]

In his subsequent analysis of other relevant texts in Chronicles, Williamson finds confirmation for his thesis.[113]

One cannot help but be impressed by the ingenuity of Williamson's thesis. Nevertheless, it will not stand up to close scrutiny. Most importantly, Williamson's argument depends completely on his claim that the conditions of the dynastic promise, which will lead to the establishment of the dynasty, are focused exclusively upon Solomon. This is true in 1 Chr 28:7–9 and 2 Chr 7:17–18, but simply false in 2 Chr 6:16.[114] Solomon prays:

---

[110]Williamson, "Eschatology," 115–154.

[111]Williamson, "Eschatology," 141.

[112]Williamson, "Eschatology," 142.

[113]Williamson, "Eschatology," 142–153.

[114]Williamson notes how the conditions of obedience are applied to Solomon "or your children" in 1 Kgs 9:6, whereas in 2 Chr 7:19 "or your children" is omitted. But the reason for this

> Now therefore, O Lord, God of Israel, keep with thy servant David my father, what thou has promised him saying, "There shall never fail you a man before me to sit upon the throne of Israel, *if only your sons* take heed to their way, to walk in my law as you have walked before me. (emphasis mine)

While this passage is taken nearly unchanged from his source, if the Chronicler had intended to show that the conditions applied only to Solomon, he would have altered his source to suit his intention as he does elsewhere.[115] In fact, the change that the Chronicler does introduce into his source material is to state the condition of obedience not in terms of "walking before me" (1 Kgs 8:25), but as "walking in my law." In the words of M. Fishbane, "In this way, the mediating position of the Torah as the condition of dynastic continuity is significantly and radically underscored."[116] This point alone is sufficient to invalidate Williamson's thesis, but there are additional problems.

For one, Chronicles never explicitly says that Solomon fulfilled the conditions of obedience, which thereby established the dynasty eternally. Admittedly, Solomon's fulfillment of this condition is possibly implied by the Chronicler's deletion of the report of his apostasy later in his reign, but one would expect such an important theme as the eternity of the dynasty to be asserted by more than mere implication. If a case is to be made on what is only implied, then when the Chronicler says at the conclusion of his account of Solomon's reign, "Now the rest of the acts of Solomon, from first to last, are they not written in the history of Nathan the prophet, and in the prophecy of Ahijah the Shilonite, and in the visions of Iddo the seer concerning Jeroboam the son of Nebat?" (2 Chr 10:29), he is implying Solomon's later apostasy. This is all the more evident since Ahijah the Shilonite's prophecy in 1 Kgs 11:33 concerns the division of Israel, "because he (Solomon) has forsaken me, and worshipped" other gods, "and has not walked in my ways, doing what is right in my sight and keeping my statutes and my

---

is that the conditions mentioned are the building of the temple and obedience; the Chronicler's primary interest is the former condition which only applied to Solomon.

[115]Williamson, "Eschatology," 139, disagrees with Mosis that 6:16 refers only to later Davidides arguing correctly that Solomon must be included in the reference to "your sons." He continues, "in fact, however, it would even seem that the reference is primarily to him for verse 15 speaks of the fact that the first part of the promise to David (that his son would build the temple) has been fulfilled 'this day'". In response, we could note that of course the first part of the promise involving the temple building will be applied exclusively to Solomon "this day," but that has no implications for the second part of the promise dealing with the obedience of David's sons.

[116]Fishbane, *Biblical Interpretation*, 386. This conditional understanding of the dynastic promise may well explain why the Chronicler deleted 2 Sam 7:14 from his source, since this deletion actually weakens the unconditional character of the promise otherwise implied.

ordinances, as David his father did."[117] That the Chronicler assumes his readers
know the content of this prophecy, and thus about Solomon's apostasy, is indicated by his appeal to it as the reason for the division of the kingdom in 2 Chr
10:15.

Besides, the emphasis on Solomon's obedience can be explained on the basis of the Chronicler's interest in idealizing Solomon for his role as the one who
built the temple and established the cult.[118] That this is the Chronicler's real interest is illustrated in David's earlier encouragement of Solomon:

> Fear not, be not dismayed; for the Lord God, even my God, is with you. *He will
> not fail you or forsake you, until all the work for the service of the house of the
> Lord is finished* (1 Chr 28:20). [emphasis mine]

Moreover, Williamson says that Solomon's role in founding the dynasty is equal
to David's. Yet when the Chronicler explains why the dynasty continued in spite
of apostate kings, he refers to David alone as the reason for a continuing dynasty
(2 Chr 21:7).

In light of these considerations, Williamson's attempt to account for the
conditional nature of the dynastic promise in terms of an eternal dynasty must be
judged unsuccessful. It is true that the Chronicler has focused the dynastic
promise largely on Solomon, but it is also true that the continuity of the dynasty is
dependent on the obedience of the later davidic kings as well. And although the
Chronicler certainly explained the long continuity of the davidic dynasty, in spite
of many apostate kings, on the basis of the dynastic promise to David, claims that
he believed in an eternal dynasty based on an unconditional dynastic promise
cannot be supported in the text.

A final issue pertaining to the interpretation of the dynastic promise is the
meaning of עד־עולם. The typical English translation of this phrase is "for ever"
or some equivalent.[119] This in turn has led biblical critics to speak of an "eternal"
davidic dynasty. For example, Williamson asks:

> whether the Chronicler thought that the promises to David, which of course
> were of eternal significance, were of such a kind as to lead him to expect the
> emergence of a king some time in the future in Jerusalem, or ... that the signifi-
> cance of these promises had been transferred to the temple and its cultus?[120]

---

[117]On the other hand, Solomon's obedience is stressed by the Chronicler (see 2 Chr 11:17).

[118]See Caquot, "Peut-on parler," 117, who states that the perfection of Solomon is a corol-
lary of the author's reverence for the cult; similarly, Braun, "Solomonic Apologetic," 512–515.

[119]See KJV, ASV, RSV, NEB, (also: "for all time," in 1 Chr 17:13,14; "in perpetuity," in
1 Chr 28:7), JB, NIV.

[120]Williamson, "Eschatology," 133.

The key assumption here is that the promises "of course were of eternal significance." I presume that this allegedly obvious "eternal significance" depends for the most part on the qualifying phrase עד־עולם. This is not, however, the only or obvious meaning of עד־עולם.

E. Jenni has made a thorough investigation of the use of the word עולם in the Hebrew Bible.[121] He identifies "remotest time," or "most distant time" as the basic meaning of the word.[122] Nevertheless, the specific temporal horizon designated by עולם must be determined by the context in which it is used. Jenni explains, "As an expression of an extreme limit, עולם can, according to the "horizon" of the speaker with regard to time, refer to a variety of remote times."[123] The time indicated, therefore, is not always unlimited or free of conditions.[124] For example, עולם is used to describe a perpetual slave (cf. Ex 21:6), whose servitude is nonetheless quite finite. In the same way, עולם can refer to the lifetime of the king (cf. 1 Kgs 1:31).[125]

Furthermore, the limit implied by עולם is not always an intrinsic physical limit, such as the span of a lifetime. M. Tsevat explains that עולם qualifies a thing "within its proper limits, physical limits in the one case—the span of a human life—religious, legal or social limits in the other—the intrinsic suppositions of the covenant."[126] An explicit illustration of this circumstance occurs in 1 Sam 2:30, where the perpetual promise to the house of Eli is revoked:

> Therefore the Lord the God of Israel declares: "I promised that your house and the house of your father should go in and out before me for ever (עד־עולם);"

[121]E. Jenni, "Das Wort ῾ōlām," im Alten Testament," *ZAW* 64 (1952) 197–248; *ZAW* 65 (1953) 1–35; "עוֹלָם," *Theologisches Handwörterbuch zum Alten Testament* (2 vols.; ed. E. Jenni and C. Westermann; München: Chr. Kaiser/Zürich: Theologischer Verlag, 1979) 2:228–243; "Time," *The Interpreter's Dictionary of the Bible* (4 vols.; ed. G. A. Buttrick; Nashville: Abingdon, 1962) 4:644.

[122]Jenni, "עוֹלָם," *Handwörterbuch*, 2:230; J. Barr, *Biblical Words for Time* (SBT 1/33; 2nd ed.; Naperville, IL: Allenson, 1969) 73, though in basic agreement with Jenni, would supplement Jenni's definition with a sense of "perpetuity," based on its use in the phrase עבד עולם ("perpetual servant").

[123]Jenni, "Time," *IBD*, 4:644; likewise, Barr, *Biblical Words*, 73, "Most important is to notice that in the sense 'the remotest time' no specification is given of how remote the time referred to is; precision of this kind may be inferred from the context, but the word itself just tells us that the remotest time relevant to the present subject is meant."

[124]H. D. Preuss, "עוֹלָם," *Theologisches Wörterbuch zum Alten Testament, Band 5* (ed. G. J. Botterweck and H. Ringgren; Stuttgart: Kohlhammer, 1986) 1148.

[125]Jenni's attempt to argue that עולם extended servitude or kingship to the next generation ("Das Wort ῾ōlām," 236) has not found wide acceptance (cf. M. Tsevat, "Studies in the Book of Samuel," *HUCA* 34 [1963] 76f; Preuss, "עוֹלָם," *TWAT*, 5:1150).

[126]Tsevat, "Studies," 76f.

but now the Lord declares: "Far be it from me; for those who honor me I will
honor, and those who despise me shall be lightly esteemed."

In this case, we could say that the limit to which עד־עולם pointed was reached.

Thus, while עד־עולם and equivalent phrases[127] may characterize "remotest
time" in terms of an open-ended or indefinite future, it need not mean
"everlasting," as the use of the terms "for ever" or "eternal" seems to imply. Jenni
speaks of the remotest time in the future imaginable.[128] Precisely how far into the
future or the past was thinkable is not clear. S. Talmon suggests that עולם would
be used to refer to times beyond the ordinary scope of Israelite temporal thinking—beyond three or four generations![129] Yet sometimes the extent of עד־עולם
is specified as much longer than four generations, exceeded 10 generations (Deut
23:4), or even 1,000 generations (Ps 105:8; 1 Chr 16:15).[130] Nevertheless, the
point remains that the precise temporal limit or limitlessness implied by עד־עולם
must be deduced from its actual use in a given passage, since it refers to the
remotest time appropriate to the context. We must ask, then, what does the
context imply about the meaning of עולם in the dynastic promises in Chronicles?

In 1 Chronicles 17, the first proclamation of the dynastic oracle and David's
prayer in response to it, עד־עולם or it equivalent is used in reference to the
dynasty in vv. 12,14,22,24,27. In none of these verses is the exact time frame of
עד־עולם specified. Only in v. 17 is another temporal phrase used which sheds
light on the implied time frame of עד־עולם. David prays: " ... thou hast also
spoken of thy servant's house for a great while to come" (למרחוק).[131] In no case
does למרחוק ever mean "eternal" or "everlasting" in the Hebrew Bible, but simply "far off."[132] Hence, since here למרחוק is used synonymously with עד־עולם,
it is doubtful whether the latter implies "eternal" or "everlasting."

In the repetition of the dynastic oracle in 1 Chr 22:10, the context does not
offer any parallel expressions to gauge the precise extent of עד־עולם. In 1 Chr
28:7, on the other hand, the promise is expressed as עד־עולם, but is then quali-

---

[127]לעולם is nearly equivalent to עד־עולם, although Jenni, "Das Wort ᶜōlām", 231–233,
notes a distinction between these two expressions in that עד־עולם emphasizes progression in a
series.

[128]Jenni, "Das Wort ᶜōlām", 233, "עולם ist hier an allen Stellen ein zeitlicher Begriff und
bezeichnet den äussersten denkbaren terminus ad quem."

[129]Talmon, "Eschatologie und Geschichte," 29–30.

[130]In Ps 89:36–37, עולם is associated with the continual existence of the sun and moon; in
1 Enoch 10:10 an eternal life is equated with 500 years.

[131]The final phrase in v. 17 unfortunately is obscure.

[132]See A. Even-Shoshan, *A New Concordance of the Bible* (Jerusalem: Kiryat Sefer, 1989)
1993; see also *KB*, vol. 2, 885; *BDB*, 935.

fied, as we observed above, by the condition of obedience.[133] This conditional expression of the promise suggests a meaning of עד־עולם as perpetual, i.e., as long as the conditions are met. Thus, in the two instances where the meaning of עד־עולם is specified by the context, it is not obvious that it must be interpreted as "eternal." In fact, the two specifications noted above allow for a finite period for עד־עולם (a long time to come or when the conditions of the covenant are no longer met).

Yet even if the meaning of the remotest time appropriate to the narrative context is debatable, we may inquire about the context of the Chronicler. The Chronicler wrote about the collapse of the monarchy under the Babylonians, and was well aware of the failure of Judean kings to fulfill the conditions of the dynastic promise. In addition, the narrative never explicitly calls for or speaks of the reemergence of the dynasty, or even the possibility of its reemergence. But more importantly, since the Chronicler lived and wrote at a time when there had been no davidic dynasty for almost two hundred years, would not the remotest time appropriate to his context be the end of the monarchy in 586 BCE? From his perspective, 586 BCE would have designated the limit of עד־עולם.

Accordingly, in my judgment, it is anything but obvious that the dynastic promises had eternal significance. This is not to say that the dynastic promises could not have been interpreted in terms of the re-establishment of the davidic monarchy, but this understanding of the Chronicler's view would have to be proven on the basis of other evidence, not on the mere repetition of the dynastic promise with the phrase עד־עולם.

b. Other Narrative Evidence

Having completed our examination of the dynastic oracle in Chronicles, we may now proceed to consider other evidence concerning the continuity of the davidic dynasty. 2 Chr 6:41–42 is a slightly altered citation of Ps 132:8–10, which occurs at the conclusion of Solomon's prayer at the dedication of the temple, with no parallel in Dtr. Von Rad claimed that the citation of Psalm 132, what he called an eschatologically charged psalm, transformed the entire context messianically. Thus, he explained v. 42, saying, "Die Bitte ... ist dem Salomo nicht nur beiläufig ausschmückend in den Mund gelegt, sondern hier hören wir einen Laut aus den theologischen Anliegen der nachexilischen Zeit."[134]

Williamson took a different approach saying that the revision of "for thy servant David's sake" (Ps 132:10) into "Remember thy steadfast love for David

---

[133]Note in 1 Chr 28:4 עד־עולם refers to David's lifetime.

[134]Von Rad, *Geschichtsbild*, 127f.

thy servant" (זכרה לחסדי דויד עבדך), was a conscious allusion on the part of the Chronicler to Isa 55:3b, which says, "and I will make with you an everlasting covenant, my steadfast, sure love for David" (ואכרתה לכם ברית עולם חסדי דוד הנאמנים). He asserts that whereas Isa 55:3b applies the davidic covenant to Israel as a whole, the Chronicler's use of the phrase חסדי דוד is an attempt to re-emphasize the royalist interpretation of the promise to David.[135]

By way of evaluation of this messianic or royalist interpretation of 2 Chr 6:41–42, we must maintain that v. 42 cannot bear the weight von Rad and Williamson place upon it. First, it may be asked why Psalm 132 should be viewed as an eschatological psalm. It may have functioned as such in the New Testament, but von Rad offers no grounds for his assumption that it was an eschatological psalm at the time of the Chronicler. On the other hand, if the Chronicler was trying to evoke the atmosphere of Psalm 132, it should be recalled that the verse immediately after the one paraphrased in Chronicles repeats the dynastic promise in unmistakably conditional terms.

As for Williamson's belief that the Chronicler is reasserting the royalist understanding of the davidic covenant in opposition to Isa 55:3b by altering Ps 132:10, it must be remembered that the connection between v. 42 and Isa 55:3b is slim, simply the phrase חסדי דוד. On the other hand, given other examples of psalms appearing in different forms in Chronicles, it may be that a different form of Psalm 132, no longer preserved, was being used.[136] At any rate, Solomon does pray that the Lord not turn away the face of his anointed one, and one may ask whether this reveals a messianic or royalist hope on the part of the Chronicler?

In my judgment, the evidence indicates that it does not. First, the Chronicler's use (or addition) of ועתה at the beginning of v. 41 has the effect of applying the paraphrase of Psalm 132 to the specific situation in the narrative context—the first dedication of the temple. Thus, even if in the pre-exilic cultic use of Psalm 132 any reigning davidic king could have been designated by the phrase "your anointed one," the only and obvious referent to the phrase in 1 Chr 6:42 is Solomon, not future kings. Quite in contrast to von Rad's assumption about Psalm 132 being an eschatological psalm, placed in the narrative context of Chronicles, its cultic use is historicized. And in light of the Chronicler's interest in music and psalmody, it is not at all surprising that he inserted a psalm at this high point in the narrative, thereby portraying Solomon as the pious king *par excellence*, who at the conclusion of his prayer, so to speak, quotes Holy Writ.

Secondly, v. 42 calls upon God not to turn away the face of his anointed one on behalf of his steadfast love for David. This makes sense applied to Solomon; it

---

[135]Williamson, "Eschatology," 145. On the interpretation of Isa 55:3b, see above, pp. 38–41.

[136]P. R. Ackroyd, *I and II Chroniclers, Ezra, Nehemiah* (London: SCM, 1973) 113.

could be applied equally well to later kings of Judah. But it is a request for the benefit of the reigning king, and in the late Persian period, there was no king and no evidence that anyone was called the "anointed one."[137] It is not a request for the benefit of the house of David generally, or toward the sons of David. It is not a request to raise up a king. Rather, it assumes there is a king, and in this sense is wholly inapplicable to the post-exilic situation, which may explain why the Chronicler historicized it. Accordingly, while the use of this psalm is entirely appropriate in the narrative context, to suggest that such a passage signals the Chronicler's hope for a davidic messiah goes far beyond the evidence in this text.

Other passages in the narrative of Chronicles are commonly cited as further proof of the Chronicler's messianic or royalist expectation. First, in king Abijah's speech to Jeroboam in 2 Chr 13:4–12, he rebukes Jeroboam saying, "Ought you not to know that the Lord God of Israel gave the kingship over Israel for ever to David and his sons by a covenant of salt" (v. 5)? And, "And now you think to withstand the kingdom of the Lord in the hand of the sons of David, ... " (v. 8a).

Many proponents of the messianic or royalist interpretation have seen this as clear proof of the Chronicler's hope for a coming davidic figure.[138] However, there seems to be a fundamental confusion inherent in their position. The question is not whether the Chronicler believed that the davidic dynasty was the divinely appointed and therefore only legitimate dynasty during the monarchy. No one, except Caquot, has questioned this.[139] Rather, the point at issue is whether the Chronicler hoped for the re-establishment of the davidic monarchy long after its collapse. The passage simply does not address this question. Williamson and others seem to believe that the eventual re-establishment of the davidic monarchy is implied by the words עד־עולם. But besides the problem associated with their interpretation of עד־עולם,[140] their conclusion overlooks other evidence.

First, we have previously argued that the Chronicler understood the davidic covenant to be conditioned on the obedience of the kings. Clearly by the time the

---

[137]In Zech. 4:14, Zerubbabel and Joshua the high priest, are wrongly designated "anointed ones" (see above, p. 60).

[138]For example, von Rad, *Geschichtsbild*, 124; Brunet, "La Théologie du Chroniste," 389; Newsome, "New Understanding," 209 n. 27; R. B. Dillard, *2 Chronicles* (WBC; Waco, TX: Word, 1987) 108; Williamson, "Eschatology," 146–147. Williamson's logic to support a royalist expectation is as follows: v. 8 declares that the Lord's kingdom is in the hands of the sons of David, and the Lord's kingdom is permanent and indestructible. Thus, he asks whether there is any indication "that the Lord will continue to express his kingship through the Davidic house," for which he finds clear affirmation in v. 5. In contrast, Caquot, "Peut-on parler," 119, suggested that Abijah's speech reflects only the views of Abijah, not the Chronicler, but this is unlikely, and Caquot offered no proof for his claim.

[139]Caquot, "Peut-on parler," 119.

[140]See above, p. 97.

Judean state and monarchy fell to Babylon, the conditions of the "covenant of salt" had been severely violated. The messianic or royalist interpretation of 2 Chr 13:5 completely ignores this fact. Secondly, within the narrative, v. 5 is used to condemn Jeroboam's usurpation of kingship in Israel. Hence, the issue is not the renewal of the monarchy, but having assumed the presence of a monarchy in Israel, the question concerns the monarchy's legitimate kings. In the time of the Chronicler, when no monarchy existed, this was a moot issue.

Thirdly, if the message of the passage for the Chronicler's audience was in fact that "the Lord God of Israel gave the kingship over Israel for ever to David and his sons by a covenant of salt," by the late Persian period, God would have violated his own "covenant of salt" for between 150 to 225 years, since the sons of David did not possess the kingship during this time. Far from inspiring hope in the Lord's re-establishment of the davidic dynasty, it would stand as an illustration of the Lord's failure to make good on his word. Abijah's statement makes no allowances for a hiatus in the continuity of davidic kingship. If one argued that by the time of the Chronicler, a hiatus in the dynasty would be implied by the new context, one could just as well argue that this new context implied that the dynasty was a matter of past glory, whose value was now embodied in the temple cult. In either case, the meaning of the passage would depend on assumptions about the context of the Chronicler and his audience, not on the internal signals within the text.

Fourthly, Abijah's speech has an identifiable and meaningful role within the overall framework of Chronicles. In this regard, Throntveit has argued that Abijah's speech functions to demarcate the beginning of the second period within the Chronicler's tripartite periodization of Israelite history. The first period, the united kingdom under David and Solomon in which all Israel worshipped at the Jerusalem temple, is followed by period two, the divided monarchy, in which the Northern Kingdom separated itself from the true cult of the Lord. Period two comes to a close when Hezekiah's speech in 2 Chr 30:6–9, inviting the Northern refugees to Judah, results in a Passover celebration that brings joy unparalleled since the time of Solomon, in effect, symbolizing a return to a united kingdom. For the Chronicler, then, the period of the divided monarchy formed a parenthesis in which the Northern Kingdom stood in rebellion against the Lord.[141]

Accordingly, the point of Abijah's speech is that the North, by rebelling against the divinely appointed davidic kings and abandoning worship in Jerusalem, was in fact rebelling against the Lord himself. Furthermore, this rebellion ceased when the Northerners in the time of Hezekiah returned to the proper worship of God in Jerusalem. Here, the logic of the narrative appropriately as-

---

[141]Throntveit, *Kings Speak*, 115–120.

sumes the presence of the perpetual davidic monarchy. But, it is what we might call narrative staging appropriate to the historical period being treated. The message of the passage, on the other hand, is a warning against rebelling against the Lord by separating oneself from the sole legitimate cult in Jerusalem, certainly a meaningful message at the time of the Chronicler.[142] But to extract v. 5 from Abijah's speech, where it has an identifiable function within the overall structure of Chronicles, and interpret it as an unmistakable indication of the Chronicler's royalist or messianic hope is mistaken.

In light of these considerations, I maintain that the passage simply has no relevance for the question about the continuation of the davidic dynasty after the destruction of Judah. The narrative's interest in the davidic monarchs and the continuity of the dynasty during the monarchy, or references to the "eternal" davidic covenant do not necessarily imply that the author hoped for a renewed davidic monarchy at some future time.

This same point is applicable to two other instances, often cited by proponents of the messianic or royalist interpretation, where the continuity of the dynasty is mentioned in the narrative of Chronicles. 2 Chr 21:7 offers an explanation of why Jehoram, a brutally evil king, was permitted to reign:

> Yet the Lord would not destroy the house of David, because of the covenant which he had made with David, and since he had promised to give a lamp to him and to his sons forever.

This verse is taken over from Dtr with two changes: 1) "Judah" becomes "house of David"; 2) "for the sake of David" becomes "because of the covenant which he had made with David." Williamson asserts that these two changes help illustrate the eternity of the davidic covenant and therefore the Chronicler's royalist expectations.[143] Likewise, in the account of Joash's accession to the throne, in 2 Chr 23:3, the high priest Jehoiada says, "Behold, the king's son! Let him reign, as the Lord spoke concerning the sons of David." Since this is not paralleled in Dtr, it has been viewed as an unmistakable testimony to the Chronicler's royalist hopes.[144]

Yet, W. E. Lemke demonstrated the danger of positing such significant thematic tendencies on the basis of minor divergences from the MT of Dtr.[145] More

---

[142] See Braun, "Solomonic Apologetic," 515f; cf. also Noth, *Chronicler's History*, 103.

[143] Williamson, "Eschatology," 148; see also, von Rad, *Geschichtsbild*, 124.

[144] Williamson, "Eschatology," 148f; von Rad, *Geschichtsbild*, 124.

[145] W. E. Lemke, "The Synoptic Problem in the Chronicler's History," *HTR* 58 (1965) 349–363. Japhet, *Ideology*, 454–456, suggests that the Chronicler's use of the phrase "house of David" may be due to his doctrine of individual retribution.

importantly, these passages testify only to the Chronicler's belief that the davidic family continued to hold the throne in Israel, in spite of threats, due to the Lord's commitment to David. They do not, however, address the question of a renewal of the dynasty about two centuries after its demise. If 2 Chr 21:7 is evidence for the Chronicler's belief that the Lord would always leave a lamp for David in Jerusalem, where was this lamp in the intervening 150–225 years between the fall of the davidic dynasty and the Chronicler own time? Nor should mention of a covenant with David in 2 Chr 21:7 be magnified in importance. As Japhet observes, 2 Chr 21:7 is unusual in that it is the only mention a covenant with David in Chronicles; she judges that "the concept of a covenant with David has no importance or theological significance in the book of Chronicles."[146]

Furthermore, Williamson claims that these three passages (2 Chr 13:5; 21:7; 23:3) "are illustrative of the three major situations through which the dynasty could pass whilst remaining intact."[147] With respect to this point, two comments are in order. First, Williamson himself intuitively recognizes that the issue for the Chronicler is whether the dynasty would remain intact, not whether, after its demise, some century or two later it would be revived. Secondly, conspicuously absent from the Chronicler's narrative is any assurance whatsoever that the dynasty survived the destruction of Judah in any form. In his account of the destruction of Judah by Nebuchadnezzar, the Chronicler totally ignores the fate of the second to last king, Jehoiachin—and for that matter, the last king, Zedekiah, even though an account was in his source. If the Chronicler chose to remind his readers of the continuity of the davidic dynasty at those times when the dynasty's future appeared most brittle, as Williamson supposes, then the Chronicler missed a crucial opportunity in his description of the end of the Kingdom of Judah, which omits any hope for the future of the dynasty.[148]

In contrast, at this very point in the book, we find an important indication of the Chronicler's actual disinterest in the re-establishment of the davidic monarchy, since instead of the account of Jehoiachin's release from captivity, the Chronicler

---

[146]Japhet, *Ideology*, 459.

[147]Williamson, "Eschatology," 149. In fairness to Williamson, it should be noted that he sees these passages as significant in confirming his earlier thesis evaluated above, not as definitive proofs in themselves.

[148]Williamson, "Eschatology," 149, calls the time prior to Joash a "period when the dynasty as a whole came as close as imaginable to total destruction." Surely, the destruction of Judah and the end of the monarchy was a time when the dynasty was closer to total destruction. In fact, the dynasty was destroyed. Williamson seems to confuse a dynasty—the continuous rule of a given family line, with the mere continued existence of a family line. Of course, the end of the family means the end of the dynasty; but the existence of the family, does not necessarily mean the continuance of the dynasty.

ends his story of Judah with an acknowledgment of Cyrus' divinely sanctioned rule over "all the kingdoms of the earth," and his intention to sponsor the rebuilding of the temple in Jerusalem (2 Chr 36:22–23).[149] The only question is whether this passage reflects the authentic thought of the Chronicler, since some have attributed it to a later redactional level.[150] But there are sound reasons for treating it as original to Chronicles.

For one, the orthography of the name Jeremiah in 2 Chr 36:22 (ירמיהו, with the long ending) is consistent with the Chronicler's usual spelling of the prophet's name (cf. 2 Chr 35:25; 36:12,21), but different from the spelling in Ezra 1:1 (ירמיה, with the short ending). Williamson accounts for this orthographic difference, as well as the different prepositions (בפי in Chronicles, מפי in Ezra), by claiming that after vv. 22–23 were added from Ezra 1:1–3a, a copyist assimilated the phrase in v. 22 to the form of the phrase found in the preceding verse.[151] But no textual evidence supports this speculation; the LXX already testifies to the different prepositions in v. 22 and Ezra 1:1. A more plausible explanation for the difference would hold that the Chronicler spelled Jeremiah in his characteristic way, and then the author of Ezra-Nehemiah, although overlapping his composition with the ending of Chronicles, employed his customary orthography.[152] For this reason, vv. 22–23 should not be deleted from the original form of Chronicles. Other alleged reasons for viewing these verses as secondary are hardly convincing.[153] We conclude, then, that the Chronicler recognized the dominion of the Persians, a viewpoint scarcely consistent with a fervent messianic or royalist hope.

---

[149]See Baltzer, "Das Ende," 39–41.

[150]A common view among those who viewed Chronicles and Ezra-Nehemiah as a single composition was that when the Chronicler's work was divided, these verses from the beginning of Ezra-Nehemiah were repeated at the end of Chronicles in order to indicate the continuation of the story in the now separated parts of the work. In this case, of course, the verses still reflected the views of the Chronicler. But even among those who view Chronicles and Ezra-Nehemiah as originally independent works, the authenticity of 2 Chr 36:22–23 is questioned. For example, Williamson and Braun are undecided about the ending of Chronicles, but seem to lean toward a position that understands these verses as indicative of the Chronicler's viewpoint. Also, although Freedman, Newsome, and Cross held these verses as original, this did not influence their view about the messianism of Chronicles.

[151]Williamson, *Israel*, 9.

[152]Japhet, "Supposed Common Authorship," 338–341, shows that the author of Ezra-Nehemiah prefers the short version of theophoric names.

[153]Williamson, *Israel*, 9–10, says that the break in the account of Cyrus' decree at ויעל is "unnatural," and it is difficult to see why the Chronicler did not include the decree in full. He asserts, too, that v. 21 provides a "more satisfying conclusion" to Chronicles. Actually, in my judgment, vv. 22–23 form a very satisfying conclusion: Chronicles culminates with the return to Judah and Jerusalem in the same way in which the genealogical section reached a climax in the listing of those who were the first to return to Judah and Jerusalem (1 Chr 9:2–32).

Thus, our examination of texts in the narrative of Chronicles dealing with the davidic dynasty suggests that the messianic or royalist interpretation of Chronicles goes far beyond the textual data. The Chronicler's mention of the on-going davidic dynasty and his characterization of it within the narrative as עד־עולם do not necessarily entail that he held messianic or royalist hopes. In addition, it ignores evidence to the contrary. In short, recognition of the divine institution and care of the davidic dynasty, along with an idealized portrait of its first two monarchs, cannot be equated with a messianic or royalist expectation.

c. 1 Chr 3:17–24

1 Chr 3:17–24 is a continuation of a davidic genealogy beginning with king Jeconiah (Jehoiachin) and extending well into the post-exilic period. Above, in the discussion concerning the date of Chronicles, I treated the textual and interpretive problems associated with this passage. Now, our task is to ascertain what these verses reveal about the continuing relevance of the davidic dynasty, particularly since some have cited this genealogy as evidence for the Chronicler's messianic expectation.[154]

To begin, we must understand the function of the genealogy as a whole, and in this regard, it may be helpful to delineate the different genealogical forms present in 3:1–24.[155] Verses 1–9 enumerate the sons and daughters of David; then in vv. 10–14, a strictly linear genealogy beginning with one of those sons, Solomon, lists successive kings of Judah; in vv. 15–24, the genealogical form is mixed, listing multiple sons of a father, but tracing further generations through only one descendant. In this mixed genealogy, vv. 15–16 list multiple sons of Josiah and Jehoiakim, all but two of whom ruled as king.[156] In vv. 17–24, the mixed genealogy continues, although those listed did not hold the office of king.

[154]Stinespring, "Eschatology," 210; cf. Williamson, "Eschatology," 129, who speaks about the genealogy as a witness to the continuing interest in the davidic line; and P. R. Ackroyd, "The Theology of the Chronicler," *LTQ* 8 (1973) 112, who, although seeing the elaboration of davidic genealogical material as secondary, counts it as evidence for concern for the davidic ideal.

[155]Genealogical form can be classified as follows: linear, which traces only one line of descent from a given ancestor; segmented, which traces more than one line of descent from a given ancestor, exhibiting branching; and mixed, which lists multiple descendants of a father, but traces further generations through only one of those descendants (see R. R. Wilson, *Genealogy and History in the Biblical World* [New Haven: Yale University Press, 1977] 8–9; Braun, *1 Chronicles*, 2).

[156]Josiah's first-born, Johanan, is otherwise unknown; his fourth son Shallum is the same person as Jehoahaz, who succeeded Josiah (cf. 2 Kgs 23:30; Jer 22:11); his third-born Zedekiah, according to 2 Kgs 24:17, succeeded his nephew Jehoiachin; according to 2 Chr 36:10, the successor of Jehoiachin was a different Zedekiah, brother of Jehoiachin.

Accordingly, in vv. 10–14, one can observe a typical function of linear genealogies, which list persons who held an important office.[157] The intention to enumerate those who held royal office is continued in vv. 15–16, but now in the form of a mixed genealogy, that form being necessary here, since more than one royal son reigned.[158] Yet, the exact function of the mixed genealogy in vv. 17–24 is unclear. It is to this issue, therefore, that our attention must turn.

One possibility would be that it too lists persons who held an important office. Usually this function is performed by a linear genealogy, but as we have seen in vv. 15–16, when circumstances require, a mixed genealogy can function in this way as well. However, the circumstances that required a mixed genealogy in vv. 15–16—more than one son of a father holding office—are not documented for vv. 17–24. In fact, except for Zerubbabel, who, according to Haggai 1:1; 2:2, was governor of Judah, there is little evidence to support the claim that those named in vv. 17–24, or the davidic house generally, provided governors for Judah during the late sixth to early fifth centuries BCE.[159] The only actual governors known for the fifth century BCE, Nehemiah and the Persian Bogoas, were certainly not Davidides. Furthermore, the listing of families in v. 21b, rather than individuals, argues against this interpretation of the genealogy's function.

Another possibility for the function of this mixed genealogy is to legitimate in some way the last named generation or person.[160] The latter possibility is made all the more plausible if the Anani in v. 24 can be identified with a certain Anani, evidently a prominent person, mentioned in a letter from Elephantine to Jewish leaders in Jerusalem dated 407 BCE.[161] On the other hand, the break in the genealogy in v. 21b, since it weakens the pedigree of the last-named generation or person, mitigates against this conclusion.

---

[157]Johnson, *Genealogies*, 71. Another function of linear genealogies is to establish a pedigree for a prominent person (cf. 1 Chr 2:10–17); segmented genealogies functioned to illustrate relationships.

[158]See Johnson, *Genealogies*, 71.

[159]Hanson, *Dawn*, 349, claims that the davidic house supplied governors for Judah, pointing to the prominence of the house of David in Zechariah 12 and the diarchic structure of the theocratic ideal with a Zadokite priest and a davidic ruler, as well as this genealogy, as evidence for his claim. Actual data, however, consists of bullae and seals referring to "Elnathan, the governor," and to "Shelomith, the mother of Elnathan," where this Shelomith is identified with Zerubbabel's daughter in 3:19, and Elnathan her husband (mother, being court language for wife) [see, Braun, *1 Chronicles*, 47, for references]. Also, storage jar impressions with the name of Hananiah and Baruch ben Shimei have been related to those names listed in vv. 17–24. It should be obvious that none of this data substantiates the claim that the Davidides were governors of Judah in the fifth century BCE.

[160]Braun, *1 Chronicles*, 5.

[161]Pritchard, *ANET*, 492.

Furthermore, if legitimizing the last named person were the only purpose of the genealogy, it is difficult to account for the presence of sons through whom the line of descent is not traced and for the families mentioned in v. 21b. In this regard, Johnson thinks that the genealogy may function to legitimize the Davidides listed in the sense of showing the size and leadership role of davidic families in the restoration community.[162] This suggestion has merit because it both comports with the general function of the genealogies of Judah and Levi in Chronicles,[163] and accounts for the significance of the house of David in the post-exilic community witnessed in Zechariah 12 and Ezra 8:2–3, and possibly in the prominence of Anani.

Moreover, this explanation of the genealogy's function allows us to speculate on the reason for the break in the genealogy caused by the listing of the four families in v. 21b. If we recall that Hattush, from the sons of Shecaniah, came from Babylon with Ezra, one might suppose that the other three families listed along with the sons of Shecaniah also came from Babylon with Ezra (since Hattush is designated the head of his father's [David's] house, it is likely that the house of David included more than just the sons of Shecaniah.) These new davidic families from Babylon may have displaced in prominence and power the older davidic families already present in Judah. Accordingly, they would have displaced them in the genealogical register. After all, the purpose of genealogies is not primarily to list flawless continuity, but to legitimize or at least acknowledge those named in the genealogy.

Thus, the clear break in the linear continuity of the genealogy caused by the listing of the four families in v. 21b would have resulted from new davidic families, recently migrated from Babylon, coming into prominence in Judah and displacing the davidic line associated with earlier returnees. This displacement may have been possible, on the one hand, because of their connection with Ezra, who certainly possessed prominence and power, evident in the successful imposition of his legal tradition on Judah, or, on the other, due to their association with the same Persian authorities who supported Ezra.[164]

In any case, if the purpose of the davidic genealogy in vv. 17–24 is to emphasize or acknowledge the size and leadership role of the house of David in the

---

[162]Johnson, *Genealogies*, 70,76.

[163]Johnson, *Genealogies*, 69.

[164]There is no way to be certain whether the four families displaced the two sons of Hananiah listed, but if they did, the activity of these four families would be dated ca. 470–450 BCE. Of course, this would imply an early date for Ezra's activity (ca. 458 BCE), and incidentally synchronizes the last-named Anani with the Anani mentioned in the Elephantine letter of 407 BCE.

post-exilic community, what implications does this have for the possibility of davidic messianism or royalism in Chronicles? As we observed, except for Zerubbabel, there is little evidence that members of these davidic families held the office of governor, or any other official political office.[165] Furthermore, the genealogy's apparent lack of interest in a linear descent of persons suggests that its purpose is not the enumeration of legitimate aspirants for the davidic throne.[166] In other words, in 3:17–24, we have an example of a familial geneal- ogy not a dynastic line.

Moreover, any suggestion of messianic or royalist hopes associated with these Davidides is wholly absent. Johnson notes that there is no assurance of blessing mentioned in the list of Davidides, adding that the list from 3:10–24 reads like an anti-climax.[167] Likewise, Braun observes, " ... the text before us (3:17–24) is silent concerning any future hope of either a political or theological nature that might be attached to the line."[168] We must conclude, therefore, that the genealogy only points to a certain prominence for davidic families in the post- exilic community, not to dynastic hopes. But even here, the prominence of the davidic families in the post-exilic community is deduced from data mostly outside of Chronicles (Zechariah 12 and Ezra 8:2b–3a); the Chronicler himself fails to single out the Davidides for special attention when he lists the first inhabitants of Jerusalem after the return (1 Chr 9:2–34).[169]

d. The Function of the Davidic Dynasty Tradition in Chronicles

If setting forth a messianic or royalist hope is not part of the Chronicler's purpose, then what role does his focus on the davidic dynasty and idealizing of David and Solomon play in Chronicles? Here it is not necessary to develop a new thesis, since we can appeal to the work of Rudolph, Ackroyd, Braun, and others.[170] In

---

[165]As noted earlier (p. 46), Zerubbabel's name was probably grafted into this davidic genealogy secondarily.

[166]In fact, although those listed in v. 21b and afterward are doubtless davidic, the break in the genealogy makes it impossible to insure that they were in anyway related to Zerubbabel or to earlier kings who traced their lineage to Solomon.

[167]Johnson, *Genealogies*, 79.

[168]Braun, *1 Chronicles*, 55; see also, R. J. Coggins, *The First and Second Books of Chron- icles* (CBC; New York: Cambridge University Press, 1976) 26; Ackroyd, *I and II Chronicles, Ezra, and Nehemiah*, 35.

[169]In 1 Chr 9:2–34, the Chronicler singles out some of the people from Judah, Benjamin, Ephraim and Manasseh, as well as priests, Levites, and other cultic functionaries. Conspicu- ously missing is a separate category for the Davidides.

[170]Rudolph, "Problems of the Books of Chronicles," 407–409; Caquot, "Peut-on parler," *passim*; Ackroyd, "History and Theology," 512–514; "The Theology of the Chronicler,"

this view of things, the Chronicler's focus on David, Solomon, and the davidic dynasty is a function of his primary interest: the legitimization and exaltation of the contemporary cultic community centered around the Jerusalem temple as the sole locus and exclusively valid organization for the worship of the Lord for all Israel.

In Chronicles, the location of the temple and the cultic personnel and procedures were divinely appointed. Thus, the temple's placement in Jerusalem and the significant role of the Levites become matters of divine choice, not historical accident. The need for the exclusive legitimization of Zion may be related to claims associated with rival Jewish cultic places or temples.[171] The effort to secure an important place for the Levites among the cultic personnel and activity is probably to be linked with internal power struggles between the Levites and Aaronic priests.[172] This latter point may explain why the author appeals to the davidic tradition for legitimizing the Levites over against the Moses/Sinai traditions, which focused on the Aaronic priests.[173] But whatever the precise circumstances and forces generating the Chronicler's position, what is crucial is that the divine will that bestowed exclusive authority on both temple and cultic organization was mediated and implemented by davidic kings, particularly David and Solomon.

David and Solomon, moreover, are not only mediators of the divine institution of the Chronicler's cultic community, their reigns represent a period in which

---

112–113; Braun, "Solomonic Apologetic," *passim*; "Rally 'Round," 512; Mason, *Preaching the Tradition*, 123–124.

[171]The hypothesis that Chronicles is essentially an anti-Samaritan polemic has rightly been discarded on the basis of the Chronicler's moderately positive attitude toward the North. Nevertheless, Chronicles implicitly still rejects all other cultic sites for the worship of the Lord, and in this sense, indeed, would have rejected Samaritan sanctuaries or cultic sites as well. But the Samaritan cultic site (or sites) may not have been the only or principal target of the Chronicler's emphasis on the singularity of the Jerusalem temple. In this regard, it may not be coincidental that ca. 408 BCE, authorities in Jerusalem refused the request of the Jewish community in Elephantine for aid in rebuilding their temple. Moreover, if other evidence—some of which dates from a later time—of Jewish temple building in Arad, near Beth-Sheva (seventh century BCE), Araq el-Emir (second century BCE), Leontopolis (ca. 160 BCE), and, of course, Shechem (late fourth century BCE) [see Stone, *Scritpure, Sects, and Visions*, 77–82, for a summary of this evidence], reflects Jewish attitudes contemporary with the Chronicles, the need for justifying Jerusalem's uniqueness as the cultic site for the worship of the Lord may have been timely.

[172]Most recently, De Vries, "Moses and David," 619–639; cf. also von Rad, *Geschichtsbild*, 119; Rudolph, "Problems of the Books of Chronicles," 407; Williamson, *1 and 2 Chronicles*, 30.

[173]De Vries, "Moses and David," 638–639.

all Israel belonged to and participated in this cultic community. In this regard, Hezekiah's policy of including Northern Israelites into the Jerusalem cult appears to represent the renewal of this ideal of a united Israel late in the monarchy. In turn, Hezekiah's policy may have provided a model for the Chronicler's own attitude toward Northern Israelites in his own day. Or more accurately, the Chronicler's own moderately open stance toward non-Judean Israelites is read back into Hezekiah's reign. In addition, by anchoring his contemporary cultic community in the traditions of the davidic kingdom, the Chronicler offered his readers a sense of continuity and identity with pre-exilic institutions.

Accordingly, the Chronicler's focus on David and Solomon, and the davidic monarchy generally, illustrates the divinely instituted exclusiveness of the Jerusalem temple and cult, and its ancient and proper status as the shrine of all Israel. To find davidic messianism or royalist hopes in this use of the davidic dynasty tradition can only be achieved at the cost of abstracting the Chronicler's focus on the davidic dynasty from its function of legitimating temple and cult. To do so, however, violates the logic of Chronicles. The failure of the davidic dynasty to live up to the conditions of the dynastic covenant and the resulting harsh judgment against Judah and its temple meant the end of davidic rule over the Lord's kingdom. The Chronicler's narrative of the end of the Kingdom of Judah offers not a glimmer of hope for the dynasty. Yet the lasting contribution of the davidic house would live on in the cult and temple.

Finally, we might observe that Chronicles, instead of passing on the tradition of David as the progenitor of a messianic line, may have been instrumental in handing on—or creating—the image of David as founder and patron of the Jerusalem cult. It is well known that in Chronicles, David's role in preparations for the building of the temple and in the arrangement of cultic organization far outstrips his role in Dtr. Wellhausen's comment about the Chronicler's David being "seen through a cloud of incense" may be an exaggeration, but nevertheless makes the point.[174] In the same way, the portrait of David and davidic kings as devotees of the cult and its ceremonies is prominent in early Judaism (cf. Ezra-Nehemiah, 1 Esdras 1, Sir 47:8–10; 11QPs[a] 27:2–11). On the other hand, there is no evidence that early Jewish interpreters of Chronicles were aware of its messianic or royalist dimension.[175]

---

[174]J. Wellhausen, *Prolegomena to the History of Ancient Israel* (reprint ed.; Cleveland and New York: World, 1957) 182.

[175]E. Ben Zvi, "The Authority of 1–2 Chronicles in the Late Second Temple Period," *JSP* 3 (1988) 59–88.

4. Summary and Conclusion

First and foremost, nowhere in Chronicles is there an explicit call for the resumption of the davidic monarchy or a direct expression of hope for a davidic messiah. The messianic or royalist interpretation of the Chronicler's ideology is derived from indirect evidence found both in the text and in hypothetical contexts. Within the text, the decisive evidence has been the repetition of the dynastic promise, the focus on the davidic monarchy throughout the narrative, along with the idealized portraits of David and Solomon, and the post-exilic davidic genealogy in 1 Chr 3:17–24. I have endeavored to show that none of these features in Chronicles implies a messianic or royalist hope on the part of the Chronicler.

The dynastic promise is focused on Solomon and his role as the temple builder, is conditioned upon the obedience of kings whose apostasy the Chronicler documents, and need not be construed as "everlasting" or "eternal." The focus on the davidic monarchy, while acknowledging the continuity of the davidic dynasty during the monarchy, is irrelevant for the question about its reemergence in the post-exilic period. Moreover, the interest in the davidic monarchy and the idealization of David and Solomon serve to legitimate the temple and cultic traditions current in the Chronicler's own time. Finally, the post-exilic davidic genealogy functions to acknowledge or legitimate the size and leadership role of davidic families in the post-exilic community; it is not a dynastic line. In addition, the messianic or royalist view cannot account for the Chronicler's recognition of Cyrus as the one possessing divinely appointed dominion over all the nations of the world. Altogether, the internal textual signals do not testify to a davidic hope on the part of the Chronicler.

Support for the messianic or royalist interpretation has also come from the supposed historical context of the Chronicler. Freedman's claim of davidic messianism in Chronicles was based on his assertion that Chronicles was to be associated with messianic hopes fixed on Zerubbabel—hopes known from the prophecies of Haggai and Zechariah. Freedman's thesis, however, founders on it circular method of establishing the messianic ideology of Chronicles, its arbitrary rejection of 1 Chronicles 1–9 from the original composition of the Chronicler, and the unsubstantiated dating of a hypothetical original version of Chronicles to ca. 520–515 BCE.

Williamson and Wright have suggested, although with the customary caveats, that the revolt against Persia led by the Sidonian Tennes in 352–347 BCE may have provided the historical setting for the Chronicler's royalist ideology. On the one hand, although possible, since Chronicles can be dated to this period, this suggestion is pure conjecture. We might add that Judean participation in an earlier revolt connected with the Sidonian king ᶜAbd-ᶜštart I in 370–362 BCE might have provided an equally suitable context for royalist ideology.

On the other hand, coins minted in Judea during these revolts do not witness to davidic royalist hopes. In the earlier revolt linked to ᶜAbd-ᶜštart I, Judean coins apparently imprint the likeness of a local ruler clad in a *kidaris*,[176] but this ruler is neither designated as royal nor davidic. Betlyon thinks this is a portrait of the high priest, who was the governor of Judah. Inscriptions on Judean coinage from the time of the Tennes revolt again reveal no hint of royalist or davidic aspirations.[177] In fact, a proposed relationship between Chronicles and known revolts is ill-conceived, for Chronicles' preoccupation with cultic organization and its lack of explicit stress on the re-establishment of the monarchy are hardly the stuff of political revolution—all the more so if one considers 2 Chr 36:22–23 original, as we have above.

Indeed, what is known about the context of Chronicles speaks against a messianic or royalist interpretation, for when Chronicles was written, sometime between ca. 435–348 BCE, the monarchy and the dynasty had been defunct for 150 to 240 years. Furthermore, the only documented messianic or royalist stirring during the Persian period, found in the prophecies of Haggai and Zechariah (1–8), lay 85 to 175 years in the past.[178] The political significance of the davidic dynasty was a distant memory. In contrast, the political importance of the priesthood is clearly implied for the time of Ezra and confirmed for the end of the Persian period.[179] It should, therefore, not be surprising that no extant Jewish literature, including Chronicles, or material evidence from the late Persian period testifies to a continuing messianic or royalist tradition connected with the davidic house.

We conclude, therefore, that neither the text nor the context of Chronicles supports a messianic or royalist interpretation. Instead, in the hands of the Chronicler the davidic dynasty tradition subserved a particular vision of the Jerusalem cultic community in the late Persian period.

---

[176]Betlyon, "Yehud Coins," 637–638, esp. n. 16; L. Mildenberg, "Yehud: A Preliminary Study of the Provincial Coinage of Judaea," *Greek Numismatics and Archaeology* (ed. O. Mørkholm and N. M. Waggoner; Wetteren: Editions NR, 1979) 183–196, believes the ruler is Persian.

[177]See Betlyon, "Yehud Coins," 638.

[178]None of the supposed contemporary messianic literature cited by von Rad, *Geschichtsbild*, 122–123, is both messianic and contemporary with Chronicles.

[179]A coin, probably dated ca. 335–331 BCE, bears the inscription יחנן הכהן (see Betlyon, "Yehud Coins," 639).

B. Zech 12:2–13:1

1. Introduction

Zech 12:2–13:1 speaks of the activity of the "house of David" and is therefore pertinent to our study of the davidic dynasty tradition in early Judaism. Indeed, some interpreters have claimed that it witnesses to a hope for the restoration of the davidic dynasty or for a davidic messiah.[180] Nevertheless, at the outset it must be admitted that Zech 12:2–13:1 confronts an interpreter with a host of textual, literary, and historical problems. There is little scholarly consensus about the meaning of this passage.[181] Attempts to relate it to specific, often hypothetical, historical settings—usually through numerous deletions and emendations of the text—have proven unconvincing,[182] largely because of the dearth of specific historical references in the text and the paucity of historical information about the Jewish community in Judah during the Persian and early Hellenistic periods.[183] Plöger and Hanson undoubtedly made an advance in understanding the text as a witness to some inner-Jewish conflict, but the specifics of their hypotheses are more difficult to substantiate.[184]

---

[180]Mitchell, *Hag, Zech, Mal, and Jonah*, 326 (restoration of dynasty); R. L. Smith, *Micah–Malachi* (WBC; Waco, TX: Word, 1984) 275 (regain leadership role, but no personal messiah); Blenkinsopp, *Prophecy*, 262 (restoration of davidic dynasty); R. C. Dentan, "Zechariah," *The Interpreter's Bible, Vol. 6* (ed. G. A. Buttrick; Nashville: Abingdon, 1956) 1107 (messianic ruler); P. Lamarche, *Zacharie IX–XIV: Structure littéraire et Messianisme* (Paris: Gabalda, 1961) 121–122 (davidic messiah).

[181]Koch, *Prophets*, 2:180, remarks with respect to Zechariah 9–14, "Nowhere do the opinions of scholars diverge so widely about prophetic writings as here, and nowhere are the findings of research so uncertain." For a summary of the history of criticism of these problems, see Eissfeldt, *Introduction*, 435–437; Plöger, *Theocracy and Eschatology*, 78–79; and Hanson, *Dawn*, 287–290. Hanson, *Dawn*, 357, calls the history of criticism of 12:2–13:1 "bewildering."

[182]See Hanson, *Dawn*, 286–292, esp. p. 287, " ... the text is tortuously forced to serve one historical hypothesis after the other."

[183]See Coggins, *Hag, Zech, Mal*, 63,71; cf. Petersen, "Zechariah," *Harper's Bible Commentary* (ed. J. L. Mays; San Francisco: Harper & Row, 1988) 747; Eissfeldt, *Introduction*, 439. Details in the text were typically associated with events known from the pre-exilic period, the Maccabean period, or one of the few incidents known from the Persian and early Hellenistic periods. The passage was then adapted and interpreted accordingly. See the review of scholarship in Plöger, *Theocracy and Eschatology*, 78–79; and Hanson, *Dawn*, 287–290.

[184]Specifically, Hanson, *Dawn*, 280–401, argued that the passage reflected one stage in the continuing conflict between two parties in post-exilic Judah, the hierocratic party and the visionary party. Set in the first half of the fifth century BCE, Zech 12:2–13:1 witnessed to the visionary party's increasing alienation from the halls of power, controlled by the hierocratic party, and the visionary's apocalyptically oriented version of its role in the establishment of the post-exilic theocracy. For a critique of Hanson's view see, R. P. Carroll, "Twilight of Prophecy or Dawn of Apocalyptic?" *JSOT* 14 (1979) 3–35.

Our treatment below will take up the problems of this text inasmuch as they bear on our more limited aim: the identity and characterization of the house of David. Accordingly, we will begin with a careful delineation and justification of the literary unit under examination, followed by a summary of the interpretation of this unit. Then, the identity and characterization of the "house of David" will be studied more closely to ascertain whether or how the davidic dynasty tradition is being used. Next, I will attempt to establish a date for the passage. Finally, in light of this study the validity of claims that Zech 12:2–13:1 witnesses to a royalist or messianic hope will be evaluated.

2. Analysis of Zech 12:2–13:1

a. Literary Context, Integrity, and Structure

It is a matter of scholarly consensus that Zechariah 9–14, whatever its present literary and theological relationship to Zechariah 1–8, contains anonymous oracles originally unrelated to those in chaps. 1–8.[185] Moreover, within chaps. 9–14 the vast majority of commentators recognize at least two independent units consisting of 9–11 and 12–14, each unit being introduced with the phrase מַשָּׂא דְבַר־יהוה. Since Malachi begins with this same superscription, it is held that three short anonymous collections were appended to the prophetic corpus.[186] In addition, still smaller literary units exist within chaps. 12–14. After the superscription in 12:1, three originally independent oracles can be distinguished: a prose oracle in 12:2–13:6, a poetic oracle in 13:7–9, and a second prose oracle in 14:1–21.[187]

---

[185]See the standard Hebrew Bible introductions; see also Coggins, *Hag, Zech, Mal*, 60–62, for a recent treatment of the issue.

[186]See for example, Fohrer, *Introduction*, 466; Eissfeldt, *Introduction*, 440; Rendtorff, *Introduction*, 240; Blenkinsopp, *Prophecy*, 259. Some have maintained that Zechariah 9–14 is a unified composition, or nearly so. Lamarche, *Zacharie IX–XIV*, esp. pp. 112–113, argued that these chapters were the product of a single author who used a rather elaborate chiastic pattern to structure his work. His view, however, has not been widely accepted (see Coggins, *Hag, Zech, Mal*, 64, for a brief review of Lamarche's thesis). Rudolph, *Hag, Sach 1–8, 9–14, Mal*, 219, saw chap. 12 as a continuation of chap. 11, the attack against Jerusalem by the nations being motivated by the breaking of the covenant with them in 11:11. His view, however, was forced to relegate the superscription in 12:1 to the status of a secondary addition, a very unlikely hypothesis.

[187]M. Saebo, *Sacharja 9–14: Untersuchungen von Text und Form* (WMANT 34; Neukirchen-Vluyn: Neukirchener Verlag, 1969) 252–309; I. Willi-Plein, *Prophetie am Ende: Untersuchungen zu Sacharja 9–14* (Köln: Peter Hanstein, 1974) 56–63. Some, however, have questioned the independence of these units. Childs, *Introduction*, 481, has pointed to the recurring phrase "in that day" both in 12:2–13:6 and 14:1–21, thereby linking them together. Likewise, the prose style and the common theme—an attack on Jerusalem by the nations—favor a connection between these two units. Thus, Plöger, *Theocracy and Eschatology*, 89, saw 12:2–14:21, apart from glosses, expounding one event; Hanson, *Dawn*, 369–371,

Several items support the independence of 12:2–13:6: it is separated from 14:1–21 by the poetic oracle in 13:7–9; the introductory formula in 14:1a signals a new oracle; and most importantly, 12:2–13:1 is characterized by an interest in the inhabitants of Jerusalem, the house of David, and the people of Judah, motifs absent in 13:7–9 and 14:1–21.

Questions about the integrity of 12:2–13:6 have generated a bewildering array of hypotheses about the formation of the text in layers and glosses.[188] Elliger would eliminate 12:2b,3b,4bα,6a,7–8 from the original layer.[189] Plöger, followed for the most part by Rudolph, thought v. 5 and v. 6b should also be deleted, and perhaps v. 4a and v. 4bβ.[190] M. Saebo presented an entirely different scenario for the formation of the unit around three speeches of the Lord in 12:3, 12:9f, and 13:2,[191] while Hanson maintained the integrity of the unit except for 12:8–9, which he thought was a later addition.[192]

In my view, this multiplicity of hypotheses demonstrates the lack of methodological controls available for reconstructing the history of the text. Similarly, Willi-Plein notes that it may be illegitimate to use criteria from the pre-exilic prophets to judge the integrity of late prophetic literature.[193] This is especially true when it is recognized that late Israelite prophecy in general,[194] and Zechariah 9–14 in particular, is characterized by the reuse of various earlier traditions.[195] Accordingly, the combination and integration of ideas and images from different traditions into a new unity here in Zech 12:2–13:6 should not be surprising, nor necessarily taken as a sign of different redactional stages in the formation of the text. In any event, the literary history of this passage is likely beyond reconstruction. Nevertheless, as Willi-Plein has observed:

---

recognized two units, but attributed them to the same group of visionaries. Accordingly, on some level, 12:2–13:6 and 14:1–21 may be more closely related.

[188]See the summary of views in Saebo, *Untersuchungen*, 255–259.

[189]K. Elliger, *Die Propheten Nahum, Habakuk, Zephanja, Haggai, Sacharja, Maleachi* (ATD 25; 7th ed.; Göttingen: Vandenhoeck & Ruprecht, 1975) 167–170; see the suggested readings in *BHS*.

[190]Plöger, *Theocracy and Eschatology*, 83; Rudolph, *Hag, Sach 1–8, 9–14, Mal,* 220.

[191]Saebo, *Untersuchungen*, 259–276.

[192]Hanson, *Dawn*, 356. For yet another redactional theory, see P. L Redditt, "Israel's Shepherds: Hope and Pessimism in Zechariah 9–14," *CBQ* 51 (1989) 631–642.

[193]Willi-Plein, *Prophetie am Ende*, 56f.

[194]Petersen, *Late Israelite Prophecy*, 15–16.

[195]See Coggins, *Hag, Zech, Mal*, 64–65; Mason, *Hag, Zech, Mal*, 79f; already Mitchell, *Hag, Zech, Mal, and Jonah*, 237–238.

Zudem muss es gewiss irgendwann—zumindest nämlich im Moment der letzten angenommenen Glossierung—eine Zeit gegeben haben, in der cap. 12 oder eine noch grössere Einheit wirklich als Einheit verstanden wurde ... [196]

Moreover, this unity is achieved by the use of the recurring phrase "in that day" (ביום ההוא) [12:3,4,6,8(twice),9,11; 13:1,2,4], which functions to join the disparate sayings.[197] A final point in favor of the integrity of 12:2–13:6 is that it makes sense as a whole—at least according to the interpretation offered below.[198]

Lastly, we must examine the structure of 12:2–13:6. Three thematic units comprise 12:2–13:6:

A. Description of a battle at Jerusalem (12:2–9)
B. Description of a mourning ritual (12:10–14)
C. Description of the purification (13:1–6)

The passage, however, does not break down evenly along these lines. 12:2–13:1 forms the first part, since it is interconnected by an interest in Jerusalem—its fate and inhabitants (12:2[twice],3,5,6,7,8,9,10,11; 13:1). On the other hand, an interest in Jerusalem is absent from 13:2–6; instead these verses apply to the land the theme of purification initiated in 13:1. In addition, 13:2–6 is set off from the preceding by an extended introductory formula ("And it will be in that day, saying of the Lord"). Thus, within the structure of this passage as a whole, 13:2–6 must be seen as a second part, which elaborates the last idea in 12:2–13:1.[199]

In light of these consideration, a basic structural outline of the passage would look like this:

I. The Final Events at Jerusalem (12:2–13:1)
A. Battle Against Jerusalem (12:2–9)
B. Mourning Rite (12:10–14)
C. Purification of House of David and Inhabitants of Jerusalem (13:1)
II. Purification of the Land (13:2–6)
A. From idols (13:2a)
B. From prophets (13:2b–6)

The following interpretation will focus on 12:2–13:1, since this part of the oracle refers to the house of David.

[196]Willi-Plein, *Prophetie am Ende*, 57.

[197]Saebo, *Untersuchungen*, 265, even suggests that the use of "in that day" forms a genre framework.

[198]Cf. also Willi-Plein, *Prophetie am Ende*, 57–58.

[199]Willi-Plein, *Prophetie am Ende*, 58; Saebo, *Untersuchungen*, 274; Plöger, *Theocracy and Eschatology*, 87.

b. Interpretation

The account of the fate of Jerusalem begins with a statement of the Lord's intention to make Jerusalem an agent of destruction against the besieging nations round about it (12:2–3). What is striking here is the declaration that Judah will be numbered among the besiegers (12:2b), a notion also present, however, in the description of the final battle at Jerusalem found in chap. 14 (see 14:14a).[200] But God fights on behalf of his city: he throws the besieging forces into tumult and bewilderment. In addition, he opens his eyes upon Judah (12:4), and this gracious action toward them prompts the chiefs/clans of Judah[201] to acknowledge and confess: "Strength is to the inhabitants[202] of Jerusalem through the Lord of hosts their God" (12:5). In light of this recognition, Judah becomes the physical agent of the Lord's attack against the nations from within the ranks of the besiegers: "I will make the clans of Judah like a blazing pot in the midst of wood, like a flaming torch among sheaves; and they shall devour to the right and to the left all the peoples round about" (12:6). Meanwhile, Jerusalem remains secure.

Then comes a curious section, where different levels of glory are apportioned to the various principals involved:

> The Lord will deliver the tents of Judah first, so that the glory of the house of David (בית־דויד) and the glory of the inhabitants of Jerusalem will not be made greater than that of Judah. On that day the Lord will put a shield about the inhabitants of Jerusalem so that the feeblest among them on that day will be like David and the house of David will be like God, like the angel of the Lord before them (12:7–8).

---

[200]In the MT, 12:2b reads: וגם על־יהודה יהיה במצור על־ירושלם. The MT appears to have conflated readings preserved, on the one hand, in the Targums and Vulgate (which lacks the preposition על before יהודה), and on the other, in the LXX and Peshitta (which lacks the preposition ב before מצור). Hence the text originally read either: 1) and Judah also will be in the siege against Jerusalem; or 2) and against Judah also will be the siege against Jerusalem. In the first, Judah is included among the besiegers against Jerusalem, while in the second, it stands with Judah against the besiegers. The first reading is to be preferred for the following reasons: 1) a siege must be against a city; it is not clear what a siege against Judah would mean; 2) v. 3b says all the nations will be gathered against *it*, referring to Jerusalem; 3) 14:14a makes the same point that Judah will be opposed to Jerusalem in the final battle of Jerusalem; 4) although Judah ultimately fights on the side of Jerusalem, it is only after a change of heart, and then they fight from within the ranks of the besiegers; 5) in v. 4aα, Judah is singled out for special treatment in the context of God's actions against the nations, indicating Judah's presence among the besieging nations.

[201]The question is whether the text should be read אַלְפֵי (chiefs) or אַלְפֵי (clans). In either case, the sense of the present interpretation is not affected.

[202]Reading אמצה as a noun meaning "strength," and לישבי, positing dittography for the MT's לי ישבי.

The details of these verses will be discussed below, but for the present, it can be observed that the text evidently reflects a certain competitive sentiment on the part of Judah over against the inhabitants of Jerusalem and the house of David. This of course comports with Judah's initial participation in the siege against Jerusalem. In any event, the Lord insures that their status will not be subordinate to the inhabitants of Jerusalem and the house of David. Nonetheless, even though the inhabitants of Jerusalem and the house of David will not acquire greater glory than Judah, they each receive varying degrees of it. The description of the final battle closes with a summary statement that God will seek to destroy all the nations that come against Jerusalem (12:9).

The next subsection describes a mourning rite which begins with the Lord pouring out a spirit of compassion and supplication upon the house of David and the inhabitants of Jerusalem (12:10aα). As a consequence, they will look upon the one whom they have pierced[203] and mourn over him (12:10aβ–14). The mourning will be of extreme magnitude (12:10b–11) and be done clan by clan alone. The procedure is specified further:

> the family of the house of David (מִשְׁפַּחַת בֵּית־דָּוִיד) alone and their wives alone; the family of the house of Nathan alone and their wives alone; the family of the house of Levi alone and their wives alone; the family of the Shimeites alone and their wives alone; all the remaining families family by family alone and their wives alone (12:12b–14).

Finally, a fountain will be opened for the house of David and the inhabitants of Jerusalem for the cleansing of sin and impurity (13:1). This theme of purification is then elaborated and applied to eliminating idols and prophets from the land (13:2–6). Thus, Zech 12:2–13:1 presents an eschatological scenario in which the Lord defeats the nations, unites and glorifies Judah and Jerusalem, and purifies the people of Jerusalem.

c. The House of David

It will be helpful to organize our discussion of the reference to the house of David around several issues: 1) who or what does the phrase "house of David" refer to; 2) how is it characterized; 3) how is its identity and characterization related to the biblical traditions about the davidic dynasty and davidic descendants.

1) Outside Zech 12:2–13:1, the phrase "house of David" occurs 19 times in the Hebrew Bible. Apart from references to a building,[204] the phrase refers to the

---

[203]Reading אֶל or אֵלַי, which refers to the same person designated by the pronominal suffix in עָלָיו in the next clause.

[204]Cf. 1 Sam 19:11; Isa 22:22.

rule,[205] the king or court,[206] or the dynasty[207] of the davidic family. Yet all these references presume a time when the house of David was in power as the ruling family in Judah or Israel. They may, therefore, be less helpful in determining the meaning of the phrase in Zech 12:2–13:1, which dates from a time during the post-exilic period when the davidic family did not provide kings for Judah.[208]

Thus, several suggestions have been made by scholars to explain its meaning. Wellhausen interpreted "house of David" simply as a term for the government in Jerusalem without genealogical relationship to the davidic family.[209] Almost all recent interpreters have rejected this theory. Instead Plöger thought "the family of David (*gens davidica*) held a position in the Jewish community corresponding to their traditional authority."[210] He apparently meant by this that as one of the eminent families, members of the family of David held leading positions in Jerusalem.[211] Hanson is more specific, claiming that "house of David" designated the governors of Judah, who were of davidic descent and allied with the hierocratic party of Jerusalem.[212] Mitchell thought it indicated that David had descendants in Palestine, "and that they still cherished hopes of the restoration of the dynasty."[213] Finally, R. Mason, after considering some of the above possibilities concluded that one cannot make a judgment, although he notes that the reference does not reflect a strongly messianic view of the davidic line.[214]

None of the above views, however, has addressed this question in the context of the social situation of post-exilic Judah. Doing so will aid in clarifying the meaning of the "house of David" in Zech 12:2–13:1. Here the work of J. P.

---

[205]Cf. 1 Sam 20:16; 2 Sam 3:1,6 (prior to the establishment of the dynasty); 1 Kgs 12:19,20,26; 14:8).

[206]Cf. Isa 7:2,13; Jer 7:2.

[207]Cf. 1 Kgs 13:2; 1 Chr 17:24; 2 Chr 21:7; also 2 Sam 7:11b. See H. A. Hoffner, "בַּיִת," *Theological Dictionary of the Old Testament, Vol 2* (rev. ed.; ed. G. J. Botterweck and H. Ringgren; Grand Rapids, MI: Eerdmans, 1975) 114f; E. Jenni, "בַּיִת," *Theologisches Handwörterbuch zum Alten Testament* (2 vols.; ed. E. Jenni and C. Westermann; München: Chr. Kaiser/Zürich: Theologischer Verlag, 1979) 1:311.

[208]Plöger, *Theocracy and Eschatology*, 85, "The reference to the house of David ... can hardly be explained from the pre-exilic situation ... ;" cf. also Mitchell, *Hag, Zech, Mal, and Jonah*, 326. For a more precise dating, see below.

[209]Cited by Mitchell, *Hag, Zech, Mal, and Jonah*, 326.

[210]Plöger, *Theocracy and Eschatology*, 85. Dentan, "Zechariah," 1107, thinks of members of the one-time royal family who occupied positions of importance.

[211]Plöger, *Theocracy and Eschatology*, 84,85.

[212]Hanson, *Dawn*, 348; Smith, *Micah-Malachi*, 275, makes a similar suggestion.

[213]Mitchell, *Hag, Zech, Mal, and Jonah*, 326.

[214]Mason, *Hag, Zech, Mal*, 117; cf. Rudolph, *Hag, Sach 1–8, 9–14, Mal*, 222, who says only that the house of David played a role in post-exilic Jerusalem.

Weinberg provides the basis for the following summary of the social structure of post-exilic Judah.[215] Weinberg identified the post-exilic Jewish community of the sixth-fourth centuries BCE as a Bürger-Tempel-Gemeinde in which the בית אבות ("house of the fathers") was the primary social unit.[216] These בית אבות were groups of families bound by common descent, each consisting of anywhere between 100 and 2800 adult male members and possessing a leader called the head of his father's house (cf. Ezra 1:5; 4:3; 8:1).[217] Moreover, this social unit functioned as an important economic institution.[218] Finally, while these social units for the most part had their roots in pre-exilic Israel and were related to the pre-exilic משפחה ("clan"),[219] they cannot be understood as a straight-line development of the old clan system, but represent a new social formation.[220] The importance of this social arrangement in the post-exilic period is well illustrated in Neh 7:61ff in the account of those excluded from Israel, because "they could not prove their fathers' houses nor their descent, whether they belonged to Israel" (Neh 7:61).

In light of the above analysis of the social context, the reference to the house of David in Zech 12:2–13:1 must be interpreted as designating a relatively large social unit consisting of several hundred or even a few thousand members, something like a clan. In fact, in 12:12 the house of David—as well as the other houses mentioned—is called a משפחה. Furthermore, 12:8 makes clear that this house of David is to be included among the inhabitants of Jerusalem.[221] Its presence in the list in 12:12–14 indicates that the house of David was one of several בית אבות living in and around Jerusalem. Not only this, the four named houses in 12:12–14 must represent the most prominent houses in Jerusalem, since they are singled out from the rest of the משפחות mentioned in 12:14. Yet, the house of

---

[215]J. P. Weinberg, "Das *bēit ʾāḇōt* im 6.–4. Jh. V.U.Z.," *VT* 23 (1973) 400–414 (=*The Citizen-Temple Community* [JSOTSup 151; JSOT Press, 1992] 49–61); see also, H. G. Kippenberg, *Religion und Klassenbildung im antiken Judäa* (2nd ed.; Göttingen: Vandenhoeck & Ruprecht, 1982) 23–41.

[216]Weinberg, "Das *bēit ʾāḇōt*," 402–404. The Bürger-Tempel-Gemeinde was a widespread form of social organization in the Persian empire (see Petersen, *Hag and Zech 1–8*, 30).

[217]Weinberg, "Das *bēit ʾāḇōt*," 405–407; see also Kippenberg, *Religion und Klassenbildung*, 37–38.

[218]Weinberg, "Das *bēit ʾāḇōt*," 49; Kippenberg, *Religion und Klassenbildung*, 40.

[219]Weinberg, "Das *bēit ʾāḇōt*," 409–414; Kippenberg, *Religion und Klassenbildung*, 23.

[220]Weinberg, "Das *bēit ʾāḇōt*," 412–413. Thus, the system of tribe-clan-house-man found in Josh 7:14ff (cf. also Judg 9:1; Num 1:17ff; 36:1), where the house was a subdivision of the clan (see Hoffner, "בַּיִת," *TDOT*, 2:114) was no longer operative.

[221]Note too that the phrase "house of David" always occurs in connection with the "inhabitants of Jerusalem."

David seems to be the most prominent, since it is listed first and receives individual billing throughout the passage. Finally, while this house of David would have its genealogical roots in the pre-exilic royal family, one must nevertheless recognize that its status and function cannot be directly inferred from pre-exilic social arrangements, but must be understood within the social structures of post-exilic Judah.

Accordingly, we may reject Wellhausen's view that the house of David referred to the current rulers in Jerusalem without davidic genealogical connections. Nevertheless, the prominence of the house of David indicated by Zech 12:2–13:1 does not imply that they supplied governors for Judah, as Hanson suggested.[222] Moreover, the phrase does not refer to a dynastic line or an individual figure, but to a clan consisting of hundreds or thousands of members. This point is further corroborated by mention of the wives of the house of David in 12:12. Thus, the "house of David" must be understood as a prominent Jerusalem clan which exercised some form of power. Yet there is little evidence that members of the house of David occupied official political office.[223] Undoubtedly, its familial lineage would entail some sense of prominence or nobility, and probably informal political power. But we might presume that the source of its power was economic, since the house of the fathers was the primary economic unit and the house of David appears to be the most prominent house.[224]

2) We must now investigate the characterization of the house of David in Zech 12:2–13:1. First, their glory, along with the rest of the inhabitants of Jerusa-

---

[222]Nor does the other evidence put forward by Hanson, *Dawn*, 348–349, support his claim. He cites as evidence the post-exilic davidic genealogy in 1 Chr 3:17–24, the prominence of the house of David in Chronicles, the pairing of a davidic figure with a priestly figure in the documents of the hierocratic party (Ezekiel 40–48; Haggai, and Zechariah), and the mention of the house of David in Zech 12:1ff. It should be obvious that none of these reasons supports his hypothesis about davidic governors in Judah to the end of the fifth century BCE. The only possible evidence for davidic governors in Judah in the post-exilic period consists of the following: 1) Zerubbabel, if davidic, was governor; 2) Zerubbabel's son-in-law, Elnathan, may have been governor (see Meyers and Meyers, *Hag, Zech 1–8*, 12–13). But even this scant evidence provides little proof when it is recognized that Zerubbabel's davidic status is doubtful, and thereby so is his son-in-law's. Plus, there is evidence to the contrary: 1) Sheshbazzar, ca. 538 BCE, was a non-davidic governor (Ezra 5:14); 2) Nehemiah, a non-Davidide, was governor from 445 BCE to sometime after 433 BCE, at a time encompassing those mentioned in the davidic genealogy of 1 Chr 3:17–24, which was cited by Hanson; 3) Bogoas, apparently a Persian, was governor ca. 407 BCE.

[223]See previous note.

[224]If we may speculate further, this economic power, and its misuse, may explain the animosity felt by the people of Judah toward the house of David and the inhabitants of Jerusalem, and why they would have participated in the siege against Jerusalem. This kind of economic tension between the nobles in Jerusalem and other Jews would be similar to that found in the account in Neh 5:1–13.

lem, is not to exceed the glory of Judah. Yet, they will have glory: while even the feeblest of the inhabitants of Jerusalem will be like David, the house of David will be like God, as the angel of the Lord before them. Interpretations of this characterization differ. It has been suggested that it alludes to the harmony of will that will exist between God and the davidic kings of the last days.[225] More common is the view that this is an allusion to the story of the exodus and elsewhere, where the Lord, as the angel of the Lord, led his people; in like manner, will the house of David lead.[226] In addition, it has been compared to the depiction of David as an angel of God.[227] Finally, it has been understood as a mythic way of expressing the heroic status of the house of David.[228]

In my judgment, to understand 12:8 properly, it is important to observe that its statements pertain to the inhabitants of Jerusalem, who are described by reference to two groups among them—the feeblest and the house of David. If the house of David is understood as the greatest among the inhabitants of Jerusalem, as we have said above, then in effect the dual reference in 12:8 forms a kind of *inclusio*, which makes a statement about the exalted status of the whole of Jerusalem by referring to its lowliest and greatest residents: the glory of the lowly will be like that of the great (like David), and the glory of the great will be like that of the greater (like God).[229] In other words, all of Jerusalem will be glorified. In this sense, to focus on the specifics of the metaphors misses the point of the rhetoric, which is simply that the house of David, the leading בית אבות in Jerusalem, will retain its prominence in the ideal future when all of Jerusalem is glorified. Hence, it will be at the head of the inhabitants of Jerusalem (לפניהם). Moreover, there is no suggestion that this glorification implies divine, royal, or messianic status. On the one hand, we must recall that an entire clan is designated; nothing is asserted about an individual. On the other, their glorification will not exceed that of Judah.

---

[225]Mason, *Hag, Zech, Mal*, 117 (though he differs in "The Relation of Zech 9–14 to Proto-Zechariah," *ZAW* 88 [1976] 235–238).

[226]Mitchell, *Hag, Zech, Mal, and Jonah*, 326; Lamarche, *Zacharie IX–XIV*, 77; Smith, *Micah-Malachi*, 275, cites Ex 32:34; 23:20; Judg 6:11; 2 Sam 14:17.

[227]Rudolph, *Hag, Sach 1–8, 9–14, Mal*, 223, citing 2 Sam 14:17,20; 19:28.

[228]A. Cody, "Zechariah," *New Jerome Bible Commentary* (ed. R. Brown, J. A. Fitzmyer, and R. E. Murphy; Englewood Cliffs, NJ: Prentice-Hall, 1990) 358.

[229]This is similar to the rhetorical form used in Isa 60:17, where bronze and iron are replaced by gold and silver, while wood and stone are replace by bronze and iron; the lesser becomes great and the great becomes greater. The point is that everything is proportionally better. See Amos 5:3 for the use of this rhetorical convention in reverse (a city of a thousand becomes a hundred, a city of a hundred becomes a ten). Again, the point is that all experience judgment.

Secondly, it is said that the house of David, along with the inhabitants of Jerusalem, will receive a spirit of compassion and supplication and then mourn for one they had pierced (12:10ff). Following this, the mourners will be cleansed from their sin and impurity (13:1). Speculation about the precise incident lying behind these statements and about the identity of the one who was pierced is rife.[230] But too little is known about the historical context to venture a reliable suggestion about the specifics here.[231] What is clear is only that the house of David, along with the rest of the inhabitants of Jerusalem, was somehow implicated in the death of the person, over whom they will now mourn with great intensity in light of the preservation of Jerusalem and their reception of the divinely given spirit of compassion.

The act of mourning will be performed individually clan by clan. Four houses or clans are specifically mentioned: the house of David, the house of Nathan, the house of Levi, and the house of Shimei. Often interpretations of this list presume royal connotations for the house of David. One view holds that the four families represent the royal house of David, one of its subsidiary branches stemming from David's son Nathan (cf. 2 Sam 5:14; 1 Chr 3:5), the priestly house of Levi, and one of its subsidiary branches stemming from Shimei (cf. Num 3:17; 1 Chr 6:26).[232] Another view takes the four houses to represent the following:[233]

> house of David = royal line
> house of Nathan = prophets
> house of Levi = Levites
> house of Shimei = temple singers

Neither of these interpretations is persuasive. Nathan and Shimei are not uncommon names in the post-exilic period (cf. Ezra 8:16; 10:23,33,38,39), and the houses associated with these names could stem from any persons with these names (note that in Ezra 8:16, a certain Nathan is numbered among the leading

---

[230]Cf. Hanson, *Dawn*, 365; Eissfeldt, *Introduction*, 439; Lamarche, *Zacharie IX–XIV*, 119–122; Plöger, *Theocracy and Eschatology*, 84–85; Mitchell, *Hag, Zech, Mal, and Jonah*, 330; Coggins, *Hag, Zech, Mal*, 69; Mason, *Hag, Zech, Mal*, 118–119; Rudolph, *Hag, Sach 1–8, 9–14, Mal*, 223–224; Blenkisopp, *Prophecy*, 263.

[231]Cf. Willi-Plein, *Prophetie am Ende*, 118, for the same judgment. Attempts to see a davidic messiah in the one who was pierced (cf. Lamarche, *Zacharie IX–XIV*, 120–122) are particularly out of place. The house of David joins in mourning over the one who is pierced; there is no hint that the person himself was from the house of David or was a messianic figure for that matter.

[232]Mitchell, *Hag, Zech, Mal, and Jonah*, 333; Plöger, *Theocracy and Eschatology*, 85; Rudolph, *Hag, Sach 1–8, 9–14, Mal*, 225; J. G. Baldwin, *Haggai, Zechariah, Malachi*, (Tyndale Old Testament Commentaries; London: Tyndale, 1972) 194.

[233]Cf. Willi-Plein, *Prophetie am Ende*, 118–119; Koch, *Prophets*, 2:181.

men). No doubt these four clans are listed because they are the largest or most powerful in Jerusalem. To theorize further about the list is speculation.[234] Accordingly, the house of David is included not because it represents the royal line, but because it is one of the powerful clans in Jerusalem at the time of this prophecy.

3) The last issue involves how the reference to the house of David is related to the biblical traditions about the davidic dynasty and davidic descendants. Our previous discussion has really answered this question already. The house of David mentioned in Zech 12:2–13:1 refers to the leading Jerusalem clan, which traced its lineage to the royal family of pre-exilic times. Hence, the relationship to the biblical tradition appears to be strictly genealogical. Nowhere in the text of Zech 12:2–13:1 is there reference to the terminology and imagery associated with the davidic dynasty tradition. Continuity with or appropriation of a royal ideology is absent; only genealogically continuity with the once royal family is indicated.

d. Date

Up to this point, I have presumed only a post-exilic date for Zech 12:2–13:1; this dating must be specified further.[235] After Stade's work at the end of the nineteenth century, it was common to date Zechariah 9–14, or parts of it, to the Greek period (ca. 300 BCE), and even the Maccabean age.[236] But this dating depended on relating vague "historical" allusions in these chapters to persons and events documented elsewhere.[237] More recent commentators have abandoned this method as too speculative and turned to other criteria.[238] Thus, Hanson and Petersen attempted to set Zech 12:2–13:6 within the development of prophecy. Hanson assigned Zech 12:2–13:6 to the first half of the fifth century BCE, noting how it represented a stage in prophetic literature midway between classical prophecy and later apocalyptic literature.[239] Petersen placed Zech 13:2–6, which is nevertheless dependent on Zech 12:2–13:1, in the late sixth to early fifth cen-

---

[234]Willi-Plein, *Prophetie am Ende*, 119, makes the same point.

[235]Eissfeldt, *Introduction*, 439, rightly observes there is no trace of a pre-exilic origin for chaps. 12–14; Childs, *Introduction*, 481, notes that a post-exilic date is supported by motifs associated with post-exilic prophecy.

[236]See Eissfeldt, *Introduction*, 436f; Hanson, *Dawn*, 288–290; Plöger, *Theocracy and Eschatology*, 78–79.

[237]Hanson, *Dawn*, 358, observed that given this method, it is no surprise that Zechariah 9–12 was often dated to the Greek period, particularly the Maccabean period, since this period is more well documented than the fourth or third centuries BCE.

[238]Cf. Coggins, *Hag, Zech, Mal*, 71; Hanson, *Dawn*, 358.

[239]Hanson, *Dawn*, 368.

tury BCE.[240] Koch opted for sometime in the Persian period (538–333 BCE), because Zechariah 9–14 betrays the same editorial hand as that in Malachi, is markedly different from hellenistic era Jewish literature like *1 Enoch* and Daniel, and lacks any clear reference to an event after 350 BCE.[241]

Although not definitive, these reasons indeed point to the Persian period. My own view would date Zech 12:2–13:1 to late fifth to early fourth centuries BCE on the following grounds. First, the idea of a siege against Jerusalem presupposes that Jerusalem existed as a walled city, and therefore reflects a time after Nehemiah's rebuilding of the walls in ca. 445 BCE. Secondly, at the time of Zech 12:2–13:1, the house of David was the leading clan in Jerusalem. A similar witness to their leading status is found in the genealogy of the davidic family in 1 Chr 3:17–24 and reference to the sons of David with Ezra in Ezra 8:2b,[242] texts that date from sometime between 458 and 348 BCE.[243] After this time, we hear nothing about the house of David. Certainly by the third century BCE it was no longer a leading family; we hear instead about the Tobiad and Oniad families.[244] Accordingly, the leading role of the house of David reflected in Zech 12:2–13:1 points to a date in late fifth to early fourth century BCE.

3. Conclusion

As stated at the beginning of this section, many interpreters have seen Zech 12:2–13:1 as a witness to davidic messianic or royalist hopes. But the foregoing study has shown that mere reference to the "house of David" does not imply a messianic or royalist hope. Here in Zech 12:2–13:1, the house of David refers to a rather large social group akin to a clan. This clan could trace its genealogy back to the pre-exilic family of David and surely was a prominent group within Jerusalem in the late fifth to early fourth centuries BCE. Moreover, this oracle proclaims that in the eschatological restoration their prominence would remain. It appears that the social hierarchy present in Jerusalem is merely idealized. There is no evidence that messianic or royalist hopes were fixed upon the house of David. No individual figure is in view—whether royal or messianic; the passage speaks of a group of people including women. In addition, the passage contains no overt expectation of a future royal or messianic rule. Allusions to earlier biblical pas-

---

[240]Petersen, *Late Israelite Prophecy*, 37; in "Zechariah," *HBC*, 747, Petersen notes that recent commentators have dated Zechariah 9–14 to the fifth or fourth centuries.

[241]Koch, *Prophets*, 2:181.

[242]Weinberg, "Das *bēit ᵓābōt*," 402, notes that the "sons of X" was another way of referring to the "house of X". Ezra 8:1ff makes this obvious.

[243]See above, p. 88, the discussion of the date of Chronicles.

[244]M. Hengel, *Jews, Greeks, and Barbarians* (Philadelphia: Fortress, 1980) 29–30.

sages associated with the royal ideology of the davidic dynasty tradition are likewise absent. Throughout Zech 12:2–13:1 the Lord is the sole agent of salvation; he works through no royal or messianic figures.

It is significant too that chap. 14 presents a similar portrait of God's decisive intervention for Israel. As observed earlier, while an independent oracle, chap. 14 is at some level to be connected with Zech 12:2–13:1.[245] Thematically the parallels are unmistakable. Besides having the linking phrase "in that day," it presents a remarkably similar eschatological scenario: the nations are arrayed against Jerusalem (v. 2), with Judah included among the attackers (v. 14); the Lord himself smites the nations by causing panic among them (vv. 12–13); Jerusalem will remain secure (v. 11b), and be purified (vv. 11a,20–21). As in Zech 12:2–13:1, the Lord is the sole agent of salvation. Moreover, v. 9 states: "And the Lord will become king over all the earth." There is no suggestion that his rule will be implemented by human agents.

Thus, as a whole the prophetic booklet in Zechariah 12–14 presents two oracles describing the final victory of the Lord on behalf of Israel. Both stress the Lord's role as savior. Neither account suggests that davidic royal or messianic figures are involved in the battle or the subsequent rule. The disproportionate amount of interest devoted to the supposed messianism of these chapters, and Deutero-Zechariah as a whole, is no doubt related to the New Testament's application of Zech 9:9 and 12:10 to Jesus (Matt 21:5; John 12:15 and 19:37, respectively).[246] To be sure, Zechariah 9–14 witnesses to royal themes (9:9) and addresses the problem of leadership in terms of shepherding (10:2–3; 11:4–17), a metaphor commonly used of kings. But there is no evidence of a hope for a davidic king or messiah. Mason's comments are an apt summary of the evidence:

> It is illegitimate to detect a Messianic figure elsewhere in deutero-Zechariah. Whatever be made of the promises concerning David in 12:8, it cannot be overlooked that the house of David needs to share in the general act of penitence which follows, nor that the context specifically states that victory will be clearly Yahweh's, so that the glory of the house of David and the inhabitants of Jerusalem shall not be unduly exalted above that of the rest of the community (v. 7). Even if v. 8 is secondary in its present position, this does not suggest that the circle responsible for the final form of these oracles saw the house of David in a traditionally Messianic way ... No reference to human leadership of any kind is found in ch. 14.[247]

---

[245]See above, n. 187.

[246]See, for example, Lamarche, whose book is entitled: *Zacharie IX–XIV: Structure littéraire et Messianisme*; see esp. pp. 121–122. It should be observed, however, that Zech. 9:9 makes no mention of a davidic king, although this is assumed by some (cf. Blenkinsopp, *Prophecy*, 260).

[247]Mason, "The Relation of Zech 9–14 to Proto-Zechariah," 237.

Finally, we can note the similarity between the situation reflected in Zech 12:2–13:1 as we have summarized it above and that indicated in 1 Chr 3:17–24 and Ezra 8:2b. In each case, the davidic family possesses social prominence but holds no official office; nor is it the object of royal or messianic speculation. Accordingly, this appears to be the status of the davidic family in the late Persian period. It is clear then that these traditions about davidic descendants have little to do with Jewish ideas from a later period about a Son of David as a messianic figure.

CHAPTER 4
Texts From the Hellenistic and
Roman Periods: Part I

The texts under study in this and the next chapter come from the Hellenistic and Roman periods. The earliest document from these periods is the Wisdom of Ben Sira, written sometime between 198–175 BCE. Sirach, therefore, represents the first witness to the davidic dynasty tradition since its use in Chronicles sometime in the late fifth to early fourth centuries BCE. This means, however, that there exists no reliable evidence about whether or how Jews may have understood the davidic dynasty tradition during a 200 year period. What little data that can plausibly be said to reflect Jewish life during the fourth or third century BCE, including some sections of *1 Enoch*, quasi-historical material from Greek historians and Josephus, and numismatic evidence, show no indication of interest in the davidic dynasty tradition or leaders connected with it in some way.[1] But the paucity of extant material precludes drawing firm conclusions from these data. In any event, Alexander's conquest of the Near East, Ptolemaic and Seleucid rule, and later the arrival of the Romans would have a profound effect on Jewish life and thinking. Within this new context, Jewish authors drew upon the davidic dynasty tradition in a variety of ways to express their ideas. In the following two chapters, therefore, I will examine relevant passages from the LXX, Ben Sira, 1 Maccabees, *Psalms of Solomon*, Qumran literature, 4 Ezra, and Josephus, in order to trace the history of the davidic dynasty tradition and to evaluate its relevance for davidic messianism in these periods.

---

[1] For literary evidence about Judaism during the fourth and third centuries BCE, see Stone, *Scriptures, Sects and Visions*, esp. 27–47; for treatment of historical sources for the period, see M. Hengel, *Judaism and Hellenism* (2 vols.; Philadelphia: Fortress, 1974) 1:255–277; for relevant numismatic evidence, see Betlyon, "Yehud Coins."

A. The Septuagint

The translation of the Hebrew Bible into Greek began as early as the third century BCE with the Torah, and before the first century BCE Greek translations of all books were probably completed.[2] Moreover, at times LXX translations are characterized by "midrashic" alterations or expansions and, consequently, indicate how the translator and his community interpreted certain biblical texts. In theory, then, the LXX translation of texts related to the davidic dynasty could illuminate how some Jews in the Second Temple period construed those passages.

In practice, however, this is not a very fruitful mode of inquiry. On the one hand, a survey of key texts related to the davidic dynasty tradition shows very little in the way of interpretive activity. On the other, formidable obstacles confront the analysis of any such interpretive translations. For one, even to speak of "the Septuagint" suggests a misleading notion about the unity of Greek translations of the Hebrew Bible, since, as Kraft notes, "there is no homogeneity among the various translation units of the collection."[3] Accordingly, each book or section of a book must be evaluated separately. Next, recovering the Old Greek or one of the early recensions from the Second Temple Period—such as the καιγε or proto-Lucian recension—for a passage is often difficult; indeed scholars are divided about the existence and status of some of these layers.[4] Even when the text of the Old Greek or one of the early recensions can be identified, it is difficult to know the date and provenance of the interpretation implied in the translation. Although the Greek translation of the Torah probably stems from Alexandria in the third century BCE, this same context cannot be assumed for other books.[5] Moreover, to clarify the import of an individual variant, it would have to be set within the overall interpretive *tendenz* of a book or section, a subject about which little is often known. Finally, differences between the Old Greek and the Hebrew of the MT that are perceived as interpretive moves on the part of the translators could at times be the result of the translator using a *Vorlage* different from the

---

[2]E. Tov, "The Septuagint," *Mikra* (CRINT 2:1; ed. M. J. Mulder; Philadelphia: Fortress/ Assen: Van Gorcum, 1988) 162.

[3]R. A. Kraft, "Septuagint: B. Earliest Greek Versions," *The Interpreter's Dictionary of the Bible, Supplementary Volume* (ed. K. Crim; Nashville: Abingdon, 1976) 811. See also, L. Greenspoon, "The Use and Abuse of the Term "LXX" and Related Terminology in Recent Scholarship," BIOSCS 20 (1987) 21–29.

[4]See M. K. H. Peters, "Septuagint," *Anchor Bible Dictionary* (6 vols.; ed. D. N. Freedman; New York: Doubleday, 1992), 5:1096–1100; Kraft, "Versions," 813.

[5]Kraft, "Versions," 813.

MT.[6] In sum, there are adequate reasons for pessimism about using the LXX for tracking the davidic dynasty tradition in early Judaism.

Nevertheless, recognizing the limited potential for unambiguous results, a few items are worthy of comment. First, a comparison of the MT and LXX for 2 Sam 7:11b reveals an interesting difference:

וְהִגִּיד לְךָ יְהוָה כִּי־בַיִת יַעֲשֶׂה־לְּךָ יְהוָה

("And the Lord announces to you that the Lord will make a house for you.")

καί ἀπαγγελεῖ σοι Κύριος ὅτι οἶκον οἰκοδομήσεις αὐτῷ

("And the Lord announces to you that *you will build a house for him.*")

The difference is clear. In the MT, God promises that he will establish a dynasty for David, while in the LXX, God announces that David will build the temple for God.[7] The significance of this difference is harder to ascertain. On the one hand, an explicit statement of the dynastic promise is now missing, but the remainder of the dynastic oracle in 2 Kgdms 7:12–16 certainly affirms the establishment of the davidic dynasty. On the other hand, interest has shifted to the building of the temple.

Recently, W. Schniedewind has argued that the LXX's revision of 2 Sam 7:11b is part of a pro-temple *tendenz* in 1–4 Kingdoms, since several other passages betray a similar shift in emphasis.[8] He suggests an Alexandrian setting for this translation, where Jews had little interest in the restoration of the davidic monarchy, yet supported the temple in Jerusalem.[9] Whether or not one accepts an Alexandrian provenance for the translation, it appears that some Jewish community that read the scriptures in Greek looked to David more as the founder of the temple and less as the progenitor of a royal line, a interpretive move similar to that proposed above for the Chronicler. But beyond this limited claim, we cannot go.

Secondly, Jer 33:14–26, a passage that strongly asserts the continuing validity of the davidic covenant, is missing from the LXX. If purposely excluded by the translator, this would at least indicate disinterest in the future implications of the davidic covenant. But as widely recognized, the version of Jeremiah in the LXX is based on a *Vorlage* different from the MT. Thus, the absence of Jer

---

[6]Cf. esp. the LXX version of Jeremiah.

[7]It should be noted that the reading present in the so-called Lucianic recension (boc_2e_2) returns to the meaning of the MT.

[8]W. M. Schniedewind, "Textual Criticism and Theological Interpretation: The Pro-Temple *Tendenz* in the Greek Text of Samuel-Kings," *HTR* 87 (1994) 107–116.

[9]Schniedewind, "Pro-Temple," 116.

33:14–26 from the LXX must be attributed to the editor of an early Hebrew version of Jeremiah.[10] Whether the oracle was unavailable to this editor or was omitted with purpose is difficult to determine. In either case, these questions no longer pertain to the period under study.[11]

Thirdly, Ezek 34:23–24 expresses the promise that the Lord will set up a new David as shepherd and prince over Israel. In the next verse (34:25) the MT and the LXX read:

... וכרתי להם ברית שׁלום

("I will make with them a covenant of peace ... ")

καὶ διαθήσομαι τῷ Δαυιδ διαθήκην εἰρήνης ...

("I will make *with David* a covenant of peace ... ")

Thus, according to the MT God will make a covenant of peace with the people; in the LXX he makes it with the new David. Assessing the significance of this difference is again problematic. For one, in a parallel passage in Ezek 37:26, the LXX follows the MT exactly and renders, "I will make with them a covenant of peace." Hence, there does not appear to be a pattern or *tendenz* in the translator's handling of texts about a new David. Moreover, it is unclear in the LXX of Ezek 34:25 whether the covenant of peace refers to a renewed davidic covenant or some other covenant. In any case, it seems that because the preceding context spoke about God raising up a new David, the translator understood the covenant mentioned in 34:25 as pertaining to this new David. The rule of a new David was therefore viewed as secured by a covenant. In spite of this added feature, however, the overall meaning of the passage remains the same.

Finally, in Jer 23:5 and Zech 3:8; 6:12, the term צמח ("branch" or "sprout") is translated in the LXX by ἀνατολή, a word often meaning "rising," as in the rising of the sun. In Zech 6:12 it is further said of the person called Ανατολή: καὶ ὑποκάτωθεν αὐτοῦ ἀνατελεῖ ("And from beneath him he will rise up."). Accordingly, since the use of the noun ἀνατολή has been perceived as unusual, and the verb ἀνατέλλω is found in Num 24:17, Ps 132:17, and Mal 3:20, it has been suggested that the LXX translators are purposely relating texts from the davidic dynasty tradition.[12]

Yet this point cannot be sustained. On the one hand, while ἀνατολή often means "a rising," it also denotes "a growing," making it an appropriate translation

---

[10]See E. Tov, "Textual and Literary Aspects," 154.

[11]See above, pp. 42–45, for a brief discussion of the date of Jer 33:14–26 and the dates of the two Hebrew editions of Jeremiah.

[12]Duling, "Promises to David," 61.

for צמח.[13] As for the verb ἀνατέλλω, it is commonly used in LXX books to render terms associated with rising celestial objects and sprouting plants,[14] and is perfectly ordinary in all the supposedly davidic promise texts cited above. Moreover, Num 24:17 and Mal 3:20 are not actually part of the davidic dynasty tradition, and while Ps 132:17 is, the Greek verb used there is ἐξανατέλλω, a cognate of ἀνατέλλω, which weakens the case that these passages are intentionally linked. But all this aside, to connect ἀνατολή or ἀνατελεῖ to Num 24:17, Ps 132:17, and Mal 3:20 ignores the fact that the LXX is a collection of books produced by different translators, who probably worked in different historical settings. There is no evidence to suggest that the translators of Jer 23:5 and Zech 3:8; 6:12 independently sought to evoke the Greek translation of Num 24:17, Ps 132:17, or Mal 3:20 when they chose a suitable Greek equivalent for צמח. What all these texts do have in common, along with dozens of others, is the idea of something rising up; it is hardly significant then that cognate Greek vocabulary occurs in them. Thus, we conclude that there is no interpretive significance to the translation of צמח as ἀνατολή.

B. The Wisdom of Jesus Ben Sira

The earliest references to the davidic dynasty tradition in the Hellenistic and Roman periods are found in the Wisdom of Jesus Ben Sira, written between 198–175 BCE. Our primary interest in this section concerns how Ben Sira appropriated the davidic dynasty tradition. An important dimension of this question is whether Ben Sira's use of the davidic dynasty tradition indicates hope for a davidic royal figure or messiah.[15] Many commentators have viewed Ben Sira this way,[16] while others have disagreed.[17] The problem of discerning Sirach's view on

[13]See *LSJ*, 123.

[14]See E. Hatch and H. A. Redpath, *A Concordance to the Septuagint* (Oxford: Clarendon, 1897; reprinted, Grand Rapids, MI: Baker, 1983) 1:83.

[15]See J. D. Martin, "Ben Sira's Hymn to the Fathers: A Messianic Perspective," *Crises and Perspectives* (OTS 24; ed. A. S. van der Woude; Leiden: Brill, 1986) 107–123, for a recent though superficial treatment of the question of davidic messianism in Ben Sira.

[16]R. Smend, *Die Weisheit des Jesus Sirach: Kommentar* (Berlin: Reimer, 1906) 452,457; Klausner, *Messianic Idea*, 254–258; M. R. Lehmann, "Ben Sira and the Qumran Literature," *RevQ* 9 (1961) 103–116; J. Priest, "Ben Sira 45,25 in the Light of the Qumran Literature," *RevQ* 5 (1964) 111–118; A. A. Di Lella, *The Hebrew Text of Sirach: A Text-Critical and Historical Study* (The Hague: Mouton, 1966) 102–103; P. W. Skehan and A. A. Di Lella, *The Wisdom of Ben Sira* (AB 39; New York: Doubleday, 1987) 526,528; S. M. Olyan, "Ben Sira's Relationship to the Priesthood," *HTR* 80 (1987) 281–286; and R. T. Siebeneck, "May Their Bones Return to Life!—Sirach's Praise of the Fathers," *CBQ* 21 (1959) 426–427, who is less certain.

[17]A. Caquot, "Ben Sira et le Messianisme," *Sem* 16 (1966) 43–68; H. Stadelmann, *Ben Sira*

this matter is due in part to an apparent lack of consistency among several passages. Nevertheless, below I will argue that his use of the davidic dynasty tradition is not contradictory and fits well Ben Sira's overall intention.

Most of the relevant texts are found within Sirach's Hymn in Praise of the Fathers (44:1–50:24). Of primary significance here is 45:25, which refers to the covenant with David. Moreover, chap. 47, which is largely devoted to the praise of David and Solomon, contains two important texts about the davidic dynasty (47:11,22). Passages in chap. 49 also shed light on Ben Sira's view of the subject. Finally, in a psalm found in the Hebrew version of Ben Sira between 51:12 and 13, there is mention of a davidic figure. Below, these texts will be considered with respect to Ben Sira's use of the davidic dynasty tradition and its implications for his attitude toward a davidic royal or messianic figure.

1. 45:25

The most important text with regard to the davidic dynasty tradition in Ben Sira is 45:25, but its interpretation presents rather complicated textual and interpretive problems. Our analysis will begin with a treatment of the textual problems, where our aim will be to recover from the witnesses in the Hebrew, Greek (LXX), and Syriac versions the original Hebrew of Ben Sira himself.[18] The texts of these versions are as follows:[19]

---

als Schriftgelehrter (WUNT 2/6; Tübingen: Mohr, 1980) 157; B. L. Mack, *Wisdom and the Hebrew Epic* (Chicago Studies in the History of Judaism; Chicago: University of Chicago Press, 1985) 35–36; T. Middendorp, *Die Stellung Jesu Ben Siras zwischen Judentum und Hellenismus* (Leiden: Brill, 1973) 174; Schürer, *History*, 2:499, who is less certain.

[18]For the Hebrew text, see I. Lévi, ed., *The Hebrew Text of the Book of Ecclesiasticus* (SSS 3; Leiden: Brill, 1904; reprint ed. 1951); other Hebrew editions are listed in M. D. Nelson, *The Syriac Version of the Wisdom of Ben Sira Compared to the Greek and Hebrew Materials* (SBLDS 107; Atlanta: Scholars Press, 1988) 2. For the Greek text, see J. Ziegler, ed. *Sapientia Iesu Filii Sirach* (Septuaginta 12:2; Göttingen: Vandenhoeck & Ruprecht, 1965). For the Syriac text (Peshitta version), see F. Vattioni, *Ecclesiastico: Testo ebraico con apparato critico e versioni greca, latina e siriaca* (Naples: Instituto Orientale di Napoli, 1968); other Syriac editions are listed in Nelson, *Syriac Version*, 19–26. Vattioni also reproduces the Latin text of Ben Sira, but the Latin version is of limited usefulness in text criticism (see below, n. 26).

[19]The following translations are intentionally literal and are not meant to prejudice the interpretation of the text given below.

וגם בריתו עם דוד
בן ישי למטה יהודה
נחלת אש לפני כבודו
נחלת אהרן לכל זרעו

And also his covenant with David
son of Jesse of the tribe of Judah
an inheritance of a fire-offering before his glory
an inheritance of Aaron to all his seed.

καὶ διαθήκην τῷ Δαυιδ
υἱῷ Ιεσσαι ἐκ φυλῆς Ιουδα
κληρονομία βασιλέως υἱοῦ ἐξ υἱοῦ μόνου
κληρονομία Ααρων καὶ τῷ σπέρματι αὐτοῦ

And a covenant with David
son of Jesse from the tribe of Judah
an inheritance of a king is a son from a son only
an inheritance of Aaron is also to his seed.

w ᵓp dwyd
br ᵓyšy
yhrtnᵓ dmlkᵓ blḥwdwhy yrt
wywrtnᵓ dᵓhrwn lh wlzrᶜh

And also David
son of Jesse
an inheritance of kings alone he inherited
but an inheritance of Aaron is to him and his seed.

It is immediately clear that the meaning of these witnesses is different. The Hebrew text without textual emendation seems to make only passing reference to the davidic covenant in v. 25a–b before returning to elaborate on the nature of the covenant with Phineas, which involves the priesthood's ministry of sacrifice (v. 25c–d [an inheritance of a fire-offering]).[20] In contrast to this, the LXX appears to set up a parallel between the inheritance of a king within the davidic covenant and the inheritance of Aaron: just as the kingship is passed only to the direct familial successor of the king, so too the inheritance of Aaron is transferred

---

[20]It is possible that the Hebrew of v. 25c should be amended to נחלת איש לפי כבודו ("an inheritance of a man according to his glory"). In this case, v. 25 as a whole sets up an antithesis between the inheritance of a king in the davidic covenant, which passes to a person based on his honor, and the inheritance of Aaron, which passes to all of his descendants. In other words, the inheritance of Aaron is transferred not by merit, but by heredity (cf. Smend, *Weisheit*, 437–438).

only to a direct familial successor. Finally, the Syriac text sets up an antithesis between the inheritance of kings, which was inherited by David alone, and the inheritance of Aaron, which is to him and his seed. In light of the above, it is apparent that a decision on the proper text will greatly affect our interpretation.[21]

Before turning to the texts themselves, some background on the various versions and their relationships is necessary. The Hebrew of 45:25 comes from a manuscript fragment found in the Cairo Geniza,[22] dated roughly between the ninth and twelfth centuries.[23] And although the authenticity of the Geniza manuscripts was debated during the first half of the twentieth century, since the work of Di Lella in 1966, a consensus about their authenticity has emerged. Wright summarizes: " ... it can be held with confidence that despite numerous errors and corruptions in the Geniza texts they *substantially* reflect the Hebrew that Ben Sira himself wrote."[24] On the other hand, 45:25 is generally recognized as a corrupt portion of the text.[25]

The LXX text represents a translation from a Hebrew text made by Ben Sira's grandson sometime between 132 and 116 BCE, i.e., some 45 to 80 years after the original composition.[26] Its precise relationship to its parent Hebrew text

---

[21]The text has been reconstructed in various ways; see Olyan, "Ben Sira's Relationship," 283–284, for a sampling.

[22]45:25 is found only in Ms B of the Geniza manuscripts of Ben Sira; 45:25 was not among the fragments found at Qumran or Masada. For a fuller treatment of the Hebrew text of Ben Sira, see Nelson, *Syriac Version*, 2–5; B. G. Wright, *No Small Difference* (SBLSCS 26; Atlanta: Scholars Press, 1989) 2–4; and Di Lella, *Hebrew Text, passim.*

[23]G. H. Box and W. O. E. Oesterley, "The Book of Sirach," *The Apocrypha and Pseudepigrapha of the Old Testament* (2 vols.; ed. R. H. Charles; Oxford: Clarendon, 1913) 1:272, (twelfth century CE); I. Lévi, *Hebrew Text*, ix, (before the twelfth century CE); Di Lella, *Hebrew Text*, 15 (end of eighth to twelfth CE).

[24]Wright, *Difference*, 3; cf. also Nelson, *Syriac Version*, 4. According to Di Lella, *Hebrew Text*, 106–107, the most common corruption is retroversion from a Syriac version. For a summary of the history of the study of the Hebrew manuscripts of Ben Sira, see Nelson, *Syriac Version*, 7–16.

[25]Cf. Box and Oesterley, *APOT*, 1:489; and also Priest, "Ben Sira 45,25," 113, for his view and others cited by him. That many such corruptions have entered the Hebrew text is noted also by Wright, *Difference*, 15.

[26]There are two forms of the Greek text of Ben Sira: GkI, found in the major uncial manuscripts (A B C S), represents the translation of the grandson, and GkII, reconstructed from Origenic and Lucianic textual traditions (Wright, *Difference*, 4–5; Nelson, *Syriac Version*, 5–6). Since GkII is a later expanded version based on an expanded Hebrew edition, it is not relevant to the present discussion; likewise, the Old Latin text (which was also used in the Vulgate) is a witness to GkII; moreover, the earliest Latin manuscripts lack the Hymn in Praise of the Fathers (cf. Wright, *Difference*, 5–6). For the date of Ben Sira's grandson, see the Prologue to Ben Sira, v. 14, and the discussion of it in Box and Oesterley, *APOT*, 1:293.

has been disputed.[27] In a recent monograph on this matter B. G. Wright counsels caution when seeking to reconstruct in general the Hebrew of Ben Sira from the Greek version, although he admits that individual passages can be successfully recovered.[28] Specifically, he notes that the grandson was inconsistent in his word choice when translating Hebrew words, but more reliable with respect to word order, especially in his avoidance of adding words not originally in the Hebrew text.[29] In any case, Wright's study means that the reconstruction of 45:25 will have to avoid generalizations about the grandson's faithfulness to the original and be firmly based on the particular textual evidence for this verse.

Finally, the Syriac Peshitta version is a translation of a Hebrew *Vorlage* made sometime between 200 and 400 CE, most likely toward the end of this period.[30] Yet, the relationship of the Syriac to the original Hebrew is complicated by the fact that the Syriac version is based on a form of the Hebrew text later than the one used by Ben Sira's grandson and influenced by a Greek version later than the grandson's.[31] Moreover, it is generally acknowledged as a rather free rendering of its exemplar.[32] Nonetheless, it remains an important witness to the Hebrew, particularly when seeking clues to the Hebrew words that lie behind the Syriac and Greek versions.[33]

Turning now to the task of reconstructing the text of 45:25, we are aided by the work of F. V. Reiterer, whose thorough study of the translation technique used in Sir 44:16–45:26 will inform the following discussion.[34] Beginning with v. 25a–b, few problems present themselves. The Hebrew and the Greek agree almost exactly, except for the omission in the Greek of the Hebrew third person pronominal suffix ("his" in "his covenant"). Reiterer suggests that the absence of

---

[27]See Wright, *Difference*, 20–23.

[28]Wright, *Difference*, 232–233. His caution is based on the grandson's rather free translation technique. This "free" technique is virtually conceded by the grandson himself in the prologue when he admits that "what was originally expressed in Hebrew does not have exactly the same sense when translated into another language."

[29]Wright, *Difference*, 234.

[30]Box and Oesterley, *APOT*, 1:288; Di Lella, *Hebrew Text*, 150; Nelson, *Syriac Version*, 19,132.

[31]Nelson, *Syriac Version*, 6–7,131–132; Wright, *Difference*, 6.

[32]Box and Oesterley, *APOT*, 1:288; Nelson, *Syriac Version*, 6.

[33]Wright, *Difference*, 237.

[34]F. V. Reiterer, *"Urtext" und Übersetzungen: Sprachstudie über Sir 44,16–45,26 als Beitrag zur Siraforschung* (ATAT 12; St. Ottilien: EOS, 1980) 30–31,225–229. Reiterer has done the kind of analysis in 44:16–45:26 that Wright, *Difference*, 8, sees as a model of proper method. For additional text critical discussion, see also Smend, *Weisheit*, 437; Middendorp, *Stellung*, 142; and Priest, "Ben Sira 45,25," 112–14. Box and Oesterley, *APOT*, 1:489, settle on an eclectic text as the basis for their English translation.

"covenant with" and "of the tribe of Judah" in the Syriac is due to its reliance on a different *Vorlage*.[35] Accordingly, v. 25a–b would have originally read:

וגם בריתו עם דוד

בן ישי למטה יהודה

Verse 25c presents the most complexity for reconstruction. The first word of the line, however, offers no problems. The witnesses read נחלת (Heb), κληρο-νομία (Gr), and *yhrtn* (Syr). Clearly the original text read נחלת.[36] For the second word, the versions read אש (Heb), βασιλέως (Gr), and *mlk* (Syr). βασιλέως and *mlk*, respectively, represent the regular translation equivalents in Ben Sira for the Hebrew word מלך.[37] Reiterer has shown that the use of a plural in Syriac (*mlk*) for an originally singular noun (מלך) is a common feature in the Syriac translation.[38] On the other hand, Ms B (אש) appears to be working from a different exemplar.[39] Ben Sira certainly wrote מלך.[40]

For the remainder of the line, there is clearly convergence in the Greek and Syriac between μόνου and *blhwdwhy*, thus representing a word in the original Hebrew meaning "only." In 49:4a *blhwd* translates the Hebrew לבד,[41] while in 30:26a (33:18a) לבדי is rendered with ἐμοὶ μόνῳ.[42] Accordingly, the original Hebrew most likely read לבדו.[43] The word כבודו (defective = כבדו) in Ms B would then be explained as a corruption of לבדו.

The final question in 25c pertains to the original Hebrew behind לפני (Heb), υἱοῦ ἐξ υἱοῦ (Gr), and *yrt* (Syr). It is unlikely that *yrt* in the Syriac had any

---

[35]Reiterer, *"Urtext"*, 225–226. Or possibly, the Syriac's dropping of "a covenant with" is explicable given its overall understanding of the verse, where the inheritance of kingship goes to David alone. Middendorp's suggestion (*Stellung*, 142) that v. 25a–b was a later addition must be rejected for lack of any textual witness for this claim.

[36]Cf. Reiterer, *"Urtext"*, 227.

[37]Cf. D. Barthélemy and O. Rickenbacher, *Konkordanz zum hebräischen Sirach mit syrisch-hebräischen Index* (Göttingen: Vandenhoeck & Ruprecht, 1973) 224. See also Reiterer, *"Urtext"*, 227.

[38]Reiterer, *"Urtext"*, 227,51.

[39]Reiterer, *"Urtext"*, 227.

[40]Smend's suggestion that אש לפני כבודו is a reference to Solomon and is therefore equivalent to מלך with the υἱοῦ ἐξ υἱοῦ of the LXX being termed "trimmings" is untenable, because the Syriac also reflects some of the so-called trimmings in *blhwdwhy*. Moreover, the Hebrew text would need several questionable emendations to make sense (לפני=איש; לפי=לפני).

[41]In 45:22, *blhwd* translates אך.

[42]In 49:4a, πάρεξ translates לבד.

[43]Cf. Reiterer, *"Urtext"*, 227.

equivalent in its *Vorlage*,[44] because *yrt* always translates either נחל or ירש, words that are in no way reflected in the Hebrew or Greek witnesses. In fact, the Hebrew and Greek lack any word at all in a corresponding position. Moreover, the presence of *yrt* alters the syntax of the verse entirely, disrupting the grammatical parallelism present in both the Hebrew and Greek witnesses of two verbless clauses in 25c and 25d.

In Ms B, לפני, if vocalized as לְפָנַי, still makes sense in the context of our previous reconstruction ("an inheritance of a king before me alone"). But against it as original is the way it breaks up the verbal and grammatical parallelism between 25c and 25d. Here, the Greek term υἱοῦ offers a more plausible counterpart to the term "seed" in v. 25d. Thus, we would expect in the original Hebrew the usual lexical equivalent for υἱοῦ, namely, the Hebrew word בן.[45] That בן was preceded by the preposition ל and followed by the pronominal suffix ו is suggested by the corresponding preposition and suffix associated with *zr*^c in v. 25d. Further, this suggested reading—לבנו—is confirmed by the way it explains the Greek version and Hebrew version in Ms B. On the one hand, לבנו, in the context of the entire line, refers to the idea of succession ("an inheritance of a king is to his son alone"), the very same idea expressed by way of "dynamic equivalence" by υἱοῦ ἐξ υἱοῦ.[46] On the other hand, לבנו could easily have been corrupted to לפני in the copying process.[47] Altogether then v. 25c would have read:[48]

נחלת מלך לבנו לבדו

Finally, the reading for v. 25d must be established. Much of this line is easily reconstructed, since the Hebrew, Greek, and Syriac witnesses all agree on the first two words and last word of the line: נחלת אהרן ... (ל)זרעו (Heb), κληρο-

---

[44]Reiterer, *"Urtext"*, 227.

[45]Cf. Barthélemy and Rickenbacher, *Konkordanz*, 56–59.

[46]Cf. Wright, *Difference*, 114–116, on the "free" translation technique of the grandson. This phrase υἱοῦ ἐξ υἱοῦ is admittedly unusual. Its use here is unique in Greek literature (based on a search of the *Thesaurus Linguae Graecae*). Yet it may not be so surprising in light of the way genealogical relationships are frequently expressed in the LXX with the form υἱὸς [name] υἱοῦ (cf. 1 Para. 6:18–32; 2 Esdr 7:1–5); nor may it be coincidental that this unusual phrase occurs in the context of the covenant with Phineas, who is often called Φινεες υἱὸς Ελεαζαρ υἱοῦ Ααρων (cf. Num 25:7,11; 31:6; Josh 22:13; Judg 20:28; 2 Esdr 7:5).

[47]Cf. Reiterer, *"Urtext"*, 227.

[48]This is the suggested original reading of I. Lévi, *Hebrew Text*, 62; and N. Peters, *Der jüngst wiederaufgefundene hebräische Text des Buches Ecclesiasticus, untersucht, heraugegeben, übersetzt und mit kritischen Noten versehen* (Freiburg: Herder, 1902), cited in Reiterer, *"Urtext"*, 227.

νομία Ααρων ... τῷ σπέρματι αὐτοῦ (Gr), and *wywrtn ᵓ dᵓhrwn ... lzrᶜh* (Syr). Here, the original of Ben Sira would have read as Ms B. The difference between the versions lies in the remainder of the line. The Syriac text reads *lh w* before *lzrᶜh*, so that the inheritance of Aaron is *to him* and his seed. Since these words are not reflected in the Hebrew and *lh* is also lacking in the Greek, they are suspect. Moreover, it is easy to imagine several ways by which this reading could have arisen. For one, in the Syriac text David is the sole recipient of the inheritance of kings. Accordingly, if the Syriac had rendered v. 25d without *lh*, it would have suggested that Aaron, as the progenitor of the line, was not himself a recipient of the inheritance, in contrast to David, the progenitor of his line, who is specifically marked out as the only recipient of the inheritance. The addition of *lh* removes this potential ambiguity. Furthermore, the language of 45:24c ("to him and his seed") may have influenced the translator here. Finally, several LXX manuscripts (A, plus several minuscules) read αὐτῷ in place of Ααρων. The Peshitta could well be a conflation of the two manuscript traditions. In any case, *lh* is secondary.

The Hebrew of Ms B reads כל before זרעו, so that the inheritance of Aaron is to *all* his seed. This reading is not paralleled in the Greek and Syriac versions, although dittography could account for its absence in those manuscript traditions. Yet its presence in the original Hebrew is doubtful, because the matter at hand is not simply the priesthood, but the high priesthood (cf. 45:24d: כהונה גדולה).[49] Given Ben Sira's reverence for that office, it is unlikely that he would claim that all of Aaron's seed receive it as an inheritance. Consequently, the presence of כל in Ms B probably reflects the changed situation in the Middle Ages where the high-priestly office had lost its importance; the covenant with Phineas was therefore applied to all the priests.

Lastly, the LXX reads καὶ before τῷ σπέρματι. A parallel expression is lacking in Ms B,[50] suggesting that καὶ had no *Vorlage* and may represent an attempt by the grandson or a later copyist to clarify the parallel relationship between the inheritance of a king and the inheritance of Aaron.[51] At any rate, a judgment about the originality of an equivalent for καὶ is of minor significance. In this textual reconstruction, I will assume no equivalent for καὶ; the precise

---

[49]So too the Syriac (*khnwt ᵓ rbt;*); the LXX speaks of the magnificence of the priesthood (ιερωσύνης μεγαλεῖον), but even the word order suggests that its *Vorlage* read as the Geniza text. Also, see below, p. 139.

[50]Here, the Syriac reads *w*, but this is necessary due to its addition of *lh*, and would not then reflect a reading in its *Vorlage*.

[51]Cf. however Wright's observation (*Difference*, p. 234) that the LXX rarely adds words to the text.

relationship between the inheritance of a king and the inheritance of Aaron will be left to the task of interpretation.

To summarize the above work of textual reconstruction, the original of Sir 45:25a–d would have read:

וגם בריתו עם דוד
בן ישי למטה יהודה
נחלת מלך לבנו לבדו
נחלת אהרן לזרעו

And his covenant with David
son of Jesse of the tribe of Judah
an inheritance of a king is to his son alone
an inheritance of Aaron is to his seed.

We turn now to the question concerning the meaning and function of the reference to the davidic covenant in 45:25. In this regard, it is important to keep in mind the entire context within which this reference to the davidic covenant occurs, namely, the covenant God made with Phineas for an eternal high priesthood (45:23–26). Phineas, described as third in glory, is praised for his act of zeal whereby he stood in the breach of the people and thus made atonement for them. Therefore, God made a covenant of peace (ברית שלום) with him to maintain the sanctuary, "which is to him and his seed, a high priesthood for ever" (כהונה גדולה עד עולם). After this comes the text under study, v. 25a–d, which is followed by a short hymn (vv. 25e–26d) that reads:[52]

> And now, may you (pl.) bless the Lord of good, who crowns you (pl.) with glory. May he give you (pl.) wisdom of heart (to judge his people with righteousness), so that your benefits and glory may not be forgotten for perpetual generations.

The background for this section is the story about Phineas in Num 25:6–13 (cf. also Ps 106:28–31). What is interesting, however, is the way Ben Sira has interpreted this biblical story. In Num 25:12–13a Phineas and his descendants are given the covenant of the priesthood forever (ברית כהנת עולם), while in Sir 45:24 he and his descendants receive the covenant of the high priesthood forever (כהנוה גדולה עד עולם).[53] Sirach's application of the covenant with Phineas to

---

[52] The textual tradition is mixed. Ms B lacks v. 26b, "to judge his ... ", but it is supplied here on the basis of the LXX reading.

[53] Some interpreters of Num 25:6–13 have suggested that the covenant made with Phineas was for the high priesthood (cf. Noth, *Numbers*, 199). But Milgrom, *Numbers*, 216–217, points out that the text does not speak about the high priesthood, and that this text originally legitimated the Zadokite priesthood as a whole as the sole priests of the temple (cf. Ezek

the high priesthood is confirmed by 50:22–24, where at the conclusion of his praise of Simon the high priest, there is a short hymn which includes lines identical to the hymn in 45:25e–26d and ends with the words, "May his kindness for Simon last and may he establish for him the covenant with Phineas which will not be cut off for him and his descendants as the days of the heavens" (50:24).[54]

Recognizing Ben Sira's construal of the covenant with Phineas leads to two other observations. First, by describing Phineas, son of Eleazar, as "third in glory" (v. 23a), Sirach draws attention to Phineas' place in the line of high-priestly succession from Aaron to Eleazar to Phineas.[55] Secondly, it becomes clear that the "you" (pl.) in the short hymn in vv. 25e–26d designates the high priest, at that time Onias III, and his descendants,[56] just as the similar lines in 50:22–24 refer to the high priest and his descendants.

Thus, the entire context concerns the high-priestly covenant, its establishment under Phineas as an eternal covenant for him and his descendants and its future under Onias III and his descendants.[57] Yet within this context Ben Sira speaks of the covenant of kingship made with David. Indeed, the mention of the davidic covenant at this point is all the more striking, because it is the only place where the chronological sequence in the Hymn in Praise of the Fathers is interrupted.[58] What is the reason for this?

44:15–16). Ben Sira's interpretation is suggested, however, by 1 Chr 5:27–29; 6:34–38, which give the genealogy of the leading (high?) priests of the pre-exilic period, and Neh 12:10–11, which carries the genealogical listing down to ca. 400 BCE.

[54]The references to Simon and the covenant with Phineas do not appear in the Greek text (only mention of Simon occurs in the Syriac). Skehan and Di Lella, *Ben Sira*, 550, suggest that the shorter version found in the Greek is a deliberate attempt to revise the text in light of the changed situation at the time of Ben Sira's grandson; similarly, T. R. Lee, *Studies in the Form of Sirach 44–50* (SBLDS 75; Atlanta: Scholars Press, 1986) 237–8, who also accounts for the originality of the Hebrew text of Ms B in terms of genre, and Mack, *Epic*, 63, who demonstrates how the connection between Simon and the covenant of Phineas is integral to the logic of the hymn as a whole (cf. also Mack, *Epic*, 28,32). Olyan, "Ben Sira's Relationship," 271, argues that the Hebrew of 50:24 is secondary, but offers no convincing reason for this and fails to deal with points made by Skehan and Di Lella, Lee, and Mack.

[55]Note how in Num 25:7,11 Phineas is described as "Phineas, son of Eleazar, son of Aaron the priest." See Skehan and Di Lella, *Ben Sira*, 513; for a different view, see Lee, *Studies*, 249–250; and Mack, *Epic*, 33, who take the line of three to be Moses-Aaron-Phineas.

[56]Skehan and Di Lella, *Ben Sira*, 514.

[57]Note how the term "glory" in v. 23b and v. 26d functions as an *inclusio* for this section on the high-priestly covenant.

[58]Mack, *Epic*, 218; J. Marböck, *Weisheit im Wendel* (BBB 37; Bonn: Hanstein, 1971) 112. David will be treated in chronological order in 47:11.

Ben Sira has referred to the davidic covenant because he wants to compare its method of succession to the method of succession appropriate to the high-priestly covenant:

נחלת מלך לבנו לבדו
נחלת אהרן לזרעו

an inheritance of a king is to his son alone
an inheritance of Aaron is to his seed

Thus, just as royal office in the davidic covenant was transferred only to the direct familial descendant of the king, so too the office of high priest in the covenant with Phineas was to be transferred only to the direct familial descendant of the high priest, not to just any descendant of Aaron.[59] Moreover, it is clear that the relationship between the two covenants must be that of comparison, rather than contrast, because in the present context the mention of the seed of Aaron refers to a single person, the high priest, not to all Aaronic priests.[60] Accordingly, the method of succession in the davidic covenant is presented as a model of proper succession for the high priesthood.

Ben Sira apparently had good reason for concern about legitimate succession within the high priesthood. Writing some time after the death of the high priest Simon II in 198 BCE, but before the hellenistic reform movement in 175 BCE, he composed his work during the high priesthood of Onias III. And while Onias III received his office through legitimate succession, by 175 BCE he was replaced by his brother Jason, who in turn was ousted by Menelaus in ca. 172 BCE. Both Jason and Menelaus took possession of the high-priestly office through bribery. It is easily conceivable that some years before the deposition of Onias III, there existed a dispute about what constituted legitimate succession of the high priesthood.[61] In light of this situation, in 45:25 Ben Sira claims that legiti-

---

[59]The davidic covenant is called the inheritance of a king and the covenant with Phineas is called the inheritance of Aaron, who according to Ben Sira was the first high priest (cf. Phineas as "third in glory," and 45:6–22). Also, the model of direct familial succession for the high priesthood had scriptural precedent (cf. Neh 12:10–11; Ex 29:30; Lev 16:32) and is reflected in 11QTemple 15:15–16.

[60]Caquot, "Ben Sira," 61–62, comes to a similar conclusion. The Hebrew text of Ms B attempted to reverse Ben Sira's interpretation of the covenant with Phineas as applying to the high priesthood by adding the word "all" before "his seed." Skehan and Di Lella's view, *Ben Sira*, 514, that there is a contrast between the davidic covenant, in which the inheritance goes to a single descendant, and the Aaronic covenant, in which the inheritance goes to all Aaron's descendants, fails to consider the overall literary context concerning the high priesthood.

[61]Box and Oesterley, *APOT*, 1:490; Smend, *Weisheit*, 438; Caquot, "Ben Sira," 60–62.

mate succession is the kind of succession known from the davidic covenant, namely, to one's direct familial descendant.

But there is more to Ben Sira's use of the davidic covenant than as a mere illustrative example of proper succession. The reason why the davidic royal covenant provided an appropriate model of succession in the high-priestly covenant was because for Ben Sira the office of high priest in his own time embodied all the offices of Israel's history, including the royal office established in the davidic covenant.[62]

In this regard, B. L. Mack has shown how the Hymn in Praise of the Fathers is a reading of the Hebrew scriptures that understood the high priesthood of Ben Sira's own time as the climax and fulfillment of all the offices and covenants of Israel's history.[63] Specifically, the structure of the hymn indicates that all the offices in Israel were established by covenants with founding figures in Israel's early history (44:17–45:26).[64] These offices and the functions associated with them were to be the means by which God fulfilled his promise of blessings for Israel. The periods of conquest, monarchy, and restoration represent a failed struggle to actualize in history this divine blessing (46:1–49:13).[65] It is only in the final scene of the hymn, depicting Simon the high priest, whose roles encompass all of the offices of Israel, that Ben Sira saw the promises of blessing and well-being come to fruition (50:1–24).[66]

Here our particular interest in Mack's thesis is in how the high priesthood embodies the office of king, secured by the davidic covenant. Mack notes that within the hymn the primary function of royal figures, and hence the office of king, is the defense of the civil and religious institutions.[67] But in 50:1–4, it is precisely this function that is attributed to Simon the high priest:

> ... who in his life repaired the house and in his time fortified the temple. He laid the foundations for the high double walls, the high retaining walls for the temple enclosure ... He considered how to save his people from ruin, and fortified the city to withstand a siege.[68]

---

[62]Mack, *Epic*, 36; see also, 55ff.

[63]Mack, *Epic*, 41,54–55.

[64]Mack, *Epic*, 39.

[65]Mack, *Epic*, 39–41,60–61.

[66]Mack, *Epic*, 41,54–56.

[67]Mack, *Epic*, 29. Cf. the characterization of David (47:1–11), Solomon (47:12–22), and Hezekiah (48:17–25).

[68]Cf. Mack, *Epic*, 35. Actually, the ruling function has its origin in Moses and is represented by the judges. Mack, *Epic*, 32, writes, "It appears, then, that Ben Sira may have seen the kings as holding an office that obtained for a chapter of Israel's history, the function of which,

Mack explains,

> Ben Sira was careful not to claim the office of the ruler-king for Simon, but it is clear that he wished his readers to understand that the primary functions of the king—building and defense of the city and temple—were to be associated with him.[69]

In other words, the office of king, secured by the davidic covenant, is for Ben Sira now located in the office of high priest. The davidic covenant, which established the royal office and functions, is thereby fulfilled in the high-priestly office.[70]

Mack's thesis gains added confirmation when it is observed that not only has the office of high priest taken on royal functions, but a key royal symbol as well. In 45:12 the praise of Aaron includes a description of his headdress. According to Ben Sira, Aaron wore a crown of gold (עטרת פז) upon his turban (מצנפת), with a flowered plate (ציץ) somehow attached.[71] On the other hand, in pentateuchal passages that describe the headdress of Aaron, one finds on his turban only the flowered plate, variously described as a ציץ (Ex 28:36–38) or נזר (Ex 29:6) or both (Ex 39:30; Lev 8:9).[72] It is not then insignificant that Ben Sira conceives of the high priest as wearing a crown of gold (עטרת פז), which is not part of the high priest's headdress in the Pentateuch and clearly a royal symbol (cf. 2 Sam 12:30; Jer 13:18; Ezek 21:31; Ps 21:4). In fact, in Ps 21:4 the exact phrase, עטרת פז, is used to describe the headdress of the—presumably davidic—king.[73]

Thus, according to Ben Sira the functions and a key symbol of davidic kingship now belong to the high priest. Hence, it is not surprising that in 45:25 Ben Sira draws upon the davidic covenant for a model of legitimate succession appropriate to the high priesthood, for the promises of the davidic covenant have been fulfilled in the post-exilic Judean high priesthood.

---

however, had its origins before that time in Moses and continued after that time in the office of the high priest."

[69]Mack, *Epic*, 35.

[70]A similar point is made by Stadelmann, *Schriftgelehrter*, 157, but on the basis of a very different reading of 45:25. See also, Martin, "Perspective," 114–116, who likewise agrees with the conclusion, but on very different grounds.

[71]The Hebrew text of Ms B is both corrupted and incomplete. The rendering here is based in part on the LXX (see Skehan and Di Lella, *Ben Sira*, 510, for a rationale for the reading).

[72]See R. de Vaux, *Ancient Israel* (2 vols.; New York: McGraw-Hill, 1961) 2:400, for נזר/ציץ as a flower.

[73]J. N. Snaith, "Biblical Quotations in the Hebrew of Ecclesiasticus," *JTS* 18 (1967) 7; see also Stadelmann, *Schriftgelehrter*, 159.

In light of the above interpretation, we can now consider what 45:25 indicates about Ben Sira's view of the davidic dynasty. First, we may observe that although there are no extant literary references to the davidic dynasty in the two centuries before Sirach, the concept had not fallen into oblivion. There is, however, no hint of any expectation of a davidic figure as in some biblical prophets. In fact, as we have said, Ben Sira evokes the davidic covenant to make a point about the covenant with Phineas and his real concern, proper succession in the high priesthood in his own day. Thus, the view of J. Priest, who sees in 45:25 an adumbration of the royal and priestly messiahs of Qumran, must be rejected.[74] Ben Sira's juxtaposition of the davidic and Aaronic covenants does not contemplate a diarchical governance, nor are there messianic overtones. 45:25 in no way suggests that Ben Sira thought the davidic monarchy was a viable political institution. Moreover, it is clear why Ben Sira here indicates no hope or expectation for a royal messiah, davidic or otherwise. As Mack has observed, " ... the theocratic ideal for the covenant community is fully constituted in this [high-priestly] office and there is no longer any need for another kind of king as well."[75]

Furthermore, this interpretation of Ben Sira's view of the davidic covenant helps explain his seemingly conflicting statements about the davidic covenant and its kings found later in the hymn. For by locating the fulfillment of the davidic covenant in the Second Temple high priesthood, Ben Sira is able to portray the davidic covenant positively as a praiseworthy part of Israel's past (47:11,22), but at the same time acknowledge that the kings of Judah came to an end (49:4–5). It is to the interpretation of these further statements about the davidic covenant and kings we now turn.

2. Other Texts in the Hymn in Praise of the Fathers

Chapter 47:1–22 extols David and Solomon, and contains two passages pertaining to the davidic dynasty. First, at the conclusion of the praise of David, we read in 47:11:

וגם ייי העביר פשעו וירם לעולם קרנו
ויתן לו חקת מלכת וכסאו הכין על ירושלם

The Lord forgave his sins and exalted forever his horn,
and gave to him a covenant of kingship and his throne he established over
    Jerusalem.

---

[74]See Priest, "Ben Sira 45,25," 116–18; all the more to be rejected is the suggestion by Lehmann, "Ben Sira and the Qumran Literature," 114, that the davidic hope is bolstered by Ben Sira.

[75]Mack, *Epic*, 86.

Here we see that Ben Sira readily recognized the honored place that davidic kingship held in the history of Israel. Beyond this, however, some have claimed that this text testifies to Ben Sira's davidic messianism.[76] Yet a careful reading proves otherwise, since only David's קרן (i.e., his horn) is exalted forever; the covenant of kingship or his dynasty is not said to be eternal.[77] Olyan thinks that קרן here refers to davidic descendants, noting that in several biblical texts קרן has a messianic nuance.[78] But in the Hebrew Bible קרן is used more generally as a metaphor for power and prestige.[79] Undoubtedly this is the connotation in Ben Sira's usage, since he consistently employs קרן with this meaning (47:5,7; 49:5).[80]

If Ben Sira's intention was to draw attention to the eternal significance of the davidic covenant, it is surprising that his praise of David lacks any reference to the throne promise given by Nathan.[81] The term translated "covenant" here is the Hebrew חק, not ברית, the latter being the word used in the biblical passages that speak about the davidic covenant.[82] Thus, David is not praised as the founder of an eternal royal line; rather his praise consists of a tribute to his role as a mighty warrior in the defense of Israel and as a patron of the cult. In this sense, Ben Sira reveals some affinity with the image of David known from the Chronicler.[83]

A second text from the praise of David and Solomon sometimes cited in favor of Ben Sira's davidic messianism is 47:22.[84] But it is likewise doubtful

---

[76]Smend, *Weisheit*, 452; Skehan and Di Lella, *Ben Sira*, 526; Olyan, "Ben Sira's Relationship," 282–83; and apparently, Martin, "Perspective," 108–109.

[77]J. A. Goldstein, *I Maccabees* (AB 41; Garden City, NY: Doubleday, 1976) 240f; Schürer, *History*, 2:499. In contrast, it may not be coincidental that in 45:7,24 the priestly covenant is explicitly designated as eternal (עד עולם/עולם). Yet, it is debatable whether the phrase עד עולם should be invested with the idea of "eternity" at all, since in 47:13, while Ben Sira says that Solomon set up a sanctuary forever (לעד), he was well aware of the destruction of Solomon's temple in 586 BCE.

[78]Olyan, "Ben Sira's Relationship," 283, citing Ezek 29:21; Ps 132:17; Ps 148:14.

[79]Caquot, "Ben Sira," 55, who cites Deut 33:17 and Ps 89:18.

[80]Caquot, "Ben Sira," 55. In 47:5 קרן is in parallelism with עז, where it clearly means "power." Also, 49:5 is especially important because it states that the קרן of the kings of Judah was given up to others; this means the davidic kings gave up their power (see below on 49:5).

[81]Caquot, "Ben Sira," 54.

[82]Wright, *Difference*, 179–180, argues that Ben Sira makes a clear distinction between חק and ברית, and never uses חק to mean "covenant"; it is only the LXX translation of חק as διαθήκη that introduces the idea of "covenant."

[83]See below, p. 151.

[84]See for example Skehan and Di Lella, *Ben Sira*, 528; Smend, *Weisheit*, 457; Olyan, "Ben Sira's Relationship," 282; Martin, "Perspective," 109–110.

whether 47:22 should be interpreted in this way. The Hebrew text is incomplete, but can be plausibly reconstructed from the LXX:[85]

> But God does not disregard his mercy, and his words do not fall to the ground. Nor does he cut off the posterity of his chosen one; nor destroy the seed of the one who loved him. And he gave to Jacob a remnant; and to David a root for him.

The passage occurs near the end of the section on Solomon. In the previous context Solomon is praised for building the temple, for his wisdom, and for his wealth (47:12–18). Then in 47:19–21, Solomon's sin with women and its consequences are mentioned:

> But you laid your loins beside women, and through your body you were brought into subjection. You put a stain upon your honor, and defiled your posterity, so that you brought wrath upon your children and they were grieved at your folly, so that the sovereignty was divided and a disobedient kingdom arose out of Ephraim.

But in contrast to Solomon's infidelity, v. 22 affirms God's abiding faithfulness. He did not cut off the posterity of his chosen one David, but left a root for him. Thus, the line of davidic kings did not end because of Solomon's sin, but continued because of God's loyalty to David. As v. 23 says, "Solomon slept with his fathers and left after him his son, ample in folly and lacking understanding, Rehoboam ... "[86]

Accordingly, Ben Sira recounts a well known phase of Israelite history (cf. 1 Kgs 11:1–13), and attributes the continuation of the davidic royal line to God's faithfulness, as 1 Kgs 11:13 does. But a mere reference to this biblical tradition need not lead to the conclusion that Ben Sira thought the davidic dynasty was eternal or looked for its continuation in his own day. Sirach was well aware of the davidic covenant and viewed it as significant part in Israel's past. But it was history. Indeed, the entire orientation of his reference to the root of David is that of the past.[87] This is underlined by the use of a verb in the past tense (Heb: ויתן; Gr: ἔδωκεν).[88] But more importantly, according to the text itself, the result of

---

[85]The last line in Hebrew reads only ... ל ... ול ויתן ל, but the parallelism suggests that the LXX preserves the original text. Interestingly, the last line of the Syriac reads: "And he gave to the house of David a great kingdom."

[86]The Hebrew text is broken, but the Greek and Syriac together suggest this reconstruction.

[87]Middendorp, *Stellung*, 67.

[88]Goldstein, *I Maccabees*, 240. Smend, *Weisheit*, 457, thinks that the LXX has wrongly taken ויתן as a preterite. But this suggestion is unwarranted, since ויתן is grammatically a converted imperfect which the LXX accurately translates as a past tense verb (cf. Caquot, "Ben Sira," 57; Schürer, *History*, 2:499).

God's faithfulness is not a messianic hope in Ben Sira's day, but the accession of Solomon's son, Rehoboam, to the throne (v. 23). In spite of a sinful king like Solomon, the dynasty continued.[89] To draw from this that Ben Sira looked for a davidic figure in his own day is unwarranted.[90]

If the above two passages are open to ambiguity with respect to Ben Sira's view of the davidic dynasty, 49:4–5 certainly clarifies his attitude toward it.

לבד מדויד יהזקיהו ויאשיהו כלם השחיתו
ויעזבו תורת עליון מלכי יהודה עד תמם
ויתן קרנם לאחור וכבודם לגוי נבל נכרי

Except for David, Hezekiah, and Josiah, all of them sinned,
and the kings of Judah abandoned the Torah of the most high, until they
    came to an end;
for he gave their power to others, and their glory to a foolish foreign nation.

Ben Sira states that the davidic line of kings came to an end (עד תמם); there is not a hint that he expected any sort of continuation.[91] It should be noted that in the Hebrew text, in contrast to the LXX, it is God who gave away the power (ויתן קרנם) and glory of the Judean kings. Moreover, Ben Sira's explanation for the end of the Judean royal line is that the majority of their kings sinned by abandoning the Torah. This suggests that Ben Sira subscribed to a conditional view of kingship known from passages such as 1 Kgs 2:4; 1 Chr 28:7,9; and Ps 132:11. In any case, he recognizes and states that davidic rule came to an end, and is completely silent about a future for the dynasty after its collapse.

---

[89]Caquot, "Ben Sira," 56, makes the observation that the last phrase of the verse is a historical illustration of the general truth about God's faithfulness stated in the previous lines (with verbs in the imperfect used as models).

[90]The logic behind applying this verse to a davidic messianic hope seems to be the following: since Ben Sira refers to divine preservation of the davidic dynasty, it is therefore a tacit reference to the unconditional davidic promises of 2 Sam 7:11ff and Psalm 89, which in turn means that Ben Sira held to these unconditional promises and must have looked for the fulfillment of them in his own day. But there are several flaws in this argument: 1) every reference to God's preservation of the davidic dynasty in the history of Israel need not be an appropriation of the unconditional promises—the Hebrew Bible itself contains different models of davidic kingship; 2) Ben Sira never refers to an unconditional eternal davidic promise; and 3) according to the above logic, only by entirely ignoring the scriptural traditions that attribute the continuation of the davidic dynasty in history to God's mercy, such as 1 Kgs 11:13, could Ben Sira show himself not to be a tradent of davidic messianism. This is an unreasonable criterion.

[91]Mack, *Epic*, 62, observes that in the Hymn in Praise of the Fathers, Ben Sira mentions seven kings, plus a collective reference here in 49:4–5, which suggests that this phase of Israelite history, having run its course, had come to completion.

Some, however, have disagreed with this last assessment, citing 49:11–12, a text concerning Zerubbabel.[92]

> How shall we praise Zerubbabel? He was like a signet upon his right hand.
> Likewise Jeshua, son of Jozedek; who in their day built a house and raised a
> temple holy to the Lord, prepared for everlasting glory.

The purported davidic messianism implicit in these verses derives from the reference to Zerubbabel as a signet—an allusion to Hag 2:23. But again, this conclusion is gratuitous. A simple reference to Hag 2:23 does not entail a messianic orientation for Ben Sira. Indeed, according to the LXX, Jeshua son of Jozedek is also viewed as a signet (cf. οὕτως Ἰησοὺς). But it is difficult to draw definitive conclusions from this about Ben Sira's own view of Jeshua as a signet, since the Hebrew text is lost for this verse. Nevertheless, Zerubbabel is clearly paired with Jeshua, and together they (οἱ) are honored for building the second temple.[93] They are praised as a pair of temple builders; Zerubbabel here does not function as an individual davidic figure. In fact, his davidic status in not mentioned in the text. To find a reference to davidic messianism here is to assert far too much on too little.

3. Lines 8 and 9 of a Hebrew Psalm

Finally, the Hebrew version of Ben Sira includes a psalm, patterned after canonical Psalm 136, in between 51:12 and 13 of the LXX version. Yet, due to its absence from both the LXX and the Syriac, its authenticity has been seriously questioned. Pertinent to this study are lines 8 and 9, which read:[94]

הודו למצמיח קרן לבית דוד כי לעולם חסדו
הודו לבוחר בבני צדוק לכהן כי לעולם חסדו

> O give thanks unto him that maketh the horn of the house of David to bud; for
> his mercy endureth for ever.
> O give thanks unto him that chose the sons of Zadok to be priests; for his
> mercy endureth for ever.

---

[92]See Smend, *Weisheit*, 473; Skehan and Di Lella, *Ben Sira*, 544; Olyan, "Ben Sira's Relationship," 282; Martin, "Perspective," 110–111.

[93]Mack, *Epic*, 43,61, observes that Zerubbabel, Jeshua, and Nehemiah are treated as a unit, and that within the literary structure of the Hymn in Praise of the Fathers they represent only a transitional phase in the movement toward an ideal order.

[94]The text and English translation are from S. Schechter and C. Taylor, *The Wisdom of Ben Sira: Portions of the Book of Ecclesiasticus* (Cambridge: Cambridge University Press, 1896 and 1899; reprint ed., Amsterdam: APA-Philo Press, 1979).

A decision on this psalm's authenticity, date, and provenance will influence our conclusions about Ben Sira's use of the davidic dynasty tradition.

Scholars are divided in their views concerning whether these lines, and the psalm generally, go back to Ben Sira.[95] Smend judged it authentic, but on the questionable grounds that the LXX passed over it as ungreek and the Syriac with its anti-Jewish bias followed suit.[96] A more thorough and critical argument for its authenticity—or at least a second century BCE date—is put forward by Di Lella. He claims that the internal evidence, citing here lines 8 and 9, demonstrates a date in the time of Ben Sira: "The mention of a Davidic Messiah and of the 'sons of Sadok' argues for a pre-Christian date of at least these verses, and presumably of the entire psalm."[97] He supports this statement by noting the prevalence of the doctrine of the davidic messiah at this time.[98] But on the contrary, there is no evidence for the prevalence of the doctrine of the davidic messiah in the second century BCE. And even if there were, the tradition of a davidic messiah (if messiah is understood as referring to an anointed one, and not necessarily to an eschatological figure) is attested in the Assyrian, Babylonian, exilic, and early post-exilic periods, as well as the first century BCE and beyond. A reference to a davidic hope could be placed in any of these periods. Moreover, given the actual lack of textual evidence for a davidic messianic hope during the fourth through second centuries BCE, Ben Sira's time provides the least likely temporal frame of reference for 51:12(8).

Di Lella's theory also rests on the mention of the "sons of Zadok," a reference to the high-priestly line that came to a definitive end by 153 BCE, when the Hasmonean Jonathan assumed the high priesthood.[99] Accordingly, Di Lella reasons that if not original with Ben Sira, the verse, and presumably the entire psalm, comes from the Qumran community, which included a number of Zadokite priests.[100] Admittedly, the mention of the 'sons of Zadok' gives some credence to

---

[95] See Di Lella, *Hebrew Text*, 101, for a more complete review of scholarly positions regarding the authenticity of the psalm.

[96] Smend, *Weisheit*, 502.

[97] Di Lella, *Hebrew Text*, 102.

[98] Di Lella, *Hebrew Text*, 102. He cites Sir 49:11; 45:25; and 47:22, texts which though mentioning the davidic line do not, as I have argued above, indicate an expectation for a davidic messiah.

[99] Di Lella, *Hebrew Text*, 103f.

[100] Di Lella, *Hebrew Text*, 104; cf. a similar suggestion by R. E. Brown, "The Messianism of Qumrân," *CBQ* 19 (1957) 63: Brown asserts that since the Hebrew version of Ben Sira containing this psalm and the Damascus Document, which is clearly associated with Qumran, were both found in the Cairo Geniza, the psalm's link to Qumran is strengthened. This reasoning is hardly convincing.

the connection between the psalm and Qumran, but this would not thereby entail a second century BCE date, let alone a date in the early decades of that century when Ben Sira wrote. For even if the Qumran connection were certain, the *terminus ad quem* for the psalm would be 68 CE, the date of the destruction of Khirbet Qumran. But the case for a Qumran connection for this reference is quite speculative, and no more convincing than Lévi's suggestion that it may simply refer to the future, drawing on the prophecy of Ezekiel.[101]

Di Lella also attempts to account for the psalm's absence in both the LXX and Syriac versions by saying that it must have been expunged from an earlier Hebrew manuscript in order to avoid offending the Hasmonean high priests, who were not of the Zadokite line.[102] But, as A. Fuchs rightly observes, the omission of line 9 because of the offense it might cause the Hasmoneans cannot account for the absence of the whole psalm from both the LXX and Syriac.[103]

Altogether, then, explanations for both the psalm's presence in Ben Sira's original composition—or at least a second century BCE date—and its absence in the LXX and Syriac are problematic. In truth, the date, provenance, and authenticity of the psalm are unknown.[104] Therefore, line 8 of 51:12 with its reference to the davidic dynasty tradition is not original to Ben Sira and, for that matter, not even clearly datable to the early Jewish period. Consequently, our understanding of Ben Sira's use of the davidic dynasty tradition must be worked out apart from this psalm.

4. Summary

Having reviewed the relevant passages, we can summarize Ben Sira's overall attitude toward the davidic covenant and the davidic dynasty which it established. On the one hand, Ben Sira praises the davidic dynasty as a divinely ordained institution given to David for the blessing of Israel. But the davidic kings faltered, already in Solomon, and even the dynasty's continuance after Solomon testified to God's mercy. Finally, however, the sins against the Torah of the majority of kings resulted in the end of the dynasty. Thus, the potential for blessing embodied in the

---

[101]Lévi, *Hebrew Text*, 74; cf. Ezekiel 40:46; 43:19; 44:15–16; 48:11.

[102]Di Lella, *Hebrew Text*, 105.

[103]A. Fuchs, *Textkritische Untersuchungen zum Hebräischen Ekklesiastikus* (Freiburg: Herdersche, 1907) 105. Fuchs also disposes of arguments for its authenticity based on a supposed anterior relationship to the Eighteen Benedictions. Nevertheless, Fuchs himself believes the psalm is pre–153 BCE; but see my argument against this position above.

[104]Due to its similarity with statements in the Eighteen Benedictions, it is more plausibly dated around the same time as that text, which cannot itself be shown to date from the early Jewish period.

davidic covenant was never achieved by the davidic kings. Yet for Ben Sira it was not the davidic covenant itself that was the problem—God had given it for Israel's good. The potential for blessing could still be realized.

Accordingly, the task for Ben Sira was to make his way through the twin realities of the good potential of the davidic covenant and the failure of the davidic dynasty. He did this not by setting his hopes on an ideal future davidic king. In fact, when Ben Sira does reflect on his hopes for the future, as he does in 36:1–17, no king, let alone a davidic king, is envisioned;[105] here his hopes are focused on other matters.[106] Instead, he transferred the functions and symbols of davidic kings to the high priesthood. In this way, the blessings of the davidic covenant could still be experienced in his own day. The fruits of the davidic covenant could be appropriated even when the dynasty itself was viewed as a past entity. In the end, therefore, Ben Sira's view is complex, but not contradictory.

Finally, we can compare Ben Sira's strategy for dealing with the davidic dynasty tradition with that of the Chronicler; this can be done on three levels. First, in Chronicles David's importance lies in his role as the founder and model patron of the Jerusalem cult. Likewise, in Ben Sira, David is praised for his cultic and liturgical activities (47:8–10).[107] And as noted previously, this image of David was even more widespread in early Jewish tradition, as in Ezra-Nehemiah, 1 Esdras 1, and 11QPs[a] 27:2–11. In each case, David's lasting contribution to Israel was in the cultic arena, not in the establishment of the an eternal dynasty to rule Israel. Secondly, for the Chronicler the davidic covenant and the dynasty it authorized served to establish and legitimate the cultic community in Jerusalem—its location, personnel, and procedures—as the exclusive shrine for all Israel. Ben Sira's interpretation of the davidic covenant is similar to this, although not identical. Ben Sira too wants to legitimate the cultic community in Jerusalem of his own time,[108] but because he sees the office of high priest as the center and guarantee of security for that community, he contends that the davidic covenant finds its proper fulfillment in the high-priestly office. In this sense, Ben Sira's goal is the same as the Chronicler's, but his tactic for achieving it is focused specifically on the office of high priest, which in turn undergirds the rest of the social and cultic order. Finally, both in Chronicles and in Ben Sira, there is a recognition

---

[105]Klausner, *Messianic Idea*, 254; Schürer, *History*, 2:499; Caquot, "Ben Sira," 45–49.

[106]These matters include the liberation of Israel, the punishment of their enemies, the exaltation of Zion, the fulfillment of prophecies, and an answer to prayer according to the blessing of Aaron for thy people. On this passage, see Caquot, "Ben Sira," 45–49.

[107]Caquot, "Ben Sira," 54,63; Mack, *Epic*, 118.

[108]Mack, *Epic*, 118.

that the davidic dynasty came to an end: neither looked for its re-establishment; neither reflects a royalist or messianic hope. In Ben Sira this fact is even more pronounced than in Chronicles, since Sirach has pointedly assigned the role once played by the davidic kings to the high priest; hence, for him there is no place for a davidic messiah.

C. 1 Maccabees 2:57

After Ben Sira, the next extant reference to the davidic dynasty tradition occurs in 1 Maccabees, a work dated to the late second or early first century BCE.[109] This reference appears in 1 Macc 2:57, within the last testament of Mattathias to his sons, where he recalls for them the example of faithfulness and zeal set by their ancestors. The text reads as follows:

$$\Delta\alpha\upsilon\iota\delta\ \dot{\epsilon}\nu\ \tau\hat{\omega}\ \dot{\epsilon}\lambda\dot{\epsilon}\epsilon\iota\ \alpha\dot{\upsilon}\tauο\hat{\upsilon}\ \dot{\epsilon}\kappa\lambda\eta\rho\nu\dot{\omega}\mu\eta\sigma\epsilon\ \theta\rho\dot{\omega}\nu\nu\ \beta\alpha\sigma\iota\lambdaε\dot{\iota}\alpha\varsigma$$
$$\epsilon\dot{\iota}\varsigma\ \alpha\dot{\iota}\hat{\omega}\nu\alpha\varsigma$$

The question before us again is how the author appropriated the davidic dynasty tradition, and in particular, whether his use reflects an expectation for a davidic royal or messianic figure.

We might begin by setting out the problem this short verse places before an interpreter. In relative isolation, 2:57 could easily be understood to express a continuing hope for the emergence of a davidic royal figure on the throne of Israel. Indeed, modern English translations of this verse, such as the RSV, seem to imply such an interpretation: "David, because he was merciful, inherited the throne of the kingdom forever."[110] Likewise, Klausner specifically points to this text as a witness to belief in "the eternity of the rule of the house David."[111]

Yet, within its context in 1 Maccabees this interpretation of 2:57 is difficult to maintain, since it is widely recognized by scholars that the purpose of 1 Mac-

---

[109]This dating is based chiefly on the reference in 1 Macc 16:24 to the chronicles of John Hyrcanus. Some suppose this indicates that 1 Maccabees was composed after his death in 104 BCE (cf. G. E. W. Nickelsburg, *Jewish Literature Between the Bible and the Mishnah* [Philadelphia: Fortress, 1981] 117; Goldstein, *I Maccabees*, 63; Schürer, *History*, 2:217). Others allow for a date late in the reign of John Hyrcanus (cf. H. W. Attridge, "Historiography," *Jewish Writings of the Second Temple Period* [CRINT 2:2; Assen: Van Gorcum/Philadelphia: Fortress, 1984] 171; J. J. Collins, *Daniel, First Maccabees, Second Maccabees* [Old Testament Message 16; Wilmington, DE: Glazier, 1981] 150). All agree that the author wrote before 63 BCE.

[110]Cf. the similar rendering by W. O. E. Oesterley, "The First Book of Maccabees," *The Apocrypha and Pseudepigrapha of the Old Testament* (2 vols.; ed. R. H. Charles; Oxford: Clarendon, 1913) 1:74.

[111]Klausner, *Messianic Idea*, 260.

cabees was to legitimate the Hasmonean dynasty.[112] This theme is amply demonstrated throughout the book. For example, the story of the defeat of Jewish forces led by non-Maccabean generals (5:55–62) ends with this comment:

> Thus the people suffered a great rout because, thinking to do a brave deed, they did not listen to Judas and his brothers. But they did not belong to the family of those men through whom deliverance was given to Israel (vv. 61–62).

Also, we hear in 14:41–49 how the Jews decided to install Simon as their leader:

> And the Jews and their priests decided that Simon should be their leader and high priest for ever until a trustworthy prophet should arise (... ἡγούμενον καὶ ἀρχιερέα εἰς τὸν αἰῶνα ἕως τοῦ ἀναστῆναι προφήτην πιστὸν) [v. 41].

> So Simon accepted and agreed to be high priest (ἀρχιερατεύειν), to be commander (στρατηγὸς) and ethnarch (ἐθνάρχης) of the Jews and priests, and to be protector (προστατῆσαι) of them all (v. 47).

Moreover, the major world powers at the time, including the Seleucids, the Romans, and even the Spartans, recognize the rights of the Hasmoneans to rule.[113] Nickelsburg summarizes the purpose of the author:

> He has recorded the history of the foundation, the succession, and the establishment of the Hasmonean house, and he has documented its legitimacy by royal decree, popular acclaim, and the attestation of the God who worked his purposes through the Hasmonean family and its early heroes.[114]

Accordingly, an author so intent on affirming the legitimacy of the Hasmonean house would not want to claim that the davidic dynasty was eternal or somehow continued to possess exclusive rights to kingship in Israel.[115]

---

[112]J. A. Goldstein, "How the Authors of 1 and 2 Maccabees Treated the 'Messianic' Promises," *Judaisms and Their Messiahs at the Turn of the Christian Era* (ed. J. Neusner, W. S. Green, and E. S. Frerichs; Cambridge: Cambridge University Press, 1987) 73; *I Maccabees*, 240; Attridge, "Historiography," 172–174; G. E. W. Nickelsburg, "1 and 2 Maccabees—Same Story, Different Meaning," *CTM* 42 (1971) 517–521; *Literature*, 114; D. Arenhoevel, *Theokratie Nach dem 1. und 2. Makkabäerbuch* (Walberger Studien 3; Nainz: Matthias-Grünewald, 1963) 40; D. J. Harrington, *The Maccabean Revolt* (Wilmington, DE: Glazier, 1988) 57–59; Schürer, *History*, 2:500; Collins, *Dan, I Mac, and II Mac*, 149,151; J. B. Bartlett, *The First and Second Books of the Maccabees* (Cambridge: Cambridge University Press, 1973) 18,213; S. Zeitlin, *The First Book of Maccabees* (New York: Harper, 1950) 31.

[113]See Attridge, "Historiography," 173–174, for references.

[114]Nickelsburg, "Same Story," 521.

[115]Goldstein, *I Maccabees*, 240: "Our author, who writes to prove the legitimacy of the Hasmonean dynasty, would not wish to assert the eternal right of the dynasty of David to rule over the Chosen People."

But the question then arises: How is one to understand this reference to David and his inheritance?[116] Goldstein has offered a plausible interpretation. After observing the variety in the textual witnesses for the crucial phrase εἰς αἰῶνας,[117] he accounts for it by arguing that the author of 1 Maccabees deliberately chose an ambiguous term—the plural form עולמים/αἰῶνας, which is comparatively rare and most often means "lifetimes," "ages," and the like, rather than "forever."[118] He notes that the singular, עולם/αἰών, which usually means "forever," is the term used in connection with biblical promises concerning an eternal davidic dynasty.[119] Consequently, Christian scribes, sensitive to the ambiguity of αἰῶνας, wished to assert unequivocally the eternal rights of davidic descendants and altered the text accordingly.[120] Goldstein, therefore, translates v. 57 as follows: "David, for his piety, received as his heritage a royal throne for ages."[121] Hence, the author would not then be asserting the eternity of the davidic dynasty, but only that it lasted for a long time. This assertion would not only seem to have history on its side, but more importantly, it would allow for a new royal line to arise, namely, the Hasmonean dynasty. On the other hand, the author speaks quite unambiguously about an everlasting priesthood given to Phineas in 2:54 (διαθήκην ἱερωσύνης αἰωνίας).[122]

Goldstein's interpretation of 2:57 has the advantage of explaining the textual variants and placing this verse within the overall intention of the book, but is weakened when it is observed that the difference in meaning between the singular and plural forms of עולם/αἰών is not clearly distinguishable.[123] Nevertheless, in

---

[116]Zeitlin, *Maccabees*, 32, claims that 2:57 is not original to the testament of Mattathias but is a later redactional addition. This view rightly has not won scholarly approval; there is absolutely no evidence for this proposal.

[117]Goldstein, *I Maccabees*, 240–41; the textual witnesses are: εἰς αἰῶνας = S La^LXGV, Lucifer (Sy II); αιωνιας = A *q* 542 56 58 106 La^M; αιωνιου = 340; εἰς αιωνα(-νας 19) αιωνος = L-19-93 (La^B Sy I); εἰς (+τον 311) αἰωνα = 55 311 (cf. W. Kappler, ed. *Maccabaeorum libri I–IV*, fasc. 1 [Septuaginta 9; Göttingen: Vandenhoeck & Ruprecht, 1936] 61).

[118]Goldstein, *I Maccabees*, 240; although he admits that sometimes the pl. form does mean "forever." 1 Maccabees was originally written in Hebrew (cf. Attridge, "Historiography," 171) and the Hebrew equivalent of αἰῶνα would be עולמים (see Jenni, "Das Wort ʿōlām," 31).

[119]Goldstein, *I Maccabees*, 240.

[120]Goldstein, *I Maccabees*, 240f.

[121]Goldstein, *I Maccabees*, 238.

[122]Goldstein, *I Maccabees*, 240.

[123]Admitted by Goldstein, *I Maccabees*, 240; J. J. Collins, "Messianism in the Maccabean Period," *Judaisms and Their Messiahs at the Turn of the Christian Era* (ed. J. Neusner, W. S. Green, and E. S. Frerichs; Cambridge: Cambridge University Press, 1987) 104, makes a similar point. See also Jenni, "Das Wort ʿōlām," 230f, who notes that the plural form of עולם is more frequent in later biblical literature, perhaps due to the influence of Aramaic, where the plural

my judgment Goldstein's intuitions are correct, but his point need not rest on the distinction between the singular and the plural forms. Both forms can mean either "a long time" or "unlimited time," and as we determined in our earlier treatment of the term עולם in the section on Chronicles, the precise semantic value of עולם must be deduced from the context.[124] Within 1 Maccabees, where the author's intention is to demonstrate the validity of the Hasmonean dynasty as rulers of Israel, and expressions of any other royal messianic hopes are absent, the context suggests that עולם/αἰών should not be taken to mean "forever." Instead, as Goldstein suggests, it refers to a long time, specifically, the lengthy period of time in which davidic kings ruled Israel and Judah.[125] In this way, the mention of David in 2:57 is a historical reference, just like all the other references to Israelite heroes made in Mattathias' testament.[126]

Collins, however, disagrees with Goldstein's assessment and suggests another interpretation of 2:57: "It is quite possible that the author of 1 Maccabees affirmed the traditional hope of the restoration of the Davidic line, but assigned it to the eschatological future."[127] Yet there are two significant flaws in this proposal. For one, as Collins himself admits, there is little concern for the eschatological future in 1 Maccabees;[128] nor does the immediate literary context of v. 57 suggest an eschatological dimension for this allusion to the davidic monarchy. In fact, as I shall point out below, the author may view the "eschatological" ideal as realized in the reign of Simon (cf. 13:36–14:15).[129] Secondly, Collins' assumption about a "traditional hope of the restoration of the Davidic line" is problematic. As I have tried to show, this putative traditional davidic hope does not exist in the early Second Temple period; at least one cannot assume it existed in order to prove that 1 Macc 2:57 is a reflection of it. Thus, we must count Collins' suggestion as unsubstantiated.

---

equivalent of עולם (עלם) appears more frequently. With respect to the plural of עולם, Jenni (p. 231) comments, "Ein Bedeutungsunterschied ist gegenüber dem Sing. kaum festzustellen" (cf. also Barr, *Biblical Words*, 70f).

[124]See above, p. 95.

[125]Schürer, *History*, 2:500, agrees with this assessment of 2:57.

[126]See below on how this historical reference functions in 1 Maccabees.

[127]Collins, "Messianism," 104; he notes that the messiah need not be the agent of salvation.

[128]Collins, "Messianism," 104; see also, D. Arenhoevel, "Die Eschatologie der Makkabäerbucher," *TTZ* 72 (1963) 257–264.

[129]Collins, *Dan, I Mac, and II Mac*, 151, himself notes that the Maccabees take on messianic dimensions in 1 Maccabees.

We can now go on to explain the positive function of this allusion to David
and his inheritance in 1 Maccabees. For this, it is necessary to pay close attention
to the immediate context—Mattathias' testament (1 Macc 2:49–68)—and its
purpose. Mattathias' testament consists largely of a catalog of past Israelite
heroes who are presented as examples of piety and action.[130] In each case, their
deed or virtue resulted in a reward. The purpose of the list within the narrative is
to spur the sons of Mattathias on to perform similar deeds and receive similar
rewards. Indeed, Mattathias sets out this purpose in v. 51, where he introduces
the catalog of heroes by saying, "Remember the deeds of the fathers, which they
did in their generations; and receive great honor and an everlasting name." He
reaffirms this intention again at the end of his speech, "My children, be coura-
geous and grow strong in the law, for by it you will gain honor" (v. 64).[131] Accordingly, the testament of Mattathias serves to set forth models of piety that the
Maccabean sons should emulate in the hope that they will attain similar rewards.[132]

In the remainder of his history, the author demonstrates how in fact the
Maccabees followed Mattathias' counsel by presenting them in terms of biblical
models of piety.[133] Our specific interest is in how the Maccabees emulate David.
In this regard, Collins thinks the reference to David's mercy is odd, because
mercy is a virtue that receives little attention elsewhere in 1 Maccabees.[134] But in
the Hebrew *Vorlage* the word translated ἐλέει was undoubtedly חסד,[135] a term
that would have alluded to David's piety and loyalty, and certainly the Maccabees

---

[130]Lee, *Studies*, 32, identifies 1 Macc 2:51–60 as a *Beispielreihe*; G. E. W. Nickelsburg,
Resurrection, Immortality, and Eternal Life (HTS 26; Cambridge, MA: Harvard University
Press, 1972) 99, compares the testament of Mattathias to *As. Mos.* 9:4, where appeal is also
made to the example of the fathers, who were obedient. Note too that the testament of Mat-
tathias is generically similar to the Hymn in Praise of the Fathers in Sirach (cf. J. D. Martin,
"Ben Sira—Child of His Time," *A Word in Season* [JSOTSup 42; ed. J. D. Martin and P. R.
Davies; Sheffield: JSOT Press, 1986] 142–145, for other catalogs of heroes in Jewish literature).

[131]Cf. also 2:61: "And so observe, from generation to generation, that none who put their
trust in him will lack strength."

[132]Cf. Goldstein, "'Messianic' Promises," 79; Nickelsburg, *Literature*, 115.

[133]A. Chester, "Citing the Old Testament," *It Is Written* (ed. D. A. Carson and H. G. M.
Williamson; Cambridge: Cambridge University Press, 1988) 150–153; Goldstein, *I Maccabees*,
7; "'Messianic' Promises," 79,93 n. 60; cf. also Attridge, "Historiography," 172; Collins, *Dan, I
Mac, and II Mac,* 151; Harrington, *Revolt,* 58f.

[134]Collins, *Dan, I Mac, and II Mac,* 152.

[135]The חסדי דוד is mentioned in Isa 55:3b; in 1 Macc 2:57 it clearly refers to David's virtue
and not to God's grace to David, i.e., it is a subjective rather than objective genitive (see P.
Bordreuil, "Les 'Grace de David' et 1 Maccabées II 57," *VT* 31 [1981] 73–75.)

are portrayed as both pious and loyal to God and the traditions of their ancestors. Similarly, in the concluding section of 4QMMT, one finds a similar reference to David's piety as the basis for divine favor: "Remember David. He was a man of pious works (חסדים), and also was delivered from many adversities and forgiven."[136]

But even more pointedly, the Maccabees are viewed in the light of David and the davidic tradition in several passages. In 4:30, when confronted with a large Syrian army, Judas prays:

> Blessed art thou, O Savior of Israel, who didst crush the attack of the mighty warrior by the hand of thy servant David, and didst give the camp of the Philistines into the hands of Jonathan, the son of Saul ...

Judas' activity in battle is reminiscent of the wars of Saul and David against the Philistines in 1–2 Samuel.[137] Moreover, the scene in which Simon is proclaimed leader by a public assembly in 1 Macc 14:41 has been compared to the elder's request to have David rule over them in 2 Sam 5:1–3.[138] Further, Simon's rule as depicted in 14:4–15 echoes the description of conditions in Solomon's reign, particularly in its parallel with 1 Kgs 4:25—conditions that were associated with the ideal future as imagined in Mic 4:4 and Zech 3:10.[139] In this regard, many commentators have observed messianic overtones in the description of Simon's reign.[140]

Altogether, by demonstrating how the Maccabees followed in the steps of their heroic ancestors, including David and Solomon, the author implies that they have obtained for themselves similar rewards.[141] Of course, one of these rewards was to rule over Israel. Attridge comments, "Here as in many comparisons with biblical prototypes, there is an implicit defense of the legitimacy of the irregular,

---

[136]There is not yet an *editio princeps* for 4QMMT; the lines cited appear on PAM 42.838, the first two lines of the large fragment on the bottom of the plate. For a transcription and English translation, see R. Eisenman and M. Wise, *The Dead Sea Scrolls Uncovered*, Rockport, MA: Element, 1992, 198–200. Interestingly, 4QMMT may have been addressed to a Hasmonean ruler (cf. L. H. Schiffman, "The New Halakhic Letter [4QMMT] and the Origins of the Dead Sea Sect," *BA* 53 [1990] 67).

[137]Bartlett, *Maccabees*, 15; Chester, "Citing," 152; see Goldstein, "'Messianic' Promises," 93 n. 60, for a list of specific references.

[138]Arenhoevel, "Eschatologie," 262.

[139]Attridge, "Historiography," 175; Nickelsburg, *Literature*, 117; "Same Story," 521; Goldstein, "'Messianic' Promises," 77.

[140]Attridge, "Historiography," 174; Collins, *Dan, I Mac, and II Mac*, 151; Nickelsburg, *Literature*, 117; Arenhoevel, *Theokratie*, 61–66; Chester, "Citing," 152.

[141]Chester, "Citing," 150; Goldstein, "'Messianic' Promises," 79.

charismatic leadership exercised by the Hasmoneans."[142] Collins has asked whether 1 Maccabees sees "the Hasmonean dynasty as a full-fledged replacement for the Davidic dynasty," as Goldstein has suggested.[143] In my judgment, this is not the way to frame the question, because it assumes, once again, a living belief that the davidic dynasty had some claim to rule during the second century BCE—an assumption for which there is no evidence.[144] In fact, the whole issue of kingship is not prominent in 1 Maccabees; rather, special attention is given to legitimizing the Hasmoneans in the office of high priest, the locus of real power and authority.[145]

Nonetheless, David, like all the other examples in Mattathias' testament, provided a model of piety leading to a reward—a model the Hasmoneans successfully emulated. This is not to say that the davidic promises or covenant were fulfilled in the Hasmonean dynasty; there is no claim to this effect. But the Hasmoneans are types of biblical heroes, whose deeds and rewards parallel those of the ancestors of old. In this way, the davidic dynasty tradition served the author of 1 Maccabees not as a promised awaiting fulfillment, but as a biblical prototype to be imitated. We might go as far as to say that the Hasmoneans are depicted as davidic in a typological sense.[146]

But it would be wrong to make too much of the influence of the davidic dynasty tradition on the author, for it must be remembered that the reference to David and his inheritance is brief and not marked out for special consideration. Inasmuch as David was one of Israel's heroic figures, he is included in the list. This observation may nevertheless be significant, because it indicates an absence

---

[142]Attridge, "Historiography," 172.

[143]Collins, "Messianism," 104; cf. Goldstein, "'Messianic' Promises," 80.

[144]Goldstein, "'Messianic' Promises," 72–73, asserts that *1 Enoch* 90:37–38 reveals an expectation for a davidic messiah, but his arguments are very tenuous, and rightly criticized by Collins (cf. "Messianism," 100–101).

[145]Cf. Horsley and Hanson, *Bandits*, 101: "Yet instead of reviving royal imagery and titles, the Hasmonean leadership assumed the high priestly role; this act witnesses to the strength and centrality of the latter and perhaps the dormancy of the former at the time." See 1 Macc 2:23–26, where Mattathias is expressly portrayed as a type of Phineas, the ancestor through whom the high priesthood was established (cf. Sir 45:23–26; 50:24 [Heb]). On the Maccabees as high priests, see Arenhoevel, *Theokratie*, 44–47. The lack of specific interest in kingship suggests that 1 Maccabees may have been written before the Hasmoneans began to designate themselves kings, which may have been as early as 104 BCE.

[146]Here, the biblical concept of a "new David" (cf. Ezek 34:23–24; 37:24–25) may ultimately lie behind this typological identification between the Hasmoneans and David. Moreover, it is interesting to speculate whether Hasmonean expansionist policy under John Hyrcanus and Alexander Jannaeus was fueled by a desire to recreate the extent of the davidic/solomonic empire.

of any concerted polemic against the validity of an eternal davidic dynasty. Apparently expectations for renewed davidic rule were not current and therefore not in need of rebuttal. Yet, an interpretation of the davidic dynasty tradition as eternally valid in a more literal, perhaps genealogical, sense would certainly pose a threat to Hasmonean royal dynastic claims. This point, as we will see in the next section, would not go unnoticed by the opponents of the Hasmoneans.

D. Psalms of Solomon 17

Within early Judaism *Pss. Sol.* 17 provides the most extensive description of an expected davidic king and his kingdom, and therefore merits detailed attention. The *Psalms of Solomon* are preserved in both Greek and Syriac versions, although their original language appears to have been Hebrew.[147] Moreover, while the composition of the *Psalms of Solomon* is dated between 80–40 BCE,[148] *Pss. Sol.* 17 can be dated between 61 and 57 BCE, since it describes Pompey's capture of Jerusalem and Aristobolus II's exile (and the puppet kingdom of Hyrcanus II), but makes no reference to the revolt of Alexander in 57 BCE.[149] The provenance is almost certainly Jerusalem or its environs.[150]

The question of authorship is debated. Traditionally the *Psalms of Solomon* were held to be the work of Pharisees, and this view still has many proponents.[151] But since the discovery of the Dead Sea Scrolls, connections between the *Psalms of Solomon* and Qumran literature have been observed, leading some to posit their origin within or close to Essene circles.[152] However, as M. de Jonge has

---

[147]R. B. Wright, "Psalms of Solomon," *The Old Testament Pseudepigrapha* (2 vols.; ed. J. H. Charlesworth; Garden City, NY: Doubleday, 1985) 2:640.

[148]O'Dell, "The Religious Background," 241; M. de Jonge, "Psalms of Solomon," *Outside the Old Testament* (Cambridge Commentaries on the Writings of the Jewish and Christian World 4; ed. M. de Jonge; Cambridge: Cambridge University Press, 1985), 161, before 40 BCE; Wright, *OTP*, 2:641, between 70–45 BCE.

[149]G. L. Davenport, "The 'Anointed of the Lord' in Psalms of Solomon 17," *Ideal Figures in Ancient Judaism* (SBLSCS 12; ed. G. W. E. Nickelsburg and J. J. Collins; Chico, CA: Scholars Press, 1980) 71.

[150]Wright, *OTP*, 2:641; de Jonge, *Outside*, 161.

[151]Wright, *OTP*, 2:642, cites this traditional view; cf. also J. Schüpphaus, *Die Psalmen Salomos* (Leiden: Brill, 1977) 127–37; G. B. Gray, "Psalms of Solomon," *The Apocrypha and Pseudepigrapha of the Old Testament* (2 vols.; ed. R. H. Charles; Oxford: Clarendon, 1913) 2:630; Nickelsburg, *Literature*, 212; see Davenport, "The 'Anointed of the Lord'," 88 n. 19, for a summary of viewpoints on authorship.

[152]O'Dell, "The Religious Background," *passim*; R. B. Wright, "The Psalms, the Pharisees, and the Essenes," *1972 Proceedings for the International Organization for Septuagint and Cognate Studies and the Society of Biblical Literature Pseudepigrapha Seminar* (SBLSCS 2; ed. R. A. Kraft; Missoula, MT: Scholars Press, 1972) *passim*; Wright, *OTP*, 2:642.

pointed out, "sectarian" tendencies so characteristic of Qumran are lacking in the *Psalms of Solomon.*[153] Consequently, J. Charlesworth counsels that one should avoid forcing the *Psalms of Solomon* into the Pharisaical or Essene camp.[154] Nevertheless, his counsel may be overly cautious, for as Nickelsburg argues, there is much in the *Psalms of Solomon* that fits what is known about the Pharisees, and nothing that does not; thus, he concludes—and in my judgment correctly—that the *Psalms of Solomon* emanate from circles close to the Pharisees.[155]

The structure of *Pss. Sol.* 17 is that of a communal lament or complaint. Its parts are as follows: opening confession (vv. 1–3), complaint (vv. 4–20), plea (vv. 21–43), and closing benediction, prayer, and confession (vv. 44–46).[156] The opening confession asserts God's eternal kingship over Israel and Israel's complete dependence on God for mercy and judgment against the nations. Moreover, these same ideas are expressed in the closing prayer and confession (vv. 45–46), indicating that the author offers his complaint and plea within the context of acknowledging God's ultimate rule and control of affairs. But it is just this conviction on the part of the author, that God's kingly rule should involve the experience of justice and mercy, or as 17:44 expresses it, "good fortune," that highlights the disparity between that good fortune and the social and political conditions that currently obtain. In light of this disparity, therefore, the psalmist offers his complaint (vv. 4–20).

The complaint begins by recalling God's promise to David concerning an eternal dynasty:

> Lord, you chose David to be king over Israel, and swore to him about his descendants forever, that his kingdom should not fail before you (v. 4).

The language in v. 4 clearly reflects the davidic dynasty tradition as articulated in texts such as 2 Sam 7:11b–16; Ps 89:3–4,19–37; and Jer 33:17.[157] The author

---

[153]De Jonge, *Outside*, 160; in addition, O'Dell's major argument against Pharisaical authorship—the strong messianic and eschatological elements which are uncharacteristic for Pharisees—is not persuasive.

[154]An editorial addition to Wright, *OTP*, 2:642.

[155]Nickelsburg, *Literature*, 204,212.

[156]This structural arrangement roughly follows the structure posited by Schüpphaus, *Psalmen Salomos*, 70–72; and Davenport, "The 'Anointed of the Lord'," 71 (see his n. 17, p. 88), although the latter wishes to identify vv. 25–44 as a prophetic response distinct from the plea; however, the form-critical indicators for such a separation are lacking, in my judgment.

[157]Note esp. the terms ὤμοσας (Ps 89:4/88:4 [נשבעתי/ὤμοσα]); σπέρματος (2 Sam 7:12; Ps 89:5/88:5 [זרעך/σπέρμα]); τοῦ μὴ ἐκλείπειν (Jer 33:17 [לא־יכרת לדוד]; cf. also 1 Kgs 8:25).

will return later to this reaffirmation of the davidic dynastic promise as the basis of his plea, but first he recounts a series of disastrous events that have led to Israel's current condition.

He describes the usurpation of the davidic royal prerogative by sinners (vv. 5–6), God's expulsion and punishment of the usurpers by the hand of a foreigner (vv. 7–10), the devastation of the land and its people by this foreigner and his Jewish proxies (vv. 11–15), the scattering of the pious (vv. 16–18a), and the utterly sinful condition of those who remain in Israel (vv. 18b–20). Easily detected behind this thinly veiled description are the events involving the rise of the Hasmonean dynasty, Pompey's capture of Jerusalem and deportation of Aristobolus II, the puppet regime of Hyrcanus II, the resulting effects on the community behind the *Psalms of Solomon*, and the sorry state in which the author found Israel.

The specifics of this complaint are important because they depict the social and political upheaval that forms the negative counterpart for the psalmist's own ideal vision of Israel, yet to be articulated, as ruled by the davidic messiah.[158] This negative state of affairs is described in further detail in other psalms, particularly *Pss. Sol.* 2, 4, and 8.[159] Moreover, it should be observed that the author's criticisms are leveled at several groups: first, at the Hasmoneans generally for their arrogance in appropriating the royal office to themselves; secondly, at Pompey, who represents foreign oppression and impiety ("his heart [was] alien to our God"); and thirdly, the impious Jews whose collaboration with gentiles has led them to every kind of sin. Altogether, the situation is marked by unrighteousness and impiety, so much so that the author's own community has been forced to flee. Whether this means physical flight or more likely non-participation in Second Temple social and cultic institutions, the author's community is utterly disenfranchised from the current form of "Israel."[160] In response to this situation, the psalmist makes his plea, which describes the expected davidic king and the Israel that will exist under his rule.[161]

---

[158]See B. L. Mack, "Wisdom Makes a Difference," *Judaisms and Their Messiahs at the Turn of the Christian Era* (ed. J. Neusner, W. S. Green, and E. S. Frerichs; Cambridge: Cambridge University Press, 1987) 38.

[159]Mack, "Wisdom Makes," 33–35, for a summary of sins alleged especially against the leaders of Israel.

[160]Cf. Mack, "Wisdom Makes," 35, who suggests that the author and his community may not only be rejecting the administration of Second Temple institutions, but the institutions themselves.

[161]The precise structure of the plea is difficult to uncover, in part because one is dealing with a Greek translation. Schüpphaus, *Psalmen Salomos*, 64, speaks of the disunity of the en-

The first request in the plea sets forth the theme for this section:

> See, Lord, and raise up for them their king, the son of David, to rule over your servant Israel in the time known to you, O God (v. 21).

This plea rests on the conviction of an eternal davidic dynasty, mentioned earlier in v. 4, and is informed by the language and concepts of biblical texts associated with the davidic dynasty tradition.[162] It is significant too that this is the only time the phrase "Son of David" occurs with reference to a messianic figure in early Jewish literature.[163] More importantly, this davidic king is depicted as God's chosen agent. In contrast to the Hasmoneans, who usurped the royal office, the davidic king will be raised up by God. Furthermore, the notion of divine legitimacy is reinforced in that the davidic monarch will appear according to the divine timetable. The issue here is clearly one of legitimacy, and the legitimacy of the Son of David to hold royal office is grounded in a divine promise.

The plea proceeds to describe the activities and character of this davidic king. In vv. 22–25, the davidic king is said to purge and destroy unrighteous rulers from Jerusalem, both gentile and Jewish. On the one hand, the language is violent, while on the other, the mission is executed by the word of his mouth: he warns nations and condemns sinners. Here, two important items must be observed. First, in this section and throughout the plea, royal power is implemented not with military force, but with the king's words (vv. 33,35,36b,43). Thus, while it is correct to view the davidic messiah in political terms, it is mistaken to understand him in military terms.[164] Furthermore, in so far as concern for purity, righteousness, and holiness overshadows ordinary political interests, M. de Jonge's comments are apt: "It is wrong to speak of a 'political' Messiah, or a warrior-King; the ideal of a righteous king and a righteous Israel stands in the centre."[165]

---

tire psalm. Thus, the structural outline for the plea followed in this paper should be considered a working hypothesis rather than a definitive statement of its form.

[162]Cf. esp. 2 Sam 7:11–14, where the same verb, קום/ἀνίστημι ("raise up"), is used.

[163]See D. C. Duling, "The Therapeutic Son of David: An Element in Matthew's Christological Apologetic," *NTS* 24 (1978) 407–408.

[164]J. H. Charlesworth, "The Concept of the Messiah in the Pseudepigrapha," *Aufstieg und Niedergang der römischen Welt, II.19.1* (ed. W. Haase; Berlin: De Gruyter, 1979) 198f, notes that the spiritual side of the messiah is primary in contrast to the portrait in *Tg. Ps.-J.* Gen 49:10: "He has girded his loins and come down, setting in order the order of battle with his enemies and killing kings with their rulers ... reddening the mountains with the blood of their slain," or in the *War Scroll* from Qumran; cf. also Wright, *OTP*, 2:645: The messiah is political and royal, though "not military in the ordinary sense of the word;" see also the next note.

[165]De Jonge, *Outside*, 161; Klausner, *Messianic Idea*, 324, makes a similar point when he

Secondly, the author takes aim at two groups: the gentiles and the sinners, the latter being Jewish opponents of the author, led undoubtedly by Hyrcanus II and his associates. Interestingly, of these two groups the Jewish opponents come in for much harsher treatment than do the gentiles. While it is true that the gentile overlords will be driven from Jerusalem and destroyed, and gentiles in general will be banished from inhabiting Israel (v. 28b), there will yet remain a positive, though subordinate, role for the gentiles (vv. 30–31), as well as a positive attitude toward them in the future kingdom ruled by the davidic monarch (v. 34b). On the other hand, the Jewish opponents, called sinners, will be driven out from the inheritance, their arrogance smashed, and their substance shattered with an iron rod (v. 24). Particularly noteworthy is how the author modifies canonical Ps 2:9 to make his point. In Ps 2:9, *the nations* are broken by the iron rod; here, the *sinners* are its victims.[166] In addition, whereas the gentiles flee at the king's warning, the sinners are condemned (v. 25). And while the gentiles have some role in the future kingdom, there appears to be no place for errant Jews. Thus, although the *Psalms of Solomon*, and particularly *Pss. Sol.* 17, are considered anti-Roman, which they are, *Pss. Sol.* 17 at least is even more virulently directed against the Jewish opponents of its author. Accordingly, this deep division between pious Jews and sinners indicates an ideology in which the author and his community no longer look for reform of the current social and political landscape, but envision a completely new configuration. Finally, besides the author's use of Psalm 2 noted above, Isaiah 11 has exerted a marked influence upon vv. 22–24, and, as we shall see, *Pss. Sol.* 17 as a whole.[167]

The remainder of the plea (vv. 26–42) articulates a vision of an ideal Israel ruled by an ideal davidic king. It begins by predicting the ingathering of Jews to Israel, where the land, free of gentiles, will once again be apportioned to the tribes (vv. 26–28).[168] This restored Israelite community will be righteous and holy: "He will not tolerate unrighteousness even to pause among them, and any person who knows wickedness shall not live with them" (v. 27a). Themes from Isa 11:3–5 (righteous rule) and Isa 11:11–12 (restoration of Israel) are present.

---

speaks of the emphasis on the 'spiritual' side of the Messiah. I take this to mean that this davidic messiah is not a type of political revolutionary, but an ideal figure, whose characteristics nevertheless have implications for the socio-political situation.

[166]Davenport, "The 'Anointed of the Lord'," 73.

[167]Verses 22–24 are shaped particularly by Isa 11:1–5; cf. Davenport, "The 'Anointed of the Lord'," 72.

[168]Cf. Ezek 45:8–9; 47:13–14,21–22, for the theme of redistribution of the land according to tribes.

But beyond the government of Israel, vv. 29–32 indicate that a universal rule is envisioned for the davidic king:[169] he will judge peoples and nations (v. 29); he will be served by gentile nations (v. 30a); he will glorify the Lord above the whole earth (v. 30b); and nations will come from all the earth to Jerusalem (v. 31). Moreover, in v. 32, when the text says, "And he will be a righteous king over them," with Davenport, we should understand the third person plural pronoun to refer not only to Jews but to the nations as well.[170] Thus, as in the prophecies of Isaiah, the nations pay homage to the glory of the Lord through a sanctified Jerusalem.[171] But in contrast to Isaiah 66, where the nations serve the Lord, here the nations serve the king,[172] a telling clue that the king is understood to be the Lord's designated agent and representative.

Beginning in v. 32, however, the focus starts to shift to the character of the davidic monarch. We may summarize the thrust of vv. 32–43 under three points. First and foremost, as already alluded to above, he is a divinely appointed king whose power and authority is based on his being anointed by the Lord and his total reliance on God. He is taught by God (v. 32a); he does not rely on weapons of war but has hope in God (vv. 33–34a,39); he does not weaken, relying on God (v. 37); God made him powerful with his holy spirit (v. 37b); the blessing of the Lord is with him (v. 38). This characteristic is best summed up in psalm's own terms: "their king shall be the Lord's Messiah" (v. 32).[173] He is God's agent who is wholly subordinate to God, for the Lord himself is his king. In this regard, Davenport's comments apply: "Consequently, the one who will occupy the throne of David will be king in a qualified sense only. He will reign under the authority of the true King, the Lord himself."[174]

---

[169]For biblical background, cf. Ps 89:27 and Ps 72:8–11.

[170]Davenport, "The 'Anointed of the Lord'," 75.

[171]See Isa 11:10; 60:1–14; 66:18, for example.

[172]Davenport, "The 'Anointed of the Lord'," 76.

[173]There is an important textual problem at this point. Nickelsburg, *Literature*, 207; Davenport, "The 'Anointed of the Lord'," 77–79; M. de Jonge, "The Expectation of the Future in the Psalms of Solomon," *Neot* 23 (1989) 100; Klausner, *Messianic Idea*, 321; and Schüpphaus, *Psalmen Salomos*, 71, hold that the proper reading is χριστὸς κυρίου = the messiah of the Lord, while Wright, *OTP*, 2:667f, argues for the validity of χριστὸς κύριος = Lord Messiah. For our purposes the proper reading makes little difference. The point is that the davidic king is wholly God's servant, empowered by him and devoted to him.

[174]Davenport, "The 'Anointed of the Lord'," 72. Cf. also Charlesworth, "Concept," 199, " ... God is clearly the actor;" de Jonge, "Expectation," 101, and Nickelsburg, *Literature*, 207. Recall that the psalm begins and ends with the confession of God's kingship. Note, too, how this reflects the theme present in the davidic dynasty tradition found in exilic texts from Ezekiel, where the vassal status of the Israelite king is emphasized.

Secondly, this Son of David is characterized in an idealized way. He is compassionate to all nations (v. 34b), he is free from sin (v. 36a), powerful in the holy spirit (v. 37b), wise in counsel (v. 37a), he will not weaken (v. 38b), he is mighty in action (v. 40a), faithful and righteous (v. 40b), and has pure words, like those of the angels (v. 43c).[175] Here we observe again that notably absent are characteristics suitable for a warrior; rather the emphasis is on righteousness, holiness, and wisdom. Further, the superlative spiritual endowments and the idealized rule attributed to this figure suggest a semi-divine character.[176] To be sure, he remains a human figure, but nevertheless appears to possess superhuman qualities.

Thirdly, like its king, the restored Israel is depicted in ideal terms: "There will be no unrighteousness among them in his day, for all will be holy."[177] Israel is called the Lord's people (v. 35b) and the Lord's flock (v. 40b).[178] They are ruled in holiness and do not stumble (vv. 41a,40d); arrogance and oppression are absent from among them (v. 41b–c). In short, the davidic king rules over a perfected Israel.[179]

Having reviewed the contents of this psalm, we can turn to the question of the function of the davidic dynasty tradition as it is appropriated here. There appear to be at least two basic intentions. Our discussion of the first can begin with an observation. *Pss. Sol.* 17 sets forth the first positive expectation of a davidic figure in the early Jewish period.[180] What accounts for this phenomenon? The answer lies close at hand, specifically, in the opposition to the Hasmonean kings reflected in *Pss. Sol.* 17:5–7.[181] Prior to Hasmonean rule, or more probably prior to their claim of royal status, the issue of kingship in Israel was a moot point. The locus of power, as illustrated in Ben Sira's work, was the high priest-hood. But the stunning rise of the Maccabean house and their appropriation of the

---

[175]Note the influence from Isa 11:1–5 and Jer 23:5–6.

[176]Nickelsburg, *Literature*, 208, "Although the messianic king will be a human being, the author attributes to him certain semi-divine characteristics that are typical of the older (especially Isaianic) oracles;" M. de Jonge, "χρίω: Apocrypha and Pseudepigrapha," *Theological Dictionary of the New Testament, Vol 9* (ed. G. W. Bromiley; Grand Rapids, MI: Eerdmans, 1964–1976) 514, "It would be out of place to speak here—as is often done—of a national, political, earthly messiah;" cf. Wright, *OTP*, 2:643, for a similar comment.

[177]Cf. Jer 23:5b; Isa 60:21.

[178]Cf. Jer 23:1–6; Ezek 34:20–24; 37:24.

[179]Once again, cf. Isa 11:11ff.

[180]The relationship between the royal messianic figures from the *Testaments of the Twelve Patriarchs* and from Qumran and davidic messianism will be taken up below, in chap. 6.

[181]Likewise Collins, *Imagination*, 114; Davenport, "The 'Anointed of the Lord'," 86.

royal title to themselves brought a changed situation: a royal model for understanding Jewish politics and society was not only possible but actual.

The Hasmoneans themselves attempted to legitimize their position by appeal
to their accomplishments, or as the author of 1 Maccabees would put it, by God's
accomplishments through them. Nonetheless, as observed earlier, this *de facto*
validation would run counter to an interpretation of the davidic dynasty tradition
that posited a continually valid davidic dynasty. It is not hard to imagine, then,
that as disenchantment and opposition to Hasmonean kings increased, the potential for exploiting this biblical resource would draw more attention. And inasmuch
as the rule of John Hyrcanus (who had not yet claimed royal status), Aristobolus
I, and later kings—especially Alexander Jannaeus—met with Jewish (Pharisaic)
opposition, an interpretation of the davidic dynasty tradition in terms of an eternally valid davidic dynasty and a future divinely legitimized davidic king could be
employed polemically against these Hasmonean kings. *Pss. Sol.* 17 provides the
first literary evidence for this strategy.

The davidic king would be all the things the Hasmonean kings were not, and
Israel would be all the things that the Maccabean kings could never make it.
Whether or not the author or community he represented literally expected this
king and his kingdom is not the point. What is at issue is a frontal assault on the
legitimacy of the Hasmonean kings by means of a powerful biblical tradition.
That this tradition had not been employed in such a way for centuries would not
diminish the evocative power of such use in the social and political circumstances
of the mid-first century BCE.

To clarify this point somewhat, let me contrast it with the argument of E.
Lohse.[182] Lohse explains that the Hasmonean kings had assumed the royal title,
though they were not of davidic descent and therefore lacked sufficient qualifications for the office. He continues, "Dieser Verlauf der Geschehnisse löste bei den
gesetzestreuen Juden bittere Enttäuschung und schweren Kummer aus."[183] In
other words, pious Jews looking for the fulfillment of the davidic hope were
disappointed when the Hasmoneans claimed royal status. But this explanation
assumes a continuing expectation for a davidic monarch among Jews, an assumption that lacks evidence. In fact, there is evidence to the contrary. According to
Josephus' report (*Ant.* 14.41), in 63 BCE a delegation of Jews came before Pompey requesting that both Aristobolus II and Hyrcanus II be deposed, because they
did not want to be ruled by a king, since it was the custom of the Jews to obey

---

[182]Lohse, "Der König," 338; cf. also K. G. Kuhn, "The Two Messiahs of Aaron and Israel,"
The Scrolls and the New Testament (ed. K. Stendahl; New York: Harper & Bros., 1957)
61–62.

[183]Lohse, "Der König," 338.

the priests. Clearly, not all Jews imagined Israel organized along monarchical lines, let alone along the lines of a davidic monarchy. Therefore, Lohse's explanation must be rejected. In my judgment, we must maintain the reverse of Lohse's view, namely, that opposition to the Hasmonean kings among the community connected to the *Psalms of Solomon* led to the emergence of an interpretation of the davidic dynasty tradition in terms of an ideology of renewed davidic kingship. This use of the davidic dynasty tradition served to articulate their opposition to the Hasmonean kings. In other words, the davidic dynasty tradition did not generate disappointment with the Hasmoneans; rather, disappointment with the Hasmoneans generated this appropriation of the davidic dynasty tradition. This then is the first way in which the davidic dynasty tradition functioned in *Pss. Sol.* 17: to undercut the legitimacy of Hasmonean leaders, who claimed royal office in Israel.

However, the deposition of the Hasmonean kings by Pompey did not bring to Israel an ideal order. Indeed, the authors of the *Psalms of Solomon* register their consternation about the man of an alien race whose oppressive rule through apostate Jewish leadership they continued to experience. This observation, then, points to the second function of this psalm and its portrayal of a davidic messiah, namely, as a response to the author's current social and political conditions. In this regard, there are two dimensions to his response: 1) destruction of the current unrighteous leadership and the evils it perpetrated; 2) inauguration of a new order under the leadership of an ideal davidic king.[184] Based on our previous analysis of the complaint and plea, we can summarize these two dimensions of the psalmist response.

In view of the havoc wrought by Pompey and the Jewish puppet regime, the Son of David would sweep away this leadership, both gentile and Jewish. With their destruction would go the impiety and unrighteousness that characterized Jewish life. In their place would be the legitimate rule of a davidic king, appointed and empowered by God, possessing the holy spirit and superhuman virtues. His ideal kingdom would be universal in extent and perfectly righteous and holy in character. Land would be equitably distributed to the tribes of Israel again, and the dispersed would return to Israel. This social and political ideal would be established and ruled by this ideal king. In fact, the link between the davidic messiah and the ideal age is such that the king is conceived of as the mediator of God's blessings to Israel and the world.[185]

---

[184]Cf. Mack, "Wisdom Makes," 38–41.

[185]Davenport, "The 'Anointed of the Lord'," 85.

Several features of this ideal vision of Israel are of particular interest. First, absent from this ideal conception are the priests and temple.[186] Holiness, which is an important characteristic of the new order, is achieved apart from priest and temple.[187] I suspect this construal of Jewish life is born out of continual frustration with the failure of the high priesthood in the Second Temple period to deliver the kind of results envisioned in Ben Sira's hymn to Simon (Sir 50:1–24). The new situation is based on a royal model of governance, which in the end is understood as representative of God's kingly rule. Moreover, a reference to the "assemblies of the pious" (v. 16) may represent an attempt to locate Jewish life in an institution other than the temple, i.e., in the synagogue.[188]

Secondly, as noted above, the kingdom is not established by force of arms, but by the word of the king, and he will rule by the strength of his word (v. 36). Verse 43 states it well:

> His words will be purer than the finest gold, the best ... His words will be as the words of the holy ones, among sanctified peoples.

Indeed, his word is marked by the power of wisdom (cf. vv. 29,35,37). In this regard, Mack has drawn particular attention to this king's possession of wisdom and his role as sage and teacher.[189] Wisdom is characterized as the "axial notion" that "has qualified every single aspect of this king's character and effectiveness."[190] Yet, Mack maintains that this stress on the wisdom of the king does not derive from "Davidic nuances." But the davidic dynasty tradition in the Hebrew Bible does characterize the ideal davidic king as endowed with wisdom, as in Jer 23:5 and especially Isa 11:2:

> And the Spirit of the Lord shall rest upon him, the spirit of wisdom and understanding, the spirit of counsel and might, the spirit of knowledge and the fear of the Lord (Isa 11:2).

As noted throughout our analysis of *Pss. Sol.* 17, Isaiah 11 had a formative influence on the conception of the Son of David there.[191] Thus, if it was the

---

[186]Mack, "Wisdom Makes," 38.

[187]Davenport, "The 'Anointed of the Lord'," 75, observes that the king is in charge of cultic matters. This is in contrast to what one finds at Qumran, where royal activities are in general under the authority of the priests.

[188]Mack, "Wisdom Makes," 37,40; cf. also de Jonge, *Outside*, 159, who suggests that the *Psalms of Solomon* were brought together for use in the assemblies of the pious.

[189]Mack, "Wisdom Makes," 39–40; cf. also, de Jonge, "Expectation," 102.

[190]Mack, "Wisdom Makes," 40.

[191]Apart from these general themes note the influence of Isa 11:4 (LXX) on v. 24b and v. 35; 11:2–5 on vv. 26–27,42; 11:1–5 on v. 29; 11:2 on v. 37.

intention of the psalmist to characterize an ideal royal figure as an embodiment of divine wisdom, the davidic dynasty tradition could provide a davidic king to fit the need. In fact, one could say that the davidic figure of Isa 11:2 provided an ideal resource within the Jewish tradition for connecting the themes of royalty and wisdom in an ideal figure.

Thirdly, we can observe some similarities between *Pss. Sol.* 17 and the thought world associated with apocalypses.[192] The historical review (vv. 5–20), which is similar to that found in Daniel and the Book of Dreams; the pattern of oppression (vv. 5–19), cosmic portents, and apostasy (vv. 18–20), followed by a call for and description of the messianic age; and the separatist tendencies of the author are all reminiscent of apocalyptic themes. This association with apocalyptic ideas has led R. B. Wright to equate the davidic figure of *Pss. Sol.* 17 with the final apocalyptic king.[193] But Nickelsburg's more moderate claim seems more to the point: "In its assertion of the final, total kingship of God, the eschatology of this psalm closely parallels many manifestations of apocalyptic eschatology, but with important distinctions," which he goes on to list.[194] Accordingly, these contacts with apocalyptic thinking are significant, particularly with respect to its influence on the depiction of the davidic figure. As M. Delcor points out: "Dans le développement de l'idée messianique la figure du Ps. XVII occupe une place intermédiaire entre les conceptions de l'Ancien Testament et celles, tardives, d'un Messie supraterrestre."[195] Possibly the harshness of the actual social and political situation confronted by the author and his complete rejection of the current leadership inspired the use of these more fantastic and idealized images which he employed in setting forth the shape of the new order.

Thus, *Pss. Sol.* 17 is the first evidence for the expression of hope for a davidic messiah in early Jewish literature. The emergence of this interpretation of the davidic dynasty tradition in the mid-first century BCE was based on the utility of the concept of a Son of David for negating the legitimacy of the Hasmonean royal house and for envisioning an ideal social and political order, free from oppression and impurity, and characterized by piety, righteousness, and wisdom.

---

[192]More affinities than admitted by Collins, *Imagination*, 113f, who sees *Pss. Sol.* 17 as only remotely related to apocalyptic literature.

[193]Wright, *OTP*, 2:646.

[194]Nickelsburg, *Literature*, 208f.

[195]M. Delcor, "Psaumes de Salomon," *Dictionnaire de la Bible, Supplément, Vol. 9* (ed. L. Pirot and A. Robert; Paris: Letouzey & Ane, 1979) 245; cf. also Collins, *Imagination*, 114, "In the first century CE, however, this traditional picture of the Messiah [in Ps. of Sol. 17] was increasingly integrated into the apocalyptic scenario ... "

Yet, once the idea of an ideal davidic messiah was conceived, as we shall see, it could be employed by others as a useful evocative symbol.[196]

---

[196]*Pss. Sol.* 18, which is later than and secondary to *Pss. Sol.* 17 (see de Jonge, "Expectation," 100) and probably composed as a conclusion to the collection of psalms (Nickelsburg, *Literature*, 209), also looks forward to the coming messiah, although with less intensity than *Pss. Sol.* 17. The messiah is not said to be davidic, but given the context of *Pss. Sol.* 18, this may be assumed. In contrast to *Pss. Sol.* 17, however, the emphasis has shifted to the ideal times of the messiah, rather than the person of the messiah about whom little is said. Although brief in its description of the reign of the messiah, *Pss. Sol.* 18 nevertheless comports with the themes in *Pss. Sol.* 17.

CHAPTER 5
Texts From the Hellenistic and
Roman Periods: Part II

A. Qumran Literature.

Among the manuscripts of the Dead Sea Scrolls, five documents contain references to the davidic dynasty tradition: 4QDibHam, 4QpGen[a], 4QFlor, 4QpIsa[a], and 4QSerek HaMilhamah.[1] Except for 4QDibHam, they are sectarian documents apparently written by and for members of the Qumran community. 4QDibHam is not specifically sectarian, but its presence in the Qumran library suggests that it nevertheless comports with the ideology of the Qumran community, although it probably had wider currency. Together, therefore, these writings contribute to a general picture of this community's interpretation of the davidic dynasty tradition. Nevertheless, each document has its own particular contours and must first be interpreted in its own integrity. In other words, we may not assume at the outset that the sect had one view of the davidic dynasty tradition, or that it functioned the same way in each particular document. With this in mind, each of the relevant passages from these texts will be taken up. In a concluding section, however, I

---

[1]In this section, I will deal only with specific references to the davidic dynasty tradition and not with general references to messianic figures in Qumran literature, such as the Messiah of Israel. Whether other messianic figures are to be equated with davidic figures is an important subject that will be treated in chap. 6. Also, passages in Qumran literature dealing with David, apart from his relevance to the dynastic tradition, are likewise outside the scope of this study. For example, 11QPs[a] 27:2–11 mentions David, but here he is characterized as a poet and composer of psalms whom God chose as a leader of his people because of his piety; this characterization is not surprising given the position of this passage at the end and climax of 11QPs[a] (see J. A. Sanders, *The Psalms Scroll of Qumran Cave 11* [DJD 4; Oxford: Clarendon, 1965] 53–64,91–93, esp. p. 58 and p. 92).

will draw together the results of these individual studies and consider the use of the davidic dynasty tradition at Qumran in general.

1. 4QDibHam^a 1/2 4:6–8 (4Q504)

1. 4QDibHam^a 1/2 4:6–8 (4Q504)

4QDibHam^a is the longest and best preserved of three exemplars of a liturgical text named by its editor "Words of the Luminaries" (דברי המארות). Discovered in 1952, portions of this document were published by M. Baillet in 1961;[2] the complete text, along with photographic plates, appeared from the same editor in 1982.[3] According to Baillet, the text contains a series of prayers for use on various days of the week.[4] Further investigation has shown that these are community prayers of supplication, similar to other Jewish prayers known as *tahanunim*.[5] Fragments one and two, when pieced together, contain portions of seven columns of text. The fourth column, lns. 6–8, mentions the covenant established with David:

ובריתכה הקימותה לדויד להיות כרעי נגיד על עמכה וישב על
כסא ישראל לפניך כול הימים

These lines have attracted little specific attention from scholars.[6] Baillet's analysis of this passage consists mostly of suggested biblical texts that provided the language used in lns. 6–8.[7] But he does make a curious observation about the phrase לפניך כול הימים (lns. 7–8). First, he notes that the words can express presence or permanent service, but then goes on to apply this idea not to the davidic dynasty, but to David himself. He comments, "Quant à la royauté éternelle de David, on en remarquera l'affirmation expresse en 1 M II 57."[8] Baillet

---

[2]M. Baillet, "Un recueil liturgique de Qumrân, grotte 4: 'Les paroles des luminaires'," *RB* 68 (1961) 195–250.

[3]M. Baillet, *Qumran Grotte 4: III (4Q482–4Q520)* (DJD 7; Oxford: Clarendon, 1982) 137–168.

[4]Baillet, DJD 7, 137. There is a reference to Wednesday (f. 3 2:5) and the Sabbath (ff. 1–2 recto 7:4) within the document. Cf. L. H. Schiffman, "The Dead Sea Scrolls and the Early History of Jewish Liturgy," *The Synagogue in Late Antiquity* (ed. L. I. Levine; Philadelphia: American Schools of Oriental Research, 1987) 40–41, who agrees with Baillet's assessment.

[5]Schiffman, "Jewish Liturgy," 41; Flusser, "Psalms, Hymns, and Prayers," 567; see now the thorough study by B. Nitzan, *Qumran Prayer and Religious Poetry* (STDJ 12; Leiden: Brill, 1994) 89–116. See below, for a more detailed discussion of the relationship between 4QDibHam and other Jewish prayers of supplication (*tahanunim*).

[6]See only Baillet's comments in "Un recueil liturgique," 221–222; and in DJD 7, 137–138, 143–145.

[7]Baillet, "Un recueil liturgique," 221–222.

[8]Baillet, "Un recueil liturgique," 222.

offers no further explanation, and unless he means by the "royauté éternelle de David" the davidic dynasty, he appears to be saying that David was conceived of as somehow having an eternal kingship. This, however, is an unlikely hypothesis that is not supported by 1 Macc 2:57.[9] It may be significant then that Baillet's comments cited above do not appear in his notes on this phrase in DJD 7.[10] Nevertheless, Baillet's view should alert us to the fact that these lines, though mentioning the davidic covenant, appear to be focused on David himself. We shall have to take up this observation again below.

On the other hand, 4QDibHam[a] has been cited by J. J. Collins and D. Dimant as evidence for the expectation of a future davidic messiah within the Qumran sect, and perhaps within the "pre-essene" group with which 4QDibHam may also have been associated.[11] G. Vermes in his English translation of 4QDibHam[a] certainly implies such a messianic interpretation when he renders 1/2 4:5–8:

> Thou hast chosen the tribe of Judah and hast established Thy Covenant with David that he might be as a princely shepherd over Thy people and sit before Thee on the throne of Israel for ever.[12]

The question before us therefore is whether in fact 4QDibHam[a] 1/2 4:6–8 reveals an expectation for a davidic messiah or whether this reference to the davidic dynasty tradition has some other function. Without a doubt, the Qumran community, at least during some points in its history, reflected on and anticipated a davidic messianic figure. This is clear from 4QpGen[a], 4QFlor, 4QpIsa[a], and 4QSerek HaMilhamah. Yet this evidence should not lead us to prejudge the meaning of 4QDibHam[a]. One cannot assume a unified messianic expectation at Qumran.[13] Thus, at least for heuristic purposes, the function of the reference to the davidic dynasty tradition in 4QDibHam[a] must be ascertained independently of any general presupposition about davidic messianism at Qumran, based as it is on references to davidic figures in other Qumran documents. Only after an independ-

---

[9]For the treatment of 1 Macc 2:57, see above, pp. 152–159.

[10]Cf. DJD 7, 145; nor do Baillet's comments about the eternal royalty of David comport well with his translation of the sentence: "Il [David] siégea sur le trône d'Israël devant Ta face en permanence," which seems to treat David's rule as a past event.

[11]D. Dimant, "Qumran Sectarian Literature," *Jewish Writings of the Second Temple Period* (CRINT 2:2; Assen: Van Gorcum/Philadelphia: Fortress, 1984) 539 n. 265; Collins, "Messianism," 105. For the pre-essene character of 4QDibHam, see Baillet, DJD 7, 137.

[12]G. Vermes, *The Dead Sea Scrolls in English* (3rd ed.; Sheffield: JSOT Press, 1987) 218; cf. also T. H. Gaster, *The Dead Sea Scriptures* (3rd ed.; Garden City, NY: Anchor Press/Doubleday, 1976) 275, for an even more "messianic" translation.

[13]See M. Smith, "What is Implied by the Variety of Messianic Figures?" *JBL* 78 (1959) 66–72, esp. p. 71; Schürer, *History*, 2:550–554, esp. pp. 551–552, and other literature cited there.

ent analysis of 4QDibHam^a can one attempt to integrate its meaning into the whole of Qumran theology or messianism. It is therefore to this independent analysis we now turn.

The context preceding lns. 6–8 concerns the choosing of Jerusalem, Israel, and the tribe of Judah. Then, lns. 6–8 read:

ובריתכה הקימותה לדויד להיות כרעי נגיד על עמכה וישב על
כסא ישראל לפניך כול הימים

Several interlocking problems of interpretation present themselves in these lines, decisions about which lead to at least three possible readings of this text. We may begin by assessing how the covenant with David is construed here. In the biblical tradition the davidic covenant is a promise made by God to David that his descendants would rule after him perpetually (cf. 2 Sam 7:11–16; Ps 89:3–4,28–37; Jer 33:20–22; cf. also *Pss. Sol.* 17:4). In contrast, in 4QDibHam^a God establishes his covenant with David so that he—David—may be a shepherd prince over Israel.[14] The covenant appears directed toward David, not his descendants. In this case, the next phrase would be understood as the confirmation of God's covenant faithfulness to David in that he sat on the throne of Israel before God all the days, i.e., to the end of his life.[15] According to this reading, the davidic covenant is directed only to the rule of David; the biblical notion that the purpose of the davidic covenant was to established the davidic dynasty is apparently set aside.

Another possible interpretation involves the idea of corporate personality. Thus, when the text says that David would be a shepherd prince over his people, within the context of the davidic covenant, it means that David would rule not only during his lifetime, but would continued to rule in and through his descendants. This then would bring the meaning of lns. 6–7 into harmony with the biblical idea of the davidic covenant, which is always directed toward David's descendants. This reading is certainly possible, but additional issues arise con-

---

[14]Baillet's transcription of the text, which I have used, runs: לדויד להיות כרעי נגיד על עמכה. However, in the word כרעי the כ is marked as doubtful. Baillet believes that it could be a מ. From the photographic plates it is impossible to see any letter at the beginning of the word. If the letter were neither a כ nor a מ, but a ז, and the final letter a ז instead of a י (ז's and י's usually being indistinguishable) then the text would read: "your covenant you established with David that his seed might be a shepherd prince over your people." A ז, however, may be too small of a letter to fit the space between the margin and the ר, although spacing between letters is not always uniform in the document. Since no letter can be identified from the photographic plates, I will continue to rely on Baillet's reading.

[15]The temporal horizon designated by the phrase כול הימים is, like that of עד־עולם, determined by the context. It can mean "lifetime," "a long time," or perpetually, "forever."

cerning it. First, in the Hebrew Bible davidic kings are not characterized as somehow embodying or representing the actual rule of David. Davidic kings were to imitate David, but they were not David ruling.[16] Nevertheless, this difference from the biblical tradition is not in itself a definitive reason against the idea of corporate personality here.

A second matter involves the implications for the immediately following clause—וישב על כסא ישראל לפניך כול הימים. Above, this clause was read as referring to David alone: "And he (David) sat upon the throne of Israel before you all the days."[17] As noted earlier, within the context of David's own rule, the phrase כול הימים would refer to all the days of David, i.e., his lifetime. But if the word David is understood to denote his corporate personality, which includes his descendants, two other readings are possible. On the one hand, it could mean: "And he (David and his descendants) sat upon the throne of Israel before you all the days." In this context, the last phrase כול הימים would presumably refer to the end of the davidic dynasty in 586 BCE, when davidic descendants ceased to sit on the throne. On the other hand, וישב could be understood, not as introducing a new independent clause, but as a continuation of the purpose clause introduced by להיות.[18] The text would then read: "that he (David and his descendants) might sit upon the throne of Israel all the days." In this rendering, כול הימים is openended, and can mean "perpetually" or "forever." This appears to be the interpretation underlying Vermes' translation cited above. It allows for an everlasting davidic covenant and is no doubt the reading adopted by those, like Collins and Dimant, who see in 4QDibHam an expectation for a future davidic messiah.[19]

---

[16]However, a possible analogy to this idea of David's corporate personality would be the concept of a typologically new David, as expressed by Hos 3:5; Jer 30:9; Ezek 34:23–24; 37:24–25.

[17]וישב in all three readings is taken as a converted imperfect. Other options are possible: it could be a non-converted perfect, interpreted as a simple past (completed action), which would not change these first two readings, or it could be a non-converted imperfect which would give it a future sense (incomplete action). However, since וישב is in sequence with הקימותה, a perfect, we are certainly correct in reading it as a converted imperfect. Note too, this perfect/converted imperfect sequence is common in the larger context (cf. אהבתה/ותבחר [lns. 4–5]; ראה/ויביאו [lns. 8,10]).

[18]See E. Kautzsch, *Gesenius' Hebrew Grammar* (2nd Eng. ed.; Oxford: Clarendon, 1910) 352 (para. 114r). R. J. Williams, *Hebrew Syntax: An Outline* (2nd ed.; Toronto: University of Toronto Press, 1976) 34 (para. 182), however, observes that use of the *waw*-consecutive breaks down in later biblical literature, such as Eccl 1:13, where two infinitive constructs are used in a purpose clause (see also, Gen 39:10b; Deut 19:9; 1 Kgs 18:42, for additional examples of two infinitive constructs in a purpose clause).

[19]But even here, one should be cautious about assuming that this mention of the davidic covenant refers to an unconditional eternal covenant with David as reflected in some biblical texts; other conceptions of the davidic covenant as conditional are prominent in the biblical

To summarize, we have before us three viable interpretations of lns. 6–8. Before proceeding, it will be helpful to review these options:

#1 And your covenant you established with David that he might be a shepherd prince over your people; and he sat upon the throne of Israel all the days (of his life).

#2 And your covenant you established with David that he (David and his descendants) might be a shepherd prince over your people; and he (David and his descendants) sat upon the throne of Israel all the days.

#3 And your covenant you established with David that he (David and his descendants) might be a shepherd prince over your people and might sit upon the throne of Israel forever.

Each reading is grammatically possible, but each has a different meaning. The first two options are oriented toward the past: the first to David's own reign; the second to the historical davidic dynasty. This of course is due to the interpretation of וישב as a converted imperfect functioning as a finite verb with a past sense. The third option is oriented toward an open-ended future. This is because וישב is understood as a converted imperfect that continues the purpose clause begun by להיות. To help adjudicate among these three options, we will have to consider the literary context in which these lines occur.

As indicated in the introduction to this section, 4QDibHam represents a collection of communal prayers of supplication for use on specific days of the week. M. R. Lehmann connected 4QDibHam to the Tahanun prayer known from tannaitic sources due to its similarities in "mood, content and vocabulary."[20] In fact, as D. Flusser points out, the prayers in 4QDibHam belong to a genre of prayer common in biblical and early Jewish sources—as well as rabbinic sources—known as *tahanunim* or prayers of supplication.[21] As examples, Flusser cites texts such as Neh 9:6–37, Dan 9:3–19, and Bar 2:6–3:8. [22] These prayers

---

tradition as well (see chap. 2). In lns. 6–8, the covenant is not qualified as conditional or unconditional.

[20]M. R. Lehmann, "A Re-interpretation of 4 Q Dibrê Ham-me²oroth," *RevQ* 5 (1964) 106–110, esp. p. 109; Schiffman, "Jewish Liturgy," 41, rightly criticizes aspects of Lehmann's thesis, yet acknowledges common motifs in 4QDibHam and rabbinic *Tahanun;* Flusser, "Psalms, Hymns, and Prayers," 571, calls 4Q DibHam a prototype for the *Tahanun.*

[21]Flusser, "Psalms, Hymns, and Prayers," 567,571; see also Nitzan, *Qumran Prayer,* 89. The term *tahanunim* derives from Dan 9:3,17.

[22]Flusser, "Psalms, Hymns, and Prayers," 570–573, also cites 3 Macc 2:1–20; 6:1–15; Esth 14:1–19 (LXX); Pr Azar; Sir 36:1–17; Jdt 9; Ezra 9:6–15; various prayers in 1 and 2 Maccabees; and *m. Ta^can.* 2:4–5.

have a basic pattern which combines three elements: 1) supplication for God's help; 2) remembrance of God's saving deeds in the past; 3) repentance and prayer for forgiveness. This pattern is noticeably present throughout 4QDibHam.[23]

The component of special interest for our analysis of 4QDibHam[a] 1/2 4:6–8 and its immediate literary context is the second element mentioned, the remembrance of God's savings deeds in the past.[24] Actually, the historical reminiscences in 4QDibHam[a] and other *tahanunim* encompass more than simply God's saving deeds; they include other acts of God, both blessing and judgment, as well as Israel's deeds of disobedience.[25] In this regard, Neh 9:6–37 presents these historical reminiscences in a pattern that is strikingly parallel to that found in 4QDibHam[a].

Neh 9:6–37 begins with a recital of God's gracious acts toward Israel, including the promise to Abraham, the Exodus and Sinai events, and the settlement in Canaan (vv. 7–25). This section ends with the words, "so they ate, and were filled and became fat (ויאכלו וישבעו וישמינו) and delighted themselves in thy great goodness" (v. 25b).[26] The next section details Israel's sins against God and God's judgment against them (vv. 26–30). But in spite of this, God does not abandon his people: "Nevertheless in thy great mercies thou didst not make an end of them or forsake them (ולא עזבתם); for thou art a merciful God" (v. 31). This then is followed by a plea for mercy in the face of Israel's current distress (vv. 32–37, esp. v. 32). The overall pattern of historical reminiscence, therefore, is: 1) God's gracious acts on Israel's behalf; 2) Israel's sin and God's judgment against it; and 3) God's non-abandonment and continued faithfulness toward Israel. Then, on the basis on this recital of past events, Israel makes its plea in its current distress.

Although the entire literary context of 4QDibHam[a] 1/2 4:6–8 is unavailable due to lacunae in the text, enough of it is preserved to see in 4QDibHam[a] 1/2 4:2–5:18 the pattern of historical reminiscence observed above. First, there is a recital of God's gracious acts toward Israel, including God's choosing of Zion as a resting place, the establishment of his covenant with David, and the revelation of his glory to the nations, who responded by bringing their treasures to Zion, along with the resulting peace and prosperity in Israel (4:2–14). In light of these bless-

---

[23]Flusser, "Psalms, Hymns, and Prayers," 567,570–571. Several of the above cited examples have only the first two elements.

[24]See Nitzan, *Qumran Prayer*, 90–99, on the component of remembrance in prayers of supplication.

[25]Cf. Flusser, "Psalms, Hymns, and Prayers," 567, who also recognizes the wider range of historical reminiscences in 4QDibHam.

[26]Cf. also Deut 31:20.

ings, the text says of Israel: "And they ate, and were filled, and became fat (ויאכלו וישבעו וידשנו) ... " (4:14), the same phrase that capped off the section on God's blessing found in Neh 9:6–37. Secondly, after a lacuna of seven lines (4:15–21), one finds a section on Israel's sin and God's judgment against them (5:1–6). Nevertheless, God does not abandon his people (5:6–14): "But in all this, you did not reject the seed of Jacob and cast away Israel to destruction ... and you did not abandon us (ולוא עזבתנו) among the nations" (5:6–8,10–11). This is followed by a plea to God in the current distress (5:15–18). Thus, not only is the pattern of historical reminiscences outlined above evident in 4QDibHam^a 1/2 4:2–5:18, but as observed, even phrases and terminology are in some cases the same in Neh 9:6–37 and 4QDibHam^a 1/2 4:2–5:18.

Accordingly, if we are correct in the present analysis of the literary structure of 4QDibHam^a 1/2 4:2–5:18, it is clear that 4:6–8—the lines that speak of the davidic covenant—falls within the section of this *tahanun* devoted to historical reminiscences. Thus, the establishment of the covenant with David and David's sitting on the throne are recited as evidence of God's gracious acts toward Israel in the past. It therefore functions as an example of divine blessing, which never-theless failed to evoke a faithful response from Israel. It is not a statement of a continuing expectation for a davidic messianic figure (option #3). To assume that these lines, which simply recount the establishment of a covenant with David, indicate Jewish messianic hopes is gratuitous, particularly in the absence of any clear indication of a unconditional future orientation in 4:6–8.[27] This messianic interpretation is all the more unlikely when it is observed that, when the text of 4QDibHam^a 1/2 5:6–14 speaks about the restoration of Israel, it is in association with adherence to the Sinai covenant; there is no mention of a restored davidic covenant or calls for God to bring forth a new seed of David.

Now, between the first two options reviewed above, both of which are ori-ented toward the past, there is some reason for preferring option #1.[28] This is because 4:6–8 is part of a characterization of a "golden age" in Israel, which also involved the revelation of God's glory to the nations, the bringing of people's treasures to Jerusalem, and peace and blessing in Israel (4:8–13). Interestingly, the language used to describe this "golden age" derives from the biblical descrip-tion of Solomon's reign (1 Kings 4–10). For instance, when 4QDibHam^a 1/2

---

[27]Note again that the alternating pattern of perfect and converted imperfect finite verbs in 4QDibHam^a 1/2 4:2–10 favors taking וישב as a converted imperfect functioning as a finite verb with a past sense: הבתה/ותבחר (lns. 4–5); הקימותה/וישב (lns. 6–7); ראו/ויביאו (lns. 8–10).

[28]The following reason is in addition to the minor objection to option #2 that it must invoke the concept of David's corporate personality, a concept not used in the biblical tradition for describing davidic kings.

4:8–12 says,

> And all the nations saw your glory which you sanctified in the midst of your people Israel and for your great name. And they brought their offerings (מנחתם): silver and gold and precious stones, along with all the treasures of their lands to honor your people and Zion, your holy city, and the house of your splendor,

it echoes 1 Kgs 4:20–5:1 (Eng: 4:20–21), which concerns all the kingdoms from the Euphrates to Egypt bringing their tribute (מנחה) to Jerusalem, and 1 Kgs 10:1–29 (esp. vv. 2,10,22,25), which pertains to the gifts of the Queen of Sheba (vv. 1–10) and indeed those of the whole earth (vv. 24–25). Likewise, 4QDibHam[a] 1/2 4:12–13, "And there was neither adversary nor misfortune" (ואין שטן ופגע רע), is equivalent to 1 Kgs 5:18 (Eng: 5:4) [אין שטן ואין פגע רע].[29] Consequently, if 4:8–12 portrays conditions in the reign of Solomon, then it would not be implausible to interpret the immediately prior lines (4:6–8) as a historical reminiscence referring to the time of David.[30] In this case, option #1 is more probable: the davidic covenant would be focused on David alone and his own rule, its dynastic implications apparently left to the side.

Finally, we must set this reference to the davidic dynasty tradition within its historical context. Baillet dated 4QDibHam[a] to ca. 150 BCE on paleographic grounds.[31] He also associated it with the Hasidim, due to the absence of a sectarian character.[32] While we must reject Baillet's attribution of this document to the Hasidim as speculative, we can agree with his observation about its non-sectarian (i.e., non-Qumranian) character. Indeed, its similarity to other *tahanunim*, in particular Neh 9:6–37, supports the view that 4QDibHam is not distinctively sectarian. Furthermore, evidence that would associate it with any particular social group or sect is lacking. We must assume that 4QDibHam included prayers that were used widely among Jews, including the Jews at Qumran, who wanted to make their pleas before God.

And as we have seen, in *tahanunim* these pleas for mercy were preceded by a recounting of God's past actions with Israel. Specifically, 4QDibHam[a] 1/2 6–8 recalls the blessings of God in the covenant with David, so that he (and perhaps his descendants) might be a prince over Israel. And he did sit on the throne of Israel all of his days—a sign of God's faithfulness. This use of the davidic dynasty

---

[29]Cf. also 1 Kgs 5:5 (Eng: 4:25).

[30]E. G. Chazon, "*4QDibHam*: Liturgy or Literature?" *RevQ* 15 (1991) 448–450, shows that the historical reminiscences in 4QDibHam are in chronological order.

[31]Baillet, DJD 7, 137. Without explanation, Vermes, *DSS in English*, 217, calls this an "exaggeratedly early date."

[32]Baillet, DJD 7, 137.

tradition is not unlike Sir 47:11,22, except here it functions in the context of a daily prayer of supplication. We conclude, therefore, that although Jews at Qumran would later reflect on a davidic messiah who was to come, this was not the purpose of 4QDibHam[a] 1/2 4:6–8.

2. *4QpGen[a] 5:1–7 (4Q252)*

Column five of 4QpGen[a] (formerly 4QPatriarchal Blessings) offers an interpretation of Gen 49:10 that expresses hope for a davidic messiah based on the everlasting validity of the davidic covenant. One of several references to a davidic messiah in Qumran literature, this passage provides important data about how the community at Khirbet Qumran interpreted the davidic dynasty tradition. A full analysis of this text has been impeded, however, by delays in the publication of 4QpGen[a]. Although the portion of 4QpGen[a] that mentions the davidic messiah was included in a preliminary publication in 1956,[33] the entire manuscript became available only when all the previously unpublished Qumran manuscripts were released to the public in 1991.[34] Consequently, analysis of this reference to the davidic dynasty tradition can only now take into account the broader literary context in which it occurs.[35]

---

[33]J. M. Allegro, "Further Messianic References in Qumran Literature," *JBL* 75 (1956) 172–76. H. Stegemann, "Weitere Stücke von 4QpPsalm 37, 4QPatriarchal Blessings, und Hinweis auf eine unedierte Handschrift aus Höhle 4Q mit Exzerpten aus dem Deuteronomium," *RevQ* 6 (1967–9) 211–17, published a transcription of part of another column, but for reasons unknown 4QpGen[a] was omitted from DJD 5, published in 1968 (cf. the comments of J. A. Fitzmyer, review of *Qumran Cave 4: I [4Q158–4Q186]* by John Allegro, *CBQ* 31 [1969] 237). By 1972 J. T. Milik had received custody of the document, stating that he hoped to publish it soon (cf. J. T. Milik, "*Milkî-ṣedeq* et *Milkî-reša[c]*, *JJS* 23 [1972] 138).

[34]Photographs of the scrolls were made available in 1991 in R. H. Eisenman and J. M. Robinson, *A Facsimile Edition of the Dead Sea Scrolls* (2 vols.; Washington, DC: Biblical Archaeology Society, 1991). The present analysis of 4QpGen[a] relies on transparencies of the manuscript provided by the Ancient Biblical Manuscript Center, Claremont, CA. A transcription of 4QpGen[a] is published in B. Z. Wacholder and M. Abegg, ed., *A Preliminary Edition of the Unpublished Dead Sea Scrolls* (2 Fasc.; Washington, DC: Biblical Archaeology Society, 1991–1992) 2:212–215; and in Eisenman and Wise, *Uncovered*, 86–87. 4QpGen[a] has now been reassigned to M. Kister for publication of the official *editio princeps* (see E. Tov, "The Unpublished Qumran Texts from Caves 4 and 11," *JJS* 43 [1992] 114).

[35]The release of the all Qumran texts revealed two other commentaries on Genesis: 4QpGen[b] (4Q253) and 4QpGen[c] (4Q254) [See S. A. Reed, *Dead Sea Scroll Inventory Project: Lists of Documents, Photographs, and Museum Plates* (Fasc. 10; Claremont: Ancient Biblical Manuscript Center, 1992) 19]. However, neither 4QpGen[b] nor 4QpGen[c] contains an interpretation of the blessing of Judah, although 4QpGen[c] preserves portions of the Blessings of Jacob from Gen 49:1–27. Moreover, despite some overlap in subject matter and wording, the three commentaries on Genesis appear to be somewhat different works (4QpGen[a] 2:5–6 overlaps with 4QpGen[c] 1:3–4, but the previous lines are different; 4QpGen[b] 1:4–5 has

4QpGen^a consists of three fragments containing a total of six successive columns of text.[36] Stegemann identified its script as herodian,[37] yielding a date for this manuscript between 30 BCE and 70 CE.[38] Many of the columns are incomplete, but the overall content of 4QpGen^a is nonetheless clear. The author cites and comments on selected passages from the book of Genesis, from Gen 6:3 at the beginning of the document to at least Gen 49:21, the last text cited in the extant portion.[39] Specifically, after an extended interpretation of the flood chronology (Gen 6–9), the author expounds on the curse of Canaan (Gen 9:24–25,27), the age of Terah (Gen 11:24–32), a covenant ceremony with Abraham (Gen 15?), Abraham's dialogue with God about Sodom and Gommorah (Gen 18:22–33), the sacrifice of Isaac (Gen 22), Isaac's sending of Jacob to Mesopotamia for a wife (Gen 28:1–4), Amalek the grandson of Esau (Gen 36:12), and finally the blessing of Jacob's sons (Gen 49:1–27).

This method of commenting on the scriptures has implications for the genre of 4QpGen^a. Although sometimes bordering on biblical paraphrase, such as one finds in *Jubilees*, the *Genesis Apocryphon*, or the Targums, 4QpGen^a nevertheless has affinities with the pesharim.[40] Indeed, the term "pesher" appears in 4:5. In addition, structural features constitutive of Qumran pesharim, such as citation of a biblical text followed by the identification and explanation of some item in the text, are found in 4QpGen^a.[41] Yet 4QpGen^a is to be distinguished from other

---

affinities with 4QpGen^a 2:4 and 4QpGen^c 15:2, but the word ישראל in its prior context [4QpGen^b 1:3] distinguishes 4QpGen^b from the others).

[36]There is no *editio princeps* for 4QpGen^a, and therefore no standardized reference system for fragments and columns. Since the three fragments are related, I will treat them as joined fragments of six columns: frg. 1 contains portions of cols. 1, 2, and the right edge of a part of col. 3; frg. 2 includes portions of the left edge of col. 3 and portions of col. 4; frg. 3 contains portions of cols. 5 and 6.

[37]Stegemann, "Weitere Stücke," 215.

[38]F. M. Cross, *The Ancient Library of Qumran and Modern Biblical Studies* (Garden City, NY: Doubleday, 1958) 88, dates herodian script from 30 BCE to 70 CE; N. Avigad, "The Paleography of the Dead Sea Scrolls and Related Documents," *Aspects of the Dead Sea Scrolls* (2nd ed.; ScrHier IV; Jerusalem: Magna Press, 1965) 72, sets the range from 50 BCE to 70 CE; J. T. Milik, *Ten Years of Discovery in the Wilderness of Judaea* (SBT 26; London: SCM/Naperville, IL: Allenson, 1959) 96 n. 1, dates 4QpGen^a (4QPatrBless) to the first century CE.

[39]It is almost certain that the whole of the Blessing of Jacob was treated in 4QpGen^a, since 4QpGen^a 4:3 introduces this section of the document with the words ברכות יעקוב. Moreover, 4QpGen^c contains citations of Gen 49:15–17,24–26.

[40]For a different assessment, cf. the comments of T. H. Lim, "The Chronology of the Flood Story in a Qumran Text (4Q252)," *JJS* 43 (1992) 295.

[41]For an analysis of the genre of Qumran pesharim, see G. Brooke, "Qumran Pesher: To-

types of Qumran pesharim, namely, from continuous pesharim, which provide a section by section commentary on a single biblical book (e.g., 1QpHab), and from thematic pesharim, which offer an interpretation of various biblical passages from different books centered on a specific theme (e.g., 4QFlor, 11QMelch).[42] Like continuous pesharim 4QpGen[a] is devoted to a single biblical book, but in contrast interprets only selected passages, making no attempt to produce a commentary on the entire book of Genesis.[43]

This interpretive approach raises an interesting question: why did the author choose to explain some passages and not others. One might suppose that the texts selected for comment were chosen on the basis of some theme. In this regard, Stegemann suggested that 4QpGen[a] was a thematic midrash centered around the idea of eschatology, since the phrase באחרית הימים ("in the last days") occurs in 3:2.[44] But Stegemann's suggestion was based on portions of the text found in preliminary publications. In light of the newly published materials, the view that eschatology is the unifying theme of 4QpGen[a] is no longer tenable, because it is clear from the newly released portions that the author takes up topics unrelated to eschatology. In fact, there does not appear to be any single unifying theme behind the author's selection of passages for commentary. We must assume therefore that 4QpGen[a] interprets selected texts in Genesis that addressed assorted issues relevant to the ideology of the Qumran community, including interest in a 360-day solar calendar, explanation of potential discrepancies in the biblical text, and speculation about the last days. Eschatology therefore is one of several themes taken up in 4QpGen[a], not its central focus as Stegemann had thought.[45] Accord-

---

wards the Redefinition of a Genre," *RevQ* 10 (1978–81) 483–503; see also, D. Dimant, "Pesharim, Qumran," *Anchor Bible Dictionary* (6 vols.; ed. D. N. Freedman; New York: Doubleday, 1992) 5:249–250.

[42]See Dimant, "Pesharim," 5:245, who lists four types of pesharim: 1) continuous pesharim; 2) thematic pesharim; 3) isolated pesharim, which involve exposition of one or two verses in a non-pesher work; 4) other pesharim, defined as the use of allusions and sobriquets that imply a certain exposition of a biblical text.

[43]Other Qumran continuous pesharim skip verses, particularly 4QpIsa[c] (cf. M. P. Horgan, *Pesharim: Qumran Interpretations of Biblical Books* [CBQMS 8; Washington, DC: Catholic Biblical Association, 1979] 95, 238), but not to the degree found in 4QpGen[a].

[44]Stegemann, "Weitere Stücke," 213f. Other early suggestions included: a pesher on patriarchal blessings (J. M. Allegro in P. Benoit, "Editing the Manuscript Fragments from Qumran," *BA* 19 [1956] 91) or on Genesis 49 (Y. Yadin, "Some Notes on Commentaries on Genesis xlix and Isaiah, from Qumran Cave 4," *IEJ* 7 [1957] 66).

[45]The Blessing of Jacob was ripe for eschatological speculation, since in Gen 49:1 Jacob is said to tell his sons what will happen to them in the latter days (באחרית הימים). But cf. *Tg.*

ingly, 4QpGen[a] represents a type of pesharim to be distinguished from continuous and thematic pesharim: a commentary on non-continuous verses within a single biblical book.

A detailed analysis of 4QpGen[a] 5:1–7 will be aided at the outset by a transcription and translation of the passage:[46]

Text

ln. 1	ממשל לישראל בהיות יהודה משבט שליט יסור [לוא]
ln. 2	המלכות ברית היא המחקק כי לדויד כסא[47] יושב י]כרת [לוא
ln. 3	צמח הצדק משיח בוא עד הרגלים המה ישראל פי[אל]
ln. 4	אשר עולם דורות עד עמו מלכות ברית נתנה ולזרעו לו כי דויד
ln. 5	שמר ה[ן]התורה עם אנשי היחד כי
ln. 6	] עמי[ם היא כנסת אנשי
ln. 7	] נתן [

Translation

ln. 1 *A ruler shall [not] depart from the tribe of Judah* (Gen 49:10aα): when Israel has
        dominion

ln. 2 one belonging to David who sits the throne [shall not be] cut off, for the *staff* is the
        covenant of kingship;

ln. 3 [the cla]ns of Israel are the *feet. Until* the messiah of righteousness *comes,* the Branch

ln. 4 of David; for to him and to his seed was given the covenant of kingship of his people for
        everlasting generations, who

ln. 5 kept [   ] the Torah with the men of the community; for

ln. 6 [peopl]es this is the assembly of the men of

ln. 7 [   ] gave

The text begins with a lemma that cites the initial phrase of Gen 49:10.[48] This citation differs from the MT in two ways: the word שליט is added and מן is prefixed to שבט instead of יהודה. Thus, 4QpGen[a] interpreted שבט to mean

---

Ps.-J. Gen 49:1 and *Frg. Tg.* Gen 49:1, which specifically state that the Blessing of Jacob should not be understood eschatologically.

[46]The translation is meant to be literal; brackets indicate lacunae or reconstruction; in the translation biblical citations are in italics.

[47]Yadin, "Some Notes," 67, suggests the reading כסא instead of בוא (for בו) as Allegro, "Further Messianic References," 172, had transcribed. Based on the photograph, the second letter is not a ו, but could be a ס, although the leather is cracked and difficult to read. Nevertheless, for sitting on the throne, we would expect עליו, not בו, (cf. for example, Jer 36:30). For יושב כסא without על, see Ps 122:5 (noted by Yadin, "Some Notes," 67).

[48]As is typical, only the first part of the text is cited, the remainder understood.

"ruler," an interpretation attested in the LXX and Targums (LXX = ἄρχων; *Tg. Onqelos* = שׁולטן). Yet the author retained the term שׁבט, but now in the phrase מִשְׁבֵּט יהודה, a move that shifted the meaning of שׁבט from "scepter" to "tribe" and reflects a paraphrase of מיהודה similar to that found in the Targums (*Tg. Onqelos* = מדבית יהודה).[49]

The initial phrase of Gen 49:10 (v. 10aα) is then interpreted as follows: בהיות לישראל ממשל [לוא י]כרת יושב כסא לדויד. The interpretation begins with the temporal phrase "when Israel has dominion," which serves to qualify the author's understanding of this verse. On the one hand, it appears to be an attempt to explain why there were no rulers belonging to David after the exile and up to the author's time: Israel did not have dominion. On the other, it indicates the time when a davidic king would again sit upon the throne perpetually: when Israel gained dominion. But when would Israel achieve this dominion?

The key to answering this question is found by relating the reference to Israel's dominion in 4QpGen[a] to similar ideas in the *War Scroll*.[50] Specifically, 1QM 1:5 and 17:7–8 assert that Israel would achieve dominion at the time of the annihilation of their enemies in the final eschatological battle between the Sons of Light and the Sons of Darkness.[51] It follows then that according to 4QpGen[a] this too would be the time when a davidic king would sit upon the throne, since Israel would at last have dominion.[52] This timetable would not preclude a role for a davidic figure prior to this eschatological victory, but asserts that it would be from that time on that a davidic king would not be cut off from the throne.

After this qualifying phrase, the author explains Gen 49:10aα with the words [לוא י]כרת יושב כסא לדויד, a close paraphrase of Jer 33:17 and 1 Kgs 2:4; 8:25; 9:5. The phrase יושב כסא designates a king, and לדויד modifies יושב.[53]

---

[49]Cf. N. Wieder, "Notes on the New Documents from the Fourth Cave of Qumran," *JJS* 7 (1956) 72 n. 9.

[50]Yadin, "Some Notes," 67.

[51]Referring to the destruction of Israel's enemies in the eschatological war, 1QM 1:5 reads: ["That shall be] ... an appointed time of dominion for all men of his [God's] lot" (וקץ ממשל לכול אנשי גורלו), and 1QM 17:8 states that the purpose of the war is "to raise ... the dominion of Israel (ממשלת ישראל) above all flesh" (cf. Y. Yadin, *The Scroll of the War of the Sons of Light Against the Sons of Darkness* [Oxford: Oxford University Press, 1962] 258, for translation).

[52]D. Schwartz, "The Messianic Departure from Judah (4Q Patriarchal Blessings)," *TZ* 37 (1981) 257–66, objected to seeing in בהיות a reference to the future, claiming instead that Israel's dominion referred to the present reign of apostate Jews whom the author called "Israel." Yet "Israel" is used in a positive sense in 4QpGen[a] 5:3 and in the phrase "dominion of Israel" in 1QM 17:8 (see previous note).

[53]See לדויד in Jer 33:17; 1 Kgs 2:4; 8:25; 9:5. When דויד modifies כסא, it is in construct (cf. Jer 36:30). The throne here is the throne of Israel, as in the texts cited above.

The point here is clear: once Israel gains dominion, a davidic king will reign perpetually.

This reading of v. 10aα is then supported by explaining the meaning of terms in v. 10aβ: כי המחקק היא ברית המלכות [אל]פי ישראל המה הרגלים. The interpretation of המחקק as a term for royal power is well attested in Second Temple texts,[54] although the specific reference to the "covenant of kingship" is a distinctive construal of המחקק.[55] ברית המלכות clearly refers to the davidic covenant (cf. esp. 2 Sam 23:5; Ps 89:4). רגלים is decoded as a reference to אלפי ישראל.[56] Eisenman and Wise translated this phrase "leaders of Israel," apparently reading אַלְפֵי.[57] This reading, however, has little to commend to it, since the resulting phrase אַלְפֵי ישראל is uncharacteristic of Qumran texts.[58] Rather אלפי ישראל refers to the organizational structure of an ideal Israel, modeled on Pentateuchal accounts of ancient Israel's wilderness journey and now represented in the Qumran community itself, for whom אפלים designated both social units and military units.[59] Thus, the covenant of davidic kingship would not be cut off

---

[54] See G. Vermes, *Scripture and Tradition in Judaism* (Studia Post-Biblica 4; Leiden: Brill, 1973) 49–55.

[55] The phrase ברית המלכות is not found in the MT, but is similar to the expression in Sir 47:11 for the davidic covenant (חקת מלכת; cf. LXX = διαθήκην βασιλέων) and is analogous to phrases used to describe the priestly covenant in Neh 13:29 (ברית הכהנה) and 1 Macc 2:54 (διαθήκην ἱερωσύνης).

[56] Yadin, "Some Notes," 67, had suggested that רגלים be read as דגלים ("banners"), arguing that 1) this reading was possible, since the resh and dalet in Qumran texts look similar; 2) that the author's biblical text read דגלים, as in the Samaritan Pentateuch; and 3) it would explain why the term in question would be identified with אלפי ישראל, since in the *War Scroll* דגלים is equated with אלפים. But Yadin's reading cannot be sustained, most of all, because the photograph clearly reveals a resh, not a dalet: The letter in question lacks a small stroke above the right edge of the horizontal stroke, this being the mark that distinguishes the dalet from the resh (for the contrast between the resh and dalet, see the word דורות in ln. 4). Moreover, the logic of the identification could be explained otherwise, since the author may have interpreted רגלים as "descendants," as the Targums do (see Deut 28:57)—descendants that would comprise the clans of Israel. In addition, a survey of other pesharim quickly reveals that the Qumran interpretation of terms in a biblical text did not need a discernible logic.

[57] Eisenman and Wise, *Uncovered*, 89.

[58] Neither אַלְפֵי nor the phrase אַלְפֵי ישראל appear among Qumran texts.

[59] For social units, see 1QS 2:21, where during assembly, after the priests and Levites entered, it says: "And all the people shall enter, third in order, one after another according to (their) thousands (לאלפים), hundreds, fifties, and tens ... " (Cf. also CD 13:1). For military units, see 1QM 5:3: "The formation shall be composed of units of a thousand men" (translation, Yadin, *War Scroll*, 278) [Cf. also 1QM 4:1,2; 6:8; 12:4; 1QSb 3:7; 11QTemple 57:4; 58:4]. Yadin, *War Scroll*, 60,53, has shown that community organization and military organization were virtually identical among the sectarians at Qumran.

from an ideal Israel, which consisted of the Qumran community and whoever might join them.

4QpGen[a] goes on to give the meaning of the difficult phrase in Gen 49:10bα, עד כי־יבא שילה, as עד בוא משיה הצדק צמח דויד.[60] Here שילה is taken as a designation for the messiah, an interpretation also attested in the Targums and rabbinic literature.[61] In particular, 4QpGen[a] describes the figure as a messiah of righteousness and as the Branch of David (צמח דויד), a title derived from Jer 23:5–6 and 33:15–17. This specific designation is no accident, however, since it was undoubtedly chosen because of its association with the concept of righteousness: both passages from Jeremiah call the davidic figure a righteous branch (צמח צדיק); both say he will execute righteousness in the land; and both give his name as "the Lord is our righteousness." Nevertheless, aside from righteousness little description of the davidic messiah is offered, at least in the extant portions of the text.

One further issue associated with this line in 4QpGen[a] is how to understand the word עד. The basic meaning of עד is "up to" or "until" some limit. Yet in Gen 49:10, עד is not meant to express an absolute limit, claiming that when Shiloh comes (however interpreted) rule would then be cut off from Judah.[62] Instead here עד specifies a relative limit, after which the prior conditions continue to obtain.[63] In other words, rule would remain with the tribe of Judah until it was somehow secured by the coming of Shiloh. Matters in 4QpGen[a] are more complicated, however. Since the author was well aware that davidic kingship had been cut off after the exile, he therefore asserted that it would not be reestablished until Israel had dominion (ln. 1). But now the time of the re-establishment of davidic kingship and the coming of the messiah would be the same, leaving no room for some prior state as implied by the word "until."

In response to this problem, D. Schwartz argued that the time of Israel's dominion referred to the time when the Jewish opponents of the Qumran sect (here called "Israel") were in control, and accordingly, it was during this time that the davidic line would be kept alive (i.e., not cut off) within the Qumran com-

---

[60]See above, pp. 23–24, for a brief summary of possible meanings of Gen 49:10.

[61]See *Tg. Onqelos, Tg. Neophiti, Tg. Pseudo-Jonathan,* and *Fragmentary Targum.* For rabbinic references, see B. Grossfeld, *The Targum Onkelos to Genesis* (Aramaic Bible 6; Wilmington, DE: Glazier, 1988) 163 n. 25. שילה was understood to mean "to whom it (the kingdom) belongs" (see *Tg. Onqelos* and *Fragmentary Tg.*).

[62]Construing עד to denote an absolute limit was behind patristic theories of supercessionism in that the scepter remained with Judah (the Jews) until it was given to Jesus the Christ, to whom it belonged (see Wieder, "Notes," 73).

[63]See Kautzsch, *Gesenius' Hebrew Grammar*, 503, para. 164*f.*

munity *until* the davidic messiah appeared at the end of days.[64] But his view cannot be sustained, since in 1QM 17:8 the dominion of Israel is understood positively,[65] and the text does not speak of the continuation of the davidic line, but of a davidic king sitting on the throne, a state of affairs for which there is no evidence at Qumran. Vander Woude's suggestion that in 4QpGen[a] 5:3 עד must be taken to mean "when" is certainly correct.[66] Thus, the overall sense of the commentary is: "A davidic king will not be cut off *when* the messiah of righteousness, the Branch of David comes."

This prediction of a coming davidic messiah is then supported by citing the gift of an everlasting covenant of kingship over the people to David and his descendants, a clear reference to the davidic covenant as expressed in 2 Sam 7:11–16 and Ps 89:4–5,20–38. The remainder of the column is riddled with lacunae and is difficult to interpret with any certainty.[67] For ln. 5, Allegro suggested adding דורש before התורה.[68] This is possible and would be similar to 4QFlor 1:11 where the Interpreter of the Law is mentioned in conjunction with the davidic messiah, but this reconstruction cannot be used with certainty. More likely, the last word in the lacuna in ln. 6 is עמים from Gen 49:10b, which is interpreted as the כנסת אנשי, probably a reference to the Qumran community. It is impossible, however, to be sure just how the assembly of men is related to the davidic messiah in 4QpGen[a].[69]

The complete interpretation of Gen 49:10 with the appropriate interpretive substitute meanings would therefore read as follows:

> When Israel has dominion, one belonging to David who sits the throne shall not be cut off, nor the covenant of kingship from among the clans of Israel, when the messiah of righteousness, the Branch of David, comes, because to him and his seed was given the covenant of kingship over his people for everlasting generations.

---

[64] Schwartz, "Messianic Departure," 260–263.

[65] See above, n. 52. In addition, "Israel" refers to the Qumran community in 4QpGen[a] 5:3.

[66] A. S. van der Woude, *Die messianischen Vorstellungen der Gemeinde von Qumran* (Assen: Van Gorcum, 1957) 170 n. 8. Van der Woude offers a lexical justification for taking עד as "when," a justification challenged by Schwartz ("Messianic Departure," 259). Yet the meaning of עד in 4QpGen[a] 5:3 does not depend on a lexical justification, but on the new midrashic context.

[67] For instance, the antecedent of אשר at the end of ln. 4 could be David, his people, or the covenant of kingship.

[68] Allegro, "Further Messianic References," 175.

[69] The MT of Gen 49:10bβ reads: ולו יקהת עמים ("And to him is the obedience of the peoples."); the LXX runs: καὶ αὐτὸς προσδοκία ἐθνῶν ("And he is the expectation of the peoples."); in rabbinic literature, יקהת was understood as יתקהת, so that "to him is the assembly of the people" (cf. van der Woude, *Vorstellungen*, 170f).

Thus, in 4QpGen^a, Gen 49:10 was read in light of the biblical tradition of a everlasting covenant of kingship to David and his seed, and particularly influenced by the language of Jer 23:5–6; 33:15–17. The re-establishment of davidic kingship would occur when Israel achieved dominion in the eschatological war against the Sons of Darkness, after which time the davidic king would rule over Israel never to be cut off again. There is little description of the davidic messiah, except to emphasize that he would be characterized by righteousness.

Turning now to the question of how this passage about the davidic messiah functioned, we may observe that interpreters have seen a polemical interest at work in the affirmation of a coming davidic king. This coming messiah of righteousness would undoubtedly pose a challenge to any currently reigning king. Yet going on to identify some particular ruler or rulers as the object of the text's polemic is a more speculative undertaking, made difficult on the one hand by the potentially multivalent nature of any reference, and on the other, by uncertainties about the date of composition of 4QpGen^a. Nonetheless, enough evidence exists to set forth some probable conclusions.

As to the date of composition of 4QpGen^a, Qumran biblical commentaries are widely believed to have been composed late in the history of the sect with most of the manuscripts representing autographs of the document.[70] Moreover, as stated above, the manuscript of 4QpGen^a dates from the herodian period (ca. 30 BCE to 70 CE). If this is the date of its composition, it is unlikely that 4QpGen^a 5:1–7 was aimed at Hasmonean priest-kings, as Vander Woude and Vermes have suggested.[71] Instead one must seek an unrighteous king standing over against the coming davidic messiah sometime between 30 BCE and 70 CE. Consequently, the most likely candidates are herodian kings or the king of the Kittim, the Roman emperor.

In this regard, Stegemann suggested that col. 4 of 4QpGen^a might provide a clue for identifying the object of 4QpGen^a's polemic.[72] Column 4, lns. 1–3 present an interpretation of Gen 36:12, which reads as follows:

---

[70]See Cross, *Ancient Library*, 84–85; Milik, *Ten Years*, 41; P. R. Davies, *Behind the Essenes* (BJS 94; Atlanta: Scholars Press, 1987) 26. Cross notes that biblical commentaries appear in only one manuscript, leading to the conclusion that the manuscripts of these commentaries are likely autographs. However, there may be exceptions to this (see Dimant, "Pesharim," 5:245). In any case, no biblical commentary comes from a manuscript prior to the herodian period.

[71]Van der Woude, *Vorstellungen*, 171; Vermes, *DSS in English*, 260.

[72]Stegemann, "Weitere Stücke," 214–17. Stegemann's argument was based on only ln. 1.

תמנע היתה פילגש לאליפז בן עשׂיו ותלד לו את עמלק הוא
אשר הכ[ן]הון] שאול כאשר דבר למושה באחרית הימים תמחה
את זכר עמלק מתחת השמים

And Timna was the concubine of Eliphaz son of Esau and she bore for him
Amalek. This is whom Saul sm[ote], according to the word of Moses: in the last
days you will blot out the remembrance of Amalek from under heaven.

After citing Gen 36:12, the text identifies Amalek as the one defeated by Saul
(1 Sam 15:1–9) in accordance with the words of Moses in Deut 25:19 (cf. also Ex
17:14). But whereas Moses told the Israelites to blot out Amalek when they had
rest from their enemies in the land of their inheritance, 4QpGen[a] states that it
should be done in the last days (באחרית הימים). Thus, 4QpGen[a] appears to be
an early example of the tradition, attested in both Jewish and Christian sources,
that numbered Amalek among Israel's eschatological enemies.[73] But who would
represent Amalek in the last days?

Stegemann observed that the reference to Amalek mentions his descent from
Esau, which is another name for Edom.[74] He then reasoned that this text could be
aimed at Herod the Great, since it was his Idumean descent that made him illegitimate to many Jews.[75] He writes:

> Im Rahmen des eschatologischen Midrasch 4Q Patriarchal Blessings würde das
> Zitat von Genesis 36,12 dann belegen, dass das von Esau (=Edom) abstam-
> mende und somit <<illegitime>> herodianische Königtum einmal <<am Ende
> der Tage>> (vergleiche באחרית הימים in Zeile 2 des neuen Fragments) ver-
> nichtet wird und das <<legitime>> Königtum eines Davididen aus dem Hause
> des Jakob-(=Israel) Sohnes 'Juda' an seine Stelle träte.[76]

Stegemann's hypothesis that Herod the Great represented the eschatological
enemy of Israel, Amalek, and was therefore the unrighteous king against which

---

[73]For Amalek as the eschatological enemy of Israel, see in Jewish sources *T. Sim.* 6:3; *Frg.*
Tg. Num 24:20; *Mek.* Ex 17:16; and in Christian sources, *Barn.* 12:9; *Just. Dial.* 49:7f.

[74]Stegemann, "Weitere Stücke," 214.

[75]Stegemann, "Weitere Stücke," 214. For Jewish opposition to Herod, cf. *Ant.* 14.403–405,
where Herod's kingship is questioned because he was a commoner and an Idumean, that is, a
half-Jew; *Ant.* 14.9 reports that Herod supported the fiction that his family belonged to the
leading Jews who returned from the Babylonian exile. Cf. also *Ant.* 15.373–374, for Josephus'
report that an Essene prophet predicted Herod's rise to kingship while he was still a boy,
because he was found worthy of this by God. This story is probably herodian propaganda
aimed at legitimating his disputed claim to the Jewish throne.

[76]Stegemann, "Weitere Stücke," 215. We should note that this thesis makes *Ant.*
15.373–374 (see previous note) especially interesting because it involves an Essene prophet
who supposedly legitimated Herod's royal position, while 4QpGen[a] may be an Essene attempt
to undermine herodian kingship.

the davidic messiah would stand is certainly plausible.[77] We might observe too that his theory comports with Josephus' report in *Ant.* 15.371 that Essenes would not take an oath of loyalty to Herod. Moreover, perhaps Stegemann's hypothesis should not be limited to Herod the Great, but extended to include herodian kings in general. Yet Stegemann himself admitted that the absence of any evidence from the Second Temple period identifying Herod directly with Amalek posed a problem for his interpretation.[78] He supposed that the identification of Herod with Amalek in 4QpGen[a] represented a distinctive Qumran version of the broader Jewish opposition to Herod.

On the other hand, Amalek could be a cipher for the Romans, or more precisely their king. For, if in 4QpGen[a] Amalek represents the eschatological enemy of Israel, according to the *War Scroll* during the herodian period this eschatological enemy was the Kittim, who were identified as the Romans at Qumran. Indeed, several times the *War Scroll* speaks about destroying the Kittim without remnant, a fate not unlike that predicted for Amalek by Moses in Deut 25:19.[79] Moreover, as 4QpGen[a] indicates, davidic kingship would be established at the time of the eschatological victory against the Kittim. In fact, the newly released document 4QSerek HaMilhamah reveals that the davidic messiah seems to have a direct role in the execution of the king of the Kittim.[80] All this suggests that Amalek may be a pseudonym for the Romans whose unrighteous king would be displaced at the coming of the messiah of righteousness, the Branch of David.[81]

Admittedly, the evidence for either herodian kings or the king of the Kittim as the object of the polemic in 4QpGen[a] is too scanty to put forward firm conclusions. Either is plausible, neither certain. Moreover, the allusive nature of these references may preclude finding a single unrighteous king. Undoubtedly, the Qumran community rejected herodian client kings and their Roman suzerains. That Gen 36:12 expressed a connection between Edom and Amalek may have been a convenient text for the author of 4QpGen[a] to condemn herodian kings of Idumean descent and the king of the Kittim, their eschatological enemy.[82]

---

[77]Matthew 2 may reflect the same tension between a davidic figure—the baby Jesus—and Herod; see Stegemann, "Weitere Stücke," 217.

[78]Nevertheless, according to Josephus (*Ant.* 2:6), Amalek was the name of a province in Idumea in his day.

[79]See 1QM 1:6; 5:10; 18:2–3.

[80]See below, p. 209. For the king of the Kittim, see 1QM 15:2.

[81]For a similar conflict between a Jewish messianic figure, Jesus, and the Roman emperor, see John 19:12–15.

[82]That Herod and the Romans would have been perceived as closely connected is clear from Josephus (*Ant.* 17.41–43), where it is reported that Herod required an oath of loyalty to Caesar and to his government. Interestingly a groups of Jews, Pharisees, committed to ancestral

In any case, we evidently have another example of the concept of a davidic messiah being used polemically to challenge the legitimacy of a reigning king. In the case of *Pss. Sol.* 17, I argued that the davidic dynasty tradition was used to oppose Hasmonean kings. Here in 4QpGen[a] it may have been used against herodian or Roman kings. But the strategy of opposition is essentially the same: these kings were declared illegitimate because their claim to royal office lacked any basis in the biblical traditions of Israel. Thus, once evoked as a means of undermining a non-davidic monarch in the Hasmonean era, the davidic dynasty tradition could be reappropriated for use against any non-davidic monarch.

Finally, the motivation for opposing herodian or Roman kings would be their unrighteousness. Herod's impiety and corruption of ancestral customs is amply attested in Josephus,[83] and one need only recall the emperor cult to demonstrate Roman irreverence in the eyes of the Jews. In contrast to these illegitimate royal figures, the Branch of David would be a monarch marked by righteousness. Nevertheless, as noted above, this is all we are told about the davidic messiah; aside from the mention of righteousness, no other attributes are ascribed to him in 4QpGen[a].

3. *4QFlorilegium 1:10–13 (4Q174)*

4QFlorilegium offers commentary on a number of scriptural passages, commentary devoted to illuminating circumstances in the last days. Of interest for the present study is 4QFlor 1:10–13, which through its interpretation of the dynastic oracle in 2 Sam 7:11–14 affirms that the Branch of David will arise in Zion at the end times. In the analysis of this text, our aim will be to understand its characterization of the davidic figure and its intention within its socio-historical context.

4QFlor consists of 26 fragments, representing at least five columns of text.[84]

---

customs and obedience to the Law refused to take this oath, predicting instead the downfall of Herod and his house. Noteworthy too is the account in *Jub.* 37:10 of the war between the sons of Esau and the sons of Jacob, where a later hand has added the Kittim to the list of mercenaries hired by the sons of Esau (cf. Yadin, *War Scroll*, 24 n. 8).

[83]*Ant.* 15.267,281; 17.150,191,304–310. On the injustice of Herod's son Archelaus, cf. *Ant.* 17.312–314.

[84]For *editio princeps*, see J. M. Allegro with A. A. Anderson, *Qumran Cave 4: I (4Q158–4Q186)* (DJD 5; Oxford: Clarendon Press, 1968), to be used with J. Strugnell, "Notes en marge du volume V des 'Discoveries in the Judean Desert of Jordan'," *RevQ* 26 (1970) 163–276. The text of 4QFlor 1:10–13 with slightly different reconstructions can be found in G. J. Brooke, *Exegesis at Qumran: 4QFlorilegium in its Jewish Context* (JSOTSup 29; Sheffield: JSOT Press, 1985) 87; and D. Dimant, "*4QFlorilegium* and the Idea of the Community as Temple," *Hellenica et Judaica* (ed. A. Caquot, M. Hadas-Lebel, and J. Riaud; Leuven-Paris: Peeters, 1986) 166–167.

Although many of the fragments are small pieces of parchment containing only a few letters, frgs. 1–3, which contain a midrash on 2 Sam 7:10–14 and Psalms 1 and 2, are relatively well-preserved. Other fragments appear to represent an interpretation of portions of Deuteronomy 33. The genre of 4QFlor is thematic pesharim, i.e., an interpretation of a collection of biblical verses from various books linked by a common theme.[85] Thus, while not devoted to a single biblical book, the style of the commentary, involving citation, identification, and explanation, is the same found in the continuous pesharim.[86] This literary form, as well as its distinctive ideological content, indicates that the provenance of 4QFlor is the community at Khirbet Qumran. The date for the composition of this document can be set at the end of the first century BCE or the first century CE. This is based on the script used in this document—early herodian formal script with some semiformal rustic elements,[87] which Cross dated between 30–1 BCE.[88] As noted earlier, since most of the pesharim are believed to be autographs, the date of the document would be the same as the manuscript. In light of additional factors, Brooke has argued for a slightly later date for this text, sometime in the first century CE.[89]

Before turning to an analysis of 4QFlor 1:10–13, we must consider the broader context in which these lines occur. The extant portion of the manuscript begins with a pesher on 2 Sam 7:10b–11aα (1:1–6). While the precise meaning of this passage is matter of debate, its general thrust is clear.[90] By linking the lemma text to Ex 15:17b–18, the author sets forth his expectation for an eschatological sanctuary, established by God and marked by purity and divine glory. This is followed by an explication of 2 Sam 7:11aβ in which the rest from enemies promised to David is taken as a pledge to give the Sons of Light rest from the entrapments of the Sons of Belial (1:7–9). Next comes the citation and interpre-

---

[85]Dimant, "Pesharim," 5:247; Brooke, *Exegesis at Qumran*, 141, prefers the generic name Qumran midrash, rather than pesher.

[86]On this style of commentary in Qumran pesharim, see Brooke, "Qumran Pesher," 494–501.

[87]Strugnell, "Notes," 177.

[88]F. M. Cross, "The Development of the Jewish Scripts," *The Bible and the Ancient Near East* (ed. G. E. Wright; Garden City, NY: Anchor Books/Doubleday, 1965) 176; see 224ff for a description of this script.

[89]Brooke, *Exegesis at Qumran*, 217, argues that on the basis of paleography, archaeology, and style, a first century CE date is preferred, its contents suggesting the second or third quarter of the first century CE; cf. also Milik, *Ten Years*, 96 n. 1, who opts for a first century CE date.

[90]For a recent discussion of these lines, see Brooke, *Exegesis at Qumran*, 178–193; Dimant, "Community as Temple," *passim*; M. O. Wise, "4QFlorilegium and the Temple of Adam," *RevQ* 15 (1991–1992) 103–132.

tation of 2 Sam 7:11b–14 (1:10–13). After this, in a midrash on Psalms 1 and 2, the author identifies the Qumran sectarians as the faithful and upright remnant of Israel (1:14–17), who in conflict with the Kittim and the Sons of Belial will pass through a period of refining in the last days (1:18–2:4).

What each section of this document has in common is an interest in the circumstances that will obtain in the last days.[91] The phrase "the last days" (אחרית הימים) occurs repeatedly, appearing in each major part of the text (1:2,12,15,19). Accordingly, each part describes some facet of the eschatological situation: the sanctuary of the Lord (1:1–6), rest from the Sons of Belial (1:7–9), human leadership (1:10–13), the character of the faithful remnant (1:14–17), and the time of refining (1:18–2:4). With this context in mind we may now turn to a detailed study of 4QFlor 1:10–13.

The text and translation of 4QFlor 1:10–13 run as follows:

Text

ln. 10　[והג]יד לכה יהוה כיא בית יבנה לכה והקימותי את זרעכה
　　　　אחריכה והכינותי את כסא ממלכתו

ln. 11　[לעו]לם אני אהיה לוא לאב והוא יהיה לי לבן הואה צמח דויד
　　　　העומד עם דורש התורה אשר

ln. 12　[יקום] בצי[ון ב]אחרית הימים כאשר כתוב והקימותי את סוכת
　　　　דויד הנופלת הואה סוכת

ln. 13　דויד הנופל[ת א]שר יעמוד להושיע את ישראל

Translation

ln. 10　*And the Lord [decla]res to you that he will build you a house. And I will raise up*
　　　　your seed after you, and I will establish the throne of his kingdom

ln. 11　*[for]ever. I will be to him a father, and he will be to me a son* (2 Sam 7:11b–14a):
　　　　this is the Branch of David who will stand with the Interpreter of the Law, who

ln. 12　[will arise] in Zi[on in] the last days, as it is written, *And I will raise up the booth of*
　　　　David which is fallen (Amos 9:11a): he is the branch of

ln. 13　David which was fallen, who will take office to save Israel.

There is little question about the restoration of lns. 10–13 except for the first word in ln. 12. Allegro proposed no reconstruction for this lacuna,[92] while Brooke argued for ימשול.[93] Strugnell restored יקום, claiming that the verb in the

---

[91]Brooke, *Exegesis at Qumran*, 144; Dimant, "Community as Temple," 181.

[92]Allegro, "Further Messianic References," 176.

[93]Brooke, *Exegesis at Qumran*, 113–114, who also cites van der Woude, Dupont-Sommer and Vermes.

pesher would parallel והקימותי in the lemma.[94] More decisive for the restoration יקום, however, is its use in the supporting biblical citation from Amos 9:11.[95] In fact, since the Hiphil form of קום occurs in 2 Sam 7:12 and Amos 9:11, there is merit in Dimant's suggestion that the lacuna could be filled with יקים, with God as subject, thereby emphasizing the divine action in raising up the davidic messiah.[96] But against this is the fact that the Branch of David, not God, is the subject of the participle העומד in ln. 11. Consequently, I have restored יקום at the beginning of ln. 12.

The structure of this passage is clear: 2 Sam 7:11b–14a is quoted, although with significant omissions; an identification is made ("this is the Branch ... Law"); and an explanation is offered ("who will arise ... days"). This explanation is supported by the citation of Amos 9:11a, which in turn is followed by an identification ("he is the booth ... fallen") and explanation ("who will take ... Israel").[97]

Turning first to the citation of 2 Sam 7:11b–14a, one sees that portions of the MT are omitted. Missing from the quotation are phrases stating that: 1) God will raise up David's seed when his days are fulfilled and he lies with his fathers; 2) this offspring will come from David's own body; and 3) this offspring will build a temple for God's name. The author of 4QFlor has therefore edited the scriptural passage to put before the reader only those portions of the text appropriate for his point.[98] The specific motivation for these omissions becomes evident when it is observed that in 2 Sam 7:11b–14, these phrases serve to anchor the dynastic promise to the time of David's immediate successor Solomon, who indeed came from David's own body and after David's death was raised up as king and built the temple. Without these phrases the dynastic promise is freed from the moorings of its historical fulfillment so that it directly addresses the eschatological situation, which is the central concern of the author.[99] Thus, we are told only that the Lord will build David a house and raise up David's seed after him to establish the throne of his kingdom forever and that the Lord will be a father to him and he a son to the Lord.

---

[94]Strugnell, "Notes," 221; cf. also Y. Yadin, "A Midrash on 2 Sam. vii and Ps. i–ii (4Q Florilegium)," *IEJ* 9 (1959) 97.

[95]Dimant, "Community as Temple," 169.

[96]Dimant, "Community as Temple," 169,183–184.

[97]Cf. Brooke, *Exegesis at Qumran*, 138.

[98]Brooke, *Exegesis at Qumran*, 111–112, claims these omissions result from intentional and creative use of homoeoteleuton and offers specific reasons for their omission.

[99]Brooke, *Exegesis at Qumran*, 163. Also, this may explain why the author of 4QFlor stopped short of citing 2 Sam 7:15.

Then, the author identifies this seed of David (זרעכה) as the Branch of David (צמח דויד) who will arise in the last days (lns. 11–12). The title צמח דויד, derived from Jer 23:5; 33:15, is the same designation used for the davidic figure in 4QpGen[a] and 4QSerek HaMilhamah.[100] Initially, two phrases describe the activity of this figure. First, it is said that he will stand with the Interpreter of the Law (ln. 11), a title used in CD 6:7 and 7:18 to refer to a historical leader of the community.[101] In 4QFlor, however, the Interpreter of the Law is an eschatological figure. Moreover, in the view of most scholars this eschatological Interpreter of the Law is priestly in character, probably a priestly messiah.[102] What is striking here, therefore, is the unexpected importation of a priestly figure into a context which speaks only about a royal davidic figure. This undoubtedly functions to relativize the importance of the davidic king. Yet this is consistent with a general lack of emphasis on the royal messiah in 4QFlor. For instance, in the interpretation of Ps 2:1–2 (lns. 18ff)—a passage brimming with royal messianic potential—the Branch of David is not mentioned. In addition, later in 4QFlor (frgs. 6–7), in a midrash on Deuteronomy 33, the role of the priestly figure is expanded, possibly as a counter-balance to talk of the royal messiah in 1:10–13.[103] A second activity attributed to the Branch of David is that he will arise in Zion in the last days. Thus, although not describing the specific role of the davidic messiah, we do learn that he will emerge and presumably have some role in Jerusalem. But, if our reconstruction of the lacuna at the beginning of ln. 12 is correct, 4QFlor does not assert that he will rule from there.

The author's interpretation of 2 Sam 7:11b–14 is then supported by an appeal to Amos 9:11a, which states that God will raise up the fallen booth of David (סכת דויד).[104] On the one hand, the connection between Amos 9:11a and 2 Sam 7:11b–14 is based on the presence of the verb קום in both texts.[105] On the other, Amos 9:11a serves to confirm the author's exegesis of 2 Sam 7:11b–14 through a

---

[100]It is almost certainly to be restored as the name of the davidic messiah in 4QpIsa[a] as well (see below, p. 201).

[101]Dimant, "Community as Temple," 183. The Interpreter of the Law in CD is often identified with the Teacher of Righteousness (cf. J. J. Collins, "Was the Dead Sea Sect an Apocalyptic Movement," *Archaeology and History in the Dead Sea Scrolls* [JSPSup 8; ed. L. H. Schiffman; Sheffield: JSOT Press, 1990] 40).

[102]Brooke, *Exegesis at Qumran*, 199–205, esp. p. 202 n. 348; Caquot, "Messianisme," 244; Dimant, "Community as Temple," 183.

[103]Brooke, *Exegesis at Qumran*, 159f.

[104]Cf., however, CD 7:16–18, where Amos 9:11 is interpreted in an entirely different manner that does not involve davidic messianism.

[105]The MT of Amos 9:11a reads אקים, but 4QFlor cites והקימותי, which is identical to the verb form used in 2 Sam 7:12.

creative reading of the term סכת. While the MT reads סֻכַּת [plene = סוּכַּת] ("booth"), the author of 4QFlor read סוֹכַת ("branch"), so that Amos 9:11a asserts that God will raise up the branch of David (סוֹכַת דיוד) that was fallen, thus substantiating the author's claim that 2 Sam 7:11–14 taught that God would raise up the eschatological Branch of David (צמח דויד).[106]

Finally, in ln. 13 the role to be fulfilled by the Branch of David is stated: יעמוד להושיע את ישראל.[107] Here, as Brooke notes, יעמוד can be taken in the sense of "to take office."[108] Moreover, the purpose for his taking office is "to save Israel." Although the nature of this salvation is not explained, based on the use of ישע elsewhere in Qumran literature, we may suppose it means that the Branch of David will deliver Israel from its enemies.[109] Specifically, when not used idiomatically or about individual persons, ישע is employed in contexts declaring God's deliverance of his people from their enemies.[110] In 1QM 10:4, within a biblical citation from Deut 20:2–4, it says, "for your God goes with you, to fight for you against your enemies, to save (להושיע) you;" likewise, 1QM 10:7–8, citing Num 10:9, reads: "you shall be remembered before your God and you shall be saved (ונושעתם) from your enemies."[111] Also, in reference to the rebellion led by Jannes against Moses and Aaron, CD 5:19 speaks of "when Israel was saved (בהושע ישראל) the first time." In each case, God is clearly the one who saves. Nevertheless, as 1QM 11:1–3 illustrates, God's deliverance is implemented through human agency; in particular, it states: "also, you delivered us many times by the hand of our kings" (11:3). Important too is that this reference to God's deliverance of Israel in the past functions to assure Israel of his coming salvation in the eschatological conflict against their enemies, in particular, the Kittim (cf. 1QM 11:7ff).[112] Consequently, it appears that the davidic messiah will "save

---

[106]L. H. Silberman, "A Note on 4Q Florilegium," *JBL* 78 (1959) 158–159.

[107]Strugnell, "Notes," 221, claims that this relative clause refers to the Interpreter of the Law, who is designated the booth of David, but see Brooke's refutation of this claim (*Exegesis at Qumran*, 113f).

[108]Brooke, *Exegesis at Qumran*, 139.

[109]Interestingly, this role of saving Israel is neither stated nor implied in the two texts treated in the pesher, although deliverance from enemies is a task customarily reserved for kings. Moreover, the task of building the temple, a role assigned to the seed of David in 2 Sam 7:13, is not attributed to the Branch of David, since according to 4QFlor God himself appears to build the eschatological sanctuary.

[110]See Brooke, *Exegesis at Qumran*, 198, for a summary of the various uses of ישע.

[111]Translation adapted from Yadin, *War Scroll*, 304.

[112]Note also that conflict between the chosen ones of Israel and the Kittim is reflected in 4QFlor 1:18–19.

Israel" by serving as God's agent of deliverance presumably in battle against their eschatological foes, the Kittim.

We may now summarize the characterization of the davidic figure in 4QFlor. The davidic messiah, called the Branch of David, was expected to arises in Zion in the last days, an expectation based on an interpretation of the dynastic oracle in 2 Sam 7:11–14, read in conjunction with Amos 9:11. He would stand or take office alongside a priestly figure, the Interpreter of the Law, a factor that would undoubtedly relativize the status of this royal figure. The Branch of David would nevertheless have an important role to play in the eschatological drama, acting as God's agent of salvation in the final conflict against Israel's enemy, the Kittim. On the other hand, the overall characterization of the davidic messiah is sparse and colorless, and nothing is said about his continuing rule.

Proceeding to the question about the function of the davidic dynasty tradition in the text before us, we may recall that as a whole 4QFlor maps out the eschatological landscape, including such matters as the sanctuary, rest for the community from its enemies, the nature of faithful Israel, the time of refining before the end, and in 1:10–13, the leadership of the community. In this way, 4QFlor is generically similar to visions of an ideal future found in the salvation oracles of the classical prophets and in the concluding scenes of restoration in Jewish apocalypses.[113] Certainly such passages have the general intention of inspiring hope and bringing comfort to those living in less than ideal, usually deprived conditions. 4QFlor would thus share such a general intention.[114] In particular, the davidic dynasty tradition contributed to this intention by supplying a vision of Israelite leadership during the last days, leadership that would bring victory to the remnant of Israel and usher in the ideal future. Moreover, the hope and comfort instilled by this image of an ideal future was secure, rooted as it was in the biblical revelation about the seed of David.

4. 4QpIsa[a] 8–10:11–24 (4Q161)

4QpIsa[a] preserves a commentary on Isa 10:21–11:5.[115] Of particular relevance is its interpretation of Isa 11:1–5 concerning a shoot from the root of Jesse. Unfortunately, the text is quite fragmentary at points so that much of potential signifi-

---

[113]Cf., for example, Isaiah 11, Amos 9:11–15; Micah 4–5; Zechariah 14; Dan 12:1–3; *1 Enoch* 10:14–11:2; 90:28–39; *2 Apo. Bar.* 29–30.

[114]Brooke, *Exegesis at Qumran*, 174, argues for a liturgical setting for 4QFlor.

[115]For the *editio princeps*, see Allegro, DJD 5, 11–15, to be used in conjunction with Strugnell, "Notes," 183–186. A text of 4QpIsa[a], which incorporates the improved readings of Strugnell, along with a different arrangement of the fragments, is available in Horgan, *Pesharim*, 15–18.

cance remains lost. Nevertheless, the extant text does shed some light on the understanding of the davidic dynasty tradition at Qumran.

This manuscript consists of ten fragments, several of which can be joined, and preserves portions of three columns of text.[116] In terms of genre, 4QpIsa[a] is a continuous pesharim in which consecutive biblical text is cited and interpreted. Like other continuous pesharim, it has the marks of Qumran ideology, indicating that its provenance is the community at Khirbet Qumran. On the basis of its script, which Strugnell designates 'rustic semi-formal' according to F. M. Cross' categories,[117] it may be dated between 30 BCE and 20 CE.[118] Finally, it is closely related to a newly released manuscript, 4QSerek HaMilhamah, which also presents an interpretation of Isa 10:33–11:1.

The following analysis will focus on 4QpIsa[a] 8 10:11 24, which cites and interprets Isa 11:1–5, but it is important at the outset to review the broader literary context in which this text appears. First, the biblical passage interpreted in 4QpIsa[a], Isa 10:21–11:5, contains a cluster of oracles dealing with the return of a remnant of Israel (10:21–23), God's judgment against Assyria (10:24–27a), an enemy's advance toward Jerusalem (10:27b–32), God's judgment against lofty ones (10:33–34), and the coming of a shoot of Jesse (11:1–5). In the eye of the Qumran interpreter, however, this passage spoke about the eschatological conflict between the faithful remnant of Israel and the Kittim. A number of passages support this conclusion.

At the beginning of this text, the commentary on Isa 10:21 mentions "men of his army" (אנשי חילו) [1:3], and the interpretation of Isa 10:22 says that many will perish (2–4:4). More decisive, however, is the interpretation of Isa 10:24–27 in 4QpIsa[a] 5–6:2–3. The biblical passage is about how Assyria will be destroyed and the burden of its oppression lifted from the remnant of Israel. In the commentary on these verses, one finds the phrase "when they return from the wilderness of the nat[ions]" (בשובם ממדבר העו]מים), the same phrase used in 1QM 1:3, where the subject is the exiles of the Sons of Light who return to join the Qumran community in the eschatological battle against the Kittim.[119] In addition, the interpretation of this passage refers to the Prince of the Congregation (נשיא העדה). Given the context, it seems likely that this figure has some role in the

---

[116]For the identification of three columns, see Horgan, 71.

[117]Strugnell, "Notes," 183.

[118]Cross, "Jewish Scripts," 176; see his p. 224f for a description of this script; Milik, *Ten Years*, 96 n. 1, suggests a first century CE date.

[119]Cf. Yadin, "Some Notes," 68.

conflict, but since the surrounding text is fragmentary, little else can be learned about the Prince of the Congregation here.[120]

Furthermore, Isa 10:27b–32, which describes an enemy's approach toward Jerusalem from the north—no doubt Assyria in its original context, is explained as a description of an enemy's advance up to the boundary of Jerusalem at the end of days (לאחרית הימים) [5–6:10]. Although a reference to the enemy's identity is lost to a lacuna, the succeeding context makes it clear that the enemy is the Kittim.[121] Specifically, 4QpIsa[a] 8–10:1–9 cites and explains Isa 10:33–34. Modern interpreters of Isaiah have debated whether these verses originally referred to the destruction of the Assyrians or the corrupt leadership in Jerusalem by the Assyrians. In 4QpIsa[a], however, no ambiguity exists; these verses promise the destruction of Israel's eschatological enemy, the Kittim.

> [*And the th*]*ickets of* [*the forest will be cut down*] *with an ax, and Lebanon by a mighty one* [*shall fall* (Isa 10:34). They are the] Kittim, wh[o] will be fa[ll] by the hand of Israel. And the poor ones [   ] all the nations, and warriors will be filled with terror, and [their] cour[age] will dissolve. [*And those who are lofty*] *in stature will be cut off* (Isa 10:33). They are the warriors of the Kitt[im] ... *And Lebanon by a mi*[*ghty one shall fall.* They are the] Kittim, who will be gi[ven] into the hand of his great ones ... when he flees before Israel (8–10:2–9).[122]

Thus, the context preceding 4QpIsa[a] 8–10:11–24 envisions a scenario for the last days in which the faithful of Israel, represented by the Qumran community, wage war against the Kittim and utterly defeat them. With this context in view, we may now turn to a detailed examination of 4QpIsa[a] 8–10:11–24.

The structure of lns. 11–24 is as follows: lns. 11–16 quote Isa 11:1–5; the next line is blank (not numbered in the transcription in DJD 5); lns. 17–21 render a commentary; lns. 21–22 cite Isa 11:3b again; and lns. 23–24 offer commentary. The preserved text of Isa 11:1–5 follows the MT very closely with only minor deviations.[123] And although the lemma itself tells us little about the specific thinking of the author, since in continuous pesharim running text is quoted, it will nevertheless be helpful to review the contents of Isa 11:1–5 as a foil against which the commentary may be placed.

---

[120]But see below on 4QSerek HaMilhamah, where the role of the נשיא העדה in the eschatological conflict is explicated.

[121]Cf. Horgan, *Pesharim*, 80–81.

[122]Following generally the reconstruction and translation of Horgan, *Pesharim*, 17–18, 75–76.

[123]See Horgan, *Pesharim*, 85–86, for deviations from the MT.

Isa 11:1 promises a coming ruler, a shoot or branch from Jesse's stump or root. Verses 2–3a go on to describe the superlative spiritual endowments this figure receives from God, including the spirit of the Lord, a spirit of wisdom, understanding, counsel, might, knowledge, and fear of the Lord. Then vv. 3b–4 describe his judging function: he will not make judgments on the basis of what is seen and heard; he will give righteousness to the poor and weak; and he will smite the earth with his word and slay the wicked with the breath of his lips. Finally, v. 5 speaks of the righteousness and faithfulness he will wear around his waist.

Having cited this biblical passage, 4QpIsa[a] goes on to comment on it. Below this commentary is presented with only the most certain reconstructions added in the lacunae:[124]

Text

ln. 17	[פשר הפתגם על צמח[דויד העומד באח[רית הימים
ln. 18	[ ] או[יבו ואל יסומכנו ב[רוח ג[בורה
ln. 19	כ[סא כבוד נזר ק[ודש]ובגדי ריקמו[ת]
ln. 20	[ ] בידו ובכול הג[וא]י[ם] ימשול ומגוג
ln. 21	כו[ל העמים תשפוט חרבו ואשר אמר לוא
ln. 22	[למראה עיניו ישפוט]ולוא למשמע אוזניו יוכיח פשרו אשר
ln. 23	[וכאשר יורוהו כן ישפוט ועל פיהם
ln. 24	[עמו יצא אחד מכוהני השם ובידו בגדי

Translation

ln. 17   [The interpretation of the matter concerns the Branch of] David who will stand in the la[st days   ]

ln. 18   [ene]mies. And God will sustain him with a [*spirit of m*]*ight* [   ]

ln. 19   [thr]one of glory, a h[oly] crown, and embroider[ed] garments

ln. 20   [   ] in his hand and over all the n[ation]s he shall rule and Magog

ln. 21   [a]ll the peoples will his sword judge, and when it says, *Neither*

ln. 22   [*with the sight of his eyes shall he judge*] nor *with the hearing of his ears shall he decide* (Isa 11:3b), the interpretation is that

ln. 23   [   ] and as they instruct him, so will he judge, and according to their command

ln. 24   [   ] with him. One of the priests of name will go out and in his hand the garments of[125]

---

[124]The text and translation are adapted from Horgan, *Pesharim*, 18,76 (although not her line numbering).

[125]Cf. Y. Yadin, *The Temple Scroll* (3 vols. with a supplement; Jerusalem: Israel Exploration Society, Archaeological Institute of the Hebrew University, Shrine of the Book, 1983)

By way of analysis, a number of points can be made. First, and most obvious, the shoot from the stump of Jesse is identified as a davidic figure, although the exact appellation for this person is lost to the lacuna in ln. 17. On the basis of 4QFlor and 4QpGen[a], Allegro suggested that this figure was also designated צמח דויד ("Branch of David") here in 4QpIsa[a].[126] This was a reasonable hypothesis at the time, especially since terminology for a shoot and branch occurs in Isa 11:1. His suggestion now appears confirmed by 4QSerek HaMilhamah 5:3, which names the shoot from Jesse in Isa 11:1 צמח דויד.

Secondly, it is said that the davidic figure will stand or take office (עמוד) in the last days (ln. 17). On the one hand, the verb עמוד is used in conjunction with the צמח דויד in 4QFlor. On the other, it is also employed in reference to the Messiah of Aaron and Israel (CD 12:23–13:1; 20:1) and the Prince of the Congregation (נשׂיא עדה) [CD 7:20]. This does not in itself imply that these titles always describe the same figure in Qumran texts. Yet it does suggest that in 4QpIsa[a], the צמח דויד was identified with at least some of the functions ascribed to these other figures, and probably with the person of the נשׂיא עדה, who is mentioned in the previous context in 4QpIsa[a] 5–6:3 and explicitly identified with the צמח דויד in 4QSerek HaMilhamah. In addition, the appearance of this davidic figure in the last days means that he will be present for the eschatological conflict.

Thirdly, little is made in the commentary of the spiritual qualities ascribed to this scion of David in Isa 11:2. Only in ln. 18 does it mention that God will sustain him with a spirit of might.[127] This is not, however, a coincidence, since might is a characteristic most suitable for a warrior and ruler, and it is precisely this figure's power and rule that is appropriate to the military conflict envisioned in the preceding context and marked out for special attention in the succeeding lines. Specifically, we should assume that the Branch of David would have played a role in the victory against the Kittim during their assault against Jerusalem alluded to in 4QpIsa[a] 5–6:5–13 and 8–10:1–9. Further, ln. 19 affirms that he will possess a throne of glory, a holy crown, and embroidered garments, all appurtenances indicative of royal status and power. In addition, ln. 20 states that he will rule over all the nations. In ln. 20 the name Magog appears, a reference to an eschatological enemy from the north based on Ezekiel 38–39, whom, according to 1QM

1:352, who reads this verse, "with him will go forth one of the priests of renown."

[126]Allegro, DJD 5, 15; likewise, Horgan, *Pesharim*, 85.

[127]Strugnell, "Notes," 185, read "Torah" instead of "might."

11:16, God delivers into the hands of his poor ones in the eschatological battle.[128] We should, therefore, assume that the Branch of David is involved in his destruction. Moreover, we learn that the sword of the davidic messiah will judge all the peoples (ln. 21). It is noteworthy here that in Isa 11:4b the davidic figure smites and slays the wicked with verbal weapons, the rod of his mouth and the breath of his lips. In the commentary, however, it appears these metaphorical weapons have been transformed into one of iron, a sword. Yet this is consistent with the militaristic tone of the entire passage. Notably absent from the pesher is any mention of this davidic figure's righteous judgments on behalf of the poor and weak. On the contrary, the primary concern in the commentary is his domination of Israel's enemies through military might.

Fourthly, the judging activity of this davidic figure comes in for special consideration in lns. 21–23. Isa 11:3b, which says the shoot of Jesse will not judge by appearance or hearsay, is repeated. In Isa 11:4a, this statement is further explicated by saying that he will give righteous judgments for the poor and the weak. But here in 4QpIsa[a] a different point is made. He will not judge according to appearance or hearsay, but "as they instruct him" and "according to their command" (על פיהם). The explicit identity of those who instruct the Branch of David is lost, but it is almost certainly the priests. On the one hand, they are the most logical group to be doing the instruction. On the other, the phrase על פיהם is often used in connection with the Sons of Zadok, the priests (1QS *passim*; 1QSa 1:2).[129] Moreover, one of the priests, who is somehow involved with the king's garments, is mentioned in ln. 24. Van der Woude summarizes:

> Doch seine Herrschaft is nicht uneingeschrankt. Als 'bras seculier' ist er den Priestern untergeben: wie sie ihn lehren, so soll er Recht sprechen ... der König den Priestern gegenüber zweitrangig ist.[130]

4QpIsa[a] gives us another glimpse of the concept of the davidic messiah at Qumran. In the main, his spiritual qualities are played down, his domination over the nations is emphasized, and his activity—at least his judging—is placed under the supervision of the priests. Thus, one finds in 4QpIsa[a] 8–10:11–24 an understanding of the davidic messiah similar to that found in 4QFlor 1:10–13. It reveals an expectation for a davidic king in the last days who will possess the marks of royal office, but the characterization of the Branch of David is on the whole sparse in contrast to the qualities ascribed to him in Isa 11:1–3a. His ruling

---

[128]In 1QM 11:16, the reference is to Gog; note too that the "poor ones" are mentioned in 4QpIsa[a] 8–10:3.

[129]Van der Woude, *Vorstellungen*, 181.

[130]Van der Woude, *Vorstellungen*, 181f.

function is important in 4QpIsa[a], yet not over Israel, but the nations. Most significant is the subordination of the royal davidic figure to the priests. Altogether, the davidic dynasty tradition functions here to provide a scriptural basis for imaging the kind of militant leader well-suited to the task of defeating the nations, and in particular, the Kittim.

5. *4QSerek HaMilhamah 5:1–6 (4Q285)*

4QSerek HaMilhamah is a fragmentary document that refers to a davidic messiah within a context that describes a war between Israel and the Kittim.[131] Unknown to the public prior to its release in 1991, this text, especially frg. 5, soon became the focus of a highly publicized debate over whether the davidic messiah mentioned in this text slays someone or is himself slain in the war with the Kittim.[132] Beyond that particular issue, however, this newly released text represents an important addition to Qumran documents describing the davidic messiah and his activities.

The manuscript consists of ten fragments, several of which can be joined together.[133] Similar handwriting and thematic congruence among the fragments indicate that they belong to one manuscript.[134] Most of the fragments include terms or phrases reflecting the subject of an eschatological war between Israel and the Kittim. Specifically, frgs. 2/7 include references to riches, booty, graves, and the slain. Fragment 3 alludes to the time of the end. Fragment 8 mentions the Kittim, while frg. 10 names Michael, the angelic leader of the Sons of Light in the

---

[131] A photograph of this text (PAM 43.325) appears in Eisenman and Robinson, *Facsimile Edition*, Plate # 1352. For a transcription of the manuscript, see Wacholder and Abegg, *Preliminary Edition*, 2:223–227; Eisenman and Wise, *Uncovered*, 27–29. The publication of an *editio princeps* has been assigned to J. J. Collins (see Tov, "Unpublished Qumran Texts," 116).

[132] For references to early press releases about this text, see G. Vermes, "The Oxford Forum for Qumran Research Seminar on the Rule of War from Cave 4 (4Q285)," *JJS* 43 (1992) 86 n. 2. Debate continued in *Biblical Archaeology Review*: see "The 'Pierced Messiah' Text—An Interpretation Evaporates, *BARev* 18:4 (1992) 80–82, where Vermes' views are summarized; J. D. Tabor, "A Pierced or Piercing Messiah?—The Verdict is Still Out," *BARev* 18:6 (1992) 58–59; and "More on the Pierced Messiah Text from Eisenman and Vermes," *BARev* 19:1 (1993) 66–67; see now M. G. Abegg, "Messianic Hope and 4Q285: A Reassessment," *JBL* 113 (1994) 81–91.

[133] Wacholder and Abegg, *Preliminary Edition*, 2:223–227, present 4Q285 in ten fragments; I will use their numbering in the following treatment. On the photographic plate, however, there are two additional fragments on the left side in the middle; yet these are so fragmentary that they add little to our knowledge of the document. On the photographic plate, frgs. 2 and 7 are joined, as are frgs. 4 and 6. Except where joined, the order of the fragments must be deduced from their contents.

[134] Cf. M. Bockmuehl, "'A Slain Messiah' in 4Q Serekh Milḥamah (4Q 285)?" *TynBul* 43 (1992) 163.

War Scroll. More substantially, frgs. 4/6 describe a military engagement between the Kittim and Israel, the forces of the latter being led by the Prince of the Congregation (נשיא העדה). Fragment 5, which will be the subject of a detailed analysis below, refers to judgment, execution, wounds, and probably the slain of the Kittim. Finally, frg. 1, which corresponds to a previously known text, 11QBer,[135] consists of a series of blessings similar to those found in 1QM and 1QSb.[136] Therefore, based on its resemblance to 1QM, particularly the last section of that document (cols. 15–19), which includes a description of the final engagement between the Sons of Light and the Kittim, I accept the proposal of Wacholder and Abegg:

> It [4QSerek HaMilhamah] is probably part of, or attached to, the end of the War Scroll, as it depicts the final battle in which the forces of Light vanquish the forces of Darkness in a sea encounter.[137]

Within the context of a war rule, however, 5:1–6 represents what Dimant calls "isolated pesharim,"[138] and as noted above, has affinities with 4QpIsa[a] 8–10.

The manuscript has been dated on paleographic grounds to the early herodian period.[139] Moreover, its focus on the Kittim, who represent the Romans, comports with a date sometime in the herodian period (30 BCE–70 CE) for the composition of 4QSerek HaMilhamah. Consistent with this dating, too, are the affinities between 4QSerek HaMilhamah and 4QpIsa[a], the latter document coming from the herodian period, and the fact that the manuscript of 11QBer, which corresponds to frg. 1 of 4QSerek HaMilhamah, has been dated to the same period.[140]

The reference to the davidic messiah occurs in frg. 5. A transcription and translation of this fragment follow:[141]

---

[135]For 11QBer, see A. S. van der Woude, "Ein neuer Segensspruch aus Qumran (11QBer)," *Bibel und Qumran* (ed. S. Wagner; Leipzig: Evangelische Haupt-Bibelgesellschaft zu Berlin, 1968) 253–258.

[136]See 1QM 12:9–15; 13:2–17; 14:4ff; 18:7–19:8, and all of 1Sb.

[137]Wacholder and Abegg, *Preliminary Edition*, 2:xv.

[138]Dimant, "Pesharim," 5:248.

[139]Abegg, "Messianic Hope," 81.

[140]See van der Woude, "Segensspruch," 254, for the date of 11QBer.

[141]For a computer enhanced image of frg. 5, see Vermes, "Oxford Forum," 87; and p. 88 for his transcription.

Text

ln. 1   [   ] [ישעיהו הנביא ונוק[פון]

ln. 2   [סבכ היער בברזל והלבנון באדירי י]פול ויצא חוטר מגזע ישי

ln. 3   [   ] צמח דויד ונשפטו את

ln. 4   [   ] [והמיתו נשיא העדה צמ[ח דויד]

ln. 5   [   ] ס[ובמחוללות וצוה כוהן]

ln. 6   [   ] ח[ללל[ין כתיים[ ]לן [

Translation

ln. 1 [   ] Isaiah the prophet: *cut [down*

ln. 2 [*shall be the thickets of the forest with an ax, and Lebanon by a mighty one shall*
        f]all. And a shoot shall come forth from the root of Jesse (Isa 10:34–11:1)

ln. 3 [   ] Branch of David; and they shall enter into judgment
                   with

ln. 4 [   ] and the Prince of the Congregation, the Bra[nch of
                   David] will kill him

ln. 5 [   ]s and with wounds. And the [   ] priest will command

ln. 6 [s]lai[n] of the Kittim [   ]

The first readable words in ln. 1, "Isaiah the prophet," were no doubt preceded by an introductory phrase such as "as written in the book of."[142] Due to the
lacuna, the opening words of the textual citation are missing, but the first readable
word in ln. 2, [י]פול, indicates that Isa 10:34 is the verse quoted.[143] The citation
continues with Isa 11:1a and probably included 11:1b, since the last half of that
verse would easily fit into the lacuna at the beginning of ln. 3.

Before turning to the exposition of this scripture in the succeeding lines, we
must note the implied significance of one of the images in Isa 10:34. Specifically,
the cedars of Lebanon were used within Jewish midrashic tradition to symbolize
enemy nations and kings, including the Romans and their king.[144] Indeed, in its
interpretation of Isa 10:34, 4QpIsa[a] identifies the cedars of Lebanon as the Kittim.[145] Consequently, although this same equivalence is not stated here in frg. 5,

---

[142]See 4QFlor 1:15 for a similar introductory phrase. Cf. Wacholder and Abegg, *Preliminary Edition*, 2:225, who fill the lacuna with similar words.

[143]Also, both Vermes, "Oxford Forum," 88; and Wacholder and Abegg, *Preliminary Edition*, 2:225, reconstruct ונוקפו, the first word of Isa 10:34, as the last word in ln. 1.

[144]R. P. Gordon, "The Interpretation of 'Lebanon' and 4Q285," *JJS* 43 (1992) 92–94; see
also, Vermes, *Scripture and Tradition*, 26–39. With respect to the Romans, Vermes, "Oxford
Forum," 89–90, observes that according to 2 *Apo. Bar.* 36–40, the messiah judges and kills the
last ruler of the world kingdom (Rome), who was symbolized by the fallen cedar of Lebanon.

[145]4QpIsa[a] 8–10:3 says of the cedars of Lebanon, "They are the Kittim who will fall by the

references to the Kittim in the context of an eschatological conflict within 4QSerek HaMilhamah make it virtually certain that the identification of cedars of Lebanon and the Kittim is implied in this text.[146]

The extant portion of the interpretation of Isa 10:34–11:1 begins in ln. 3 with the words צמח דויד, a designation for the davidic messiah familiar from 4QpGen[a], 4QFlor, and 4QpIsa[a]. Thus, like 4QpIsa[a] 8–10:17, the present text identifies the figure promised in Isa 11:1 with the Branch of David. In addition, ln. 4 indicates that this figure also bears the title נשיא העדה.[147] Hence, for the first time in a Qumran document, the figure designated by the title צמח דויד is definitively identified with the נשיא העדה, even though this identification was often already assumed in discussions of Qumran messianism.[148] Moreover, certainty about this equivalence enhances our understanding of the role of the davidic messiah in 4QSerek HaMilhamah, since the activities of the Prince of the Congregation related in frgs. 4/6 can without reservation be ascribed to the davidic figure. Thus, in 6:1–2 the Prince of the Congregation is paired with all Israel and associated with the defeat of evil, and in 4:2–6 he is connected with a successful military engagement near the Mediterranean coast before returning to dry land and having a male person brought before him.

The interpretation of the biblical passage continues with the words ונשפטו את ("they will enter into judgment with")[ln. 3].[149] The third person plural subject of this verb is not stated, and could be either the davidic messiah and his forces or some other unspecified subject—probably the Kittim.[150] The former interpretation is to be favored, however, because it is consistent with the judging activities attributed to the davidic figure in Isa 11:3–4 and 4QpIsa[a] 8–10:21.[151] The plural form of the verb is used because the Prince of the Congregation leads all the Sons of Light in executing judgment upon their enemies.[152]

---

hand of Israel;" likewise, 4QpIsa[a] 8–10:8 explains, "They are the Kittim who will be given into the hand of the great ones."

[146]Gordon, "Interpretation of 'Lebanon'," 94.

[147][צמן appears at the end of ln. 4, contrary to the transcription in Wacholder and Abegg, *Preliminary Edition*, 225. This is undoubtedly the beginning of the phrase צמח דויד, used here in apposition to נשיא העדה.

[148]Both titles appear in 4QpIsa[a] (5–6:3 and 8–10:17), but are not explicitly related.

[149]See Bockmuehl, "A Slain Messiah?" 164 n. 26, for a justification of this understanding of the Niphal of שפט with את.

[150]For the latter possibility, see Tabor, "Verdict," 58. Tabor's suggestion is based on reading the verb המיתו in ln. 4 as a third person plural verb, a reading that I will reject below.

[151]4QpIsa[a] 8–10:21 says of the davidic messiah: "[al]l the peoples his sword will judge."

[152]Bockmuehl, "Slain Messiah?" 164f; see his references from 1QM. That the Prince of the

Line four contains the much debated term וֶהֱמִיתוֹ, which can be vocalized either וֶהֱמִיתוֹ ("and he will kill him") or וְהֵמִיתוּ ("and they will kill"). If the former reading, the phrase following this verb, נשׂיא העדה, would serve as its subject, the object being some male adversary mentioned in the preceding lacuna.[153] If the latter reading, then an unspecified third person subject would be acting upon the נשׂיא העדה, yielding the slain messiah that sparked the controversy over this text. Either vocalization is grammatically possible, and the absence of the direct object marker before נשׂיא העדה cannot be used to rule it out as the direct object, since not infrequently in Qumran texts the object marker is omitted. Consequently, to adjudicate between the alternatives, one must appeal to context, in which case the former reading, וֶהֱמִיתוֹ , is to be preferred.[154]

First, frg. 5 offers an interpretation of Isa 10:34–11:1. Isa 10:34 describes the falling of Lebanon, which, as noted above, was taken in Jewish midrashic tradition to refer to the destruction of Israel's enemies, in some cases even the Kittim. In addition, Isa 11:1 tells of a triumphant davidic figure, one of whose activities is "to slay the wicked" (ימית רשׁע) [Isa 11:4b]. Thus, since the lemma involves the twin motifs of a triumphant davidic figure who slays the wicked and the destruction of Israel's enemies, it is overwhelmingly more probable that the interpretation of these verses in frg. 5 concerns the davidic Prince of the Congregation slaying the Kittim, or here, their leader, rather than the Kittim slaying the Prince of the Congregation.[155]

Secondly, in other Qumran texts, the titles צמח דויד and נשׂיא העדה designate triumphant figures. Most importantly, according to 4QpGen[a] Israel's victory against its enemies in the eschatological battle marks the time when Israel gains dominion, the time when davidic kingship will not be cut off.[156] Given this scenario, it is unlikely that the davidic messiah is killed by the Kittim in battle. Moreover, in 4QpIsa[a] the davidic messiah is said to be sustained by a spirit of

---

Congregation and all Israel act in concert is supported by 4Q285 4:6, where a plural subject brings a male person before the Prince of the Congregation, and 6:2, where the Prince of the Congregation and "all Israel" are mentioned together.

[153]Bockmuehl, "Slain Messiah?" 165, correctly observes that the phrase ונשׁפטו את in ln. 3 requires an adversary named in the following lacuna, a designation that would serve as the antecedent of the pronominal suffix in והמיתו.

[154]See Vermes, "Oxford Forum," 85–90; Bockmuehl, "Slain Messiah?" 165–166; Wacholder and Abegg, *Preliminary Edition*, 2:xv. Beyond the specific citations, the following analysis of ln. 4 is indebted to the articles by Vermes and Bockmuehl.

[155]The leader is likely the king of the Kittim, known from 1QM 15:2, who may also be the male person brought before the נשׂיא העדה in frg. 4 ln. 10 (cf. Vermes, "Oxford Forum," 89).

[156]See above, p. 184.

might, to receive a throne of glory and a holy crown, and to rule over all the nations, while his sword judges all the peoples.[157] Similarly, according to 1QSb 5:20–29, the נשיא העדה will among other things establish the kingdom of his people forever, bring death to the ungodly, and be served by rulers of nations. None of these portrayals of the צמח דויד or נשיא העדה is consistent with an interpretation of 4QSerek HaMilhamah 5:4 that posits the execution of the davidic messiah by the Kittim. Admittedly, we should not move too quickly to harmonize every reference to a davidic messiah in Qumran texts into a synthetic depiction of that figure; yet neither should we accept antithetical characterizations of any figure unless there is clear evidence to do so.

In this regard, arguments supporting נשיא העדה as the object of the slaying are not convincing. For one, Eisenman and Wise contend that since צמח דויד is in apposition to נשיא העדה, taking נשיא העדה as the subject of והמיתו makes for clumsy Hebrew.[158] Yet one finds the very same grammatical construction in 4QpGen[a] 5:3–4, where צמח דויד is in apposition to משיח הצדק, yet משיח הצדק is the subject of the verb it follows.[159] Another purported reason is based on the supposition that והמיתו might share the same third person plural subject as ונשפטו in ln. 3.[160] But this is hardly a compelling point, since the reverse—that the subject has changed—is equally plausible.[161] Lastly, J. D. Tabor argues that while the Qumran community believed in the ultimate victory of their messiah, several texts support the idea of a temporary triumph of evil. In particular, he cites 4Q171, a commentary on various Psalms that speaks of a righteous one being put to death, and 11QMelch, which quotes Dan 9:25, where a coming messiah is subsequently "cut off" (cf. Dan 9:26).[162] In response, two points can be made. First, T. H. Lim has shown convincingly that 11QMelch is not about a dying messiah.[163] Secondly, while the Qumran community may have accounted for the suffering of its members in terms of the temporary triumph of evil, none of the texts cited by Tabor applies this principle to the Branch of David or Prince of the Congregation. In fact, as we have seen above, the Branch of David and the

---

[157]See above, p. 201.

[158]Eisenman and Wise, *Uncovered*, 24; see also, Tabor, "Verdict," 58, who states that a subject elongated by words in apposition should come before the verb.

[159]The entire clause in 4QpGen[a] 5:3–4 reads: עד בוא משיח הצדק צמח דויד.

[160]Tabor, "Verdict," 58.

[161]On the subject of ונשפטו, see above p. 206.

[162]Tabor, "Verdict," 58

[163]T. H. Lim, "11QMelch, Luke 4 and the Dying Messiah," *JJS* 43 (1992) 90–92.

Prince of the Congregation appear within contexts characterized by triumph; there is no evidence for a temporary defeat of these figures in any Qumran text.[164]

For these reasons, the weight of probability falls heavily to the side of the reading וֶהֱמִיתוֹ. Hence, ln. 4 reveals that in the battle with the Kittim, the Prince of the Congregation, the Branch of David, executes a male person, almost certainly his counterpart among the enemy forces, the king of the Kittim.

Line five contains the word ובמחוללות ("and with wounds") and may describe details of the execution referred to in ln. 4.[165] Further, the end of ln. 5 reads "and a priest shall command" (וצוה כוהן). It is possible that the next word, missing because of the lacuna at the beginning of ln. 6, is הרואש ("chief"),[166] since in the *War Scroll* the high priest has a significant role in the conduct of the war.[167] Whatever the case, the appearance of a priestly figure in a context where the davidic messiah is active is not surprising. 4QpIsa[a] 8–10:24 and 4QFlor 1:11 also speak of a priestly figure in conjunction with the davidic messiah. Moreover, a priest giving commands is consistent with the actions of the priests known from 1QM, where they are portrayed as regulating activities in the war against the Kittim.[168] Finally, ln. 6 apparently refers to the slain of the Kittim,[169] a phrase familiar from the *War Scroll*,[170] but the immediate context of this reference is missing. Nevertheless, mention of dead enemy soldiers does reinforce the above analysis that the entire theme of frg. 5, indeed of 4QSerek HaMilhamah as a whole, is one of defeat for the Kittim and victory for the Sons of Light.[171]

We are now in a position to summarize the characterization of the davidic messiah in 4QSerek HaMilhamah. First, the davidic figure bears the titles צמח דויד and נשיא העדה, designations familiar from other Qumran documents, but

---

[164]Tabor, "Verdict," 58, claims that 4QIsa[a] 8–10, a context that mentions the davidic messiah, tells of the Kittim crushing the humble. Although this is Allegro's reading of 4QIsa[a] 8–10:3 (DJD 5, p. 13), in reality the key words are virtually unreadable (see DJD 5, Plate V). For an alternate reconstruction of the same line, see Horgan, *Pesharim*, 75,83, who reads: "The Kittim, who will fall by the hand of Israel" (frgs. 7–10, ln. 7 in Horgan's numbering).

[165]Wacholder and Abegg, *Preliminary Edition*, xv, suggest that ובמחוללות should be translated "dancing women" (Ex 15:20; Judg 21:23), a reference to the celebrations accompanying the victory of the Sons of Light.

[166]Cf. Wacholder and Abegg, *Preliminary Edition*, 225. Vermes, "Oxford Forum," suggests השם for the lacuna, thus "priest of renown."

[167]See 1QM 15:4ff; 16:11ff; 18:5–6; 19:11–13.

[168]See for example, 1QM 7:8ff; 10:2.

[169]Vermes, "Oxford Forum," 88.

[170]1QM 16:8; 19:13.

[171]The eschatological blessings in frg. 1 are a further indication that the entire context of 4QSerek HaMilhamah is one of victory and blessing.

never before explicitly applied to the same figure. Secondly, the Branch of David will participate in the eschatological war against the Sons of Darkness, especially against the Kittim. In particular, in association with all Israel, in order to smite evil, he will take part in a successful battle near the Mediterranean, then head inland, where a male person will be brought before him (frgs. 4/6). And if we are correct to suppose that frg. 5 describes events subsequent to those reflected in frgs. 4/6,[172] in accordance with Isa 10:34–11:1 the davidic messiah and his army will go on to execute judgment against their enemy, and more particularly, the Branch of David will slay the king of the Kittim. On the whole, therefore, the davidic messiah has a militant, even violent role attributed to him—a role that stands in contrast to the less martial characterization of the davidic figure in *Pss. Sol.* 17.[173] In sum, according to 4QSerek HaMilhamah the davidic messiah plays a significant leadership role in the final conflict between the Sons of Light and the Kittim.

Noteworthy here is that in 4QSerek HaMilhamah the role assigned to the davidic Prince of the Congregation in the war against the Kittim is decidedly more extensive than that attributed to him in the extant portions of 1QM. In the *War Scroll* from Cave 1, one learns only that the Prince of (All) the Congregation will have written upon his shield his name, the names of Israel, Levi, and Aaron, the names of the twelve tribes, and the names of the commanders of those tribes (1QM 5:1–2). The conduct of the war is in the hands of the chief priest and his fellow priests.[174] Yet 4QSerek HaMilhamah deals with the final military engagement against the Kittim, a topic described in the last section of 1QM, which is truncated. So, it is possible that 4QSerek HaMilhamah contains material once included in the final section of 1QM, which is no longer extant. On the other hand, 4QSerek HaMilhamah could be a different recension of the war rule, which in contrast to 1QM attributed a significant role to the davidic messiah.[175] In any case, at some stage in the development of ideas about the eschatological war

---

[172]The order of the fragments must be deduced from their contents. Accordingly, it seems reasonable to place frgs. 4/6, which discuss a battle, before frg. 5, which involves the execution of the enemy leader.

[173]In 4Q Serek HaMilhamah, articulation of the davidic messiah's militancy nonetheless falls short of the violence attributed to the messiah in *Tg. Ps.-J.* Gen 49:10: "He has girded his loins and gone down to battle against his enemies, destroying kings and their power, and there is neither king nor power that can withstand him. He reddens the mountains with the blood of their slain. His garments are saturated with blood, like those of him who presses the grapes."

[174]P. R. Davies, *1QM, the War Scroll from Qumran* (BibOr 32; Rome: Biblical Institute Press, 1977) 35.

[175]Texts from Cave 4 show that different recensions of the *War Scroll* existed (cf. P. R. Davies, "War Rule," *Anchor Bible Dictionary* [6 vols.; ed. D. N. Freedman; New York: Doubleday, 1992] 6:875).

between the Sons of Light and the Sons of Darkness, the Qumran community found an important place for the davidic messiah.

Lastly, then, we may ask about the function of the davidic dynasty tradition in 4QSerek HaMilhamah. In this regard, since we have assumed that this text represents a portion of a war rule, we must begin by considering the overall purpose of war rules at Qumran. Accordingly, 1QM, the most complete example of a war rule at Qumran, describes an eschatological conflict between cosmic forces of good and evil. This is especially true of cols. 1,15–19, columns with the most similarities to motifs in 4QSerek HaMilhamah.[176] Moreover, although scholars have debated whether 1QM is a pragmatic manual for an actual war or an idealistic document describing an imaginative battle,[177] it certainly reflects—as well as encourages—belief in the ultimate triumph of God and the vindication of his people against the forces of evil in the world. In this respect, 1QM has rightly been compared to the descriptions of eschatological conflict found in apocalyptic literature.[178]

Yet in contrast to the apocalyptic scenario one finds in Daniel 11–12, where the human subjects aligned with God and his purposes play a rather passive role, in 1QM human agents take part in the execution of divine judgment against evil. In this sense, 1QM is closer to the Animal Apocalypse (*1 Enoch* 85–90) in which human military activity, along with angelic assistance, serves as a means by which God implements his judgment (see *1 Enoch* 90:13–19).[179] Hence, in 1QM faithful Israel, with the help of Michael and his angelic forces, fight against the earthly forces of Belial, most notably the Kittim or Romans. Thus, not only does 1QM envision God's decisive judgment against evil, but it finds a place for faithful Israel in the execution of that judgment on the earth.

In 1QM faithful Israel no doubt consists of the Qumran sect and those who might join them from the exiled Sons of Light, who would return from the Wilderness of Nations (1QM 1:3).[180] Furthermore, as noted earlier, 1QM places human leadership of these Sons of Light in the hands of the chief priest and his fellow priests. In contrast, 4QSerek HaMilhamah ascribes at least a significant

---

[176]1QM appears to be a composite document with cols. 2–9 representing a nationalist conflict between Israel and the nations, and cols. 1, 15–19 describing a cosmic battle between the Sons of Light and the Sons of Darkness, each with its earthly and heavenly participants (see Davies, *1QM, passim*, esp. p. 123–124).

[177]Cf. Davies, "War Scroll," *ABD*, 6:876.

[178]Collins, *Imagination*, 126.

[179]In *1 Enoch* 90:13–19, the ram with the large horn represents Judas Maccabees. Cf. Collins, *Imagination*, 56, who refers to the militant role of the righteous in the Animal Apocalypse.

[180]Davies, *1QM*, 115.

measure of human leadership to the davidic messiah. Here, the notion of davidic leadership in the struggle against the forces of evil, especially the Kittim, was inspired by the davidic dynasty tradition as expressed in Isa 10:34–11:1. The davidic dynasty tradition thereby supplied biblical warrant for imagining the kind of human leader that would stand at the head of God's people in the eschatological war—a human leader equipped to cut down the leader of the Kittim. We may conclude, therefore, that inasmuch as war rules at Qumran functioned to engender hope for the eventual overthrow of evil powers in the world, the davidic dynasty tradition contributed to this purpose by furnishing a militant royal figure who would lead the earthly forces of light in this victory.

6. The Davidic Messiah at Qumran

It has been the method of this study to avoid a synthetic approach in examining Qumran documents that use the davidic dynasty tradition and to evaluate each text in its own integrity. In light of these individual studies, however, it is now possible to draw some general conclusions about how this tradition functioned at Qumran. Accordingly, we can begin by noting that of the five documents considered, 4QDimHam clearly stands apart from the others: its date of composition is earlier (ca. 150 BCE); its ideology lacks the distinguishing features of Qumran thought; and its use of the davidic dynasty tradition is retrospective, with no expectation for a coming davidic messiah. On the other hand, among the other texts studied there is a striking convergence of data. 4QpGen[a], 4QFlor, 4QpIsa[a], 4QSerek HaMilhamah not only share the same date of composition (ca. 30 BCE–70 CE), provenance (Qumran community), and literary genre (pesharim, an isolated pesharim in the case of 4QSerek HaMilhamah), but employ the same title for the davidic messiah and posit similar ideas about him. Thus, at least for the stage of Qumran thought represented by these documents, a reasonably coherent notion about a davidic messiah emerges. Consequently, there is warrant for attempting to formulate a synthetic portrait of this figure known at Qumran as the Branch of David (צמח דויד).

First, the Branch of David would arise and take office in the last days, an expectation supported by an appeal to various scriptures, including Gen 49:10, Jer 33:17, 2 Sam 7:11–14, Amos 9:11, and Isa 10:34–11:5. In particular, his appearance was viewed as the fulfillment of the davidic covenant. As to his character, only two qualities are ascribed to him: righteousness and might, the latter characteristic receiving particular emphasis in light of the militant role reserved for the davidic messiah. God, it is said, would be the source of his power. It is noteworthy too that the many spiritual endowments associated with the shoot of Jesse in Isa 11:2–3a are not explicitly attributed to the Branch of David.

Also, the Branch of David is identified with the Prince of the Congregation. Nevertheless, the depiction of his person is on the whole limited and colorless.

With respect to the role and activities of the davidic messiah, the texts present a more elaborate portrait. He will arise in Zion and, according to 4QpIsa[a], seems to be involved in repulsing an attack of the Kittim against Jerusalem. Whether actually participating in that particular battle, the Branch of David nonetheless plays a major role in the eschatological war against the Kittim and others pitted against the remnant of Israel. He judges the nations with his sword, decimating the enemy forces as one hacks down a forest with an ax. He then personally executes the king of the Kittim. The activity of the davidic messiah in the final conflict against the Sons of Darkness is so significant, he is said "to save Israel." Altogether a distinctively militant portrayal of the Branch of David is articulated.

Moreover, it is at the time of this victory over the Kittim that dominion returns to Israel and davidic rule is restored, never to be cut off. As for the nature of the davidic messiah's reign, it will be universal, over all the nations, and will display the marks of royal splendor—a throne of glory, a holy crown, and fine clothing. Also, given the character of the messiah himself, one would assume that his kingdom would be distinguished by righteousness and might. Beyond this, however, details about his rule are conspicuously absent. Interestingly, nothing is said about his actual governance over Israel. Judgments made by the Branch of David will be in accordance with the instructions and commands of the priests. Indeed, at every turn his royal authority is relativized by the dominate role of priestly figures. He stands not alone, but with the Interpreter of the Law, a priestly messiah. Even during the war with the Kittim, priests give the commands. The davidic messiah is plainly subordinate to the authority of the priests.

However, this subordination of the royal messianic figure is consonant with other passages in Qumran documents. For example, in 1QSa 2:11–17, where the community sits according to rank, the priests all sit ahead of the Messiah of Israel, a royal figure. Likewise, at the community meal the priest partakes first, and then the Messiah of Israel (1QSa 2:17–21). Moreover, in 1QSb the order of blessings is that of the high priest, the other priests, and then the Prince of the Congregation. This is not to say that the royal figures depicted in these texts are simply to be equated with the davidic messiah;[181] rather it reveals a unmistakable trend at Qumran to subordinate royal figures to priestly figures. This construal of royal figures is similar to that found in Ezekiel 40–48, where the status and role of the נשיא was strictly limited within a vision of Israel dominated by priests. Moreover, this is generically similar to traditions found in Zechariah 1–8 and the

---

[181] See below, pp. 232–246, for a discussion of this issue.

editorial framework of Haggai about dual leadership in the post-exilic community under Zerubbabel and Joshua the high priest.[182] The relativized status of the davidic messiah at Qumran no doubt was influenced by these biblical passage.

To sum up our observations about the function of these texts referring to the davidic messiah, we can say that they were utilized, on the one hand, to challenge the legitimacy of herodian or Roman kings, and on the other, to provide a vision of Israelite kingship in the last days. In this latter regard, the davidic king's primary duty was to lead the Sons of Light to victory against their eschatological enemies and then rule in royal splendor. Such an image of freedom from foreign domination would serve to bring hope and comfort to the community as they lived in the present evil age. The davidic dynasty tradition therefore provided the resources for imagining the kind of human leader appropriate to the eschatological scenario as conceived at Qumran.

Finally, we may compare the understanding of the davidic messiah in Qumran texts to that found in *Pss. Sol.* 17. First, in both cases the expectation for a davidic messiah—the Son of David in *Pss. Sol.* 17, the Branch of David at Qumran—is supported by an appeal to biblical texts about an ongoing davidic covenant (2 Sam 7:11–16; Psalm 89; Jer 33:17), along with related scriptures, especially Isaiah 11. In Qumran documents he is explicitly an eschatological figure, coming in the last days; on the other hand, in *Pss. Sol.* 17 the time of his coming is not designated the last days, though he is nevertheless a final ideal king. The difference here is probably due to the broader eschatological visions held by the respective communities behind these documents, with a more unambiguous apocalyptic eschatology represented at Qumran.[183]

Secondly, while the characterization of the davidic messiah at Qumran is limited and colorless, including only righteousness and might, in *Pss. Sol.* 17 one finds an elaborate depiction of him. In addition to righteousness and power, the qualities of compassion, sinlessness, holiness, wisdom, faithfulness, and purity are attributed to him. On the whole, in *Pss. Sol.* 17 there is a more idealized characterization of the davidic messiah than at Qumran.

Thirdly, both figures are viewed as instrumental in ridding Israel of foreign enemies, in particular, the Romans. Yet the militancy of the Branch of David at Qumran is more pronounced, in part because description of his military activities predominates, but also because he uses real weapons as opposed to the sword of his mouth. Indeed, according to *Pss. Sol.* 17, the davidic messiah even has

---

[182]Note, however, that originally that these figures were not necessarily messianic, nor the royal figure davidic (see above, pp. 45–60).

[183]For Qumran as an apocalyptic community, see Collins, "Apocalyptic Movement?" *passim.*

compassion on the nations. Furthermore, in *Pss. Sol.* 17 apostate Jews are also singled out as the object of the davidic messiah's cleansing actions, while in Qumran texts these are not said to fall within the purview of his activities. There the focus of his actions remains on the nations.

Fourthly, in both Qumran documents and *Pss. Sol.* 17, the rule of the davidic messiah extends over all the nations; it is universal. At Qumran, however, little is said about the nature of this rule, and statements about the governance of the Branch of David over Israel are strangely absent. The opposite is true in *Pss. Sol.* 17, where the focus is on the Son of David's reign over Israel and the ideal conditions that will obtain among God's people at that time. The davidic messiah is the shepherd of the Lord's flock and mediates divine blessings to an ideal Israel. Fifthly, whereas *Pss. Sol.* 17 envisions a davidic messiah with independent authority where no priests are in view, at Qumran priestly figures stand in high relief with the Branch of David occupying a limited and subordinate position: he takes office alongside the Interpreter of the Law and issues judgments according to the instructions of the priests.

We may account for these dissimilar images of the davidic messiah in *Pss. Sol.* 17 and Qumran documents by recalling that in *Pss. Sol.* 17 the ideal Israel was envisioned in terms of a royal model of society: the king was the one who mediated the blessings of righteousness, holiness, and wisdom. Priests seemed to have no place. In contrast, priests and priestly concerns dominated at Qumran and influenced the sect's vision of a perfected Israel.[184] Nevertheless, they did find the tradition of an ongoing davidic dynasty useful, but as a community with a priestly consciousness they were cautious in their appropriation of this concept, lest the importance of a royal figure overshadow the preeminence of the priests. Although this royal figure is said to play a crucial role in the eschatological events, an independent and autonomous davidic messiah would not have been congruent with the self-understanding of the Qumran community. Consequently, the Qumran sect maintained a hope for the davidic messiah, but portrayed him in a limited fashion, circumscribed his role, relativized his status alongside a priestly messianic figure, and subordinated his authority to the priests. In this way, the image of the davidic messiah at Qumran subserved the goals and self-understanding of the sect.

Lastly, the function of the davidic dynasty tradition in *Pss. Sol.* 17 was to attack the legitimacy of Hasmonean monarchs and to set forth a vision of Israelite life, free from foreign domination and marked by righteousness, holiness, and wisdom. Similarly, at Qumran the davidic dynasty tradition was also used polemically to challenge the rule of herodian or Roman kings and aided in the

---

[184]This model of Israelite life is similar to the one reflected in Sir 45:25.

construction of an eschatological scenario that entailed defeat of enemies and universal rule for Israel. The difference between the use of the davidic dynasty tradition in *Pss. Sol.* 17 and Qumran documents therefore lies not so much in the function of the tradition, but, as noted above, in the divergent visions of the character and role of the davidic messiah within their respective images of the future.

B. 4 Ezra 12:32

A significant use of the davidic dynasty tradition occurs in 4 Ezra. This apocalypse, preserved in Latin as well as other versions, ultimately goes back to a Semitic, and probably Hebrew, original.[185] Its composition can be dated to the last decades of the first century CE or shortly thereafter.[186] The provenance is probably Palestine.[187] In this regard, its messianic expectations are similar to those found in the early parts of the Talmud and Midrash, and thus it may have some connection with rabbinic circles.[188] Yet the precise identity and social setting of the author and his community are notoriously hard to establish.[189]

Mention of the posterity of David takes place within the interpretation of the well-known eagle vision.[190] The vision itself (11:1–12:3) describes a many winged, multi-headed eagle that reigns over the earth, each wing or head taking its turn at ruling before disappearing. Its dominion is oppressive. Then, "a creature like a lion was roused out of the forest, roaring ... he uttered a man's voice to the eagle, and spoke ..." (11:37). Speaking for the Most High, the lion indicts the eagle for its crimes (11:40–43) and pronounces judgment against it (11:45–46), a judgment which is fulfilled (12:1–3).

Ezra requests an interpretation of the vision (12:4–9), which is given (12:10–34). The eagle is identified with the fourth kingdom mentioned in Daniel, here, understood to be Rome. The various wings and heads appear to represent assorted Roman leaders and their oppressive rules. Then the lion is explained:

---

[185]B. M. Metzger, "The Fourth Book of Ezra," *The Old Testament Pseudepigrapha* (2 vols.; ed. J. H. Charlesworth; Garden City, NY: Doubleday, 1985) 1:519; M. E. Stone, *Fourth Ezra* (Hermeneia; Minneapolis: Fortress, 1990) 10–11.

[186]Stone, *Fourth Ezra*, 10; J. M. Myers, *I and II Esdras* (AB 42; Garden City, NY: Doubleday, 1974) 129; Metzger, *OTP*, 1:520; Klausner, *Messianic Idea*, 349.

[187]Metzger, *OTP*, 1:520. Stone, *Fourth Ezra*, 10, is less certain.

[188]Klausner, *Messianic Idea*, 350; see also Stone, *Fourth Ezra*, 40, on connections with rabbinic teachings.

[189]M. E. Stone, "The Question of the Messiah in 4 Ezra," *Judaisms and Their Messiahs at the Turn of the Christian Era* (ed. J. Neusner, W. S. Green, and E. S. Frerichs; Cambridge: Cambridge University Press, 1987) 216–220; but see below, p. 221.

[190]For a detailed discussion of this passage, see Stone, *Fourth Ezra*, 343–380.

this is the Messiah whom the Most High has kept until the end of days, who will arise from the posterity of David, and will come and speak to them; he will denounce them for their ungodliness and for their wickedness, and will cast up before them their contemptuous dealings. For he will set them living before his judgment seat, and when he has reproved them, then he will destroy them. But he will deliver in mercy the remnant of my people, those who have been saved throughout my borders, and he will make them joyful until the end comes, the day of judgment, of which I spoke to you at the beginning (vv. 32–34).[191]

Several observation concerning this figure's characterization can be noted. First, the image of a lion, possibly derived from Gen 49:9–10, is applied to this davidic figure.[192] Moreover, he is called "the seed (Syr: *zr^ch*) of David" and specifically named the messiah (Lat: *unctus*; Syr: *msyh^ɔ*) [12:32]. In addition, while the lion is said to utter a man's voice, implying the humanity of this posterity of David, this messianic figure is also described as "being kept until the end of days," a phrase taken by M. E. Stone to imply his preexistence.[193] Further, he is active at the "end of days," yet prior to the last judgment, suggesting a temporary messianic kingdom comparable to that mentioned in 4 Ezra 7:26ff.[194] Finally, this figure is said to arise (Lat: *suscitatus*) from the forest.[195]

Most important, however, is the role of this figure. In the vision itself, the lion's sole function is to speak words of indictment and judgment to the eagle. This results, first, in the disappearance of the remaining head and wings of the eagle, "so that the whole earth, freed from violence, may be refreshed and relieved, and may hope for the judgment and mercy of him who made it," and secondly, in the burning of its body, though the agent of its destruction is not indicated here.

Yet, in the interpretation of the vision his role is expanded. To be sure, his reproving of the fourth kingdom remains an important function.[196] Beyond this,

---

[191]The phrase mentioning the seed of David is missing in the Latin version, but present in the Syriac and other versions; there is little doubt about its presence in the original (cf. M. E. Stone, "The Concept of the Messiah in 4 Ezra," *Religions in Antiquity* [Studies in the History of Religions 14; ed. J. Neusner; Leiden: Brill, 1968] 311).

[192]Note that Gen 49:9–10 was associated with the davidic king in 4QpGen^a 5:1–7.

[193]Stone, "Concept," 310; Mowinckel, *He That Cometh*, 334, holds that this preexistence should be understood as being part of God's plan, not necessarily objective existence, though he admits that this fine distinction would have no doubt been lost. Myers, *Esdras*, 127, likewise thinks the messiah is understood to be pre-existent.

[194]In 4 Ezra 11:44 and 12:32, his activity is at the end, while in 12:34, he makes the people joyful until the end comes, the day of judgment. Cf. Stone, "Concepts," 296, for a discussion of 4 Ezra's use of the term "end."

[195]Interestingly, the verb *suscitare* is the same verb used in the Vulgate translation of הקימתי in 2 Sam 7:12 and הקמתי in Jer 23:5.

[196]Cf. 12:31, which refers to his speaking and reproving; in 12:32, he will come and speak

however, he will set his adversaries living before his judgment seat, reprove them, and destroy them, and will deliver in mercy the remnant of the people and make them joyful. Thus, in the interpretation, and in contrast to his role as merely a spokesperson of judgment in the vision itself, this figure actually is the judge who denounces and sentences, as well as executioner and deliverer. Notably absent for this davidic messiah is any military function, even though this vision's political implications are unmistakable.[197] Yet, as Stone points out, this messianic figure is never spoken of as a king; he never rules over people. On the contrary, his activities, which are largely directed against Rome, are formulated in legal terms.[198]

Further light may be shed on the conception of the davidic messiah in 12:32 by looking at another passage involving a messianic figure in 4 Ezra 13.[199] Here the figure is a man from the sea, whose description echoes that of the Son of Man in Daniel 7. In the vision, a large crowd of men amass to make war against this figure (13:5,8). When they attack, the man exhales a fire storm that—without weapons of war—annihilates the attackers, after which a peaceable multitude is gathered to him.[200]

Having seen this vision, Ezra requests (vv. 14–20) and is granted an interpretation of it (vv. 21–53). But because the interpretation is so loosely fitted to the vision itself and otherwise conforms to the author's viewpoint elsewhere in 4 Ezra, Stone has argued that "the author is here writing his own interpretation to a previously existent allegory."[201] Specifically relevant for this study is the fact that the interpretation of the vision describes the function of the man from the sea in much the same way as the function of the davidic figure is set forth in chap. 12: "The understanding of this man in the interpretation, however, is substantially that of the Messiah in chaps. 11–12."[202] For example, the man from the sea is explained as he:

---

to them, denounce them, and cast up before them their ungodliness.

[197]Cf. Charlesworth, "Concept," 206, who remarks that this figure is not militant in the ordinary sense.

[198]Stone, "Question," 215.

[199]For a summary of the messiah in 4 Ezra as a whole, see M. E. Stone, *Features of the Eschatology of IV Ezra* (HSS; Atlanta: Scholars Press, 1989) 131–133.

[200]For the flaming breath that destroys the enemy, see Isa 11:4b.

[201]Stone, "Concept," 306, who rightly rejects the source theories of Box; for a detailed discussion of this issue, see Stone, *Fourth Ezra*, 11–23, esp. pp. 11–13.

[202]Stone, "Concept," 309; cf. also Collins, *Imagination*, 166; and Charlesworth, "Concept," 205. Note too that the judicial role of the man from the sea is very similar to the role of the one like a Son of Man in Daniel 7.

whom the Most High has been keeping for many ages ... and he, my son, will reprove the assembled nations for their ungodliness (this was symbolized by the storm), and will reproach them to their face with their evil thoughts and with the torments with which they are to be tortured (which were symbolized by the flames); and he will destroy them without effort by the law (which was symbolized by the fire). And as for your seeing him gather to himself another multitude that was peaceable, these are the ten tribes which were led away from their own land into captivity ... (13:26a,37–40a).

This characterization is heavily influenced by Isaiah 11 as was the characterization in 4 Ezra 11–12, and although the man from the sea is not explicitly called the messiah or labelled as a davidic figure, there is no doubt that he is understood as a symbol for the messiah.[203]

Therefore, it becomes clear that the davidic figure of chap. 12 and the man from the sea are understood by the author of 4 Ezra as having the same function, or conversely, that the messianic figure that would be active at the "end" could be described in terms of a davidic descendant or in terms of a cosmic figure like the man from the sea. Consequently, although the two images originated in different complexes of tradition, in 4 Ezra they have coalesced.[204] Going a step further Collins remarks, "The two strands of tradition have been fused so that both have been transformed."[205]

This fusion of a cosmic figure with a davidic descendant has been viewed by some as a contradiction. G. H. Box, for instance, who posited source theories and frequent editorial adjustments in 4 Ezra, believed that the phrase in 12:32, "whom the Most High has kept until the end of days," was secondary, because davidic descent did not allow for the transcendence implied in that phrase.[206] J. Keulers also noted this apparent inconsistency, but solved it in the other direction, saying, "Man hat die davidische Herkunft des Messias hier als starres Dogma zu betrachten, das seine eigentliche Bedeutung eingebüsst hat ..."[207]

Stone is less disturbed by the association of heavenly origin and davidic (and earthly) descent for a messianic figure, comparing it to a similar kind of mixing of characteristics found in the Melchizedek figure known from *2 Enoch*

---

[203]Stone, "Concept," 307; and Charlesworth, "Concept," 205, observe that the man from the sea is identified as 'my son', a title already used for the messiah in 7:28–29. Note, too, that "my son" (*filius*) is probably the Latin translation of the Greek παῖς (cf. Collins, *Imagination*, 244 n. 25; but see Klausner, *Messianic Idea*, 358, for another view.)

[204]See Collins, *Imagination*, 166, for his remark about the coalescence of messianic figures.

[205]Collins, *Imagination*, 167.

[206]G. H. Box, *The Ezra-Apocalypse* (London: Pitman, 1912) xxiii–xxiv, cited in Stone, "Concept," 297.

[207]J. Keulers, *Die eschatologische Lehre des vierten Esrabuches* (Biblische Studien 20:2,3; Freiburg: Herder, 1922) 115.

and 11QMelch.[208] He adds, however, that the reference to davidic descent is traditional and not a central concept of the book.[209] Given the paucity of material about a davidic messiah in Second Temple literature, it is not clear what Stone means by "traditional," but his point about it not being a central concept is true, even though the strong influence of Isaiah 11 on the description of the figure suggests more overtones of the davidic dynasty tradition than a surface reading might suggest. Nevertheless, whether or not it is a central concept, the text itself indicates, as we have said above, that the messianic figure in 4 Ezra could be described in both davidic and cosmic terms. The contradiction perceived by modern interpreters was presumably not understood as such by the author.

Accordingly, in addition to the point we have made above, we can sum up the depiction of the davidic messiah by noting that his prime function is to judge and destroy the Romans. Of course, this political theme is not surprising in the wake of the Jewish defeat by the Romans in 70 CE. Yet other themes are absent: military images are lacking, little is said about the messianic age that is inaugurated, and nothing is said about this messiah's reign. In this regard, Stone's observations are apt: the messiah in 4 Ezra lacks royal characteristics and the author does not envision the future state as monarchical.[210] The other main function ascribed to this figure is the ingathering of the remnant of Israel. Yet, given the limited scope of salvation described elsewhere in 4 Ezra,[211] it is doubtful whether this even includes all of Israel. But here this whole subject is left vague.

A further issue concerns the precise function of the davidic dynasty tradition in 12:32. If the davidic descent of the messiah cannot be explained as merely traditional, we must seek another reason for its use here in the characterization of the messianic figure. Stone, citing 4 Ezra 7:29, observes that the messiah of 4 Ezra dies. He writes, "Consequently it seems clear that the restoration of the ideal situation of the Davidic monarchy did not play a major role in the author's expectations for his ideal future polity."[212] This conclusion gains further support when we recall that nothing is said about the davidic messiah's reign or kingdom. The focus is wholly on the destruction of the enemy, Rome. The contours of Jewish life after the destruction of the enemy are simply described as a time of joy for the remnant of Israel.

---

[208]Stone, "Concept," 297.

[209]Stone, "Concept," 311.

[210]Stone, *Fourth Ezra*, 42,41.

[211]For instance, 7:45–74.

[212]Stone, "Question," 219; on the limited role for the messiah in 4 Ezra, see Stone, *Fourth Ezra*, 41.

Moreover, since the elimination of Rome is understood in judicial terms, it becomes clear why the davidic dynasty tradition in Isa 11:1–5, especially 11:3b–5, has had a primary influence. There the shoot from the stump of Jesse is described as a righteous judge who will "smite the earth with the rod of his mouth and with the breath of his lips he shall slay the wicked." Thus, the characterization of the messiah as a descendant of David, construed in terms of Isa 11:3b–5, would reinforce the messiah's role as the one who judges and destroys the nations, in this case, Rome. In addition, by understanding the davidic messiah according to Isa 11:3b–5, the author could easily assimilate this davidic figure to the cosmic figure—the man from the sea, who like his counterpart, the Son of Man in Daniel 7, was likewise involved in judging and destroying oppressive nations. Hence, the function of the davidic dynasty tradition in 4 Ezra is to aid in the characterization of the messiah as the righteous judge and destroyer of Israel's oppressor. In this regard, although it is difficult to establish the identity of the author, it appears that he must have perceived the crisis facing his community as very grave, since his interests are directed entirely toward the destruction of Rome, with little consideration about the nature of life in Israel beyond this.[213]

Finally, some connections with other passages need to be noted. The text which has the most in common with 4 Ezra 11–12 is *Pss. Sol.* 17. In both, the messiah purges unrighteous rulers by his word, one of his primary functions is judging, the restoration of Israel is a significant theme, a political orientation is present, and Isaiah 11 has marked influence. And whereas *Pss. Sol.* 17 is marked by some apocalyptic ideas, 4 Ezra is itself an apocalypse. Moreover, as mentioned above, the fusion of a davidic and a cosmic figure in 4 Ezra represents a further heightening of the superhuman description of the messiah found in *Pss. Sol.* 17. Nevertheless, in *Pss. Sol.* 17, davidic descent stands as a central feature of the description, unlike its less prominent role in 4 Ezra. Likewise, the messiah's attributes, his ruling function, and the messianic kingdom all receive attention in *Pss. Sol.* 17, while in 4 Ezra these are notably muted or absent.

Furthermore, the depiction of the davidic figure in 4 Ezra is politically charged, as it was in the Qumran texts about the Branch of David; likewise his role as judge is prominent in both contexts. In addition, the influence of Isaiah 11 is present in 4 Ezra and Qumran texts. But in contrast to ideas in Qumran texts, 4 Ezra appears to have no interest in priestly figures alongside the davidic messiah, and in this way, stands quite apart from a central concern at Qumran.

---

[213]See Stone, *Fourth Ezra*, 40–42, on the limited results in seeking to determine a social context and function for 4 Ezra.

C. Josephus

Josephus, like the author of 4 Ezra, stands at the end of the period under study, but represents a very different view of the davidic dynasty tradition than one finds in 4 Ezra. Yet, unlike many of the other texts reviewed in this study, Josephus' view of the davidic dynasty tradition does not seem to have attracted the attention of scholars. While there are more general studies treating Josephus' use of the Jewish scriptures,[214] and examinations of his portrayal of various scriptural heroes,[215] there exists to my knowledge no work specifically devoted to Josephus' interpretation of David or the davidic dynastic tradition.[216] In light of the absence of prior work on this topic, the approach pursued below will be to analyze passages from Josephus pertaining to the davidic dynasty tradition and to assess his understanding of it. Following this, I will show how Josephus' interpretation of this biblical tradition fits well his overall approach to biblical history.

Josephus' comments about the davidic dynasty all appear in his work *The Jewish Antiquities*, a history of the Jewish people written in 93–94 CE,[217] which in the first eleven books is essentially a paraphrase of biblical material. Taken together the various references to the davidic dynasty tradition form a coherent view that depicts the davidic dynasty as a glorious phase in the history of Israel which nevertheless came to an end because of the failure of the davidic kings to obey the law of Moses. This construal is evident in the very first reference to the davidic dynasty in the *Antiquities*, where, at the conclusion of his account of the story of Ruth, Josephus paraphrases Ruth 4:17: "Of Obed was born Jesse, and of him David, who became king and bequeathed his dominion to his posterity for one and twenty generations" (*Ant.* 5.336).[218] Josephus' point here is to show how God can promote a person, like David, descended from ordinary folk like Ruth and Boaz, to greatness (*Ant.* 5.337). Yet, this passage indicates that Josephus conceived of the davidic dynasty as a finite stage in the history of Israel. There were twenty-one kings and the dynasty came to an end. Indeed, this passage is all

---

[214]See for example H. W. Attridge, *The Interpretation of Biblical History in the Antiquitates Judaicae of Flavius Josephus* (HDR 7; Missoula, MT: Scholars Press, 1976); S. Rappoport, *Agada und Exegese bei Flavius Josephus* (Vienna: Kohut, 1930); for other works, see L. H. Feldman, *Josephus and Modern Scholarship (1937–1980)* (Berlin: De Gruyter, 1984) 121–130.

[215]See Feldman, *Modern Scholarship*, 143–190.

[216]C. R. Holladay, Theios Aner *in Hellenistic-Judaism* (SBLDS 40; Missoula, MT: Scholars Press, 1977) 75–77, devotes a very brief section to Josephus' portrayal of David.

[217]H. W. Attridge, "Josephus and His Works," *Jewish Writings of the Second Temple Period* (CRINT 2:2; Assen: Van Gorcum/Philadelphia: Fortress, 1984) 210–211.

[218]English translations of Josephus are from the LCL.

the more noteworthy, since Josephus' comment about the length of the davidic dynasty is in no way paralleled in Ruth 4:17, where only a bare genealogy is given.

This understanding of the davidic dynasty as a finite stage in the history of Israel is illustrated in other passages as well. When he narrates the end of the kingdom of Judah, Josephus remarks:

> Thus, then, did the kings of David's line end their lives; there were twenty-one of them including the last king and they reigned altogether for five hundred and fourteen years, six months and ten days (*Ant.* 10.143).

In addition, it is clear why Josephus treats the davidic dynasty as having ended and does not indicate any expectation for the resumption of davidic kingship. For him the monarchy was a phase in the governance of Israel, preceded by the rule of judges and followed by the leadership of high priests and Hasmonean kings:

> For the high priests were at the head of affairs until the descendants of the Asomonaean family came to rule as kings. Before the captivity and deportation they were ruled by kings, beginning first with Saul and David, for five hundred and thirty-two years, six months and ten days; and before these kings the rulers who governed them were the men called judges and monarchs, and under this form of government they lived for more than five hundred years after the death of Moses and the commander Joshua (*Ant.* 11.112).[219]

Moreover, Josephus' conception of the davidic dynasty as a glorious but finite stage in the life of Israel is borne out in his handling of the biblical passages about the davidic covenant and specific davidic kings. On the one hand, he interprets these passages so as to emphasize the long length of the davidic dynasty, its greatness and splendor, and maybe most importantly, that it was conditioned on the faithfulness of its kings to the law of Moses. On the other hand, he avoids blanket statements about the eternity of the royal line and never characterizes the dynastic promise to David in terms of a covenant. The various passages from the *Antiquities* cited below illustrate these themes.

The themes of great length, greatness and renown, and conditionality are introduced by Josephus in his version of the anointing of David by Samuel (cf. 1 Sam 16:1–13). In the biblical account, Samuel merely anoints David (1 Sam 16:13); in the *Antiquities*, after Samuel anoints David, Josephus adds:

> He also exhorted him to be righteous and obedient to His commandments, for so would the kingship long continue to be his, and his house would become splendid and renowned ... he would in his lifetime attain glorious fame and bequeath it to his posterity (*Ant.* 6.165).

---

[219]Cf. also *Ant.* 10.151, where Josephus refers to those who were high priests "in the period of the kings" (ἐπὶ τοῖς βασιλεῦσι).

Whether the length of the kingship here refers to David's own reign or that of his dynasty is not clear.[220] Yet in either case, kingship is conditioned on David's righteousness and obedience.

We encounter similar ideas in Josephus' account of the dynastic promise given through the prophet Nathan (cf. 2 Sam 7:11–16; 1 Chr 17:10–15):

> ... He said, after David's death at an advanced age and at the end of a long life, the temple should be brought into being by his son and successor to the kingdom, whose name would be Solomon, and whom He promised to watch over and care for as a father for his son, and to preserve the kingdom for his children's children and transmit it to them, but He would punish him, if he sinned, with sickness and barrenness of soil. When David heard this from the prophet, he rejoiced greatly to know assuredly that the royal power would remain with his descendants and that his house would become glorious and renowned (*Ant.* 7.93–95).

Here, in contrast to the biblical account, Josephus offers a weaker version of the divine promise: there is no mention of a covenant; it is said that the kingdom will be preserved for Solomon's children's children instead of forever (עד־עולם); and the unconditional nature of the promise, made explicit in the biblical account, is left unstated.[221] Characteristically, Josephus again draws attention to the glory and renown that would attend the davidic house. Here it is not specifically stated that the dynastic promise is conditional—only the prosperity under Solomon is contingent on obedience,[222] but as we will see in the next few passages examined, the conditional character of the dynasty is clearly stipulated, while references to the unconditional eternity of davidic kingship are omitted from Josephus' paraphrase of the biblical text.

In this regard, a comparison between a verse from the biblical account of David's exhortation to Solomon and Josephus' paraphrase of it shows how

---

[220]For Josephus, however, the notion of a davidic dynasty is already assumed before the story of God's promise of a dynasty given through the prophet Nathan. Thus, when David is anointed king over all Israel in Hebron (2 Sam 5:3; 1 Chr 11:3), Josephus goes beyond the biblical text in saying that David was made king, "together with his sons" (*Ant.* 7.53).

[221]Note too how the filial relationship between God and the king is weakened in Josephus' version, where God will only watch over Solomon as a father for his son, instead of the biblical notion of God being a father to the king and the king being a son to God.

[222]Cf. also *Ant.* 7.373 in David's commendation of Solomon to the people, where he says, "I pray, then, that the prosperity which He Himself has declared He will send during Solomon's reign will be diffused throughout the entire land and continue with it for all time. These things will be assured and will come to a happy issue, if you show yourself to be pious and just, my son, and an observer of our country's laws. Otherwise, if you transgress them, you must expect a worse fate."

Josephus avoids reference to the eternity of the dynasty. In 1 Chr 22:10 in a reference to the dynastic promise, it reads:

> He shall be my son, and I will be his father, and I will establish his royal throne in Israel for ever.

Josephus paraphrases in *Ant.* 7.337:

> and promised to watch over him like a father, and bring prosperity to the country of the Hebrews in his reign.

Thus, instead of a royal throne forever, the dynastic promise pledges prosperity for Solomon.

The explicitly conditional nature of the davidic dynasty is well illustrated in Josephus' version of David's dying charge to Solomon (cf. 1 Kgs 2:1–4). After exhorting Solomon to obey the commandments set down by Moses, he continues:

> do not neglect them by yielding either to favour or flattery or lust or any other passion, for you will lose the goodwill of the Deity toward you, if you transgress any of His ordinances, and you will turn his kind watchfulness into a hostile attitude. But, if you show yourself to be such as you should be and as I urge you to be, you will secure the kingdom to our line, and no other house than we shall be lords over the Hebrews for all time (*Ant.* 7.384–385).

If Solomon is righteous, he will secure the kingdom for the davidic line. This is clearly a conditional arrangement. Likewise, Josephus in his account of God's promise to Solomon given in a dream (cf. 1 Kgs 9:4–9) highlights the conditional nature of the kingship:

> as for the king himself, God said that if he abided by his father's counsels, He would first raise him to a height and greatness of happiness beyond measure, and that those of his own line should for ever rule the country and the tribe of Judah. If, however, he should be faithless to his task and forget it and turn to the worship of foreign gods, He would cut him off root and branch and would not suffer any of their line to survive ... (*Ant.* 8.126–127).

In the last two examples, Josephus' paraphrase of the biblical text simply retains the conditional notion of davidic kingship stated in his source, although in the latter case, Josephus is noticeably more explicit about the fate of the dynasty in the face of disobedience ("He would cut him off root and branch and would not suffer any of their line to survive"). This is significant, however, since in the absence of clear affirmations of the unconditional nature of the davidic dynasty, Josephus' retention and heightening of the conditional promises found in Dtr and Chronicles is determinative.[223] In effect, the potential ambiguity about the status

---

[223]In *Ant.* 8.113, Josephus does not explicitly say the kingship is conditional, but it appears

of the davidic dynasty in Josephus' sources, where both conditional and unconditional promises exist, is removed. For Josephus, the fate of the davidic dynasty
rests on the faithfulness of its kings to God's law given by Moses.

In this regard, one can see how Josephus' conception of the davidic dynasty
fits his overall theological interpretation of Jewish history. In a study of the
interpretive scheme used by Josephus in *The Jewish Antiquities*, H. W. Attridge
has pointed to the concept of providence (πρόνοια) as the fundamental theological theme of the work.[224] Attridge notes how God's providence toward Israel is
expressed in benefactor/alliance terminology, which replaces the covenant language of Josephus' biblical source.[225] Important is Attridge's explanation for this
change:

> A second possible explanation, which affects primarily the alliance language, is
> that this terminology does not imply any necessary, formal, long-term or auto-
> matic commitment on the part of God to act on behalf of the Israelites.[226]

He goes on to say:

> A special relationship between God and Israel exists, but it is not stressed in the
> *Antiquities*. In fact it is limited by another factor which also explains the basis
> for that relationship. This is the fact that the major component in God's provi-
> dential care for the world is His retributive intervention to reward the righteous
> and punish the wicked. His special concern for Israel is ultimately due to the
> special virtue of the people or its leaders.[227]

Accordingly, it is not just for the davidic dynasty tradition that Josephus avoids
the idea of a everlasting unconditional covenant, but he avoids it completely in his

---

to be implied. In Solomon's prayer at the dedication of the temple, he asks God to "increase
our house for ever, as Thou didst promise David, my father, both in his lifetime and when he
was near death, saying that the kingship should remain among us and that his descendants
should transmit it to numberless successors." But this is qualified in the next sentence: "These
things, therefore, do Thou grant us, and to my sons give that virtue in which Thou delightest."
Hence, Josephus considers the continuance of the dynasty closely associated with the virtue of
the kings. Also, in *Ant.* 9.145, in his account of Queen Athalia's unsuccessful attempt to stamp
out the davidic line, Josephus quotes the high priest Jehoida as he presents the young king
Joash to the people: "This is your king from that house, which, as you know, God foretold to
us should rule for all time to come." The context is such that one would not expect a statement
about the conditional nature of the dynasty; yet neither is the dynasty explicitly said to be
unconditionally guaranteed. Given Josephus' overall understanding of the conditional nature of
the dynasty, this passage must also be viewed in that context.

[224] Attridge, *Interpretation*, 71–76; "Josephus," 218–219.

[225] Attridge, *Interpretation*, 78–80.

[226] Attridge, *Interpretation*, 82.

[227] Attridge, *Interpretation*, 83.

interpretation of Jewish history. Virtue, not divinely initiated select status, is what makes the relationship between God and the Jews unique. It is not, therefore, surprising that Josephus applies the same criterion of retributive justice to the davidic monarchy as he does to the rest of Jewish history.

Of course, the idea of retributive justice is present in Dtr and Chronicles, but as Attridge observes with respect to Josephus' handling of his sources, Josephus not only adopts but reinforces this theology of retributive justice.[228] Indeed, this is precisely what we noted above concerning Josephus' redaction of the biblical passages dealing with the davidic dynastic promise: the conditional conception of kingship, contingent as it is on the obedience or virtue of the kings, was repeated or heightened.[229] And since Josephus was well aware of the failings of Solomon and later davidic kings, the end of the davidic dynasty after twenty-one kings would be an example of God's providential activity of rewarding virtue and punishing disobedience. Consequently, we see that Josephus' interpretation of the davidic dynasty tradition is actually a specific instance of his overall interpretive program in the *Antiquities*.

This last observation leads us then to a better understanding of the positive function of Josephus' interpretation of the davidic dynasty tradition. For him, most importantly, it provides a moral lesson. God rewards those who obey his laws and punishes those who do not. This is how Josephus states his purpose in the *Antiquities*:

> But, speaking generally, the main lesson to be learnt from this history by any who care to peruse it is that men who conform to the will of God, and do not venture to transgress laws that have been excellently laid down, prosper in all things beyond belief, and for their reward are offered by God felicity; whereas, in proportion as they depart from the strict observance of these laws, things (else) practicable become impracticable, and whatever imaginary good thing they strive to do ends in irretrievable disaster (*Ant.* 1.14).

This moralizing is a dominant theme throughout the *Antiquities*.[230] But again, it is not surprising that Josephus' interpretation of the davidic dynasty tradition contributes to this more general intention. Yet, another motif present in Josephus' construal of the davidic dynasty serves a different aim in the *Antiquities*. Specifically, Josephus' emphasis on the long length and splendor of the davidic dynasty

---

[228]Attridge, *Interpretation*, 84–87, esp. p. 86.

[229]Attridge, *Interpretation*, 91, notes that in Moses' speech from Deuteronomy, "the special relationship of God to Israel is mentioned, but the conditional nature of that relationship is emphasized," depending on conformity to God's will.

[230]See Attridge, *Interpretation*, 109–144, for a discussion of this theme in the *Antiquities*, along with examples.

undoubtedly contributed to his apologetic purpose of presenting a favorable portrait of Judaism to his Greco-Roman readers.[231]

Thus, as stated at the outset, Josephus viewed the davidic dynasty as a glorious phase in Jewish history that came to an end due to the disobedience of its kings.[232] It is now clear that this portrait of the davidic dynasty tradition fit Josephus' theological conception of divine providence and his moralizing and apologetic purposes in the *Antiquities*. On the other hand, there is not a trace of davidic messianism in the *Antiquities*. Unlike his near contemporary, the author of 4 Ezra, Josephus had no expectations for a Jewish messiah, davidic or otherwise. In fact, in *The Jewish War* Josephus applies an undetermined biblical text about a world ruler, which was interpreted by some of his contemporaries as referring to a Jewish figure, to Vespasian, the Roman general and emperor to be:[233]

> But what more than all else incited them to war was an ambiguous oracle, likewise found in their sacred scriptures, to the effect that at that time one from their country would become ruler of the world. This they understood to mean someone of their own race, and many of their wise men went astray in their interpretation of it. The oracle, however, in reality signified the sovereignty of Vespasian, who was proclaimed Emperor on Jewish soil (*J.W.* 6.312–313).

That Josephus thought that Vespasian was a "messiah" is doubtful.[234] Nevertheless, his interpretation of the scriptural oracle as referring to Vespasian is reminiscent of the position espoused by Deutero-Isaiah, that Cyrus was the Lord's designated messiah and world ruler (Isa 44:28–45:1).[235]

Whether Josephus' interpretation of the davidic dynasty tradition is uniquely his or represents that of other thoroughly hellenized Jews is difficult to say.

---

[231]Cf. Schürer, *History*, 1:48, who characterizes the purpose of the *Antiquities* as that of eliciting "from the cultivated world respect for the much calumniated Jewish people." For the Greco-Roman audience of the *Antiquities*, see Schürer, *History*, 1:48; Attridge, "Josephus," 217.

[232]Note that this is similar to the interpretation of the davidic dynasty found in Ben Sira (see above, pp. 150–151).

[233]This text in *The Jewish War* is significant for investigating whether the messianic beliefs of the Jewish revolutionaries involved davidic hopes, and thus it will be dealt with in this context later in chap. 6.

[234]See M. de Jonge, "Josephus und die Zukunftserwartungen seines Volkes," *Josephus-Studien: Untersuchungen zu Josephus, dem antiken Judentum und dem Neuen Testament* (ed. O. Betz, K. Haacker, and M. Hengel; Göttingen: Vandenhoeck & Ruprecht, 1974) 209–210.

[235]Cf. also 2 Chr 36:23, where it says that the Lord gave Cyrus all the kingdoms of the earth. Whether Josephus had this precedent in mind is difficult to say, but in *J.W.* 3.351–354, Josephus attributes his skill in divining the fate of Vespasian as the future emperor (cf. *J.W.* 3.400–402) to his priestly status and *knowledge of the prophecies in the sacred books*.

Nevertheless, he stands as an example of a Jew at the end of the first century CE who did not share a belief in the davidic messianism that would ultimately characterize both Christianity and later rabbinic Judaism.

CHAPTER 6
Davidic Figures and Other Royal
Messianic Figures

In the previous three chapters, the history of the davidic dynasty tradition has been traced through the period of early Judaism. Several passages described a davidic messianic figure variously called the Son, Branch, or Seed of David. Yet, one hears of other royal messianic figures in early Jewish literature and history, such as the Messiah of Israel in Qumran literature, the Messiah of Judah in the *Testaments of the Twelve Patriarchs,* and Simon bar Giora in Josephus. The question before us in the present chapter, therefore, is how these other figures relate to the specifically davidic messianic figures previously discussed.

It is important to raise this question because it is not uncommon for some of these other royal messianic figures to be labelled "davidic," even when they are not identified as such. Behind this identification no doubt lies in part the assumption that hope for a davidic messiah was "traditional," i.e., a continuous, widespread, dominant, and in some cases uniform, expectation among Jews in the Second Temple period. Hence, all royal figures are viewed through the lens of this traditional expectation. In the present study, this assumption about a traditional davidic messianic hope has been questioned. In fact, as the previous chapters illustrate actual data for a such a hope is sparse. Therefore, it may not be taken for granted that all royal messianic figures were davidic messiahs. In this regard, already in 1959 M. Smith warned against harmonizing differing messianic conceptions:

> Though unjustified, the tacit presupposition of uniformity is common, witness the many articles which take for granted that the data are to be harmonized ... But the manifest diversity of the material requires us first to make complete and

distinct accounts of each separate title, and not to impose on any document any concept it does not clearly contain.[1]

The present chapter is an attempt to heed Smith's warning. The plan of the chapter is as follows. I will consider royal messianic figures mentioned in texts from Qumran and the Messiah of Judah known from the *Testaments of the Twelve Patriarchs*. In each case, I will assess how these royal figures are related, if at all, to davidic messianism. Then, in the final section of this chapter, I will briefly draw attention to some other royal messianic figures known from early Jewish literature and history, who are clearly not davidic, in order to illustrate how hopes for a royal messiah could be based on other models of kingship present in the biblical tradition.

A. Royal Messiahs at Qumran

One dimension of Qumran theology that has generated an enormous amount of scholarly interest is the variety of messianic conceptions present in the texts from Qumran.[2] A number of messianic figures, some priestly or royal, others prophetic or cosmic, played a role in the world of Qumran thought. It is not our goal here, however, to enter into the broader discussion of Qumran messianism; rather it is to focus only on those figures who possess royal—or at least leading lay politi-cal—status. Yet even in this more limited area one finds diversity: beyond the messiah, the Branch of David, one reads of the Messiah of Israel and the Prince of the Congregation. We may add to these another conception of a royal figure, not often dealt with in this context—the ideal king described in the "Statutes of the King" section of the *Temple Scroll*.[3]

---

[1]Smith, "Variety of Messianic Figures?" 71 n. 28; cf. also J. J. Collins, "Patterns of Escha-tology at Qumran," *Traditions in Transformation* (ed. B. Halpern and J. D. Levenson; Winona Lake, IN: Eisenbrauns, 1981) 351–375, esp. pp. 372–373, who observes the diversity of eschatological expectations at Qumran.

[2]See J. A. Fitzmyer, *The Dead Sea Scrolls: Major Publications and Tools for Study* (rev. ed.; SBLRBS 20; Atlanta: Scholars Press, 1990) 164–167, for a partial list of publications pertaining to Qumran messianism. For a recent treatment, see L. H. Schiffman, "Messianic Figures and Ideas in the Qumran Scrolls," *The Messiah* (ed. J. H. Charlesworth; Minneapolis: Fortress, 1992) 116–129.

[3]Other examples of davidic messianism in the scrolls have been claimed, but have not re-ceived broad acceptance; see Smith, "Variety of Messianic Figures?" 66–67; Brown, "The Messianism of Qumrân," 66–78. Also, it is unclear whether the figure who is designated "Son of God" in 4Q246 should be construed as a Jewish royal messiah (see E. Puech, "Fragment d'une apocalypse en Araméen [4Q246=ps Dan[d]] et le 'Royaume de Dieu'," *RB* 99 [1992] 98–131). Recently, J. J. Collins, "The *Son of God* Text from Qumran," *From Jesus to John* (JSNTSup 84; ed. M. C. De Boer; Sheffield: JSOT Press, 1993) 65–82, has argued that in 4Q246 the "Son of God" is a Jewish messiah, even a davidic messiah. However, the latter claim rests mainly on the link between the term "son" and the davidic dynasty tradition, and on

The question before us, then, is how these other royal figures are related to the davidic dynasty tradition, and in particular, to the davidic messiah described in 4QpGen[a], 4QFlor, 4QpIsa[a], and 4QSerek HaMilhamah.

Before attempting to answer this question, however, it will be helpful to consider some methodological issues raised by this diversity of royal figures. We can begin by noting that there has been a tendency to identify various royal figures; in particular, it is common for the Messiah of Israel and the Prince of the Congregation to be identified with the Branch of David.[4] On the other hand, as Smith and others have cautioned, we should not move so quickly to harmonize these different figures into one synthetic royal messiah for the Qumran community.[5] But how then should one account for the diversity of royal figures? Smith's own solution to this problem was that eschatology was "a comparatively arbitrary and individual matter ... about which the opinions of different members might, and did, differ quite widely ... "[6] Thus, differing and even conflicting messianic conceptions could stand side by side.[7] Another strategy for dealing with different

---

the similarity between 4Q246 and Luke 1:32–33. This appears to me to be too ambiguous a basis on which to identify the "Son of God," as a davidic messiah. In any case, if this claim were sustained, it would not substantially affect the thesis developed below.

[4]In older works see, for example, van der Woude, *Vorstellungen*, 185; Brown, "The Messianism of Qumrân," 57–58, who thought that the Prince of the Congregation was davidic, but was cautious about identifying the Messiah of Israel with the Prince of the Congregation; in a later article, however, Brown counts both the Prince of the Congregation and the Messiah of Israel as davidic (see "J. Starcky's Theory of Qumran Messianic Development," *CBQ* 28 [1966] 51,55); see also D. Barthélemy and J. T. Milik, *Qumran Cave I* (DJD 1; Oxford: Clarendon, 1955) 128–129. In more recent studies, see Schürer, *History*, 2:550–552; S. Talmon, "Waiting for the Messiah: The Spiritual Universe of the Qumran Covenanters," *Judaisms and Their Messiahs at the Turn of the Christian Era* (ed. J. Neusner, W. S. Green, and E. S. Frerichs; Cambridge: Cambridge University Press, 1987) 122; Dimant, "Sectarian Literature," 524.

[5]Smith's comments cited above were especially directed toward the study of Qumran messianism (see above, p. 231). For similar more recent cautions about relating different figures too readily, see Caquot, "Messianisme," 235; Schiffman, "Messianic Figures," 129; J. H. Charlesworth, "From Messianology to Christology: Problems and Prospects," *The Messiah* (ed. J. H. Charlesworth; Minneapolis: Fortress, 1992) 26.

[6]Smith, "Variety of Messianic Figures?" 72. Caquot, "Messianisme," 235, takes a similar position holding that as a haggadic matter, messianic speculation would have been free, as it appears to be in Tannaitic sources.

[7]The issue of differing royal messianic figures is related to the question of diverse eschatologies in the Dead Sea Scrolls. On the latter issue, see J. J. Collins, "Patterns," *passim*, who attempts to find an underlying consistency among the various eschatological conceptions; and P. R. Davies, "Eschatology at Qumran," *JBL* 104 (1985) 39–55.

messianic conceptions is to do so in terms of development. The first and most extensive proposal in this vein was made by J. Starcky, who proposed four stages in the development of Qumran messianism.[8] The specifics of Starcky's thesis foundered, however, on problems surrounding his dating of documents.[9] Nevertheless, the basic approach he employed was correct. Indeed, at least allowing for the development of ideas at Qumran is a recognized axiom of research.[10]

Yet attempting to trace the evolution of Qumran thought—even in the limited area of royal figures—raises questions that introduce more complexity.[11] One such question pertains to the dating of documents, or individual passages within a document, when a text is composite. Accordingly, in the following analysis it will be important not only to examine the various references to royal figures, but to assign approximate dates to these references. A second concern is whether all the Dead Sea Scrolls can be attributed to the community at Qumran. With respect to the texts dealt with below, all either reflect the specific ideology of the group at Qumran or, in the case of CD and 11QTemple, at least emanate from closely related groups, whether temporally prior or geographically separate from the Qumran community. In light of these points, therefore, I will proceed as follows: I will summarize the references to and characterizations of these royal figures, observing the dates of these references and considering how they relate to the davidic dynasty tradition; then, I will evaluate how these other royal figures relate to davidic messianism in the development of ideas about royal figures at Qumran.

To begin, then, the "Statutes of the King," in the *Temple Scroll* (11QTemple 56:12–59:21) consists of a set of laws that in effect describe an ideal Jewish king.[12] It opens with a slightly modified citation of Deut 17:14–20 and proceeds to present additional laws dealing with the royal army and guard, a judicial council, requirements in marriage, relations with subjects, and rules for war. It ends with a passage stating the curses and blessings that will result from disobe-

---

[8]Starcky, "Les Quatre Étapes du Messianisme à Qumran," *RB* 70 (1963) 481–505.

[9]On Starcky's dating of CD, see Brown, "Starcky's Theory," 52–57; on his dating of 1QM, see Dimant, "Sectarian Literature," 540 n. 267.

[10]Charlesworth, "Messianology," 26, writes, "... all work on the theology of the Dead Sea Scrolls is confused if it does not allow for diversity and development in the community," citing the attested variety in the community, redactions and additions to texts, and the long length of time Qumran was occupied. Cf. also Davies, "Eschatology," 45.

[11]Cf. Schiffman, "Messianic Figures," 116–117, on the complexity of studying Qumran messianism in general.

[12]M. Hengel, J. H. Charlesworth, and D. Mendels, "The Polemical Character of 'On Kingship' in the Temple Scroll: An Attempt at Dating 11QTemple," *JJS* 37 (1986) 38, comment that the author of 11QTemple takes a more practical and less utopian approach to Jewish politics. Nevertheless, the king in the *Temple Scroll* is still an ideal figure. For the text, as well as introductory material and commentary, see Yadin, *Temple Scroll*.

dience and faithfulness, respectively.[13] Several features of this section are pertinent to the image and role of the ideal king.

First, this king is clearly subordinated to priests.[14] Several passages illustrate this point. Thus, in contrast to Deut 17:18, where the king writes for himself a copy of this law, in 11QTemple 56:20–21 it says, "they shall write for him this law." The "they" who write the law are almost certainly the priests, who are in charge of the law.[15] Moreover, although the king is a military leader, in matters of war he is wholly dependent on the high priest:

> And he (the king) shall not go out until he comes before the high priest, who shall inquire for him by the judgment of the Urim and the Thummim. At his word he shall go out, and at his word he shall come in, both he and all the people of Israel with him ... (58:18–20).

Finally, the king's judicial powers are limited by a judicial council composed of 12 leaders of the people, 12 priests, and 12 Levites.

> They shall sit together with him for judgment and the law, that his heart may not be lifted up above them, and that he may not do anything by any counsel apart from them (57:13–14).

While membership on the judicial council is not limited to priests, it provides yet another venue for priestly oversight of royal activities. Thus, like the Branch of David, the ideal king in the *Temple Scroll* is subordinated to the priests, even in battle.

Secondly, the "Statutes of the King" lays out certain qualifications for the king. He must be an Israelite, one from among his brethren and no foreigner (56:14–15). No other tribal or familial qualifications are stipulated, however. His wife must be an Israelite and also from his father's family, but again no particular family is stated. What is of interest here is that no davidic or Judean lineage is required for the king. While it is true that the requirement of only being Jewish derives from Deut 17:15, the author did not hesitate to expand upon the provisions in Deut 17:14–20 in other matters. Yet, in this case no other genealogical conditions for kingship—davidic or otherwise—are added.[16]

---

[13]See Yadin, *Temple Scroll*, 1:346, for a complete outline of the contents of the "Statutes of the King."

[14]Similarly, Hengel, Charlesworth, and Mendels, "Polemical," 32; Yadin, *Temple Scroll*, 1:352.

[15]Hengel, Charlesworth, and Mendels, "Polemical," 32, suggest that those who write the law are either the priests or the scribes in the presence of the priest.

[16]L. H. Schiffman, "The King, His Guard, and the Royal Council in the *Temple Scroll*," *Proceedings of the American Academy for Jewish Research* (Jerusalem/New York: American

Thirdly, the final segment of the "Statutes of the King" (59:13–21) consists of curses and blessings upon the king:

> And the king whose heart and eyes strayed wantonly from my commandment, there shall be found nobody for him to sit on the throne of his fathers all the days, for I will cut off his descendants for ever from ruling over Israel. But if he will walk in my statutes, and will observe my commandments, and will do what is right and good in my sight, a man of his sons shall not be cut off from sitting on the throne of the kingdom of Israel for ever ... (59:13–18).

What is significant about this declaration of curses and blessings is the explicitly conditional understanding of Jewish kingship that is presupposed by it. Dynastic continuance depends only on obedience; disobedience would mean the end of the dynasty. This is obviously contrary to notions about an eternal davidic covenant or a guaranteed davidic dynasty. In fact, the phrases used to explain the results of royal disobedience express the opposite of what is promised in portions of the davidic dynasty tradition that speak about the unconditional perpetuity of the dynasty. A comparison of Jer 33:17 with 11QTemple 59:14–15 will illustrate this:

לא־יכרת לדוד איש ישב על־כסא בית־ישראל (Jer 33:17)[17]

לוא ימצא לו איש יושב על כסא אבותיו כול הימים (11QTemple 59:14f)

כי לעולם אכרית זרעו ממשול עוד על ישראל (11QTemple 59:15)

> For David a man who sits upon the throne of the house of Israel shall not be cut off (Jer 33:17).
> For him a man who sits upon the throne of his fathers will not be found forever (11QTemple 59:14f).
> For I will cut off his seed from ruling over Israel forever (11QTemple 59:15).

In 11QTemple 59:14f, the reversal is accomplished by substituting the word ימצא for יכרת; in 11QTemple 59:15, the promise is reversed by omitting the negative לא. Moreover, in both phrases from 11QTemple, the ultimacy of the action is intensified by indicating that the end of the dynasty is permanent (כול הימים and לעולם/עוד). Consequently, in the "Statutes of the King" we find a very different interpretation of Jewish kingship from that underlying a continuing davidic dynasty or a revival of it in a davidic messiah. This of course fits our

---

Academy for Jewish Research, 1987) 256, attributes the absence of reference to davidic descent to the author's attempt to avoid anachronisms. Hengel, Charlesworth, and Mendels, "Polemical," 31,35,38, think that 11QTemple is a practical document that had to deal with real—Hasmonean—kings.

[17]Cf. similar phrases in 1 Kgs 2:4; 8:25; 9:5.

observation above that the qualifications for the king in 11QTemple do not include davidic lineage.[18]

Thus, the evidence requires us to conclude that the ideal royal figure of 11QTemple was not understood as a davidic king. Nor is he legitimately called a messiah, since he is not an eschatological figure.[19] In these respects, the ideal king of the *Temple Scroll* is quite distinct from the Branch of David identified in other texts. On the other hand, like the davidic messiah at Qumran he is placed under the supervision of the priests. This we will see is a consistent motif in the way royal figures are treated in Qumran texts. The *Temple Scroll* dates from the second half of the second century BCE,[20] and therefore represents a case where, at this stage in Qumran thought, hopes were not pinned on a davidic messiah, or apparently any messiah at all.

With regard to the Messiah of Israel, there are six references in texts from Qumran. Four of these are found in the Damascus Document.[21] CD 12:23–13:1 speaks of the members of the Qumran community as those who will walk in certain statutes during the age of wickedness "until the coming of the Messiah of Aaron and Israel" (עד עמוד משוח אהרן וישראל). Similarly, in 14:19, although the context is fragmentary, there is mention of an exact statement of rulings that are prescriptive "[until the coming of Messia]h of Aaron and Israel."[22] In 19:10–11 the text refers to a time of visitation when those who hesitate will be given over to the sword "at the coming of the Messiah of Aaron and Israel" (בבוא משיח אהרן וישראל). And in 19:21–20:1, one hears of apostates who will not be counted among the council of the people "from the day of the gathering of the teacher of the community until the coming of the Messiah from Aaron and from Israel" (עד עמוד משוח מאהרן ומישראל).

---

[18]Thus, the failure to require the ideal king to be a davidic descendant is not due to an effort to avoid anachronisms, as Schiffman suggests (see above, n. 16), but the entire theory of Jewish kingship is different from one that posits the eternal validity of the davidic dynasty.

[19]Schiffman, "Messianic Figures," 127, notes that the *Temple Scroll* as a whole is not eschatological. Charlesworth, "Messianology," 25, observes that the *Temple Scroll* does not contain one reference to the "Messiah."

[20]For this date of 11QTemple, see Yadin, *Temple Scroll*, 1:386–390; most recently, M. O. Wise, *A Critical Study of the Temple Scroll From Qumran Cave 11* (Studies in Ancient Oriental Civilization 49; Chicago: Oriental Institute of the University of Chicago, 1990) 200, suggests a date of ca. 150 BCE; for a later dating, see Hengel, Charlesworth, and Mendels, "Polemical," 38 (103/2–88 BCE).

[21]The text of CD is from C. Rabin, *The Zadokite Documents* (Oxford: Clarendon, 1954).

[22]See Rabin, *Zadokite Documents*, 71; and Vermes, *DSS in English*, 99, for reconstruction of the lacuna.

Another reference to the Messiah of Israel occurs in 1QS 9:9b–11, where the community is instructed to maintain the original precepts in which it was first taught "until the prophet shall come and the Messiahs of Aaron and Israel" (עד בוא נביא ומשיחי אהרון וישראל).[23] Finally, 1QSa 2:11b–22 sets forth the protocol for an eschatological banquet.[24] Here, only after the priest, perhaps a priestly messiah, and his retinue have been seated may the Messiah of Israel and his associates enter. Likewise, the priest is the first to extend his hand in blessing over the bread; then the Messiah of Israel offers his blessing.

In light of these references we can now summarize some of the characteristics of the Messiah of Israel. For one, he is always mentioned along with and second to a priestly figure—the priest in 1QSa 2:11b–22, the Messiah of Aaron elsewhere.[25] Further, the coming of the Messiah of Israel represents a decisive moment in the course of events that can be designated eschatological: the community must remain faithful to certain legal norms until this time (CD 12:23–13:1; 14:19; 1QS 9:9b–11); it appears to mark the end of the age of wickedness (CD 12:23–13:1); it is connected with a visitation in which some will be given over to the sword (CD 19:10–11); and it brings final exclusion of apostates (CD 19:21–20:1).[26] Likewise, the Messiah of Israel plays a role at the eschatological feast (1QSa 2:11b–22). Other than this, a specific description of this figure is lacking.[27] In particular, nowhere is davidic status attributed to or implied for the Messiah of Israel;[28] nor is the davidic dynasty tradition invoked.

Accordingly, we conclude that the Messiah of Israel should not be conceived as a davidic figure, and therefore not identified with the Branch of David. Nevertheless, some interesting generic similarities exist between the Messiah of

[23]The text of 1QS is from M. Burrows, *The Dead Sea Scrolls of St. Mark's Monastery* (vol. 2; fasc. 2; New Haven: American Schools of Oriental Research, 1951).

[24]The text of 1QSa is from Barthélemy and Milik, DJD 1, 108–118. Cf. Collins, "Patterns," 356–358, for a discussion of how this eschatological banquet was proleptically experienced at Qumran.

[25]Although the singular משיח is used in the passages in CD, the grammar allows for two figures, and this is a widely accepted interpretation: cf. for example Brown, "The Messianism of Qumrân," 54–55; van der Woude, *Vorstellungen*, 29; Collins, "Patterns," 354, esp. n. 8; Talmon, "Waiting, 122.

[26]See P. R. Davies, *The Damascus Covenant* (JSOTSup 25; Sheffield: JSOT Press, 1982) 180, for this explanation of CD 19:21–20:1.

[27]It is unlikely that CD 14:19 attributes to the Messiah a role in atoning for sins; the context is far too fragmentary to make any claim (see Rabin, *Zadokite Documents*, 70–71, esp. p. 71 n. 19). As Collins, "Patterns," 355–356, notes, there is little emphasis on the personalities and activities of the messiahs at Qumran beyond that they will come.

[28]See similar observations by Caquot, "Messianisme," 238; and Schiffman, "Messianic Figures," 119,120,121.

Israel and the Branch of David. Both are eschatological figures and both appear alongside priestly figures. Further, although the Messiah of Israel is not explicitly described as a military figure, as is the Branch of David, his appearance is connected with some people being given over to the sword. In any case, the Messiah of Israel appears far less militant than the Branch of David. All documents that refer to the Messiah of Israel—CD, 1QS, and 1QSa—were composed ca. 100 BCE or earlier,[29] and consequently offer another instance where davidic messianism is not in evidence in this phase of Qumran thought.

Another royal figure, the Prince of (All) the Congregation, is mentioned in five passages. Since references to this figure are found in texts that date from different periods and the relationship between this figure and the davidic dynasty tradition is more complicated than was the case for the previous two royal figures, each text must be examined separately. One reference occurs in CD 7:19–20, which provides an interpretation of Num 24:17: "A star shall come forth out of Jacob and a scepter shall rise out of Israel." Whereas the star is identified with the Interpreter of the Law (cf. 7:18), the scepter is specified as the Prince of All the Congregation (נשיא כל העדה) [7:20]. It is further said that when he arises "he shall strike violently all the sons of Seth" (Num 24:17). Moreover, the literary context reflects divine eschatological vindication, indicating that the Prince is rightly viewed as a messiah. Accordingly, in this text from ca. 100 BCE, the Prince of All the Congregation is portrayed as a militant messianic figure who is juxtaposed to a priestly figure, the Interpreter of the Law. There is not, however, any suggestion that the Prince possesses davidic status.

Another passage referring to this same individual is 1QM 5:1–2, where it is stated that on the sh[ield] of the Prince of All the Congregation (נשיא כול העדה) should be written his name and the names of Israel, Levi, Aaron, the twelve tribes, and the twelve chiefs of their tribes.[30] Yet apart from this, the Prince of All the Congregation appears to play no part in military maneuvers, which are in the hands of the priests in the *War Scroll*. In fact, there is no description of the Prince's character or role, and he is not mentioned again in the remainder of the manuscript, a surprising feature in light of the warlike role ascribed to the Prince in CD 7:20. Consequently, here we learn little about the Prince of All the Con-

---

[29]For the dates of CD and 1QS, see Dimant, "Sectarian Literature," CD (not later than 100 BCE), p. 490; 1QS (second half of second century BCE), p. 498; for 1QSa, see Schiffman, "Eschatological Community," 8. The manuscript containing 1QS, 1QSa, and 1QSb has been dated to ca. 100–75 BCE and is a copy from an earlier exemplar.

[30]For the text, see Yadin, *War Scroll*, 279.

gregation. Included in this silence is any connection to the davidic dynasty tradition.

Assigning a date to the *War Scroll* is problematic. Based on its script, the manuscript of 1QM has been dated to the second half of the first century BCE, but one fragment of the *War Scroll* from Cave 4, or at least an earlier recension of it (4QMᶜ), dates to the first half of the second century BCE.[31] In addition, 1QM in its present form is composite, comprised of sections which come from different periods. In this regard, Davies has argued that cols. 2–9, which include the reference to the Prince of All the Congregation, represent an early section of the *War Scroll*, portions of which go back to the aftermath of the Maccabean Wars, the whole of cols. 2–9 dating well before the Roman occupation of Palestine.[32] Accordingly, the reference to the Prince of All the Congregation in 1QM should be dated no later than the first quarter of the 1st century BCE, and possibly earlier.[33] Thus, for this time period the *War Scroll* provides no evidence that the Prince of All the Congregation was conceived of as a davidic messiah.

Next there is an extended passage in 1QSb 5:20–29 concerning the blessing of the Prince of the Congregation.[34] After the blessing of the community, high priest, and priests, it says, "The Master shall bless the Prince of the Congregation (נשׂיא העדה), who [...], so that he may establish the kingdom of his people forever" (lns. 20–21). In lns. 21–22, the Prince's ruling functions are described in language borrowed in part from Isa 11:4a. Furthermore, in the blessing itself, portions are based on Isa 11:2b,4b–5 (lns. 24–26). Altogether, in this passage the Prince of the Congregation is characterized as one who judges with righteousness, is exalted by God, crushes the ungodly, is served by foreign rulers, and possesses superlative spiritual endowments—all so that he may establish the kingdom of God's people. Moreover, ln. 23 asserts that the Prince will establish his [holy] covenant in a time of oppression for those who seek God, which seems to indicate that the Prince of the Congregation is an eschatological figure. This is by far the fullest description of the Prince of the Congregation both in terms of his person and role. He is clearly a military figure, but also a ruler over the nations and Israel. He is not explicitly subordinated to the priests, but since his blessing comes after that of the high priest and priests, a subordinate status is implied.

In this passage, the Prince of the Congregation has some features that may be related to the davidic dynasty tradition. For one, his title, Prince (נשׂיא), is

---

[31] See Dimant, "Sectarian Literature," 515.

[32] Davies, *1QM*, 66–67.

[33] Also, literary affinities with 1QS and 1QH support a date ca. 100 BCE (see Dimant, "Sectarian Literature," 516).

[34] The text of 1QSb is from Barthélemy and Milik, DJD 1, 127–128.

used as a title for a new David in Ezek 34:24; 37:25.[35] On the other hand, the title נשׂיא is used in contexts apart from any connection to David or the davidic dynasty tradition. For instance, in Ezekiel 40–48, נשׂיא refers to a secular leader whose powers are severely limited with respect to the priesthood and who lacks any overt connection to the davidic dynasty tradition.[36] Given the subordination of the Prince of the Congregation to the priests at Qumran, he appears to be a figure closely related to the נשׂיא of Ezekiel 40–48. More importantly, however, in Ezra 1:8 נשׂיא is used as a title for Sheshbazzar, who is clearly not a davidic figure.[37] Also, Simeon bar Kosiba, or bar Kokhba, designated himself נשׂיא ישׂראל on coins minted during the Second Jewish Revolt (132–135 BCE).[38] There is no evidence that he viewed himself as a davidic messiah or of davidic descent.[39]

Nevertheless, the fact remains that the term נשׂיא has some connection to the davidic dynasty tradition. But, of course, any term for a royal figure, whether it be מלך, משׁיח, נגיד, or נשׂיא, has some connection with the davidic dynasty tradition, though none is limited to that tradition. What term could the Qumran community have given its chief non-priestly leader which could not be plausibly related to davidic dynasty tradition? נשׂיא is certainly not a major term for davidic kings in the Hebrew Bible. Hence, to relate the Prince of the Congregation to davidic messianism on the basis of the title נשׂיא alone is unwarranted. As Starcky suggested, the term נשׂיא may have been preferred over מלך in order distinguish this ideal royal figure from the Hasmonean monarchs who, beginning with Aristobulus I, sported the title מלך,[40] and therefore was not employed because the Prince was viewed as a davidic messiah.

Yet another link with the davidic dynasty tradition exists in 1QSb 5:20–29. In his characterization of the Prince of the Congregation the author uses language taken from Isa 11:2–5, a passage that describes a shoot from the stump of Jesse.

---

[35]See Barthélemy and Milik, DJD 1, 129; Brown, "The Messianism of Qumrân," 57; Schürer, *History*, 2:550. נשׂיא is also used once for Solomon in 1 Kgs 11:34.

[36]See above, pp. 30–32.

[37]See above, p. 32, esp. n. 81.

[38]L. Mildenberg, "Bar Kokhba Coins and Documents," *Harvard Studies in Classical Philology* 84 (1980) 313–314.

[39]Mildenberg, "Coins and Documents," 314–315. Rabbinic reports that Rabbi Akiva proclaimed bar Kosiba the messiah are of disputed historical authenticity (see A. Reinhartz, "Rabbinic Perceptions of Simeon bar Kosiba," *JSJ* 20 [1989] 171–194. Reinhartz argues that bar Kosiba was perceived by some of his contemporaries as a messiah [not necessarily a davidic messiah], but as an explanation of his success [p. 193]).

[40]Starcky, "Les Quatre Étapes," 488.

Moreover, as we have seen above, in 4QpIsa[a] this passage is interpreted in terms of a davidic messiah. This has led many scholars to conclude that here in 1QSb the Prince of the Congregation is a davidic messiah.[41] But this deduction may be too facile.

For one, it is worth observing that nowhere in the text does it actually state that the Prince is a davidic messiah. And, while it is true that the author paraphrases parts of Isa 11:2–5 in his description of the Prince of the Congregation, it is significant that he omits any reference to Isa 11:1, where the shoot from the stump of Jesse is mentioned.[42] A specific connection to the davidic figure is therefore lacking. This becomes all the more important when it is recognized that symbols and images originally associated with a particular biblical figure could be reapplied to a new figure. In fact, in *T. Levi* 18 allusions from Isa 11:9 (*T. Levi* 18:5) and Isa 11:2 (*T. Levi* 18:7), as well as Num 24:17 (*T. Levi* 18:3), are used to characterize a new priest![43] In that case, allusions from Isaiah 11 are utilized quite apart from connotations of davidic status. In other words, using imagery from the davidic dynasty tradition to describe a person does not mean that person is a davidic messiah.

Furthermore, the characterization of the Prince of the Congregation in 1QSb 5:20–29 is really a pastiche of images from various biblical texts. For example, in ln. 26 the images of "horns of iron and shoes of bronze" come from Mic 4:13,[44] where they are applied to the daughter of Zion, and the symbol of the scepter (ln. 27) probably derives from Num 24:17, which refers to a royal figure who is not davidic. What warrant is there for selecting only the allusions that derive from texts related to the davidic dynasty tradition, like Isa 11:2–5, as determinative for the identity of this figure? In this regard, much of the imagery about royal power and persons in the Hebrew Bible is found in texts originally associated with davidic kings. Must we assume that because the author of 1QSb did not com-

---

[41]For example, Brown, "The Messianism of Qumrân," 57; Schürer, *History*, 2:550; Dimant, "Sectarian Literature. " 524; Schiffman, "Messianic Figures," 122.

[42]Starcky, "Les Quatre Étapes," 488.

[43]This use of terms from Isaiah 11 is not limited to the Greek *Testament of Levi*, since in 4QT Levi ar[a] 1:14 language from Isa 11:2 occurs in Levi's prayer. Also, according to J. C. Greenfield and M. E. Stone, "Remarks on the Aramaic Testament of Levi from the Geniza," *RB* 86 (1979) 215,223, in the Aramaic *Testament of Levi* known from the Cairo Geniza, which is very similar to the fragments of the Aramaic *Testament of Levi* discovered at Qumran and loosely related to the Greek *Testament of Levi* from the *Testaments of the Twelve Patriarchs*, "royal terminology is consistently applied to Levi" (p. 219).

[44]Starcky, "Les Quatre Étapes," 488, observes that the celebrated prediction about a ruler from Bethlehem Ephrathah in 5:1 (Eng 5:2) is not taken up here.

pletely avoid evocative images from these texts that he meant the Prince of the Congregation was a davidic messiah?

Consequently, we must conclude that the title נשׂיא and imagery from Isa 11:2–5 do not constitute sufficient evidence for construing the Prince of the Congregation in 1QSb as a davidic messiah. This is because both items were used for non-davidic persons and a clear indication of davidic status is absent—particularly the author's failure to cite Isa 11:1. Since the composition of 1QSb is dated to ca. 100 BCE, it too provides no evidence for davidic messianism at Qumran at this time.[45]

In 4QSerek HaMilhamah 5:4 the Prince of the Congregation (נשׂיא העדה) is not only mentioned, but explicitly identified with the Branch of David. Since I have treated this text in detail in the previous chapter, further discussion of it here is unnecessary, except to recall that 4QSerek HaMilhamah dates to herodian period (ca. 30 BCE–70 CE). Finally, within a fragmentary context, 4QpIsa[a] 5–6:3 mentions the Prince of the Congregation (נשׂיא העדה) in its interpretation of Isa 10:28–32.[46] No information about this figure can be gleaned because of the broken context. But since this reference to the Prince occurs in the same context as a reference to the Branch of David (4QpIsa[a] 8–10:11–24), and because these figures are identified in 4QSerek HaMilhamah, a text closely related thematically to 4QpIsa[a], we should assume their identification in 4QpIsa[a] as well. As noted in the previous chapter, 4QpIsa[a] has been dated to between 30 BCE–20 CE.

To sum up the preceding treatment of the Prince of the Congregation, we see that in CD, 1QM, and 1QSb, the Prince is not understood as a davidic messiah. On the other hand, in 4QpIsa[a] and 4QSerek HaMilhamah the Branch of David and the Prince of the Congregation are identified. To explain this difference the dates of the various documents must be taken into account. CD, 1QM, and 1QSb all date to ca. 100 BCE, while 4QpIsa[a] and 4QSerek HaMilhamah are dated to the herodian period. Accordingly, it seems the Prince of the Congregation was only interpreted as a davidic messiah in the herodian period and not before.

To clarify this matter further, we must broaden the argument. First, all references to the Branch of David come from the herodian period,[47] and only in these herodian era texts is the Prince of the Congregation identified with the davidic messiah. Secondly, in documents dating from ca. 100 BCE and before, no royal

---

[45]1QSb is found in the same manuscript as 1QS and 1QSa, which is dated to ca. 100–75 BCE and copied from an earlier exemplar.

[46]The text of 4QpIsa[a] is from Allegro, DJD 5, 12.

[47]See the section on Qumran literature in chap. 5 for the dates of references to the Branch of David.

figure, whether the ideal king of the *Temple Scroll*, the Messiah of Israel, or the Prince of the Congregation, is presented as a davidic messiah. This evidence leads to the conclusion that davidic messianism did not arise at Qumran until the herodian period (35 BCE–70 CE).[48] After the concept of a davidic messiah was introduced at Qumran, however, at least one of the earlier royal figures, the Prince of the Congregation, was identified with him—or perhaps more accurately, assimilated to him, a development not surprising given some of the similarities in character and role between the Branch of David and the Prince of the Congregation. Both were militant, both envisioned as rulers, and both subordinated to the priests. In any event, in the earlier phases of the Qumran community, other models of royal leadership based on Deut 17:14–20, Num 24:17, and Ezek 40–48 inspired the Qumran community's understanding of royal figures. Only later, in the herodian era, was the davidic dynasty tradition utilized to fashion the conception of a davidic messiah.[49]

Moreover, this conclusion serves to explain certain seemingly anomalous features of Qumran thought. For one, it accounts for why David, though mentioned in a number of Qumran texts, is never the subject of messianic speculation. Specifically, CD 5:5, while defending David's righteousness, in no way relates him to a future ideal king.[50] Likewise, in 1QM 11:1–3 David is not associated with eschatological hopes; in particular, he is not linked to the Prince of All the Congregation mentioned in 1QM 5:1, a striking omission, since in 11:1–3 David is presented as an example of military success rooted in his trust in God. Nor are any of the psalms that are attributed to David in Qumran psalters messianic.[51] Furthermore, in the concluding section of 4QMMT, David is held up as a model of piety, whom the recipient of the letter is encouraged to remember.[52] There is

---

[48]It is of course possible that davidic messianism was introduced at Qumran sometime between ca. 100 and 35 BCE, but no documents support this.

[49]Starcky, "Les Quatre Étapes," 500, had posited only a revival of davidic messianism in the herodian period, since he thought the Prince of the Congregation in 1QSb was probably davidic, although he appeared puzzled about his identity there, stating, "Il est pourtant curieux que l'auteur évite de nommer David ou Juda," and noting the author's failure to cite Isa 11:1 and Mic 5:1 (p. 488). Caquot, "Messianisme," 245, seems to suspect that davidic messianism may have arisen at Qumran only in the herodian period when he writes about davidic messianism in that period: " ... je chercherais dans des contingences plus immédiates *la naissance* ou la renaissance de cette forme de messianisme" (emphasis mine). Cf. also, Liver, "Doctrine of the Two Messiahs," 159–163, who observes that the Messiah of Israel and the Prince of the Congregation are not explicitly characterized as davidic figures and suggests that texts which mention a branch of David may come from a later time.

[50]Cf. Schiffman, "Messianic Figures," 119.

[51]Charlesworth, "Messianology," 25.

[52]4QMMT is available on PAM 42.838; for a transcription and English translation, see

no hint of davidic messianism implied here. In fact, if the recipient of the halakhic letter preserved in 4QMMT was a Hasmonean ruler, as some propose, David is set forth as an example for a non-davidic Jewish ruler.[53] Also, in a prose composition near the end of 11QPs[a] (col. 27, lns. 2–11), David is characterized as a wise and righteous psalmist whose many compositions derived from his prophetic gift. This association of David with liturgical matters is reminiscent of the portrayal of David in Chronicles and Sir 47:8–10, and appears to be part of a broader tradition about David unrelated to his role as progenitor of a messianic line.[54] Thus, the reason why David is never the subject of messianic speculation in the aforementioned texts may be because CD, 1QM, 4QMMT, and the contents of 11QPs[a] were written ca. 100 BCE or earlier,[55] well before the rise of davidic messianism at Qumran.

In addition, if davidic messianism is a phenomenon of the herodian period at Qumran, it explains why 4QTestimonia, a document listing messianic proof-texts that dates from before 100 BCE, offers Num 24:15–17 as the text in support of a royal messiah.[56] As Caquot has noted, this is not a passage well suited to a specifically davidic messiah.[57] Furthermore, the above conclusion might explain why in 1QM the Prince of All the Congregation is not davidic, while in 4QSerek HaMilhamah he is, the latter being a portion of a war rule from the herodian period. Finally, the conclusion that speculation about a davidic messiah appears at Qumran only in the herodian period comports with the broader thesis of this study

---

Eisenman and Wise, *Uncovered*, 198–200.

[53]For a Hasmonean king as the recipient of 4QMMT, see Schiffman, "Halakhic Letter," 67. E. Qimron and J. Strugnell, "An Unpublished Halakhic Letter from Qumran," *Biblical Archaeology Today* (ed. J. Amitai; Jerusalem: Israel Exploration Society/Israel Academy of Sciences and Humanities, 1984) 400, make a similar suggestion.

[54]Cf. G. W. E. Nickelsburg, "The Bible Rewritten and Expanded," *Jewish Writings of the Second Temple Period* (CRINT 2:2; ed. M. E. Stone; Philadelphia: Fortress/Assen: Van Gorcum, 1984) 139–140. For the text of 11QPs[a] 27:2–11, see Sanders, DJD 4, 92.

[55]As noted above, CD and the *War Scroll* date to ca. 100 BCE. While 11QPs[a] dates to the first half of the first century CE, other psalters from Cave 4 date as early as the mid-second century BCE and the contents of 11QPs[a] go back to the second century BCE (see P. W. Skehan, "Qumran and Old Testament Criticism," *Qumrân: Sa piété, sa théologie et son milieu* [BETL 46; ed. M. Delcor; Paris: Duculot/Leuven: University Press, 1978] 168,181). For the date of 4QMMT, Qimron and Strugnell, "Halakhic Letter," 401, think the text goes back to the earliest phase of the Qumran sect; Schiffman, "Halakhic Letter," 70, supports this dating.

[56]On the function of Num 24:15–17 in 4Q Testimonia, see Dimant, "Sectarian Literature," 518; and Vermes, *DSS in English*, 295.

[57]Caquot, "Messianisme," 238.

that davidic messianism is absent in the Second Temple period until its appearance in *Pss. Sol.* 17 in the middle of the first century BCE.

Why did davidic messianism arise at Qumran in the herodian period? Here we may recall the discussion about the Branch of David in chapter five, where it was argued that the interpretation of the davidic dynasty tradition in terms of an expectation for a davidic messiah served to challenge the legitimacy of either herodian or Roman kings and to describe a mighty Jewish monarch whose identity was suited to the task of destroying Roman legions. The davidic dynasty tradition provided the scriptural resources for depicting such a figure. Whether the Qumran community was in any way influenced by *Pss. Sol.* 17, where the idea of a davidic messiah had already been broached in the middle of the first century BCE, cannot be determined.[58]

B. The Messiah of Judah in the Testaments of the Twelve Patriarchs

In the *Testaments of the Twelve Patriarchs*, several passages mention a future king from the tribe of Judah—a king who is usually referred to as the Messiah of Judah.[59] The question to be considered in this section, therefore, is how the Messiah of Judah is related to the davidic dynasty tradition, in particular, whether he is a davidic figure? Again it is common for scholars to identify the Messiah of Judah with a davidic messiah.[60] Yet, we must test whether this identification is based on what the texts actually say about this figure, or merely on the assumption of a traditional davidic hope.[61]

The whole question is complicated, however, by uncertainty about the history of the composition of the *Testaments*.[62] Briefly, two major hypotheses exist:

---

[58]See above, pp. 214–216, for similarities between the davidic messiah at Qumran and in *Pss. Sol.* 17.

[59]This title is never used for the future king from Judah; in fact, the term "messiah" never occurs in the *Testaments*. But if "messiah" is taken to refer to a human eschatological savior figure, the designation may not be inappropriate (cf. Collins, *Imagination*, 236 n. 90).

[60]G. R. Beasley-Murray, "The Two Messiahs in the Testaments of the Twelve Patriarchs," *JTS* 48 (1947) 1; Liver, "Two Messiahs," 173; van der Woude, *Vorstellungen*, 209; Kuhn, "Two Messiahs of Aaron and Israel," 57,61; A. Hultgård, *L'eschatologie des Testaments des Douze Patriarches* (2 vols.; Acta Universitatis Upsaliensis, Historia Religionum 6; Stockholm: Almquist & Wiksell, 1977) 1:169; "The Ideal 'Levite', the Davidic Messiah, and the Savior Priest in the Testaments of the Twelve Patriarchs," *Ideal Figures in Ancient Judaism* (SBLSCS 12; ed. G. W. E. Nickelsburg and J. J. Collins; Chico, CA: Scholars Press, 1980) 95–99.

[61]Cf., for example, the assumption of Liver, "Two Messiahs," 173, "But it is hardly credible that in the *Testament of Judah* there should be no messianic expectations for the House of David."

[62]For a brief survey of recent views on the *Testaments*, see J. J. Collins, "Testaments: II.

one construes the *Testaments* as Jewish compositions—sometimes with several Jewish stages from the early second century BCE to the beginning of the first century CE—that were subsequently interpolated by a Christian writer; the other understands the *Testaments* as second century CE Christian compositions that utilized Jewish sources and traditions, some of which may even have been in testamentary form.[63] Thus, everyone agrees that in their final form the *Testaments* are Christian in character, and also that they include Jewish material: the debate concerns what specific content, the amount and form of which, that should be attributed to the various Jewish or Christian stages.[64] Accordingly, for passages that make use of the davidic dynasty tradition, we will have to assess what stratum of the *Testaments* they belong to.

A second problem involves precisely what kind of messianism is present in the *Testaments*. Probably the most widely held position, especially since the Qumran discoveries, is that from the beginning the *Testaments* expressed an expectation for two messiahs—a priestly messiah from Levi and a royal messiah from Judah.[65] In contrast, R. H. Charles thought that the original *Testaments* anticipated only a priestly messiah from Levi; he considered passages mentioning a royal messiah from Judah as first century BCE additions.[66] More recently, based

---

The Testamentary Literature in Recent Scholarship," *Early Judaism and Its Modern Interpreters* (ed. G. W. E. Nickelsburg and R. A. Kraft; Philadelphia: Fortress/Atlanta: Scholars Press, 1986) 268–276; for a comprehensive survey of scholarship on the *Testaments*, see H. D. Slingerland, *The Testaments of the Twelve Patriarchs: A Critical History of Research* (SBLMS 21; Missoula, MT: Scholars Press, 1977); cf. also M. de Jonge, "The Interpretation of the Testaments of the Twelve Patriarchs in Recent Years," *Studies in the Testaments of the Twelve Patriarchs* (SVTP 3; ed. M. de Jonge; Leiden: Brill, 1975) 189, who says the whole question of the composition and origin of the *Testaments* is open.

[63]Collins, "Testaments," 268, remarks that the first view is represented in various ways by R. H. Charles, J. Becker, A. Hultgård, and H. C. Kee, the second, by M. de Jonge and his students. He also notes that a third hypothesis, represented by Dupont-Sommer, Philonenko, Kuhn, Liver, and van der Woude, that the *Testaments* are Essene documents, has few recent advocates; see J. Becker, *Untersuchungen zur Entstehungsgeschichte der Testamente der zwölf Patriarchen* (AGJU 8; Leiden: Brill, 1970) 149–151; and M. de Jonge, "Two Messiahs in the Testaments of the Twelve Patriarchs?" *Jewish Eschatology, Early Christian Christology and the Testaments of the Twelve Patriarchs* (NovTSup 63; Leiden: Brill, 1991) 193, for criticism of the theory of an Essene or Qumran origin for the *Testaments*.

[64]Cf. similar comments in M. de Jonge, "Interpretation," 189–190.

[65]Beasley-Murray, "Two Messiahs," *passim*; Kuhn, "Two Messiahs of Aaron and Israel," 57–58; van der Woude, *Vorstellungen*, 190–216; Liver, "Two Messiahs," 163–179.

[66]R. H. Charles, "The Testaments of the Twelve Patriarchs," *The Apocrypha and Pseudepigrapha of the Old Testament* (2 vols.; ed. R. H. Charles; Oxford: Clarendon, 1913) 2:294.

on analysis of the Aramaic *Testament of Levi*, Stone and Greenfield have made a similar suggestion.[67] Hultgård, on the other hand, put forth a complex theory that posited an early stage of tradition (second century BCE) that mentioned only an idealized Levite, followed by a phase (early first century BCE) in which the Messiah of Judah stood alongside the ideal Levite, which was succeeded by a still later Jewish stage (beginning of first century CE) that anticipated a "savior priest," who possessed priestly, royal, and angelic features.[68] Becker, on the other hand, relegated all messianic statements in the *Testaments* to a small and late layer,[69] while de Jonge held that no messianism existed at all until the Christian stage, where there is only one messiah, Jesus Christ.[70]

Thus, some scholars think the notion of a Messiah of Judah is original to the *Testaments*, while others variously see it as a later Jewish development. Still others reject the notion of a Messiah of Judah in any Jewish stage. Nevertheless, although these different views have implications for any discussion of the identity of the Messiah of Judah, it is not the task of the present study to argue for one particular position about the overall messianism in the *Testaments*. For the present purpose we are considering a very limited set of questions: 1) do passages that refer to a future king (or kingship) from Judah ever characterize him (or it) as davidic? 2) if such passages exist, should they be ascribed to a Jewish phase of the *Testaments*?

When the question is limited in this way, many passages can be eliminated from the scope of our inquire, since they have absolutely no connection to the davidic dynasty tradition. Some simply predict that the tribe of Judah will possess kingship in Israel or that salvation will come through Judah.[71] For example, *T. Iss.* 5:7–8 reads:[72]

---

[67]Stone and Greenfield, "Remarks," 219.

[68]Hultgård, *L'eschatologie*; "Ideal," *passim*.

[69]Becker, *Untersuchungen*, 405.

[70]De Jonge, "Two Messiahs?" *passim*, esp. p. 192; in Jewish traditions behind the *Testaments*, de Jonge finds only a special role for the tribes of Levi and Judah; Collins, *Imagination*, 112, agrees that in their final form, there is one messiah who is Christ, but thinks it probable that this was an adaptation of an earlier expectation of two messiahs.

[71]In some of these passages, Christian composition or redaction may be reflected (cf. for example *T. Naph* 8:2).

[72]Translations of the *Testaments* are from H. C. Kee, "Testaments of the Twelve Patriarchs," *The Old Testament Pseudepigrapha* (2 vols.; ed. J. H. Charlesworth; Garden City, NY: Doubleday, 1985) 1:782–828. For the Greek text of the *Testaments*, see M. de Jonge with H. W. Hollander, H. J. de Jonge, and Th. Korteweg, *The Testaments of the Twelve Patriarchs: A Critical Edition of the Greek Text* (PVTG 1:2; Leiden: Brill, 1978).

> And Levi and Judah were glorified by the Lord among the sons of Jacob. For the Lord made choice among them: and to one he gave the priesthood, and to the other the kingship. Therefore, obey them ...

Likewise, *T. Naph.* 8:2:

> Accordingly, command your children to unite with Levi and Judah, for through Judah salvation will arise for Israel and in him Jacob will be blessed.

Similar passages occur in *T. Levi* 2:11; *T. Dan* 5:4,10; *T. Naph.* 5:1–7; and *T. Jud.* 17:5–6.[73] Other texts do mention a messianic figure associated with Judah (or Judah and Levi), but the characterizations of this figure are devoid of features that can plausibly be linked to the davidic dynasty tradition. *T. Sim.* 7:1–2 and *T. Gad* 8:1 illustrate this class of texts:

> And now, my children, obey Levi and by Judah you will be redeemed. And do not exalt yourselves over these two tribes, because from them will arise for you the salvation of God. For the Lord will raise up from Levi someone as a high priest and from Judah someone as a king, God and man. He will save all the nations and the people of Israel (*T. Sim.* 7:1–2).

> And tell these things to your children, that they should honor Judah and Levi, because from them the Lord will raise up a savior for Israel (*T. Gad* 8:1).

Analogous passages are found in *T. Rub.* 6:11–12 and *T. Levi* 8:14.

When the above mentioned passages are eliminated as irrelevant to the present inquiry, three texts remain that speak of a king or kingship from Judah: *T. Jos.* 19:8–12; *T. Jud.* 24:1–6; and *T. Jud.* 21:1–22:3. These texts use or are said to use the davidic dynasty tradition. Therefore, I will examine them for evidence of this tradition, and for those that indicate such use, I will attempt to determine their provenance—specifically whether they reflect a Jewish or Christian stratum of the *Testaments*.

T. Jos. 19:8–12 reads as follows:

> And I saw that from Judah was born a virgin, wearing a linen (Armenian version: multi-colored) robe. And from her came forth a spotless lamb (ἀμνὸς ἄμωμος), and on its left was something like a lion. And all the wild beasts rushed against it, and the lamb defeated them and destroyed them, trampling them under foot. And the angels and men and all the earth rejoiced about him. These things will happen in their appointed time, in the last days. Therefore, my children, keep the commandments of the Lord and honor Judah and Levi, because from them the lamb of God will arise, by grace saving all the nations and Israel. For his kingdom is an eternal kingdom, which is not shaken. My

---

[73]Cf. also *Jub.* 31:11–20.

kingdom among you will end as a watchman's hut, because after summer it disappears.

Hultgård argues that *T. Jos.* 19:8–12 "clearly mentions the Davidic messiah."[74] He bases this assertion on three observations.[75] First, in the Armenian version of v. 8 the virgin is wearing a "multi-colored" robe instead of a linen one. Hultgård prefers this as the original reading and connects it with davidic royal contexts in Ps 45:15, Ezekiel 16, and 4QpIsa[a]. Secondly, the role of the lamb in destroying the wild beasts, who represent the enemies of Israel, is the role performed by the davidic messiah in other contexts such as *Pss. Sol.* 17:24–25. Thirdly, in the Greek text the lamb is said to be "spotless," a quality characteristic of the davidic messiah in *Pss. Sol.* 17:36 and 1QSb 5:22.

None of these points is persuasive, however. Hultgård's preference for the Armenian text is gratuitous.[76] And even if the text had originally read "multi-colored," this term, although used in the context of royalty, is not limited to davidic contexts, as even Ezekiel 16 (a text cited by Hultgård!) demonstrates. Moreover, the role of destroying Israel's enemies is not limited to the davidic messiah, but is characteristic of other messianic figures such as the Son of Man in Daniel 7. Finally, it is true that the davidic messiah in *Pss. Sol.* 17:36 is said to be without sin, but to go on to imply from this that the "spotless lamb" in *T. Jos* 19:8 is clearly a davidic figure is simply unwarranted.[77]

Nevertheless, Hultgård's argument is really beside the point, since *T. Jos* 19:8–12 is thoroughly Christian.[78] For example, the phrase "spotless lamb" (ἀμνὸς ἄμωμος) is a designation for Christ in early Christian writings (cf. 1 Pet 1:19),[79] and is connected to the "lamb of God" referred to in *T. Jos* 19:11, another patently Christian phrase. Likewise, mention of a virgin, salvation by grace, and the salvation of the nations marks this passage out as the work of a Christian

---

[74]Hultgård, "Ideal Levite," 95.

[75]Hultgård, "Ideal Levite," 96–99.

[76]Cf. de Jonge, "Two Messiahs?" 192f, who criticizes Hultgård generally for *ad hoc* selection of readings from the Armenian version; see also, Becker, *Untersuchungen*, 59–66; Collins, "Testaments," 271, who notes that recent research confirms de Jonge's low estimation of the value of the Armenian version as an independent witness to the text.

[77]The same is true about 1QSb 5:22, where the Prince of the Congregation is said to be without sin, and this figure is not even davidic.

[78]H. W. Hollander and M. de Jonge, *The Testaments of the Twelve Patriarchs: A Commentary* (SVTP 8; Leiden: Brill, 1985) 407–409; cf. Becker, *Untersuchungen*, 243, who cites de Jonge with approval.

[79]Cf. Hollander and de Jonge, *Commentary*, 408, for other citations in later Christian literature.

author.[80] Moreover, the identify and role of this messiah is similar to that of Jesus in the book of Revelation,[81] and his kingdom even replaces the kingdom of Judah (19:12). If there ever existed a Jewish substratum in this section—possibly in Joseph's call to honor Judah and Levi (v. 11)—it is clear that none of the supposed davidic features can be attributed to the Second Temple Jewish phase.

A second text that could reflect use of the davidic dynasty tradition is *T. Jud.* 24:4–6. In order to provide a context for these verses, the following excerpt cites *T. Jud.* 24:1–6, where Judah says:

> And after these things a star will rise up for you from Jacob in peace, and a man from my seed will arise as the sun of righteousness, walking with the sons of men in humility and righteousness, and no sin will be found in him. And the heavens will be opened to him to pour out the blessing of the spirit of the holy father. And He will pour out the spirit of grace upon you. And you will be to him sons in truth, and you will walk in his commandments from first to last. This is the branch (βλαστὸς) of God most high, and this is the spring of life for all flesh. Then the scepter (σκῆπτρων) of my kingdom will shine, and from your root (ῥίζης) will be a stem (πυθμὴν). And in him will come (ἀναβήσεται) a rod (ῥάβδος) of righteousness for the nations, to judge and save all those who call upon the Lord.

Here the Messiah of Judah is designated ὁ βλαστὸς (v. 4). Hultgård pointed to the use of this term within a davidic context in Ezek 17:23 (LXX).[82] H. C. Kee connected βλαστὸς to the name for the davidic messiah in Isa. 11:1; Jer 23:5; 33:15; and Zech 3:8; 6:12.[83] Yet the term βλαστὸς occurs in none of these texts in the LXX, although it is found in the Greek translation of Isa 11:1 by Symmachus.[84] In this respect, Isa 11:1 provides a suitable background for other terms in *T. Jud.* 24:4–6, including ῥίζης (v. 5), ῥάβδος (v. 6), and ἀναβήσεται (v. 6). Thus, language from the davidic dynasty tradition may have been used here to characterize the Messiah of Judah. But an even more likely source for the terminology of *T. Jud.* 24:4–6 is Gen 49:9–10a, where it is said:

> a whelp of a lion is Judah, from a branch (MT: טרף; LXX: βλαστὸς), my son, you have come up. A scepter shall not depart from Judah, nor the ruler's staff from between his feet.

Gen 49:9–10a could account for the terms βλαστὸς (v. 4), σκῆπτρων (v. 5), ῥάβδος and ἀναβήσεται (v. 6).

---

[80]Cf. Hollander and de Jonge, *Commentary*, 408–409.

[81]Cf. especially Revelation 5 and 12–14.

[82]Hultgård, *L'eschatologie*, 1:212

[83]See Kee, "Testaments," 1:801 n. c.

[84]Hultgård, *L'eschatologie*, 1:212.

Nonetheless, since it is possible that the davidic dynasty tradition in Isa 11:1 may have influenced the language of *T. Jud.* 24:4–6, it must be asked whether this text should be assigned to a Jewish or Christian redactional layer. In this regard, we conclude that it is almost certainly the work of a Christian author or editor. Hollander and de Jonge have shown how the whole of 24:1–6 is full of early Christian terminology and allusions.[85] Specifically in vv. 4–6, notions like Jesus as the branch (βλαστὸς) and spring (πηγὴ) of life abound in second century Christian writers; so too, images of Christ as scepter and as growing from a root are equally common.[86] Thus, even if it could be confirmed that *T. Jud.* drew on language from Isa. 11:1, the verses in which this language occurs appear to be from the pen of a Christian writer.

The third and final passage we must consider is *T. Jud.* 21:1–22:3. It begins with the well-known verses about the subordination of the kingship to the priesthood, where Judah says:

> And now, children, love Levi, that you may endure, and do not exalt yourselves above him, that you may be utterly destroyed. For to me the Lord gave the kingship and to him the priesthood, and he subordinated the kingship to the priesthood (21:1–2).

It proceeds in 21:6–22:1 to describe the degradation of the kingship among Judah's descendants in terms that recall the history of the davidic monarchy. It continues:

> And by men of foreign nations my kingship will be ended, until the salvation of Israel comes, until the appearing of the God of righteousness, so that Jacob may rest in peace and all the nations. And he will guard the power of my kingdom forever, for by an oath the Lord swore to me that my kingship would not cease from my seed all the days, forever (22:2–3).

Of course, in this passage, from the fictive historical perspective of the sons of Jacob, Judah's kingship included the reign of the davidic monarchs. Consequently, when the future of Judah's kingship is described, as it is in *T. Jud.* 21:6–22:1, allusions to the davidic monarchy are to be expected. But this in itself does not imply that Judah's kingship is limited to the davidic line within the tribe of Judah. Indeed, at least one factor argues that the author did not intend to limit Judah's kingship to the davidic family, since Judah himself is identified as a king (*T. Jud.* 1:6; 12:6; 15:1–3; 17:5–6); he even possessed a crown (*T. Jud.* 12:6). At

---

[85]Hollander and de Jonge, *Commentary*, 227–228. Becker, *Untersuchungen*, 323, thought vv. 1–4 were Christian, while vv. 5–6 were a secondary Jewish redaction; Hultgård, "Ideal Levite," 96, claimed the whole was Jewish with some Christian interpolation.

[86]Hollander and de Jonge, *Commentary*, 228.

best, allusions to the historical davidic monarchy leave open the possibility that a future king from the tribe of Judah would also come from the line of David, but this is by no means required.

More importantly, however, some scholars have seen a promise of a coming davidic messiah in *T. Jud.* 22:2–3. In particular, 22:2b is said to be reminiscent of Jer 23:6a, a passage which predicts the coming of a branch for David,[87] and 22:3b is understood as a reference to the davidic dynastic promise found in various biblical passages such as 2 Sam 7:11–16, Ps 89:2–5,35–38, and Jer 23:6; 33:15–17, as well as *Pss. Sol.* 17:4b.[88] To be sure, at some points the language of *T. Jud.* 22:2–3 is similar to these texts, especially to *Pss. Sol.* 17:4b. But *T. Jud.* 22:2–3 contains many echoes of Gen 49:10 (LXX), particularly with respect to the promise given to Judah, and thus it appears that this biblical text provided the resources for the author's conception of the Messiah of Judah (parallel words and ideas are underlined):

ἕως τοῦ ἐλθεῖν τὸ σωτήριον Ισραήλ, ἕως παρουσίας τοῦ θεοῦ τῆς δικαιοσύνης ... καὶ πάντα τὸ ἔθνη ... ὅρκῳ γὰρ ὤμοσέ μοι κύριος μὴ ἐκλεῖψαι τὸ βασίλειον μου ἐκ τοῦ σπέρματός μου πάσας τὰς ἡμέρας, ἕως τοῦ αἰῶος (T. Jud. 22:2b–3).

οὐκ ἐκλείψει ἄρχων ἐξ Ιουδα καὶ ἡγούμενος ἐκ τῶν μηρῶν αὐτοῦ, ἕως ἂν ἔλθῃ τὰ ἀποκείμενα αὐτῷ, καὶ αὐτὸς προσδοκία ἐθνῶν (Gen 49:10 [LXX]).

Nevertheless, Gen 49:9–10 cannot account for every aspect of *T. Jud.* 22:2–3, particularly the notion of the Lord himself making the oath, as well as the specific reference to the perpetuity of the promise. Hence, this may suggest the influence of ideas from texts associated with the davidic dynastic promise cited above. This influence does not necessarily imply that the promised kingship of Judah is identical with davidic kingship, since, as *T. Levi* 18:7 shows, language from the davidic dynasty tradition could be employed to characterize a non-davidic figure (the Messiah of Levi).[89] Yet, there remains here at least a possible connection between the kingship of Judah and the davidic dynasty tradition.

---

[87]Hultgård, *L'eschatologie,* 1:169.

[88]Hultgård, *L'eschatologie,* 1:169; Kee, "Testaments," 801, marginal note; Hollander and de Jonge, *Commentary,* 224.

[89]See above, p. 242.

The question now is whether this connection between the kingship of Judah and the davidic dynasty tradition can be attributed to a Jewish stage of the *Testaments*. Hollander and de Jonge viewed the entire passage as Christian;[90] Becker too saw 21:1–22:3 as a supplement and did not attributed it to any Jewish stage.[91] Hultgård, on the other hand, claimed that this text could only be explained on a Jewish basis.[92] Yet Hultgård's argument assumed that this entire passage was a polemic against Hasmonean kings. Specifically, he contended that 22:2a—"And by men of foreign nations/tribes (ἀλλοφύλοις) my kingship will be ended"— alluded to the usurpation of royalty by the Hasmoneans.[93] But of course the Hasmoneans did not end (συντελεσθήσεται) the kingship of Judah; rather this verse obviously refers to the events of 586 BCE, when the kings of Judah were "ended" by Nebuchadnezzar (cf. Sir 49:5). Hultgård's theory is therefore untenable.

Nevertheless, while there is no necessity for interpreting this passage on a Jewish basis, it is possible to do so. In this case, 22:2–3 asserts that God would appear and guard the power of Judah's kingdom forever, because he had promised this. God himself, then, would be the active agent throughout the passage. Equally plausible, however, is the interpretation of this text on a Christian basis.[94] In this case, the God of righteousness in v. 2b and the subject of v. 3a (αὐτὸς) would be the Messiah of Judah, Jesus Christ, the one from Judah's seed to whom the kingdom was promised (v. 3b). Similarly, the term *parousia*, rest for all the nations, and the eternal character of the messiah's kingdom (v. 3a) would be viewed as a reflection of the Christian tradition. But again, none of these concepts is inconsistent with a Jewish origin. Likewise, Gen 49:10 is associated with the messiah in both early Jewish and second century Christian writings.[95] Consequently, on the basis of the evidence in the text, it is not possible to assign *T. Jud.* 24:4–6 with certainty to either a Jewish or Christian level of composition or redaction.[96] Therefore, possible allusion to the davidic dynasty tradition in a

---

[90]Cf. Hollander and de Jonge, *Commentary*, 222–224.

[91]Becker, *Untersuchungen*, 318; cf. also p. 404, where *T. Jud.* 21:1–22:3 is not listed among supplementary texts that are Jewish.

[92]Hultgård, *L'eschatologie,* 1:168f.

[93]Hultgård, *L'eschatologie,* 1:169.

[94]See de Jonge, "Two Messiahs?" 197; Hollander and de Jonge, *Commentary*, 223–224.

[95]Cf. citations in Hollander and de Jonge, *Commentary*, 224.

[96]Similar passages in the *Testaments* (*T. Jud.* 23:5–24:6; *T. Ben.* 9:1–3; *T. Zeb.* 9:8; cf. also *T. Jos.* 19:12) speak of the advent of Christ and his salvation, after the exile, but others (*T. Dan* 5:10f; *T. Naph.* 4:4–5) do not characterize this salvation in an exclusively Christian manner.

Jewish phase of the *Testaments* cannot be ruled out. On the other hand, positive evidence for identifying a Messiah from Judah as davidic in a Jewish stage of the *Testaments* is also lacking.

To summarize, based on the analysis of the relevant evidence, we must conclude that the case for identifying the Messiah of Judah as a davidic figure is very weak. In passages mentioning a king (or kingship) from Judah, only *T. Jud.* 24:4–6 and *T. Jud.* 22:2–3 contain a possible connection with the davidic dynasty tradition. Of these, the former is clearly Christian, while the latter could be, although a Jewish origin cannot be ruled out for it. The weight of evidence requires us, therefore, to refrain from labeling the Messiah of Judah a davidic figure in any Jewish phase of the *Testaments*.

Finally, as noted earlier, it is not even certain whether the *Testaments* ever contained a pre-Christian Jewish expectation for a Messiah of Judah. In this regard, de Jonge's thesis that there is no messianism in the *Testaments*—associated with Judah or anyone else—until the Christian stage is, in my judgment, quite probable.[97] Nevertheless, if one could posit an expectation for the Messiah of Judah in a Jewish stage, as many scholars do,[98] it would provide another model of royal messianism that was non-davidic in orientation.

C. Other Royal Messiahs and Models of Jewish Kingship

Above I have argued that the Messiah of Judah—if indeed this is a pre-Christian figure, the Messiah of Israel, the ideal king from the *Temple Scroll*, and, prior to the herodian period, the Prince of the Congregation were not identified as davidic messiahs. This is significant because it indicates that during the Second Temple period Jews could imagine royal messianic figures quite apart from the biblical tradition of a davidic covenant and dynasty. Specifically, the figures mentioned above are rooted in models of kingship based on Gen 49:9–10, Num 24:17, Deut 17:14–20, and Ezek 40–48. In other words, the notion of a davidic covenant and dynasty was only one among several biblical prototypes of kingship employed by Jews when they reflected on royal messianic figures. In this final section, additional examples of royal messianic figures, based on still other biblical models of kingship, will be reviewed. Specifically, the King from the Sun in *Sib. Or.* 3 and the various popular royal messiahs mentioned by Josephus will be considered.[99]

---

[97]Cf. de Jonge, "Two Messiahs?" *passim.*

[98]See above, p. 247.

[99]The white bull in *1 Enoch* 90:37 probably does not represent the messiah, but a new Adam (see M. Black, *The Book of Enoch or I Enoch* [Leiden: Brill, 1985] 279–280), or some other antediluvian patriarch (see J. C. VanderKam, *Enoch and the Growth of an Apocalyptic Tradi-*

Each case offers evidence for royal messianism in the Second Temple period rooted not in the davidic dynasty tradition, but in an alternative conception of Jewish kingship.

1. Sibylline Oracles 3

The first example of a non-davidic royal messianic figure comes from *Sibylline Oracles* 3.[100] These oracles are the product of Egyptian Judaism sometime during the middle of the second century BCE.[101] In vv. 652–656, hope is expressed for a King from the Sun. In the lines immediately preceding this passage (vv. 635–651), eschatological portents are predicted. Then the text reads:

> And then God will send a King from the sun (ἀπ᾽ ἠελίοιο) who will stop the entire earth from evil war, killing some, imposing oaths of loyalty on others; and he will not do all these things by his private plans but in obedience to the noble teachings of the great God.[102]

It is clear that this King from the Sun, who brings peace and stability in the midst of eschatological upheaval in obedience to God, is a type of messiah.[103] Moreover, the identity of this figure is clarified when it is observed that the phrase King from the Sun is used in the Potter's Oracle to designate an Egyptian king.[104] Furthermore, during the Hellenistic period, the Ptolemaic kings had appropriated to themselves aspects of the old Egyptian royal ideology.[105] All this suggests, therefore, that the royal messiah envisioned in *Sib. Or.* 3:652–656 is a Ptolemaic monarch, a king of Egypt.[106]

---

tion [CBQMS 16; Washington, DC: Catholic Biblical Association, 1984] 168). The white bull does not represent a davidic figure as Goldstein, "'Messianic' Promises," 72–73, suggests (cf. Collins, "Messianism," 100–101; and VanderKam, *Enoch*, 168).

[100]V. Nikiprowetzky, *La Troisième Sibylle* (Études Juives IX; Paris: Mouton, 1970) 135–136, suggests that the figure in *Sib. Or.* 3:286–287 is a davidic messiah; this view is not widely held, however, and is refuted by the analysis given below.

[101]J. J. Collins, *The Sibylline Oracles of Egyptian Judaism* (SBLDS 13; Missoula, MT: Scholars Press, 1974) 33.

[102]English translations are from J. J. Collins, "Sibylline Oracles," *The Old Testament Pseudepigrapha* (2 vols.; ed. J. H. Charlesworth; Garden City, NY: Doubleday, 1985) 1:317–472. For the Greek text see, J. Geffcken, *Die Oracula Sibyllina* (GCS 8; Leipzig: Hinrichs, 1902).

[103]Schürer, *History*, 2:501.

[104]Collins, *Sibylline Oracles*, 41. Collins cites other close parallels in Egyptian literature.

[105]Collins, *Sibylline Oracles*, 42.

[106]Collins, *Sibylline Oracles*, 43.

This identification of the King from the Sun is confirmed beyond doubt by three other passages in *Sib. Or.* 3 that correlate eschatological transformation with the seventh king of Egypt, who will be a Greek (v. 193; v. 318; v. 608). For instance, vv. 191–194 read:

> Every kind of deceit will be found among them until the seventh reign, when a king of Egypt, who will be of the Greeks by race, will rule. And then the people of the great God will again be strong.

Collins considers this evidence and concludes:

> It is difficult, if not impossible, to distinguish between the king of Egypt, during whose reign will occur the beginning of the messianic age, and the Egyptian royal figure who ushers in that age. The remarkable conclusion which follows from this is that the sibyllist not only draws on Egyptian terminology to express the Jewish expectation of a messiah, but that the king whom he expected to usher in the messianic age would in fact be a king of Egypt, numbered from the line of the Greeks.[107]

Within the context of *Sib. Or.* 3, however, a messianic hope associated with a gentile king is not as peculiar as it might first appear, since in a description of the restoration after the Babylonian exile, where mention of a king can only refer to Cyrus, the Persian monarch who freed the Jews from exile, vv. 286–287 say:

> And then the heavenly God will send a king and will judge each man in blood and the gleam of fire.[108]

Thus, the messianic conceptions of the author of *Sib. Or.* 3:652–656 appear to have been influenced by the biblical model of royal messianism known from Deutero-Isaiah, where Cyrus, a gentile king, is heralded as the messiah of the Jews (Isa 44:28–45:1; cf. also 2 Chr 36:22–23).[109] This biblical example of divine salvation through a gentile king would be the obvious prototype for the author of *Sib. Or.* 3:652–656, who looked for salvation from the seventh Ptolemaic king of Egypt.[110] Accordingly, it is clear that messianic expectations among

---

[107]Collins, *Sibylline Oracles*, 43; see "Sibylline Oracles," *OTP*, 1:356, for a summary of this position; cf. also Schürer, *History*, 2:501.

[108]See Collins, *Sibylline Oracles*, 38–39, for a discussion of this text. Schürer, *History*, 2:501; and H. C. O. Lanchester, "The Sibylline Oracles," *The Apocrypha and Pseudepigrapha of the Old Testament* (2 vols.; ed. R. H. Charles; Oxford: Clarendon, 1913) 2:384, also identify the king as Cyrus; *contra* J. Noland, "*Sib. Or. III*, An Early Maccabean Messianic Oracle," *JTS* 30 (1979) 158–166, esp. p. 165, who thinks this passage is in keeping with a davidic hope.

[109]Collins, *Sibylline Oracles*, 43. Note too that this is similar to Josephus' view of the Roman emperor Vespasian (see above, p. 228).

[110]It may be noted further that this messianism is not peripheral to the message of *Sib. Or.*

Egyptian Jews in the middle of the second century BCE could flourish quite apart from the davidic dynasty tradition.[111]

2. Popular Messianic Figures in Palestine

Another biblical model of Jewish kingship is reflected in the various popular messianic movements which appeared in Palestine just prior to and during the first century CE. R. A. Horsley, whose work represents the most recent and thorough study of these popular movements and their leaders, has identified five figures who are properly characterized as royal messiahs.[112] Three of these, Judas the son of Hezekiah, Simon, Herod's servant, and Athronges, emerged during the unrest which followed the death of Herod the Great (4 BCE). Two others, Menachem, son of Judas the Galilean, and Simon bar Giora, made claims to royal power at the time of the great Jewish revolt against Rome (66–70 CE).[113] Below, I will briefly review the evidence for these figures and then consider the biblical model of Jewish kingship which seems to have influenced this form of royal messianism.

In his account of the political and social unrest after Herod's death, Josephus writes:

> Then there was Judas, the son of the brigand chief Ezekias ... This Judas got together a large number of desperate men at Sepphoris in Galilee and there made an assault on the royal palace ... He became an object of terror to all men by plundering those he came across in his desire for great possessions and his ambition for royal rank (*Ant.* 17.271–272).

Josephus continues:

> There was also Simon, a slave of king Herod ... Elated by the unsettled conditions of affairs, he was bold enough to place the diadem on his head, and having got together a body of men, he was himself also proclaimed king by them in their madness, and he rated himself worthy of this beyond anyone else (*Ant.* 17.273–274).

3; Collins, *Sibylline Oracles*, 35, describes one of this work's major concerns as "royal eschatology."

[111]We may note too that Philo, a later representative of Egyptian Judaism, never refers to the davidic dynasty in his discussion of an ideal state; rather he grounds his discussion in Pentateuchal laws and bases legitimate kingship on merit (cf. H. A. Wolfson, *Philo* [2 vols.; rev. ed.; Cambridge, MA: Harvard University Press, 1948] 2:333).

[112]See Horsley and Hanson, *Bandits*, 88–134. See also, M. Hengel, *The Zealots* (Edinburgh: T. & T. Clark, 1989) 290–302.

[113]Simon bar Kokhba represents a still later example of a royal messiah (132–135 CE), but he lies outside the temporal limits of the present study.

A final figure is then described:[114]

> Then there was a certain Athronges, a man distinguished neither for the position of his ancestors nor by the excellence of his character, nor for any abundance of means but merely a shepherd completely unknown to everybody ... This man had the temerity to aspire to the kingship ... Athronges himself put on the diadem and held a council to discuss what things were to be done, but everything depended on his own decision. This man kept his power for a long while, for he had the title of king and nothing to prevent him from doing as he wished (*Ant.* 17.278–281).

Horsley has summarized the character of these three popular movements by observing that they were oriented around a charismatic king of humble origin, who organized bands of peasants with the goal of overthrowing herodian and Roman power.[115]

Josephus mentions two others who sought Jewish kingship later, during the great revolt against Rome. After Jewish insurgents had begun their attack on Jerusalem, they were joined by the Sicarii, urban terrorist led by Menachem, who was the son of Judas the Galilean—founder of the Fourth Philosophy. Menachem quickly led his followers to Masada, where they plundered Herod's armory (*J.W.* 2.433). Josephus reports:

> he (Menachem) returned like a veritable king (οἷα δὴ βασιλεὺς) to Jerusalem, became the leader of the revolution, and directed the siege of the palace (*J.W.* 2.434).

Shortly after this, however, Menachem was murdered by rebels loyal to another leader. Accordingly, due to the brevity of Menachem's royal leadership and the unprecedented nature of messianic claims among the Sicarii, Horsley rightly calls Menachem's bid for power a messianic incident rather than a movement.[116]

In contrast, Simon bar Giora, a native of Gerasa, represents a full-fledged messianic figure who emerged two years into the revolt. After organizing a band of revolutionaries, he hooked up with the Sicarii, who by this point were holed up at Masada. Josephus writes:

> His efforts to tempt them (the Sicarii) to greater enterprises were, however, unsuccessful ... He, on the contrary, was aspiring to despotic power and cherishing high ambitions; accordingly ... he withdrew to the hills, where, by

---

[114]Josephus suggests in *Ant.* 17.285 that others, beyond the three persons mentioned, aspired to Jewish kingship: "Anyone might make himself king as the head of a band of rebels."

[115]Horsley and Hanson, *Bandits*, 114–117

[116]Horsley and Hanson, *Bandits*, 118.

> proclaiming liberty for slaves and rewards for the free, he gathered around him the villains from every quarter (*J.W.* 4.507–508).

Horsley connects Simon's proclamation of freedom to contemporary Jewish messianic expectations.[117] Moreover, Josephus reports that his followers obeyed him like a king (*J.W.* 4.510). Further, we learn of Simon that after plundering the countryside and capturing the town of Hebron, he went on to Jerusalem, where he established his supremacy as leader of the insurgents.

But most important for understanding Simon's royal messianic role is the story of his activities after the fall of Jerusalem. Josephus explains that Simon was unable to escape from the city through underground passages.

> Thereupon, Simon . . . dressed himself in white tunics and buckling over them a purple mantle arose out of the ground at the very spot whereon the temple formerly stood (*J.W.* 7.29).

Simon then surrendered to the commanding officer and was put in chains. Subsequently, he was taken to Rome and ritually executed at the climax of the victory procession (*J.W.* 7.153–155). Horsley observes that Simon's ceremonial surrender and execution "reveal both that Simon understood himself as the messiah and that the conquering Romans recognized him as the leader of the nation."[118]

Having reviewed the data about the popular royal messiahs, we can proceed now to ask what understanding of Jewish kingship may have motivated them to contend for the crown. In this regard, Hengel maintains that at least some of the popular messianic figures claimed davidic descent, thereby invoking the davidic dynasty tradition.[119] He offers four reasons: 1) early Jewish tradition, i.e., pre-rabbinic tradition, attributed davidic descent to the war messiah; 2) the importance the New Testament attaches to Jesus' davidic lineage points to the kind of messianic hopes that were generally current in the first century CE; 3) Hegesippus reports that after the conquest of Jerusalem Vespasian sought after Jews of davidic descent in order to eliminate those of royal lineage; 4) at this time the lineage of leading personalities was followed with particular interest.[120]

None of these reasons is compelling, however. As for Hengel's first reason, as we have seen in the earlier portions of this study, the attribution of davidic descent to a war messiah in early Judaism is in reality quite infrequent. Moreover, even if there were a dominant expectation for a messiah of davidic descent, that in no way would imply that these popular royal contenders must have fit that

---

[117]Horsley and Hanson, *Bandits*, 122.

[118]Horsley and Hanson, *Bandits*, 126.

[119]Hengel, *Zealots*, 298.

[120]Hengel, *Zealots*, 298–300.

expectation.[121] Secondly, Christian claims about Jesus' davidic status cannot be used to establish what general Jewish messianic expectations were like in the first century CE. Indeed, the tendency to read Jewish expectations through the lens of the New Testament has resulted in an undue emphasis on Hengel's first reason. Thirdly, the historical validity of Hegesippus' report is suspect. It is very likely that Hegesippus' account of the search for davidic descendants, *who were purportedly relatives of Jesus*, by Vespasian and later emperors is to be regarded as an apologetic legend designed to support Christian claims that Jesus was the davidic messiah.[122] Finally, as for Hengel's assertion that the lineage of leading personalities was followed, this is attested in the Second Temple period for priests, especially the high priests, but ascription of davidic lineage to notable figures, such as Hillel, appears to be the result of ideological, rather than genealogical, interests.[123] Thus, none of Hengel's arguments offer support for his case that these popular messiahs claimed davidic descent.

Quite the contrary, evidence that these popular messiahs appealed to the davidic dynasty tradition to support their bid for Jewish kingship is entirely lacking. Hengel accounts for this by discounting Josephus as a reliable source for genealogical claims made by popular messiahs. To be sure, Josephus, the only source for our knowledge of these figures, is by no means an unbiased writer. He tends to cast Jewish conceptions in Hellenistic terms, and in particular, seems to avoid Jewish messianic language.[124] Hence, whatever one says about these popular figures is dependent on critical judgments concerning Josephus' accounts. Yet, there is no obvious reason why Josephus would decline to mention appeals to the davidic dynasty tradition by these popular messiahs, especially since all the popular movements failed.

Furthermore, Josephus is really not all that reticent about the nature of popular messianic hopes. In particular, to account for Jewish revolutionary fervor

---

[121]Cf. Horsley and Hanson, *Bandits*, 89,110, esp. p. 92, who note the distinction between the images of messianic figures produced by literate groups and actual concrete popular messiahs.

[122]Schürer, *History*, 1:528.

[123]Horsley and Hanson, *Bandits*, 91,132 n. 7. Some families in the first century BCE appear to have traced their lineage to the "house of David" (see D. Flusser, "Jesus, His Ancestry, and the Commandment of Love," *Jesus' Jewishness* [ed. J. H. Charlesworth; New York: Crossroad, 1991] 158–159, who points to an ossuary inscription: שלבי דיד ["those of the house of David"]), but there is no evidence that these families supplied any leading personalities. I suspect that this reference to the "house of David" is similar in nature to the one in Zech 12:7–13:1 (see above, pp. 117–123).

[124]Horsley and Hanson, *Bandits*, 110,114; Hengel, *Zealots*, 291, esp. n. 339.

in the revolt against Rome, he explains:

> But what more than all else incited them to the war was an ambiguous oracle, likewise found in their sacred scriptures, to the effect that at that time one from their country would become ruler of the world. This they understood to mean someone of their own race, and many of their wise men went astray in their interpretation of it (*J.W.* 6.312–313).

While it impossible to be sure what scripture Josephus is referring to here, suggested texts include Num 24:17–24 and Daniel 2.[125] Nevertheless, it is virtually impossible for the oracle to have been one connected with the davidic dynasty tradition, since it does not appear to limit the genealogy of the future king beyond that of Jewish descent and must have been sufficiently general in nature for Josephus to have applied it to Vespasian (cf. *J.W.* 6.313). Neither of these observations comports well with an oracle that predicted a world king of exclusively davidic lineage.[126] At any rate, if Josephus was willing to impart the kind of information about Jewish messianic beliefs found in *J.W.* 6.312–313, it is not clear why he would suppress appeals to the davidic dynasty tradition, if indeed popular messiahs ever made such appeals. In fact, we see that for several of the royal contenders, Josephus does refer to their family background, but never links anyone to the house of David or even to the tribe of Judah. Specifically, for Athronges, Josephus characterizes him as "a man distinguished neither for the position of his ancestors ..." (*Ant.* 17.278).[127]

More important, however, than the absence of any evidence linking these popular messiahs to the davidic dynasty tradition is the positive evidence for the biblical prototype of kingship that appears to have influenced these royal messiahs and their movements. Here Horsley has pointed to the tradition of popular kingship reflected in the Hebrew scriptures.[128] As examples of this tradition, one can cite Abimelech (Judg 9:1–22),[129] and David, during his initial rise to royal

---

[125]De Jonge, "Josephus und die Zukunftserwartungen," 210; Hengel, *Zealots*, 237–240.

[126]Hengel, *Zealots*, 300, suggests that the davidic claims of the popular messiahs might be associated with this oracle mentioned by Josephus, even though he would tend to connect the oracle with Num 24:17–24 (see also *Zealots*, pp. 237–240).

[127]Judas is identified as the son of Hezekiah, and Menachem as the son of Judas the Galilean. Further, Hengel, *Zealots*, 299, himself admits that Simon ben Giora, whose father's name implies that he was a proselyte, would have been an exception to his contention that the popular messiahs claimed davidic descent.

[128]Horsley and Hanson, *Bandits*, 92–102.

[129]Horsley and Hanson, *Bandits*, 93, identify Abimelech only as a brigand, in contrast to a king, but this is unwarranted in light of Judg 9:6,22, where Abimelech is clearly made king and rules Israel.

office (1 Samuel 17–2 Samuel 5).[130] Moreover, after the rise of the davidic dynasty ideology and its claim of an everlasting royal line, earlier ideas about a conditional monarchy continued to live on in the Northern Kingdom of Israel, from Jeroboam down to the fall of Samaria,[131] and were not even completely displaced in the Southern Kingdom of Judah, as portions of the Dtr and Psalm 132 indicate.[132]

Horsley characterizes this tradition of popular kingship as conditional, based on popular election, and revolutionary: it was conditional, in that it was subject to certain covenantal requirements (cf. 1 Sam 10:25; Deut 17:14–20); based on popular election, as in the case of Saul (1 Sam 10:20–24), David (2 Sam 2:4; 5:1–3), and Jeroboam (1 Kings 12:20); and revolutionary, since it was a way of establishing freedom from foreign domination.[133] Accordingly, this biblical model of popular kingship offered a suitable prototype for the royal messianic figures around the first century CE, who vied for kingship not through dynastic claims, but by popular appeal as advocates of the lower class and opponents of foreign domination. These kings, of humble origins themselves, who organized peasants against oppressive powers find their closest parallels in the biblical figures of popular kingship cited above.

Finally, that these popular royal messiahs stood in the tradition of popular kingship rather than davidic messianism may be related to the fact that several were non-Judeans: Judas and Menachem were from Galilee and Simon bar Giora from Gerasa.[134] We may observe that the texts which set forth a hope for a davidic messiah—*Pss. Sol.* 17, Qumran texts, and 4 Ezra—were Judean in provenance or connected to affairs in Jerusalem. In addition, in ancient Israel the official davidic royal ideology had never taken hold in the Northern Kingdom and was unpopular even among elements in Judea.[135] One wonders whether Jews outside Judea and Jerusalem ever looked upon the davidic dynasty tradition as a viable biblical model for Jewish kingship. In any case, the royal messianic figures active around the first century CE did not invoke the davidic dynasty tradition, but

---

[130]It is important to distinguish here between David as an example of popular kingship in his rise to power, and the davidic dynasty tradition, which was a wholly different ideology of kingship that attempted to secure the monarchy for the house of David.

[131]Cf. Horsley and Hanson, *Bandits*, 96; Cross, *Hebrew Epic*, 219–273.

[132]Cf. Cross, *Hebrew Epic*, 219–273, 285–289; on these texts, see above, chap. 2.

[133]Horsley and Hanson, *Bandits*, 94–96.

[134]The regional origin of Simon, Herod's servant, and Athronges is not stated, although Simon had adherents among the Pereans (*Ant.* 17.276).

[135]Horsley and Hanson, *Bandits*, 96–98.

instead were influenced by another biblical conception of kingship—that of popular kingship.

D. Conclusion

The purpose of this chapter was to assess how royal messianic figures from early Jewish literature and history were related to the davidic dynasty tradition. We have seen that the Messiah of Judah, the Messiah of Israel, the ideal king from 11QTemple, and, prior to the herodian period, the Prince of the Congregation should not be identified as davidic messiahs. In fact, these figures were based on non-davidic models of Jewish kingship derived from Gen 49:9–10, Num 24:17, Deut 17:14–20, and Ezek 40–48. Likewise, still other prototypes of Jewish kingship are reflected in *Sib. Or.* 3, where a gentile king like Cyrus was the antici-pated messiah, and in the popular royal messiahs around the first century CE, who stood in the biblical tradition of popular kingship. Thus, while davidic messianism would eventually become "traditional" in both rabbinic Judaism and Christianity, the Judaism of the Second Temple period had no such standardized expectation. Instead one finds different biblical models of kingship reflected in Jewish thought on the subject of royal messiahs. In the early Jewish period, messianism rooted in the davidic dynasty tradition is certainly represented, but it must be understood as one among several types of royal messianism. It therefore cannot be construed as the "traditional" type of Jewish messianic expectation in early Judaism.

CHAPTER 7
Summary and Conclusion

The purpose of this study has been two-fold: first, to offer a history of the davidic dynasty tradition in early Judaism, and second, to evaluate whether there existed in this period a widespread, continuous, dominant, or uniform expectation for a davidic messiah. With regard to these two matters, I can now summarize the results of the preceding chapters and state my conclusions.

The analysis of the davidic dynasty tradition in the biblical material prior to the late Persian period indicated that the tradition of a davidic dynasty was marked by diversity. Not even in the pre-exilic texts, which came from a time when there were sitting davidic kings, was there a wholly consistent understanding of the davidic dynasty. Specifically, the dynasty could be construed as either conditional or unconditional, and not always in terms of a covenant agreement. Nor was the davidic dynasty the only model of Israelite kingship available, as Deut 17:14–20, Gen 49:8–12, Num 24:17–19, and Isa 32:1–8 revealed.

In exilic texts, the davidic dynasty tradition proved durable, adaptable, or expendable. While expectation for a renewed davidic monarchy was possibly attested in Ezek 17:22–24, other interpretations of the tradition were present: Ezek 34:23–24; 37:24–25 and Jer 30:9 spoke of a figure typologically similar to David, the "new David;" in the theocracy described in Ezekiel 40–48, there was a place for a נשיא, but he was not specifically davidic; in Isa 55:3b, the promise to David was transferred to the people of Israel; and in Jeremiah 40–41 and the final edition of Dtr, hope for the restoration of the davidic dynasty was given up.

Evidence for the use of the davidic dynasty tradition in texts from the early post-exilic period was sparse. Only Jer 33:14–26—if indeed it is correctly dated to the early post-exilic period—revealed hope for the re-establishment of the davidic dynasty by strongly asserting the continuing validity of the davidic covenant. Beyond this, there was an exhortation to observe the Sabbath in Jer

17:19–27, where the continuity of the pre-exilic davidic monarchy was viewed as dependent on Israel's faithfulness to the Sabbath command. Haggai and Zechariah 1–8 did pin royalist hopes on Zerubbabel, but never characterized him as a davidic figure. Indeed, the only evidence that Zerubbabel was of davidic lineage came from 1 Chr 3:19, a passage we judged to be historically unreliable. Finally, mention of the "booth of David" in Amos 9:11–15 was taken as a reference to Jerusalem, not to the davidic dynasty.

This evidence indicated that the biblical tradition about the davidic dynasty was marked by diversity, providing later authors with a rich array of concepts and terminology upon which to draw. To reduce the biblical tradition of the davidic dynasty to an unconditional everlasting covenant promise, as one finds in 2 Sam 7:11–16 and Psalm 89, would be an unwarranted limitation of the textual evidence. Moreover, the exilic and post-exilic usage of the davidic dynasty tradition illustrated ways in which the tradition could be interpreted in the absence of the davidic monarchy, and indicated that at the dawn of the early Jewish period evidence for an ongoing davidic royalist or messianic hope was very limited. All this served to emphasize the need to ask how references to the davidic dynasty tradition were employed in early Jewish literature.

In the period of early Judaism, the davidic dynasty tradition was interpreted and applied in numerous ways. First, in Chronicles, which we took as an essentially unified composition to be dated to ca. 400 BCE, the narrative focused on the davidic dynasty, especially its first two kings, David and Solomon. It was argued that the davidic dynasty tradition functioned to legitimate and exalt the cultic community in Jerusalem as the exclusively valid place and organization for Israelite worship of the Lord. The kings of the davidic dynasty, in particular, David and Solomon, were depicted as the divinely appointed founders and patrons of this cultic community. This message may have been motivated by the presence of rival Jewish temples in the early Jewish period. On the other hand, neither the repetition of the dynastic oracle, along with other evidence from the history of the monarchy, nor the davidic genealogy in 1 Chr 3:17–24 pointed to a royalist or messianic hope on the part of the Chronicler. These texts could be used to support a davidic royalist or messianic expectation only at the cost of abstracting them from their literary context and function within Chronicles as a whole and by placing them in some hypothetical historical setting.

Zech 12:2–13:1, which also dated from ca. 400 BCE, witnessed to a significant role for the "house of David" in post-exilic Jerusalem. Yet we argued that within the social configuration of Judah in the late Persian period, "house of David" referred to a large clan-like group that, while genealogically related to the pre-exilic family of David, was not to be identified with the pre-exilic royal house. No royal or messianic figure was in view; no allusion to the davidic royal ideology was in evidence; no call for the restoration of the monarchy was present. This text indicated that the families who could trace their lineage to the pre-exilic davidic families enjoyed social and economic prominence in post-exilic Jerusalem, but, in effect, Zech 12:2–13:1 was not an interpretation of the davidic dynasty tradition.

Looking to the LXX to track the interpretation of the davidic dynasty tradition yielded few results. This was due in part to the infrequency of interpretive activity in texts pertaining to the davidic dynasty tradition, but also to difficulties in determining the significance and provenance of translations that did deviate from the text of the MT. Only the LXX translation of 2 Samuel 7:11b offered potentially useful evidence, since it appeared to indicate a shift in interest among Jews who read the scriptures in Greek from David as progenitor of a royal line to David as builder of the Jerusalem temple.

About two hundred years after the composition of Chronicles and Zech 12:2–13:1, Ben Sira (198–175 BCE) offered an interpretation of the davidic dynasty tradition. On the one hand, Sirach could portray the davidic covenant and kingship as a praiseworthy part of Israelite history (47:11,22), even though he believed the davidic monarchy had come to an end because its kings had abandoned the Torah (49:4–5). On the other hand, for Ben Sira the davidic covenant found its ultimate fulfillment in the Second Temple high priesthood, the office which had taken over the functions and symbols of the pre-exilic davidic monarchy. In particular, Ben Sira maintained that in the uncertainty surrounding the high priesthood following the death of Simon II, the mode of familial succession known from the davidic dynasty was to be employed in high priestly succession (45:25). Ben Sira's ideal Israel had no place for a king, let alone a davidic king. The psalm found between 51:12 and 13 in the Hebrew version of Ben Sira was deemed not original to Ben Sira, and may not even date from the early Jewish period.

In 1 Macc 2:57, the testament of Mattathias cited David, who inherited a throne of a kingdom in perpetuity, as a model of piety to be emulated by Mattathias' sons, the Maccabees, in the hope that they would receive a similar reward. The author of 1 Maccabees, who wrote at ca. 100 BCE in order to legitimate the Hasmonean dynasty, then proceeded to demonstrate how the Maccabean ancestors indeed followed in the footsteps of David and other biblical heroes and thus won for themselves the right to rule the kingdom of Israel. Accordingly, David's inheritance of a dynasty provided a biblical prototype that was successfully imitated by the Maccabees.

Pss. Sol. 17, which was composed ca. 60 BCE and probably emanated from Pharisaical circles, provided the first evidence in the early Jewish period of hope for a davidic messiah, named here, the Son of David. This hope was based on an interpretation of the davidic dynasty tradition that posited an eternally valid dynastic promise on the basis of which God would raise up an ideal davidic king—a king who would rule Israel and the world. The catalyst for this interpretation was the rise of the Hasmoneans and their claim to kingship. As opposition to the Hasmoneans increased, this reading of the davidic dynasty tradition functioned to attack the legitimacy of the Hasmoneans, exploiting the contradiction between an eternally valid davidic dynasty and Hasmonean rule. Moreover, the characterization and role of this Son of David served to articulate the author's vision of an ideal social and political order, free from foreign oppression and full of righteousness, holiness, and wisdom. Indeed, the davidic king, who was ascribed every kind of charismatic endowment—but especially wisdom and righteousness, would be the mediator of these divine blessing. On the other hand, temple and priests had no place in this ideal Israel.

Among the documents found at Qumran, 4QDibHam[a] represented a prayer of supplication (*tahanun*), which was probably used more widely among Jews and dated from ca. 150 BCE. Mention of the covenant made with David and David's sitting on the throne all the days occurred in a specific portion of the *tahanun* devoted to the remembrance of God's saving deeds in the past, deeds which nevertheless failed to evoke a faithful response from Israel. Yet God remained faithful to Israel, and this acknowledgment provided the context for Israel's plea for help in its current distress. To have understood this reference to the davidic dynasty tradition as evidence of hope for a davidic messiah would have violated its context and function within a prayer of supplication. This interpretation of 4QDibHam[a] was therefore rejected.

Other Qumran documents, which reflected the specific ideology of the Qumran sect, revealed an expectation for a davidic messiah in the last days. In 4QpGen[a] (ca. 30 BCE–70 CE), Gen 49:10 was read in terms of an everlasting davidic covenant, on the basis of which the messiah of righteousness, the Branch of David, would come. The reign of the davidic messiah would begin when Israel achieved dominion in the eschatological war against the Sons of Darkness and would never be cut off. Little else was said about this davidic figure, however. It was suggested that within its socio-historical context this interpretation of the davidic dynasty tradition was used polemically to challenge the legitimacy of herodian or Roman kingship due to their unrighteous rule.

4QFlor 1:10–13 (ca. 30 BCE–70 CE) also understood the davidic dynasty tradition in terms of an everlasting davidic dynasty. Specifically, 2 Sam 7:11b–14 was interpreted in conjunction with Amos 9:11a to reveal the coming of the Branch of David, who would stand with the Interpreter of the Law and take office to save Israel. The unexpected importation of a priestly figure (the Interpreter of the Law) alongside this royal messiah highlighted the relativized status of the

Branch of David in Qumran thought. Yet the davidic messiah would act as God's agent of salvation in the final conflict against Israel's enemies and therefore was an important component in the author's vision of the eschatological landscape. Beyond this, however, the depiction of the Branch of David was rather vague.

On the basis of its interpretation of Isa 11:1–5, 4QpIsa^a 8–10:11–24 (ca. 30 BCE–20 CE) spoke of a militant davidic figure whose sword would judge the nations, especially the Kittim. The spiritual qualities attributed to the davidic figure in Isa 11:1–5 were largely passed over, with the exception of might, since the davidic messiah's key role was the exercise of military power. Moreover, the Branch of David would possess the signs of royal office. Most importantly, however, Isa 11:3b was radically reinterpreted in order to place the judging activities of the davidic messiah under the guidance and supervision of the priests.

In 4QSerek HaMilhamah (ca. 30 BCE–70 CE), the davidic messiah was identified with the Prince of the Congregation and depicted as the leader of the Sons of Light in the eschatological war against the Kittim. In particular, the Branch of David executed judgment against the nations and killed the king of the Kittim. In contrast to 1QM, therefore, 4QSerek HaMilhamah attributed a significant role in the conflict to a human military leader who would act as God's agent of judgment. In this way, this document engendered hope for the ultimate overthrow of oppressive political powers.

The Qumran texts considered testified to the importance of davidic messianism in the ideology of the Qumran community. Yet, our analysis of references to other royal messianic figures at Qumran indicated that, whereas the ideal king in the *Temple Scroll* and the Messiah of Israel were not characterized as davidic figures, the Prince of the Congregation was portrayed as a davidic messiah only in texts dating from the herodian period. Indeed, we observed that texts reflecting hope in a davidic messiah all dated from the herodian period, and therefore concluded that before this time, the characterizations of royal figures at Qumran were derived from other models of Jewish kingship. In short, davidic messianism emerged at Qumran only during the herodian period.

In 4 Ezra 12:32 (ca. 100 CE), the messiah in the eagle vision was said to come from the seed of David. The role of this messiah was to deliver Israel from the oppressive rule of the nations, especially Rome, and to gather the remnant of Israel; yet his activities were characterized in largely judicial, rather than military, terms. Moreover, this davidic messiah was described as preexistent and performed the same role as the cosmic messianic figure in 4 Ezra 13, the man from the sea. This illustrated how various messianic motifs could be intertwined in the characterization of an ideal figure. The davidic status of the messiah in 4 Ezra 12 did not seem to be of central significance; yet the davidic dynasty tradition from

Isa 11:1–5 aided the author in portraying the messiah as a righteous judge of Israel's oppressors.

Finally, in *The Jewish Antiquities* (93–94 CE), Josephus depicted the davidic dynasty as a glorious phase in the history of Israel, which nevertheless came to an end because of the failure of the davidic kings to obey the laws of Moses. This construal of the davidic dynasty tradition fit Josephus' overall theological interpretation of Jewish history, which understood God as exercising his providential care over Israel through retributive justice: blessing virtue and punishing disobedience. The failure of the davidic dynasty thereby provided a moral example of how God punished disobedience. On the other hand, Josephus' glorious portrayal of the davidic dynasty helped him present a favorable picture of Judaism to his Greco-Roman readers. There was no davidic messianism in Josephus; for world political leadership this Jewish historian looked to the Roman emperor Vespasian.

In light of this summary of the background, content, and function of the davidic dynasty tradition in early Judaism, we can conclude the following. First, the davidic dynasty tradition was interpreted in a variety of ways according to the intention of the literary work in which it was used and served a meaningful function within the socio-historical setting in which that work was composed. Reference to the davidic dynasty tradition was not limited to "messianic" interpretations.

Secondly, in six texts, *Pss. Sol.* 17, 4QpGen^a, 4QFlor, 4QpIsa^a, 4QSerek HaMilhamah, and 4 Ezra, the davidic dynasty tradition was interpreted to express hope for a davidic messiah. Yet, one finds different characteristics and functions ascribed to the davidic messiah in individual texts, except for a reasonably consistent portrayal of this figure in the four texts from Qumran. Consequently, although there are generic similarities among the various concepts of a davidic messiah, the evidence demonstrates that no uniform conception of a davidic messiah existed in early Judaism.

Thirdly, there existed in early Judaism no continuous, widespread, or dominant expectation for a davidic messiah. Indeed, after the expression of hope for the restoration of the davidic dynasty in some biblical texts from the exilic and post-exilic periods, the first evidence for davidic messianism is found in *Pss. Sol.* 17, which dates from the middle of the first century BCE. As we have argued, the idea of a davidic messiah first emerged in the first half of the first century BCE, in order to articulate Pharisaic opposition against the ruling Hasmoneans. After this, davidic messianism also appears in the ideology of the Qumran community in the herodian period. The last evidence of davidic messianism in the early Jewish period comes from 4 Ezra (ca. 100 CE), where it is no longer a central motif. Thus, the evidence for davidic messianism in the Second Temple period is limited to three communities, all of Palestinian provenance, active between ca. 60 BCE and 100 CE. Other royal messiahs known from the literature and history of early Judaism are not to be identified as davidic messiahs. On the contrary, figures such as the Messiah of Israel, the ideal king of the *Temple Scroll*, the initial conception of the Prince of the Congregation, the Messiah of Judah, the King from the Sun, and the popular royal messiahs from Palestine demonstrate how other biblical models of royalty could be utilized to articulate notions of Jewish kingship.

Accordingly, since there never existed a continuous, widespread, dominant, or uniform expectation for a davidic messiah in early Judaism, scholarly discourse should dispense with the idea of a "traditional" davidic hope for this period. Nor can appeal to such a traditional hope serve as a resource for explaining why some early Christians came to designate Jesus as Son of David, or why davidic messianism played an important role in rabbinic Judaism. Interpretations of earliest Christology or rabbinic messianism that rely on a straight line development of "traditional" davidic messianism, rooted in the biblical material, carried on through the Second Temple period, and taken over by earliest Christianity or formative Judaism, must be rejected. Scholars will have to investigate specifically how the davidic dynasty tradition was interpreted and applied in various early Christian and rabbinic texts in terms of the particular characterizations and functions ascribed to the davidic messiah. Only in this way would one be able to explain how and why davidic messianism became an important idea for these two religious traditions that emerged from early Judaism.

Bibliography

Abegg, M. G. "Messianic Hope and 4Q285: A Reassessment." *JBL* 113 (1994) 81–91.

Ackroyd, P. R. "Chronicles, I and II." *The Interpreter's Dictionary of the Bible, Supplementary Volume*, 156–158. Edited by K. Crim. Nashville: Abingdon, 1976.

Ackroyd, P. R. "History and Theology in the Writings of the Chronicler." *CTM* 38 (1967) 501–515.

Ackroyd, P. R. "The Historical Literature." *The Hebrew Bible and Its Modern Interpreters*, 297–323. Edited by D. A. Knight and G. M. Tucker. Chico, CA: Scholars Press, 1985.

Ackroyd, P. R. "The Theology of the Chronicler." *LTQ* 8 (1973) 101–116.

Ackroyd, P. R. *Exile and Restoration*. OTL. Philadelphia: Westminster, 1968.

Ackroyd, P. R. *I and II Chroniclers, Ezra, Nehemiah*. London: SCM, 1973.

Ackroyd, P. R. *The Age of the Chronicler*. Aukland: Colloquiem, Australian and New Zealand Theological Review, 1970.

Allegro, J. M. "Further Messianic References in Qumran Literature." *JBL* 75 (1956) 172–187.

Allegro, J. M. Report in Benoit, P. "Editing the Manuscript Fragments from Qumran." *BA* 19 (1956) 75–96.

Allegro, J. M. with A. A. Anderson. *Qumran Cave 4: I (4Q158–4Q186)*. DJD 5. Oxford: Clarendon Press, 1968.

Andersen, F. I. and D. N. Freedman. *Hosea*. AB 24. Garden City, NY: Doubleday, 1980.

Arenhoevel, D. "Die Eschatologie der Makkabäerbucher." *TTZ* 72 (1963) 257–269.

Arenhoevel, D. *Theokratie Nach dem 1. und 2. Makkabäerbuch*. Walberger Studien 3. Nainz: Matthias-Grünewald, 1963.

Attridge, H. W. "Historiography." *Jewish Writings of the Second Temple Period*, 157–184. CRINT 2:2. Edited by M. E. Stone. Assen: Van Gorcum/Philadelphia: Fortress, 1984.

Attridge, H. W. "Josephus and His Works." *Jewish Writings of the Second Temple Period*, 185–232. CRINT 2:2. Edited by M. E. Stone. Assen: Van Gorcum/Philadelphia: Fortress, 1984.

Attridge, H. W. *The Interpretation of Biblical History in the Antiquitates Judaicae of Flavius Josephus*. HDR 7. Missoula, MT: Scholars Press, 1976.

Avigad, N. "The Paleography of the Dead Sea Scrolls and Related Documents." *Aspects of the Dead Sea Scrolls*, 56–87. 2nd edition. ScrHier IV. Jerusalem: Magna Press, 1965.

Baillet, M. "Un recueil liturgique de Qumrân, grotte 4: 'Les paroles des luminaires'." *RB* 68 (1961) 195–250.

Baillet, M. *Qumrân Grotte 4: III (4Q482–4Q520)*. DJD 7. Oxford: Clarendon, 1982.

Baldwin, J. G. "*ṣemaḥ* as a Technical Term in the Prophets." *VT* 14 (1964) 93–97.

Baldwin, J. G. *Haggai, Zechariah, Malachi*. Tyndale Old Testament Commentaries. London: Tyndale, 1972.

Baltzer, K. "Das Ende des Staates Juda und die Messias-Frage." *Studien zur Theologie der alttestamentlichen Überlieferungen*, 33–43. Edited by R. Rendtorff and K. Koch. Neukirchen: Neukirchener Verlag, 1961.

Barr, J. *Biblical Words for Time*. SBT 1/33. 2nd edition. Naperville, IL: Allenson, 1969.

Barth, H. *Die Jesaha-Worte in der Josiazeit*. WMANT 48. Neukirchen-Vluyn: Neukirchener Verlag, 1977.

Barthélemy, D. and J. T. Milik. *Qumran Cave I*. DJD 1. Oxford: Clarendon, 1955.

Barthélemy, D. and O. Rickenbacher. *Konkordanz zum hebräischen Sirach mit syrisch-hebräischen Index*. Göttingen: Vandenhoeck & Ruprecht, 1973.

Barthélemy, D. *Critique textuelle de l'ancien Testament*. Fribourg: Éditions Universitaires/Göttingen: Vandenhoeck & Ruprecht, 1982.

Bartlett, J. B. *The First and Second Books of the Maccabees*. Cambridge: Cambridge University Press, 1973.

Beasley-Murray, G. R. "The Two Messiahs in the Testaments of the Twelve Patriarchs." *JTS* 48 (1947) 1–12.

Becker, J. *Untersuchungen zur Entstehungsgeschichte der Testamente der zwölf Patriarchen*. AGJU 8. Leiden: Brill, 1970.

Begg, C. T. "The Significance of Jehoiachin's Release: A New Proposal." *JSOT* 36 (1986) 49–56.

Ben Zvi, E. "The Authority of 1–2 Chronicles in the Late Second Temple Period." *JSP* 3 (1988) 59–88.

Berger, P.-R. "Zu den Namen ששבצר und שנאצר." *ZAW* 83 (1971) 98–100.

Betlyon, J. W. "The Provincial Government of Persian Period Judea and the Yehud Coins." *JBL* 105 (1986) 633–642.

Beuken, W. A. M. *Haggai-Sacharja.* SSN. Assen: Van Gorcum, 1967.

Beyse, K.-M. *Serubbabel und die Königserwartungen der Propheten Haggai und Sacharja.* Stuttgart: Calwer, 1972.

Black, M. *The Book of Enoch or I Enoch.* Leiden: Brill, 1985.

Blenkinsopp, J. *A History of Prophecy in Israel.* Philadelphia: Westminster, 1983.

Blenkinsopp, J. *Ezra-Nehemiah.* OTL. Philadelphia: Westminster, 1988.

Bloch, R. "Midrash." *Approaches to Ancient Judaism: Theory and Practice*, 29–50. BJS 1. Edited by W. S. Green. Missoula, MT: Scholars Press, 1978.

Bockmuehl, M. "'A Slain Messiah' in 4Q Serekh Milḥamah (4Q 285)?" *TynBul* 43 (1992) 155–169.

Bordreuil, P. "Les 'Grace de David' et 1 Maccabées II 57." *VT* 31 (1981) 73–76.

Box, G. H. *The Ezra-Apocalypse.* London: Pitman, 1912.

Box, G. H. and W. O. E. Oesterley. "The Book of Sirach." *The Apocrypha and Pseudepigrapha of the Old Testament.* 2 vols., 2:268–517. Edited by R. H. Charles. Oxford: Clarendon Press, 1913.

Braun, R. "A Reconsideration of the Chronicler's Attitude toward the North." *JBL* 96 (1977) 59–62.

Braun, R. "Chronicles, Ezra, and Nehemiah: Theology and Literary History." *Studies in the Historical Books of the Old Testament*, 52–64. VTSup 30. Leiden: Brill, 1979.

Braun, R. "Solomon, the Chosen Temple Builder: The Significance of 1 Chronicles 22, 28, and 29 for the Theology of Chronicles." *JBL* 95 (1976) 581–590.

Braun, R. "Solomonic Apologetic in Chronicles." *JBL* 92 (1975) 502–514.

Braun, R. "The Message of Chronicles: Rally 'Round the Temple." *CTM* 42 (1971) 502–514.

Braun, R. *1 Chronicles.* WBC. Waco, TX: Word, 1986.

Bright, J. *A History of Israel.* 3rd edition. Philadelphia: Westminster, 1981.

Bright, J. *Jeremiah.* AB 21. Garden City, NY: Doubleday, 1965.

Brooke, G. J. *Exegesis at Qumran: 4QFlorilegium in its Jewish Context.* JSOTSup 29. Sheffield: JSOT Press, 1985.

Brooke, G. "Qumran Pesher: Towards the Redefinition of a Genre." *RevQ* 10 (1978–81) 483–503.

Brown, R. E. "J. Starcky's Theory of Qumran Messianic Development." *CBQ* 28 (1966) 51–57.

Brown, R. E. "The Messianism of Qumrân." *CBQ* 19 (1957) 53–81.

Brunet, A.-M. "La Théologie du Chroniste: Théocratie et Messianisme." *Sacra Pagina: Miscellanea Biblica Congressus Internationalis Catholici de Re Biblica.* 2 vols., 1:384–397. BETL 12–13. Edited by J. Coppens, A. Descamps, É. Massaux. Gembloux: Duculot, 1959.

Burger, C. *Jesus als Davidssohn.* FRLANT 98. Göttingen: Vandenhoeck & Ruprecht, 1970.

Burrows, M. *The Dead Sea Scrolls of St. Mark's Monastery.* 2 vols. New Haven: American Schools of Oriental Research, 1951.

Caquot, A. "Ben Sira et le Messianisme." *Sem* 16 (1966) 43–68.

Caquot, A. "Peut-on parler de messianisme dans l'oeuvre du Chroniste?" *RTP* 99 (1966) 110–120.

Caquot, A. "Le messianisme qumrânien." *Qumrân: Sa piété, sa théologie et son milieu,* 231–247. BETL 46. Edited by M. Delcor. Paris: Leuven University Press, 1978.

Carroll, R. P. "Twilight of Prophecy or Dawn of Apocalyptic?" *JSOT* 14 (1979) 3–35.

Carroll, R. P. *From Chaos to Covenant.* London: SCM, 1981.

Carroll, R. P. *Jeremiah.* OTL. Philadelphia: Westminster, 1986.

Charles, R. H. "The Testaments of the Twelve Patriarchs." *The Apocrypha and Pseudepigrapha of the Old Testament.* 2 vols., 2:282–367. Edited by R. H. Charles. Oxford: Clarendon Press, 1913.

Charlesworth, J. H., ed. *The Messiah.* Minneapolis: Fortress, 1992.

Charlesworth, J. H. "The Concept of the Messiah in the Pseudepigrapha." *Aufstieg und Niedergang der römischen Welt, II.19.1,* 188–218. Edited by H. Temporini and W. Haase. Berlin: De Gruyter, 1979.

Charlesworth, J. H. "From Messianology to Christology: Problems and Prospects." *The Messiah,* 3–35. Edited by J. H. Charlesworth. Minneapolis: Fortress, 1992.

Chazon, E. G. "*4QDibHam*: Liturgy or Literature?" *RevQ* 15 (1991) 447–455.

Chester, A. "Citing the Old Testament." *It Is Written,* 141–169. Edited by D. A. Carson and H. G. M. Williamson. Cambridge: Cambridge University Press, 1988.

Childs, B. S. *Introduction to the Old Testament as Scripture.* Philadelphia: Fortress, 1979.

Clements, R. E. *Isaiah 1–39.* NCB. Grand Rapids, MI: Eerdmans, 1980.

Cody, A. "Zechariah." *The New Jerome Bible Commentary,* 352–359. Edited by R. E. Brown, J. A. Fitzmyer, and R. E. Murphy. Englewood Cliffs, NJ: Prentice-Hall, 1990.

Coggins, R. J. *Haggai, Zechariah, Malachi.* Old Testament Guides. Sheffield: JSOT Press, 1987.

Coggins, R. J. *The First and Second Books of Chronicles.* CBC. New York: Cambridge University Press, 1976.

Collins, J. J. "Messianism in the Maccabean Period." *Judaisms and Their Messiahs at the Turn of the Christian Era,* 97–109. Edited by J. Neusner, W. S. Green, and E. S. Frerichs. Cambridge: Cambridge University Press, 1987.

Collins, J. J. "Patterns of Eschatology at Qumran." *Traditions in Transformation,* 351–375. Edited by B. Halpern and J. D. Levenson. Winona Lake, IN: Eisenbrauns, 1981.

Collins, J. J. "Sibylline Oracles." *The Old Testament Pseudepigrapha.* 2 vols., 1:317–472. Edited by J. H. Charlesworth. Garden City, NY: Doubleday, 1985.

Collins, J. J. "Testaments: II. The Testamentary Literature in Recent Scholarship." *Early Judaism and Its Modern Interpreters,* 268–285. Edited by G. W. E. Nickelsburg and R. A. Kraft. Philadelphia: Fortress/Atlanta: Scholars Press, 1986.

Collins, J. J. *Daniel, First Maccabees, Second Maccabees.* Old Testament Message 16. Wilmington, DE: Glazier, 1981.

Collins, J. J. *The Apocalyptic Imagination.* New York: Crossroad, 1984.

Collins, J. J. *The Sibylline Oracles of Egyptian Judaism.* SBLDS 13. Missoula, MT: Scholars Press, 1974.

Collins, J. J. "Was the Dead Sea Sect an Apocalyptic Movement." *Archaeology and History in the Dead Sea Scrolls,* 25–51. JSPSup 8. Edited by L. H. Schiffman. Sheffield: JSOT Press, 1990.

Collins, J. J. "The *Son of God* Text from Qumran." *From Jesus to John,* 65–82. JSNTSup 84. Edited by M. C. De Boer. Sheffield: JSOT Press, 1993.

Conrad, E. W. "The Community as King in Second Isaiah." *Understanding the Word,* 99–111. JSOTSup 37. Edited by J. T. Butler, E. W. Conrad, and B. C. Ollenburger. Sheffield: JSOT Press, 1986.

Coutier, G. P. "Jeremiah." *The New Jerome Bible Commentary,* 265–297. Edited by R. E. Brown, J. A. Fitzmyer, and R. E. Murphy. Englewood Cliffs, NJ: Prentice-Hall, 1990.

Cross, F. M. "A Reconstruction of the Judaean Restoration." *JBL* 94 (1975) 4–18.

Cross, F. M. "The Development of the Jewish Scripts." *The Bible and the Ancient Near East,* 133–202. Edited by G. E. Wright. Garden City, NY: Anchor Books/Doubleday, 1961.

Cross, F. M. *Canaanite Myth and Hebrew Epic.* Cambridge, MA: Harvard University Press, 1973.

Cross, F. M. *The Ancient Library of Qumran and Modern Biblical Studies.* Garden City, NY: Doubleday, 1958.

Cullmann, O. *The Christology of the New Testament*. NTL. Revised edition. Philadelphia: Westminster, 1963.

Curtis, E. L. and A. A. Madsen. *A Critical and Exegetical Commentary on the Books of Chronicles*. ICC. Edinburgh: T. & T. Clark, 1910.

Dalman, G. *The Words of Jesus*. Edinburgh: T. & T. Clark, 1909.

Davenport, G. L. "The 'Anointed of the Lord' in Psalms of Solomon 17." *Ideal Figures in Ancient Judaism*, 67–92. SBLSCS 12. Edited by G. W. E. Nickelsburg and J. J. Collins. Chico, CA: Scholars Press, 1980.

Davies, P. R. *The Damascus Covenant*. JSOTSup 25. Sheffield: JSOT Press, 1982.

Davies, P. R. *Behind the Essenes*. BJS 94. Atlanta: Scholars Press, 1987.

Davies, P. R. *1QM, the War Scroll from Qumran*. BibOr 32. Rome: Biblical Institute Press, 1977.

Davies, P. R. "War Rule." *Anchor Bible Dictionary*. 6 vols., 6:875–876. Edited by D. N. Freedman. New York: Doubleday, 1992.

Davies, P. R. "Eschatology at Qumran." *JBL* 104 (1985) 39–55.

De Vries, S. J. "Moses and David as Cult Founders in Chronicles." *JBL* 107 (1988) 619–639.

Delcor, M. "Psaumes de Salomon." *Dictionnaire de la Bible, Supplément Vol. 9*, 214–245. Edited by L. Pirot and A. Robert. Paris: Letouzey & Ane, 1979.

Dentan, R. C. "Zechariah." *The Interpreter's Bible, Vol. 6*, 1051–1114. Edited by G. A. Buttrick. Nashville: Abingdon, 1956.

Di Lella, A. A. *The Hebrew Text of Sirach: A Text-Critical and Historical Study*. The Hague: Mouton, 1966.

Dietrich, W. *Prophetie und Geschichte: Eine redaktionsgeschichtliche Untersuchung zum deuteronomistischen Geschichtswerk*. FRLANT 108. Göttingen: Vandenhoeck & Ruprecht, 1972.

Dillard, R. B. *2 Chronicles*. WBC. Waco, TX: Word, 1987.

Dimant, D. "Qumran Sectarian Literature." *Jewish Writings of the Second Temple Period*, 483–550. CRINT 2:2. Edited by M. E. Stone. Assen: Van Gorcum/Philadelphia: Fortress, 1984.

Dimant, D. "Pesharim, Qumran." *Anchor Bible Dictionary*. 6 vols., 5:244–251. Edited by D. N. Freedman. New York: Doubleday, 1992.

Dimant, D. "*4QFlorilegium* and the Idea of the Community as Temple." *Hellenica et Judaica*, 165–189. Edited by A. Caquot, M. Hadas-Lebel, and J. Riaud. Leuven-Paris: Peeters, 1986.

Duling, D. C. "The Therapeutic Son of David: An Element in Matthew's Christological Apologetic." *NTS* 24 (1978) 392–410.

Duling, D. C. "Traditions of the Promises to David and His Sons in Early Judaism and Primitive Christianity." Ph.D. dissertation, University of Chicago, 1970.

Duling. D. C. "The Promises to David and Their Entrance into Christianity—Nailing Down a Hypothesis." *NTS* 20 (1973) 55–77.

Eichrodt, W. *Ezekiel.* OTL. Philadelphia: Westminster, 1970.

Eisenman, R. and M. Wise. *The Dead Sea Scrolls Uncovered.* Rockport, MA: Element, 1992.

Eisenman, R. H. and J. M. Robinson. *A Facsimile Edition of the Dead Sea Scrolls.* 2 vols. Washington, DC: Biblical Archaeology Society, 1991.

Eissfeldt, O. "The Promises of Grace to David in Isaiah 55:1–5." *Israel's Prophetic Heritage,* 196–207. Edited by B. W. Anderson and W. Harrelson. London: Harper & Brothers, 1962.

Eissfeldt, O. *The Old Testament: An Introduction.* New York: Harper & Row, 1965.

Elliger, K. *Die Propheten Nahum, Habakuk, Zephanja, Haggai, Sacharja, Maleachi.* ATD 25. 7th edition. Göttingen: Vandenhoeck & Ruprecht, 1975.

Emmerson, G. I. *Hosea: An Israelite Prophet in Judean Perspective.* JSOTSup 28. Sheffield: JSOT Press, 1984.

Even-Shoshan, A. *A New Concordance of the Bible.* Jerusalem: Kiryat Sefer, 1989.

Feldman, L. H. *Josephus and Modern Scholarship (1937–1980).* Berlin: De Gruyter, 1984.

Fishbane, M. *Biblical Interpretation in Ancient Israel.* Oxford: Clarendon, 1985.

Fitzmyer, J. A. Review of *Qumran Cave 4: I (4Q158–4Q186)* by John M. Allegro. *CBQ* 31 (1969) 235–238.

Fitzmyer, J. A. *The Dead Sea Scrolls: Major Publications and Tools for Study.* Revised edition. SBLRBS 20. Atlanta: Scholars Press, 1990.

Flusser, D. "Psalms, Hymns and Prayers." *Jewish Writings of the Second Temple Period,* 551–577. CRINT 2:2. Edited by M. E. Stone. Assen: Van Gorcum/Philadelphia: Fortress, 1984.

Flusser, D. "Jesus, His Ancestry, and the Commandment of Love." *Jesus' Jewishness,* 153–176. Edited by J. H. Charlesworth. New York: Crossroad, 1991.

Fohrer, G. *Introduction to the Old Testament.* Nashville: Abingdon, 1968.

Freedman, D. N. "The Chronicler's Purpose." *CBQ* 23 (1961) 436–442.

Friedman, R. *The Exile and Biblical Narrative.* HSM. Chico, CA: Scholars Press, 1981.

Fuchs, A. *Textkritische Untersuchungen zum Hebräischen Ekklesiastikus.* Freiburg: Herder, 1907.

Fuller, R. H. *The Foundations of New Testament Christology.* New York: Scribner's Sons, 1965.

Gaster, T. H. *The Dead Sea Scriptures.* 3rd edition. Garden City, NY: Anchor Press/Doubleday, 1976.

Geffcken, J. *Die Oracula Sibyllina.* GCS 8. Leipzig: Hinrichs, 1902.

Gese, H. *Der Verfassungsentwurf des Ezechiel.* BHT 25. Tübingen: Mohr, 1957.

Goldstein, J. A. "How the Authors of 1 and 2 Maccabees Treated the 'Messianic' Promises." *Judaisms and Their Messiahs at the Turn of the Christian Era,* 69–96. Edited by J. Neusner, W. S. Green, and E. S. Frerichs. Cambridge: Cambridge University Press, 1987.

Goldstein, J. A. *I Maccabees.* AB 41. Garden City, NY: Doubleday, 1976.

Gordon, R. P. "The Interpretation of 'Lebanon' and 4Q285." *JJS* 43 (1992) 92–94.

Gray, G. B. "Psalms of Solomon." *The Apocrypha and Pseudepigrapha of the Old Testament.* 2 vols., 2:625–652. Edited by R. H. Charles. Oxford: Clarendon Press, 1913.

Greenfield, J. C. and M. E. Stone. "Remarks on the Aramaic Testament of Levi from the Geniza." *RB* 86 (1979) 214–230.

Greenspoon, L. "The Use and Abuse of the Term 'LXX' and Related Terminology in Recent Scholarship." BIOSCS 20 (1987) 21–29.

Grossfeld, B. *The Targum Onkelos to Genesis.* Aramaic Bible 6. Wilmington, DE: Glazier, 1988.

Haas, L. "Bibliography on Midrash." *The Study of Ancient Judaism I: Mishnah, Midrash, Siddur,* 93–103. Edited by J. Neusner. New York: Ktav, 1981.

Hahn, F. *The Titles of Jesus in Christology.* London: Lutterworth, 1969.

Hanson, P. D. *The Dawn of Apocalyptic.* Revised edition. Philadelphia: Fortress, 1979.

Harrelson, W. "Nonroyal Motifs in the Royal Eschatology." *Israel's Prophetic Heritage,* 147–165. Edited by B. W. Anderson and W. Harrelson. New York: Harper & Brothers, 1962.

Harrington, D. J. *The Maccabean Revolt.* Wilmington, DE: Glazier, 1988.

Hatch, E. and H. A. Redpath. *A Concordance to the Septuagint.* Oxford: Clarendon, 1897. Reprint edition, Grand Rapids, MI: Baker, 1983.

Hayes, J. H. *Amos, the Eighth Century Prophet: His Times and Preaching.* Nashville: Abingdon, 1988.

Hayes, J. H. and S. A. Irvine. *Isaiah the Eighth Century Prophet.* Nashville: Abingdon, 1987.

Heinemann, J. *Prayer in the Talmud.* SJ 9. Berlin: De Gruyter, 1977.

Hengel, M. *Jews, Greeks, and Barbarians.* Philadelphia: Fortress, 1980.

Hengel, M. *The Zealots.* Edinburgh: T. & T. Clark, 1989.

Hengel, M., J. H. Charlesworth, and D. Mendels. "The Polemical Character of 'On Kingship' in the Temple Scroll: An Attempt at Dating 11QTemple." *JJS* 37 (1986) 28–38.

Hengel, M. *Judaism and Hellenism.* 2 vols. Philadelphia: Fortress, 1974.

Hillers, D. R. *Micah.* Hermeneia. Philadelphia: Fortress, 1984.

Hoffner, H. A. "בַּיִת." *Theological Dictionary of the Old Testament, Vol. 2,* 107–116. Revised edition. Edited by G. J. Botterweck and H. Ringgren. Grand Rapids, MI: Eerdmans, 1975.

Holladay, C. R. Theios Aner *in Hellenistic-Judaism.* SBLDS 40. Missoula, MT: Scholars Press, 1977.

Holladay, W. L. *Jeremiah 1.* Hermeneia. Philadelphia: Fortress, 1986.

Holladay, W. L. *Jeremiah 2.* Hermeneia. Philadelphia: Fortress, 1989.

Hollander, H. W. and M. de Jonge. *The Testaments of the Twelve Patriarchs: A Commentary.* SVTP 8. Leiden: Brill, 1985.

Horgan, M. P. *Pesharim: Qumran Interpretations of Biblical Books.* CBQMS 8. Washington, DC: Catholic Biblical Association, 1979.

Horsley, R. A. and J. S. Hanson. *Bandits, Prophets, and Messiahs.* San Francisco: Harper & Row, 1985.

Hultgård, A. "The Ideal 'Levite', the Davidic Messiah, and the Savior Priest in the Testaments of the Twelve Patriarchs." *Ideal Figures in Ancient Judaism,* 93–110. SBLSCS 12. Edited by G. W. E. Nickelsburg and J. J. Collins. Chico, CA: Scholars Press, 1980.

Hultgård, A. *L'eschatologie des Testaments des Douze Patriarches.* 2 vols. Acta Universitatis Upsaliensis, Historia Religionum 6. Stockholm: Almquist & Wiksell, 1977.

Japhet, S. "The Supposed Common Authorship of Chronicles and Ezra-Nehemiah Investigated Anew." *VT* 18 (1968) 330–371.

Japhet, S. *The Ideology of Chronicles and Its Place in Biblical Thought.* Beiträge zur Erforschung des Alten Testaments und des Antiken Judentums. Frankfurt am Main: Peter Lang, 1989.

Jenni, E. "Das Wort ʿōlām im Alten Testament." *ZAW* 64 (1952) 197–248, *ZAW* 65 (1953) 1–35.

Jenni, E. "עוֹלָם." *Theologisches Handwörterbuch zum Alten Testament.* 2 vols., 2:228–243. Edited by E. Jenni and C. Westermann. München: Chr. Kaiser/Zürich: Theologischer Verlag, 1979.

Jenni, E. "בַּיִת." *Theologisches Handwörterbuch zum Alten Testament.* 2 vols., 1:307–313. Edited by E. Jenni and C. Westermann. München: Chr. Kaiser/Zürich: Theologischer Verlag, 1971.

Jenni, E. "Time." *The Interpreter's Dictionary of the Bible.* 4 vols., 4:642–649. Edited by G. A. Buttrick. Nashville: Abingdon, 1962.

Johnson, M. D. *The Purpose of Biblical Genealogies.* SNTSMS 8. Cambridge: Cambridge University Press, 1969.

Jonge, M. de, with H. W. Hollander, H. J. de Jonge, and Th. Korteweg. *The Testaments of the Twelve Patriarchs: A Critical Edition of the Greek Text.* PVTG 1:2. Leiden: Brill, 1978.

Jonge, M. de. "Josephus und die Zukunftserwartungen seines Volkes." *Josephus-Studien: Untersuchungen zu Josephus, dem antiken Judentum und dem Neuen Testament,* 205–219. Edited by O. Betz, K. Haacker, and M. Hengel. Göttingen: Vandenhoeck & Ruprecht, 1974.

Jonge, M. de. "χρίω: Apocrypha and Pseudepigrapha." *Theological Dictionary of the New Testament, Vol 9,* 511–517. Edited by G. W. Bromiley. Grand Rapids, MI: Eerdmans, 1964–1976.

Jonge, M. de. "Psalms of Solomon." *Outside the Old Testament.* Cambridge Commentaries on the Writings of the Jewish and Christian World 4. Edited by M. de Jonge. Cambridge: Cambridge University Press, 1985.

Jonge, M. de. "The Interpretation of the Testaments of the Twelve Patriarchs in Recent Years." *Studies in the Testaments of the Twelve Patriarchs,* 183–192. SVTP 3. Edited by M. de Jonge. Leiden: Brill, 1975.

Jonge, M. de. "The Use of the Word 'Anointed' in the Time of Jesus." *NovT* 8 (1966) 132–148.

Jonge, M. de. "Two Messiahs in the Testaments of the Twelve Patriarchs?" *Jewish Eschatology, Early Christian Christology and the Testaments of the Twelve Patriarchs,* 191–203. NovTSup 63. Leiden: Brill, 1991.

Jonge, M. de. "The Expectation of the Future in the Psalms of Solomon." *Neot* 23 (1989) 93–117.

Josephus [Works]. Translated by H. St. J. Thackeray, R. Marcus, A. Wikgren, and L. Feldman. 10 vols. LCL. Cambridge, MA: Harvard University Press/London: Heinemann, 1926–65.

Kaiser, O. *Isaiah 1–12.* OTL. Philadelphia: Westminster, 1972.

Kaiser, O. *Isaiah 13–39.* OTL. Philadelphia: Westminster, 1974.

Kappler, W., ed. *Maccabaeorum libri I–IV.* Fasc. 1. Septuaginta 9. Göttingen: Vandenhoeck & Ruprecht, 1936.

Kautzsch, E. *Gesenius' Hebrew Grammar.* 2nd English edition. Oxford: Clarendon, 1910.

Kee, H. C. "Testaments of the Twelve Patriarchs." *The Old Testament Pseudepigrapha*. 2 vols., 1:776–828. Edited by J. H. Charlesworth. Garden City, NY: Doubleday, 1985.

Keil, C. F. *The Books of Chronicles*. Edinburgh: T. & T. Clark, 1872.

Keulers, J. *Die eschatologische Lehre des vierten Esrabuches*. Biblische Studien 20:2,3. Freiburg: Herder, 1922.

Kippenberg, H. G. *Religion und Klassenbildung im antiken Judäa*. 2nd edition. Göttingen: Vandenhoeck & Ruprecht, 1982.

Klausner, J. *The Messianic Idea in Israel: From Its Beginning to the Completion of the Mishnah*. New York: Macmillian, 1955.

Koch, K. *The Prophets*. 2 vols. Philadelphia: Fortress, 1983.

Kraft, R. A. "Septuagint: B. Earliest Greek Versions." *The Interpreter's Dictionary of the Bible, Supplementary Volume*, 811–815. Edited by K. Crim. Nashville: Abingdon, 1976.

Kuhn, K. G. "The Two Messiahs of Aaron and Israel." *The Scrolls and the New Testament*, 54–64. Edited by K. Stendahl. New York: Harper & Bros., 1957.

Lamarche, P. *Zacharie IX–XIV: Structure littéraire et Messianisme*. Paris: Gabalda, 1961.

Lanchester, H. C. O. "The Sibylline Oracles." *The Apocrypha and Pseudepigrapha of the Old Testament*. 2 vols., 2:368–406. Edited by R. H. Charles. Oxford: Clarendon Press, 1913.

Lee, T. R. *Studies in the Form of Sirach 44–50*. SBLDS 75. Atlanta: Scholars Press, 1986.

Lehmann, M. R. "A Re-interpretation of 4 Q Dibrê Ham-me'oroth." *RevQ* 5 (1964) 106–110.

Lehmann, M. R. "Ben Sira and the Qumran Literature." *RevQ* 9 (1961) 103–116.

Lemke, W. E. "The Synoptic Problem in the Chronicler's History." *HTR* 58 (1965) 349–363.

Levenson, J. D. "From Temple to Synagogue: 1 Kings 8." *Traditions in Transformation*, 143–166. Edited by B. Halpern and J. D. Levenson. Winona Lake, IN: Eisenbrauns, 1981.

Levenson, J. D. "The Davidic Covenant and Its Modern Interpreters." *CBQ* 41 (1979) 205–219.

Levenson, J. D. "The Last Four Verses in Kings." *JBL* 103 (1984) 353–361.

Levenson, J. D. *Theology of the Program of Restoration of Ezekiel 40–48*. HSM 10. Atlanta: Scholars Press, 1976.

Levey, S. H. *The Messiah: An Aramaic Interpretation*. Cincinnati: Hebrew Union College Press, 1974.

Lévi, I., ed. *The Hebrew Text of the Book of Ecclesiasticus*. SSS 3. Leiden: Brill, 1904. Reprint edition, 1951.

Lim, T. H. "The Chronology of the Flood Story in a Qumran Text (4Q252)." *JJS* 43 (1992) 288–298.

Lim, T. H. "11QMelch, Luke 4 and the Dying Messiah." *JJS* 43 (1992) 90–92.

Liver, J. "The Doctrine of the Two Messiahs in Sectarian Literature in the Time of the Second Commonwealth." *HTR* 52 (1959) 149–185.

Liver, J. *The House of David from the Fall of the Kingdom of Judah to the Fall of the Second Commonwealth and After* [Hebrew, with an English summary]. Jerusalem: Magnes, 1959.

Lohse, E. "Die König aus Davids Geschlect—Bemerkungen zur messianischen Erwartung der Synagoge." *Abraham unser Vater*, 337–345. Edited by O. Betz, M. Hengel, and P. Schmidt. Leiden: Brill, 1963.

Long, B. O. "2 Kings." *Harper's Bible Commentary*, 323–340. Edited by J. L. Mays. San Francisco: Harper & Row, 1988.

Longenecker, R. N. *The Christology of Early Jewish Christianity.* SBT 2/17. London: SCM, 1970.

Mack, B. L. "Wisdom Makes a Difference." *Judaisms and Their Messiahs at the Turn of the Christian Era*, 15–48. Edited by J. Neusner, W. S. Green, and E. S. Frerichs. Cambridge: Cambridge University Press, 1987.

Mack, B. L. *Wisdom and the Hebrew Epic.* Chicago Studies in the History of Judaism. Chicago: University of Chicago Press, 1985.

Marböck, J. *Weisheit im Wendel.* BBB 37. Bonn: Hanstein, 1971.

Martin, J. D. "Ben Sira's Hymn to the Fathers: A Messianic Perspective." *Crises and Perspectives*, 107–123. OTS 24. Edited by A. S. van der Woude. Leiden: Brill, 1986.

Martin, J. D. "Ben Sira—Child of His Time." *A Word in Season*, 141–161. JSOTSup 42. Edited by J. D. Martin and P. R. Davies. Sheffield: JSOT Press, 1986.

Mason, R. A. "Prophets of the Restoration." *Israel's Prophetic Tradition*, 137–154. Edited by R. J. Coggins, A. Phillips, and M. Knibb. Cambridge: Cambridge University Press, 1982.

Mason, R. A. "The Purpose of the 'Editorial Framework' of the Book of Haggai." *VT* 27 (1977) 413–421.

Mason, R. A. *The Books of Haggai, Zechariah, and Malachi.* CBC. Cambridge: Cambridge University Press, 1977.

Mason, R. *Preaching the Tradition.* Cambridge: Cambridge University Press, 1990.

Mason R. A. "The Relation of Zech 9–14 to Proto-Zechariah." *ZAW* 88 (1976) 227–239.

Mastin, B. A. "A Note on Zechariah VI 13." *VT* 26 (1976) 113–116.

Mayes, A. D. H. *The Story of Israel between Settlement and Exile.* London: SCM, 1983.

Mays, J. L. *Amos.* OTL. Philadelphia: Westminster, 1969.

Mays, J. L. *Hosea.* OTL. Philadelphia: Westminster, 1969.

Mays, J. L. *Micah.* OTL. Philadelphia: Westminster, 1976.

McEvenue, S. E. "The Political Structure in Judah from Cyrus to Nehemiah." *CBQ* 43 (1981) 353–364.

McKane, W. *Jeremiah.* 2 vols. ICC. Edinburgh: T & T Clark, 1986.

McKenzie, J. L. "Royal Messianism." *CBQ* 19 (1957) 25–52.

Metzger, B. M. "The Fourth Book of Ezra." *The Old Testament Pseudepigrapha.* 2 vols., 1:517–559. Edited by J. H. Charlesworth. Garden City, NY: Doubleday, 1985.

Meyers C. L. and E. M. Meyers. *Haggai, Zechariah 1–8.* AB 25B. Garden City, NY: Doubleday, 1987.

Middendorp, T. *Die Stellung Jesu Ben Siras zwischen Judentum und Hellenismus.* Leiden: Brill, 1973.

Mildenberg, L. "Yehud: A Preliminary Study of the Provincial Coinage of Judaea." *Greek Numismatics and Archaeology,* 183–196. Edited by O. Mørkholm and N. M. Waggoner. Wetteren: Editions NR, 1979.

Mildenberg, L. "Bar Kokhba Coins and Documents." *Harvard Studies in Classical Philology* 84 (1980) 311–335.

Milgrom, J. *Numbers.* Jewish Publication Society Torah Commentaries. Philadelphia: Jewish Publication Society, 1990.

Milik, J. T. *Ten Years of Discovery in the Wilderness of Judaea.* SBT 26. London: SCM/Naperville, IL: Allenson, 1959.

Milik, J. T. "*Milkî-ṣedeq et Milkî-reša*ᶜ. *JJS* 23 (1972) 95–144.

Miller, J. M. and J. H. Hayes. *A History of Ancient Israel and Judah.* Philadelphia: Westminster, 1986.

Mitchell, H. G., *et al. Haggai, Zechariah, Malachi, and Jonah.* ICC. New York: Charles Scribner's Sons, 1912.

Moran, W. L. "Gn 49,10 and its Use in Ez 21,32." *Bib* 39 (1958) 405–425.

"More on the Pierced Messiah Text from Eisenman and Vermes." *BARev* 19:1 (1993) 66–67.

Mosis, R. *Untersuchungen zur Theologie des chronistischen Geschichtswerkes.* Freiburger Theologische Studien 92. Freiburg: Herder, 1973.

Mowinckel, S. *He That Cometh.* Nashville: Abingdon, 1954.

Mowinckel, S. *The Psalms in Israel's Worship.* 2 vols. Nashville: Abingdon, 1962.

Muilenburg, J. "The Book of Isaiah, 40–66." *The Interpreter's Bible, Vol. 5*, 419–773. Edited by G. A. Buttrick. Nashville: Abingdon, 1956.

Myers, J. M. *I and II Esdras*. AB 42. Garden City, NY: Doubleday, 1974.

Myers, J. M. *I Chronicles*. AB 12. Garden City, NY: Doubleday, 1965.

Nelson, M. D. *The Syriac Version of the Wisdom of Ben Sira Compared to the Greek and Hebrew Materials*. SBLDS 107. Atlanta: Scholars Press, 1988.

Neusner, J. "Mishnah and Messiah." *Judaisms and Their Messiahs at the Turn of the Christian Era*, 265–282. Edited by J. Neusner, W. S. Green, and E. S. Frerichs. Cambridge: Cambridge University Press, 1987.

Neusner, J. *Messiah in Context*. Philadelphia: Fortress, 1984.

Newsome, J. D. "Toward a New Understanding of the Chronicler's Purpose." *JBL* 94 (1975) 201–217.

Nicholson, E. W. *Preaching to Exiles*. Oxford: Basil Blackwell, 1970.

Nickelsburg, G. E. W. "1 and 2 Maccabees—Same Story, Different Meaning." *CTM* 42 (1971) 515–526.

Nickelsburg, G. E. W. *Jewish Literature Between the Bible and the Mishnah*. Philadelphia: Fortress, 1981.

Nickelsburg, G. E. W. *Resurrection, Immortality, and Eternal Life*. HTS 26. Cambridge, MA: Harvard University Press, 1972.

Nickelsburg, G. W. E. with R. A. Kraft. "Introduction: The Modern Study of Early Judaism." *Early Judaism and Its Modern Interpreters*, 1–30. Edited by G. W. E. Nickelsburg and R. A. Kraft. Philadelphia: Fortress/Atlanta: Scholars Press, 1986.

Nickelsburg, G. W. E. "The Bible Rewritten and Expanded." *Jewish Writings of the Second Temple Period*, 89–156. CRINT 2:2. Edited by M. E. Stone. Philadelphia: Fortress/Assen: Van Gorcum, 1984.

Nikiprowetzky, V. *La Troisième Sibylle*. Études Juives IX. Paris: Mouton, 1970.

Nitzan, B. *Qumran Prayer and Religious Poetry*. STDJ 12. Leiden: Brill, 1994.

Noland, J. "*Sib. Or. III*, An Early Maccabean Messianic Oracle." *JTS* 30 (1979) 158–166.

Noordtzij, A. "Les Intentions du Chroniste." *RB* 49 (1940) 161–168.

North, R. "The Theology of the Chronicler." *JBL* 82 (1963) 369–381.

Noth, M. *Numbers*. OTL. Philadelphia: Westminster, 1968.

Noth, M. *The Chronicler's History*. JSOTSup 50. Sheffield: JSOT Press, 1987.

Noth, M. *The Deuteronomistic History*. JSOTSup 15. Sheffield: JSOT Press, 1981.

O'Dell, J. "The Religious Background of the Psalms of Solomon (Re-evaluated in the Light of the Qumran Texts)." *RevQ* 3 (1961) 241–257.

Oesterley, W. O. E. "The First Book of Maccabees." *The Apocrypha and Pseudepigrapha of the Old Testament*. 2 vols., 1:59–124. Edited by R. H. Charles. Oxford: Clarendon Press, 1913.

Olyan, S. M. "Ben Sira's Relationship to the Priesthood." *HTR* 80 (1987) 261–286.

Overholt, T. W. "Jeremiah." *Harper's Bible Commentary*, 597–645. Edited by J. L. Mays. San Francisco: Harper & Row, 1988.

Peters, N. *Der jüngst wiederaufgefundene hebräische Text des Buches Ecclesiasticus, untersucht, heraugegeben, übersetzt und mit kritischen Noten versehen*. Freiburg: Herder, 1902.

Petersen, D. L. "Zechariah." *Harper's Bible Commentary*, 747–752. Edited by J. L. Mays. San Francisco: Harper & Row, 1988.

Petersen, D. L. "Zerubbabel and Jerusalem Temple Reconstruction." *CBQ* 36 (1974) 366–372.

Petersen, D. L. *Haggai and Zechariah 1–8*. OTL. Philadelphia: Westminster, 1984.

Petersen, D. L. *Late Israelite Prophecy*. SBLMS 23. Missoula, MT: Scholars Press, 1977.

Plöger, O. *Theocracy and Eschatology*. Richmond: John Knox, 1968.

Polzin, R. M. *Late Biblical Hebrew: Toward an Historical Typology of Biblical Hebrew Prose*. HSM 12. Missoula, MT: Scholars, 1976.

Porter, J. R. "Old Testament Historiography." *Tradition and Interpretation*, 125–162. Edited by G. W. Anderson. Oxford: Oxford University Press, 1979.

Porton, G. G. "Diversity in Postbiblical Judaism." *Early Judaism and Its Modern Interpreters*, 57–80. Edited by G. W. E. Nickelsburg and R. A. Kraft. Philadelphia: Fortress/Atlanta: Scholars Press, 1986.

Preuss, H. D. "עוֹלָם." *Theologisches Wörterbuch zum Alten Testament, Band 5*, 1144–1159. Edited by G. J. Botterweck and H. Ringgren. Stuttgart: Kohlhammer, 1986.

Priest, J. "Ben Sira 45,25 in the Light of the Qumran Literature." *RevQ* 5 (1964) 111–118.

Pritchard, J. B., ed. *Ancient Near Eastern Texts Relating to the Old Testament*. 2nd edition. Princeton: Princeton University Press, 1955.

Puech, E. "Fragment d'une apocalypse en Araméen (4Q246=ps Dan^d) et le 'Royaume de Dieu'." *RB* 99 (1992) 98–131.

Qimron, E. and J. Strugnell, "An Unpublished Halakhic Letter from Qumran." *Biblical Archaeology Today*, 400–407. Edited by J. Amitai. Jerusalem: Israel Exploration Society/Israel Academy of Sciences and Humanities, 1984.

Rabin, C. *The Zadokite Documents*. Oxford: Clarendon, 1954.

Rad, G. von. "The Deuteronomic Theology of History in *I and II Kings*." *The Problem of the Hexateuch and other essays*, 205–221. London: Oliver & Boyd, 1966.

Rad, G. von. *Das Geschichtsbild des chronistischen Werkes*. Stuttgart: Kohlhammer, 1930.

Rad, G. von. *Deuteronomy*. OTL. Philadelphia: Westminster, 1966.

Rad, G. von. *Genesis*. Revised edition. OTL. Philadelphia: Westminster, 1972.

Rad, G. von. *Old Testament Theology*. 2 vols. New York: Harper & Row, 1965.

Rappoport, S. *Agada und Exegese bei Flavius Josephus*. Vienna: Kohut, 1930.

Redditt, P. L. "Israel's Shepherds: Hope and Pessimism in Zechariah 9–14." *CBQ* 51 (1989) 631–642.

Reed, S. A. *Dead Sea Scroll Inventory Project: Lists of Documents, Photographs, and Museum Plates*. 10 Fascs. Claremont: Ancient Biblical Manuscript Center, 1992.

Reinhartz, A. "Rabbinic Perceptions of Simeon bar Kosiba." *JSJ* 20 (1989) 171–194.

Reiterer, F. V. *"Urtext" und Übersetzungen: Sprachstudie über Sir 44,16–45,26 als Beitrag zur Siraforschung*. ATAT 12. St. Ottilien: EOS, 1980.

Rendtorff, R. *The Old Testament: An Introduction*. Philadelphia: Fortress, 1986.

Riley, W. *King and Cultus in Chronicles*. JSOTSup 160. JSOT Press, 1993.

Roberts, J. M. "Isaiah 33: An Isaianic Elaboration of the Zion Tradition." *The Word of the Lord Shall Go Forth*, 15–25. Edited by C. L. Meyers and M. O'Connor. Winona Lake, IN: Eisenbrauns, 1983.

Rothstein, J. W. and J. Hänel. *Das erste Buch der Chronik*. KAT 17. Leipzig: Deichertsche, 1927.

Rudolph, W. "Problems of the Books of Chronicles." *VT* 4 (1954) 401–409.

Rudolph, W. *Chronikerbücher*. HAT 21. Tübingen: Mohr, 1955.

Rudolph, W. *Haggai, Sacharja 1–8, Sacharja 9–14, Maleachi*. KAT 13/4. Gütersloh: Gütersloher Verlagshaus Gerd Mohn, 1976.

Rudolph, W. *Micha, Nahum, Habakuk, Zephanja*. KAT 13/3. Gütersloh: Gütersloher Verlagshaus Gerd Mohn, 1975.

Saebo, M. "Messianism in Chronicles?" *HBT* 2 (1980) 85–109.

Saebo, M. *Sacharja 9–14: Untersuchungen von Text und Form*. WMANT 34. Neukirchen-Vluyn: Neukirchener Verlag, 1969.

Sanders, J. A. "Adaptable for Life: The Nature and Function of Canon." *Magnalia Dei: The Mighty Acts of God*, 531–560. Edited by F. M. Cross, W. E. Lemke, and P. D. Miller, Jr. Garden City, NY: Doubleday, 1976.

Sanders, J. A. *Canon and Community*. Philadelphia: Fortress, 1984.

Sanders, J. A. *The Psalms Scroll of Qumran Cave 11*. DJD 4. Oxford: Clarendon, 1965.

Sarna, N. "Psalm 89: A Study in Inner Biblical Exegesis." *Biblical and Other Studies*, 29–46. Edited by A. Altmann. Cambridge: Harvard University Press, 1963.

Sauer, G. "Serubbabel in der Sicht Haggais und Sacharjas." *Das Ferne und Nahe Wort*, 199–207. Edited by F. Maass. Berlin: Töpelmann, 1967.

Schechter, S. and C. Taylor. *The Wisdom of Ben Sira: Portions of the Book of Ecclesiasticus*. Cambridge: Cambridge University Press, 1896 and 1899. Reprint edition, Amsterdam: APA-Philo Press, 1979.

Schiffman, L. H. "The Dead Sea Scrolls and the Early History of Jewish Liturgy." *The Synagogue in Late Antiquity*, 33–48. Edited by L. I. Levine. Philadelphia: American Schools of Oriental Research, 1987.

Schiffman, L. H. "The King, His Guard, and the Royal Council in the *Temple Scroll*." *Proceedings of the American Academy for Jewish Research*, 237–259. Jerusalem/New York: American Academy for Jewish Research, 1987.

Schiffman, L. H. *The Eschatological Community of the Dead Sea Scrolls*. SBLMS 38. Atlanta: Scholars Press, 1989.

Schiffman, L. H. "The New Halakhic Letter (4QMMT) and the Origins of the Dead Sea Sect." *BA* 53 (1990) 64–73.

Schiffman, L. H. "Messianic Figures and Ideas in the Qumran Scrolls." *The Messiah*, 116–129. Edited by J. H. Charlesworth. Minneapolis: Fortress, 1992.

Schniedewind, W. M. "Textual Criticism and Theological Interpretation: The Pro-Temple *Tendenz* in the Greek Text of Samuel-Kings." *HTR* 87 (1994) 107–116.

Schüpphaus, J. *Die Psalmen Salomos*. Leiden: Brill, 1977.

Schürer, E. *The History of the Jewish People in the Age of Jesus Christ (175 B.C.–A.D. 135)*. 3 vols. Revised English edition. Edited by G. Vermes, F. Millar, and M. Black. Edinburgh: T. & T. Clark, 1973–1987.

Schwartz, D. "The Messianic Departure from Judah (4Q Patriarchal Blessings)." *TZ* 37 (1981) 257–266.

Seybold, K. "Die Königserwartung bei den Propheten Haggai und Sacharja." *Judaica* 28 (1972) 69–78.

Siebeneck, R. T. "May Their Bones Return to Life!—Sirach's Praise of the Fathers." *CBQ* 21 (1959) 411–428.

Silberman, L. H. "A Note on 4Q Florilegium." *JBL* 78 (1959) 158–159.

Skehan, P. W. and A. A. Di Lella. *The Wisdom of Ben Sira*. AB 39. New York: Doubleday, 1987.

Skehan, P. W. "Qumran and Old Testament Criticism." *Qumrân: Sa piété, sa théologie et son milieu*, 163–182. BETL 46. Edited by M. Delcor. Paris: Duculot/Leuven: University Press, 1978.

Slingerland, H. D. *The Testaments of the Twelve Patriarchs: A Critical History of Research.* SBLMS 21. Missoula, MT: Scholars Press, 1977.

Smend, R. *Die Weisheit des Jesus Sirach: Kommentar.* Berlin: Reimer, 1906.

Smith, J. Z. "Sacred Persistence." *Approaches to Ancient Judaism: Theory and Practice*, 11–28. BJS 1. Edited by W. S. Green. Missoula, MT: Scholars Press, 1978.

Smith, M. "What is Implied by the Variety of Messianic Figures?" *JBL* 78 (1959) 66–72.

Smith, R. L. *Micah-Malachi.* WBC. Waco, TX: Word, 1984.

Snaith, J. N. "Biblical Quotations in the Hebrew of Ecclesiasticus." *JTS* 18 (1967) 1–12.

Stadelmann, H. *Ben Sira als Schriftgelehrter.* WUNT 2/6. Tübingen: Mohr, 1980.

Stansell, G. "Isaiah 32: Creative Redaction in the Isaian Tradition." *SBL 1983 Seminar Papers*, 1–12. Edited by K. Richards. Chico, CA: Scholars Press, 1983.

Starcky, J. "Les Quatre Étapes du Messianisme à Qumran." *RB* 70 (1963) 481–504.

Stegemann, H. "Weitere Stücke von 4QpPsalm 37, 4QPatriarchal Blessings, und Hinweis auf eine unedierte Handschrift aus Höhle 4Q mit Exzerpten aus dem Deuteronomium." *RevQ* 6 (1967–9) 193–227.

Stinespring, W. F. "Eschatology in Chronicles." *JBL* 80 (1961) 209–219.

Stone, M. E. "The Concept of the Messiah in 4 Ezra." *Religions in Antiquity*, 295–312. Studies in the History of Religions 14. Edited by J. Neusner. Leiden: Brill, 1968.

Stone, M. E. *Features of the Eschatology of IV Ezra.* HSS. Atlanta: Scholars Press, 1989.

Stone, M. E. *Fourth Ezra.* Hermeneia. Minneapolis: Fortress, 1990.

Stone, M. E. "The Question of the Messiah in 4 Ezra." *Judaisms and Their Messiahs at the Turn of the Christian Era*, 209–224. Edited by J. Neusner, W. S. Green, and E. S. Frerichs. Cambridge: Cambridge University Press, 1987.

Stone, M. E. *Scripture, Sects, and Visions.* Philadelphia: Fortress, 1980.

Strugnell, J. "Notes en marge du volume V des 'Discoveries in the Judean Desert of Jordan'." *RevQ* 26 (1970) 163–276.

Stuart, D. K. *Hosea-Jonah.* WBC. Waco, TX: Word, 1987.

Tabor, J. D. "A Pierced or Piercing Messiah?—The Verdict is Still Out." *BARev* 18:6 (1992) 58–59.

Talmon, S. "Eschatologie und Geschichte im biblischen Judentum." *Zukunft: Zur Eschatologie bei Juden und Christen*, 13–50. Schriften der Katholischen Akademie in Bayern 98. Edited by R. Schnackenburg. Düsseldorf: Patmos, 1980.

Talmon, S. "Types of Messianic Expectation at the Turn of the Era." *King, Cult and Calendar: Collected Studies*, 202–224. Jerusalem: Magnes, 1986.

Talmon, S. "Waiting for the Messiah: The Spiritual Universe of the Qumran Covenanters." *Judaisms and Their Messiahs at the Turn of the Christian Era*, 111–137. Edited by J. Neusner, W. S. Green, and E. S. Frerichs. Cambridge: Cambridge University Press, 1987.

Throntveit, M. A. "Linguistic Analysis and the Question of Authorship in Chronicles, Ezra and Nehemiah." *VT* 32 (1982) 201–216.

Throntveit, M. A. *When Kings Speak: Royal Speech and Royal Prayer in Chronicles*. SBLDS 93. Atlanta: Scholars, 1987.

Tov, E. "Some Aspects of the Textual and Literary History of the Book of Jeremiah." *Le Livre de Jérémie*, 145–167. BETL 54. Edited by P.-M. Bogaert. Leuven: University Press, 1981.

Tov, E. "The Septuagint." *Mikra*, 161–188. CRINT 2:1. Edited by M. J. Mulder. Philadelphia: Fortress/Assen: Van Gorcum, 1988.

Tov, E. "The Unpublished Qumran Texts from Caves 4 and 11." *JJS* 43 (1992) 101–136.

Tsevat, M. "Studies in the Book of Samuel." *HUCA* 34 (1963) 71–82.

Tucker, G. M. "Hosea." *Harper's Bible Commentary*, 707–715. Edited by J. L. Mays. San Francisco: Harper & Row, 1988.

Tuell, S. S. *The Law of the Temple in Ezekiel 40–48*. HSM 49. Atlanta: Scholars Press, 1992.

Unterman, J. *From Repentance to Redemption*. JSOTSup 54. Sheffield: JSOT Press, 1987.

VanderKam, J. C. *Enoch and the Growth of an Apocalyptic Tradition*. CBQMS 16. Washington, DC: Catholic Biblical Association, 1984.

VanderKam, J. C. "Joshua the High Priest and the Interpretation of Zechariah 3." *CBQ* 53 (1991) 553–570.

Vattioni, F. *Ecclesiastico: Testo ebraico con apparato critico e versioni greca, latina e siriaca*. Naples: Instituto Orientale di Napoli, 1968.

Vaux, R. de. *Ancient Israel*. 2 vols. New York: McGraw-Hill, 1961.

Veijola, T. *Die Ewige Dynastie*. Annale Academiae Scientiarum Fennicae, Series B 193. Helsinki: Academia Scientiarum Fennica, 1975.

Vermes, G. "Bible and Midrash: Early Old Testament Exegesis." *The Cambridge History of the Bible: Vol I*, 199–231. Edited by P. R. Ackroyd and C. F. Evans. Cambridge: Cambridge University Press, 1970.

Vermes, G. *Jesus the Jew*. London: Collins, 1973.

Vermes, G. *The Dead Sea Scrolls in English*. 3rd edition. Sheffield: JSOT Press, 1987.

Vermes, G. *Scripture and Tradition in Judaism*. Studia Post-Biblica 4. Leiden: Brill, 1973.

Vermes, G. "The Oxford Forum for Qumran Research Seminar on the Rule of War from Cave 4 (4Q285)." *JJS* 43 (1992) 85–94.

Vermes, G. "The 'Pierced Messiah' Text—An Interpretation Evaporates." *BARev* 18:4 1992 80–82.

Volz, P. *Jesaia II*. KAT 9. Leipzig: A. Deichert, 1932.

Wacholder, B. Z. and M. Abegg, eds. *A Preliminary Edition of the Unpublished Dead Sea Scrolls*. 2 Fasc. Washington, DC: Biblical Archaeology Society, 1991–1992.

Wegner, P. D. *An Examination of Kingship and Messianic Expectation in Isaiah 1–35*. Lewiston, NY: Mellen, 1992.

Weinberg, J. P. "Das *bēit ʾābōt* im 6.–4. Jh. V.U.Z." *VT* 23 (1973) 400–414.

Weinberg, J. P. *The Citizen-Temple Community*. JSOTSup 151. JSOT Press, 1992.

Weiser, A. *The Psalms*. OTL. Philadelphia: Westminster, 1962.

Welch, A. C. *Post-Exilic Judaism*. Edinburgh: Blackwood & Sons, 1935.

Wellhausen, J. *Prolegomena to the History of Ancient Israel*. Reprint edition. Cleveland and New York: World, 1957.

Westermann, C. *Genesis 37–50: A Commentary*. Minneapolis: Augsburg, 1986.

Westermann, C. *Isaiah 40–66*. OTL. Philadelphia: Westminster, 1969.

Wieder, N. "Notes on the New Documents from the Fourth Cave of Qumran." *JJS* 7 (1956) 71–76.

Willi-Plein, I. *Prophetie am Ende: Untersuchungen zu Sacharja 9–14*. Köln: Peter Hanstein, 1974.

Williams, R. J. *Hebrew Syntax: An Outline*. 2nd edition. Toronto: University of Toronto Press, 1976.

Williamson, H. G. M. "Eschatology in Chronicles." *TynBul* 28 (1979) 115–154.

Williamson, H. G. M. *1 and 2 Chronicles*. NCB. Grand Rapids, MI: Eerdmans, 1982.

Williamson, H. G. M. *Israel in the Books of Chronicles*. Cambridge: Cambridge University Press, 1977.

Wilson, R. R. *Genealogy and History in the Biblical World*. New Haven: Yale University Press, 1977.

Wise, M. O. *A Critical Study of the Temple Scroll From Qumran Cave 11.* Studies in Ancient Oriental Civilization 49. Chicago: Oriental Institute of the University of Chicago, 1990.

Wise, M. O. "4QFlorilegium and the Temple of Adam." *RevQ* 15 (1991–1992) 103–132.

Wolff, H. W. "Das Kerygma des deuteronomistischen Geschichtswerks." *ZAW* 73 (1961) 171–186.

Wolff, H. W. *Hosea.* Hermeneia. Philadelphia: Fortress, 1974.

Wolff, H. W. *Joel and Amos.* Hermeneia. Philadelphia: Fortress, 1977.

Wolff, H. W. *Micah the Prophet.* Philadelphia: Fortress, 1981.

Wolfson, H. A. *Philo.* 2 vols. Revised edition. Cambridge, MA: Harvard University Press, 1948.

Woude, A. S. van der. *Die messianischen Vorstellungen der Gemeinde von Qumran.* Assen: Van Gorcum, 1957.

Woude, A. S. van der. "Ein neuer Segensspruch aus Qumran (11QBer)." *Bibel und Qumran,* 253–258. Edited by S. Wagner. Leipzig: Evangelische Haupt-Bibelgesellschaft zu Berlin, 1968.

Wright, B. G. *No Small Difference.* SBLSCS 26. Atlanta: Scholars Press, 1989.

Wright, J. W. "The Origin and Function of 1 Chronicles 23–27." Ph.D. dissertation, University of Notre Dame, 1989.

Wright, R. B. "Psalms of Solomon." *The Old Testament Pseudepigrapha.* 2 vols., 2:639–670. Edited by J. H. Charlesworth. Garden City, NY: Doubleday, 1985.

Wright, R. B. "The Psalms, the Pharisees, and the Essenes." *1972 Proceedings for the International Organization for Septuagint and Cognate Studies and the Society of Biblical Literature Pseudepigrapha Seminar,* 136–154. SBLSCS 2. Edited by R. A. Kraft. Missoula, MT: Scholars Press, 1972.

Yadin, Y. "A Midrash on 2 Sam. vii and Ps. i–ii (4Q Florilegium)." *IEJ* 9 (1959) 95–98.

Yadin, Y. "Some Notes on Commentaries on Genesis xlix and Isaiah, from Qumran Cave 4." *IEJ* 7 (1957) 66–68.

Yadin, Y. *The Temple Scroll.* 3 vols. with a supplement. Jerusalem: Israel Exploration Society, Archaeological Institute of the Hebrew University, Shrine of the Book, 1983.

Yadin, Y. *The Scroll of the War of the Sons of Light Against the Sons of Darkness.* Oxford: Oxford University Press, 1962.

Yee, G. A. *Composition and Tradition in the Book of Hosea.* SBLDS 102. Atlanta: Scholars Press, 1987.

Zeitlin, I. M. *Jesus and the Judaism of His Time.* Cambridge: Polity, 1988.

Zeitlin, S. *The First Book of Maccabees.* New York: Harper, 1950.

Ziegler, J., ed. *Sapientia Iesu Filii Sirach*. Septuaginta 12:2. Göttingen: Vandenhoeck & Ruprecht, 1965.

Zimmerli, W. *Ezekiel 1*. Hermeneia. Philadelphia: Fortress, 1979.

Zimmerli, W. *Ezekiel 2*. Hermeneia. Philadelphia: Fortress, 1983.

Indexes

Subject

Aaron, 48,133–134,138–141,143,151,196,
201,210,237–239
Alexander Jannaeus, 158,166
Alexander the Great, 82,127
Amalek, 181,189–190
apocalyptic eschatology, 71,74,112,169,
211,214, 221
apocalyptic literature, 123,169,211
Aristobolus I, 166
Aristobolus II, 159,166
Athronges, 258–259,262–263

booth of David, 61–63,193,195–196,266
Branch of David, 22,45,54,183,186–187,
190–191,193–197,200–202,205–206,
208–210,212–215,221,231–233,235,
237–239,243–244,246,253,268–269

Christology, 3–4,271
clan, 18,117,199–124,266
crown, 56–59,143,200–201,208,213,252,
260
Cyrus, 40,73,82,102–103,110,228,257,264

Darius, 46,82
David, 2,13–15,18,23,25,27–29,36,38–39,
47–50,55,67,69,71–73,89–90,92–94,
96–98,100,102,107–110,116,121,129,
132–133,138,140,142,144–147,150,
155–158,172–176,178–179,187,192,
194,222–225,241,244,262–263
as king, 15–17,24,29,33,47,50,160,173,
222–224,245,266

as psalmist, 171,245
as patron of cult, 109,129,145,151,267
horn of, 16,25,144–145,148
house of, 13–14,20,26,33–34,55,62–63,
65,67,71–72,75–76,89,96,99,101,105–
106,109,111–125,129,146,148,152,
193–194,223–225,246,261–263,266
inheritance of, 134,136,153,155,158
lamp for, 14,16,101–102
type of/"new," 17–18,20,24,27–29,31,33,
41,50,69,74,130,158,175,241,265
throne of, 19,21–22,63–64,107,152,154,
164,178,267,268
davidic
covenant, 2,14–16,39–41,45,67,69–70,
90,98–102,129–133,139–146,150–
151,158,172–180,185,187,223,236,255,
267–268
dynastic promise, 2,14–16,22,24,27,30,
34–35,38–40,43–44,48,–50,55,61–63,
75,88,90–94,96,98,125,131,145,147,
158,160,194,223,225,227,236,253,265
genealogy, 27,31,66,104,106,109–110,
120,266
messiah, 2,4–9,18,40–41,55–56,60,66–
67,76–77,99,109,111,125,131–132,149,
152,158,161–162,167,169,173,175,180,
186–188,190–191,194–197,202–204,
206–216,218–221,228,231–234,236–
237,240–246,250–251,253,255–256,
261,263–265,267–271
messianism, 3–6,66,68,73–74,107,109–
110,131,144–145,147–148,165,173,

295

195,228–229,232,234,239,241,243–
246,263–264,269–271
Deuteronomistic History, 12,14,22–23,33–
38,41,44,82,89–90,97,101,109,225,227,
263,265

Egypt, 22,26,179,256–257
Essenes, 190
eternal, 34–36,41,89,92–94,96–97,101,
110,139–140,145–146,151,153–154,
159–160,162,166,173,175,236–237,
249,254,268
Ezra, 72,81,84–87,91,106,111,124,216,
218

Galilee, 258,262
Gedaliah, 32–33,37

Hasmoneans, 149–150,152–155,157–159,
161–162,165–167,169,188,191,215,
223,235,241,245,254,267–268,270
Herod, 189–191,258–259,263
Hezekiah, king, 21,17,48,100,109,142,147
high priesthood, 58,138–144,149,151,158,
166,168,267
high priests, 52,55,75,82,98–99,101,111,
139–143,149–151,153,158,209–211,
213–214,223,225,235,240,261
holiness, 162,165,168,214–215,268
Hyrcanus II, 159,161,163,167

Interpreter of the Law, 187,193–196,208,
239

Jacob, 15,23–24,48,81,146,178,180–182,
190,239,249,251–252
Jehoiachin, 21,25,27,32,35–37,43,46–48,
73,83,86,102,104
Jeroboam, 93,99–100,263
Jerusalem, 13–15,18,20,34,36,40,42–45,
51,55,61–63,65,71,73,87,94,96,100–
103,105,107–109,111,113–125,129,
144,151,159,161–164,174,178–179,
195198–199,201,213,259–260,263,266,
267
Jesse, 18,20,26,133,139,197–198,200–202,
205,212,221–222,241–242
Jesus Christ, 125,186,190,248,251–252,
254,260–261,271
John Hyrcanus, 152,158,166
Jonathan Maccabee, 149

Josephus, 1,3,5,7,9,82,127,166,189–190,
222–229,231,255,257–262,270
Joshua son of Jehozadak, 52,53,55–60,66,
99,214
Josiah, 17,21,34,104,147
Judah
son of Jacob, 23–24,180,186,248–249,
251–255
kingdom of, *see Southern Kingdom*
tribe of, 133,136,139,173–174,183,186,
225,246–249,252–253,262
Judas, son of Hezekiah, 258,262
Judas Maccabee, 153,157,211
Judas the Galilean, 258–259,262–263

King from the Sun, 255–257,271
Kittim, *see Romans*

last days, 17,24,121,182,186,189,191,193–
195,197,199–202,212,214,217,219,249,
268
Law, 14,22–23,64,90,92–93,156,190,219,
222–223,226–227,235,258,270
lion, 23,216–217,249,251

man from the sea, 218–219,221,269
Mattathias Maccabee, 152–153,155–156,
158,267
Menachem, 258–259,262–263
Messiah of Israel, 9,171,213,231–233,237–
239,244,255,264,269,271,
Messiah of Judah, 9,231,232,246–255,264
Michael, the archangel, 203,211
midrash, 1,182,192–193,195,205,207,216,
Mishnah, 4–5,7
Moses, 14,81,108,140,142,189–190,196,
222–223,225–227,233,270

nations, the, 16,20,23,39,40,46,49–51,61,
110,113,116–117,125,160,162–165,
177–179,199,201–203,205,207,209,
211,213–214,218,221,240,249–252,
254,269
nasi/Prince, 17,19,21,27–32,40–41,57,63,
130,173–174,198–199,201,203,205–
210,212–213,232–233,239–245,250,
255,264–265,269,271
Nebuchadnezzar, 21,25–26,48,102,254
Nehemiah, 43,46,61,65,72,81,85,105,120,
124,148

Northern Kingdom/Israel, 17,19,22–23,29,
  42,45,48,79,81–82,100,108–109,263

Persians, 40,50,75,82,103,105–106,111,
  119–120,257
Pharisees, 6,159–160,190
Philo, 1,5,258
Phineas, 133,137–141,144,154,158,
popular messiahs, 258–264,271
priesthood, 52,111,133,138–139,154,249,
  252
priests, 30,43–44,105,107–108,138–141,
  148–149,153,167–168,185,188,200,
  202–203,205,209–211,213,215,235,
  237–242,244,248–249,261,268,269
Prince of the Congregation, 198–199,201,
  203,205–210,212–213,232–233,239–
  245,250,255,264,269,271
Ptolemaic kingdom, 127,256,257

Qumran, 1,3,5,6,9,127,134,144,149–150,
  159–160,162,165,168,,171–216,221,
  231–247,263,268–270

righteousness, 18–22,25,42,45,139,162–
  163,165,167,169,183,186–188,190–
  191,200,202,212–215,223–225,240,
  244–245,251–252,254,268,270
Romans/Kittim, 2,127,153,163,188,190–
  191,193,196–199,201,203–215,220,
  228,240,246,257,259–260,268–270
Rome, 184,205,216,218,220–221,258–
  260,262,269

Samaritans, 76,82,108
Saul, 23,48,157,189,223,263
scepter, 23–24,186,239,242, 251–252
seed of David, 146,178,87,194–197,217,
  231,269
Seleucid kingdom, 127,153
Septuagint, 9,23,42,59,83–85,103,116,
  127–134,136–139,143,145–150,168,
  176,183,185,187,251,253,267
shepherd, 17,22,25,27–29,40–41,125,130,
  173–174,176,215,259
Sheshbazzar, 32,120,241
Sicarii, 259

signet, 21,25,46–47,49,51,148
Simon, Herod's servant, 258,263
Simon bar Giora, 231,258–260,262–263
Simon bar Kosiba/Kokhba, 241,258
Simon II, 140–143,168,267,
Simon Maccabee, 153,155,157
Sinai Covenant, 26,38,108,177–178
Solomon, 13,28,48,69,71,73–75,79,89–90,
  92–94,97–98,100,108–110,132,136,
  142,144–147,150,157–158,178,199,
  194,224–225,227,241,266
Son of David, 4–8,126,162,164,167–169,
  214–215,231,267–268,271
Son of Man, 218,221,250
Sons of Darkness, 184,188,209–211,213,
  268
Sons of Light, 184,192,198,203–204,206,
  209–211,214,269
Sons of Zadok, 148–149,202
Southern Kingdom/Judah, 14,17–18,21,
  25–27,29,32–36,42,45–46,48–50,58,
  63–64,71,73,75,85,98,100–107,109,
  111–112,114,116–121,125,144–145,
  147,155,223,254,263,266
sprout, 16,25,45,54–55,58,130–131
star, 24,239,251

tahanun prayer, 172,176–179,268
Teacher of Righteousness, 195,237
temple, 13,14,30,38,46,48–49,51–54,57–
  60,66,71–75,77,80,89–90,92–94,97–98,
  100,103,108–110,122,129,139,142–
  143,145–146,148,168,194,196,224,260,
  266,268
theocracy, 30,41,70–71,76–77,112,265

Vespasian, 228,257,260–262,270

wisdom, 20–21,139,146,165,168–169,200,
  214–215,268

Zedekiah, 21–22,25–27,32,102,104
Zerubbabel, 21,32,43,45–53,55–60,66–67,
  70,72,74,76,79–81,84–86,91,98,105,
  107,110,120,148,213,266
Zion, 26,48,51,55,62,108,151,177,179,
  191,195,197,212,242

References

HEBREW BIBLE

Genesis
6:3   181
6–9   181
9:24–25   181
9:27   181
11:24–32   181
15   181
18:22–33   181
22   181
28:1–4   181
36:12   181,188–190
39:10b   175
49:1   182
49:1–27   180–181
49:8   23
49:8–12   23,25,265
49:9   23
49:9–10   217,253,255,
             264
49:9–10a   251
49:10   18,23–25,180,
             183–184,186–
             188,212,252,
             254,268
49:10aα   183–185
49:10aβ   23,185
49:10b   187
49:10bα   186
49:10bβ   187
49:11   24
49:12   24
49:15–17   181
49:21   181
49:24–26   181

Exodus
15:17b–18   192
15:20   209
17:14   189
20:8–11   64
21:6   95
23:20   121
28:36–38   143
29:6   143
29:30   141
32:34   121
39:30   143

Leviticus
8:9   143
16:32   141

Numbers
1:17ff   119
3:17   122
10:9   196
24:14b   24
24:15–17   245
24:17   24,130–131,239,
             241,244,255,264
24:17–19   24–25,265
24:17–24   262
25:6–13   139
25:7   137,140
25:11   137,140
25:12–13a   139
36:1   119

Deuteronomy
4:25–31   38
4:29–31   36
4:31   38
5:12–14   64
5:12–15   64
17:14   22–23
17:14–20   22,24–25,234–
             235,244,255,
             263–265
17:15   22,235
17:18   235
17:20   23
19:9   175
20:2–4   196
23:4   96
25:19   189–190
30:1–10   36,38
30:3–7   38
31:20   177
33   192,195
33:2   47
33:17   145

Joshua
7:14ff   119
22:13   137

Judges
5:4–5   47
6:11   121
9:1   119
9:1–22   262
9:6   262
9:22   262
20:28   137
21:23   209

1–2 Samuel 25

1 Samuel
2:28   48
2:30   95
10:20–24   263
10:24   48
10:25   263
15:1–9   189
16:1–13   223
16:8–10   47
16:13   223
17–*2 Sam* 5 263
19:11   117
20:16   118

2 Samuel
2:4   263
3:1   118
3:6   118
5:1–3   157,263
5:3   224
5:14   122
6:21   47
7   47,90
7:10–14   192
7:10b–11aα   192
7:11ff   147
7:11–14   162,191,196,
             197,212
7:11–16   15,18,24,34,36,
             38–39,49–50,62,
             68,88,174,187,
             214,224,253,266
7:11aβ   192
7:11b   13,118,129,267
7:11b–14   193–195,268
7:11b–14a   193–194
7:11b–16   13,24,160

7:12	88,160,194–195, 217	11:12	13	10:27b–32	198–199
7:12–13	13	11:13	145,147	10:28–32	243
7:13	196	11:32	48	10:33	199
7:14	13,15,19,93	11:33	93	10:33–34	20,198–199
7:14b	89	11:34	28,48,241	10:33–11:1	198
7:14b–15	13	11:36	48	10:33–11:10	19,66
7:15	39,194	12:19	118	10:34	199,205,207
7:16	13,39,89	12:20	118,263	10:34–11:1	205–207,210– 212
7:14b–16	15	12:26	118	10:34–11:5	212
11:11	62	13	13	11	163,168,195, 214,219,220– 221,242
12:30	143	13:2	118		
14:17	121	14:8	118	11:1	18,20,24,200– 201,206–207, 242–243,251– 252
23:1–7	14f	15:4	14,24,36,38		
23:5	24–25,39,53,185	15:32	13		
		15:34–36	13		
1–2 Kings	34,45,49	18:42	175	11:1ff	165
				11:1–5	163,165,168, 197–199,221, 269–270
1 Kings		*2 Kings*	73		
1:31	95	4:23	64		
2:1–4	14,24,225	8:19	14,24,36,38	11:1b	205
2:4	43,45,147,184, 236	23:30	104	11:2	20,168–169,201, 242
		24:9	36		
4–10	178	24:17	104	11:2–3a	200,212
4:20–5:1	179	25:8	36	11:2–5	168,241–243
4:25	157	25:24	37	11:2b	240
5:5	179	25:25–26	37	11:3–4	206
5:18	179	25:27–30	32,34–38,41	11:3–5	163
8:16	47	25:37–30	37	11:3b	199,202,269
8:23	15			11:3b–4	200
8:25	14,24,35,37,43, 45,93,160,184, 236	*Isaiah*	91	11:3b–5	20,221
		1–39	18	11:4	168
		1:8	62	11:4a	202,240
8:33–34	36	1:13	64	11:4b	202,207,218
8:46ff	38	2:2–4	47	11:4b–5	240
8:46–53	36,38	4:2	54	11:5	200
8:48	38	7:2	118	11:6–9	20
9:3–9	14,24	7:13	118	11:9	242
9:4–9	225	8:23–9:6	18,19	11:10	20,25,164
9:5	43,45,184,236	8:23–9:1	19	11:11–12	163
9:6	92	9:2–4	19	11:11–16	20
10:1–10	179	9:5	19	16:5	18,62
10:1–29	179	9:5–6	19,24	22:22	117
10:2	179	9:6a	20	24–27	66
10:10	179	9:6b	20	32:1–8	20–21,25,265
10:22	179	10:21	198	32:1	21
10:24–25	179	10:21–23	198	40–55	66
10:25	179	10:21–11:5	197–198	40–66	63
11	13	10:22	198	40:3–5	47
11:1–13	146	10:23–11:10	20	43:10	40
11:12–36	24,36,38	10:24–27	198		
		10:24–27a	198		

43:14–17	47	23:5–6	22,43,45,66,165,	17:1–21	25
44:8	40		186,188	17:3	26
44:28	40	23:5b	165	17:4–6	25
44:28–45:1	228,257	23:6	42,253	17:6	53
45:1	40,73	23:6a	253	17:7–10	26
45:1–2	47	23:33–40	66	17:11–13	26
49:7	48	25:9	48	17:11–21	25
55:1–5	40	27:6	48	17:15–21	26
55:3–5	38–41	30:9	17–18,27,33,41,	17:22	26
55:3a	39,41		175,265	17:22–23	26
55:3b	39,98,156,265	31:35–37	45	17:22–24	25–26,28,31,41,
55:4	39	33	20		265
55:5	39	33:14	43	17:23	26,251
55:5a	40	33:14–16	45	17:24	26
55:5b	40	33:14–26	42–45,66,129,	19:1	28
56–66	66		130,265	21:30	28
58:12	61–63	33:15	43,53–54,195,	21:30–32	25
60:1–14	164		251	21:31	143
60:17	121	33:15–16	42	28:12	49
60:21	165	33:15–17	186,188,253	29:21	55,145
66	164	33:16	42	34:1–16	27
66:18	164	33:17	43–45,160,184,	34:15	28
			212,214,236	34:17–22	26
Jeremiah	73,91	33:17–18	45	34:20–24	165
2–20	45	33:18	42–43	34:23	33
7:2	118	33:19–26	45	34:23f	18,33,41
12:6	37	33:20–22	174	34:23–24	17,27,29,31,50,
13:18	143	33:21	44		130,175,265
17:19–20	65	33:23–24	66	34:24	28–29,33,165,
17:19–23	63	33:24	48		241
17:19–26	65	33:26	45	37	20
17:19–27	63–67,265f	36:30	183–184	37:15–20	29
17:20–21	64	38–39	201	37:21–28	29
17:21	64	39–41	33	37:24f	18,33,41
17:21–22	64	40–41	32,41,66,265	37:24–25	17,27,29,31,175,
17:24–26	63	41:1	33		265
17:25	63,65–66	49:19	48	37:24–28	50
17:25–26	64–65	50:44	48	37:24b	29
17:27	63–65	52	32,41	37:24b–28	30
22:1–9	21,24	52:10–11	32	37:25	29,130,241
22:4	22	52:31–24	32	37:26	29,130
22:5	22,53–54			37:27a	29
22:11	104	*Ezekiel*	91	37:28b	29
22:24	47,49	1–37	31	38–39	66
22:24–30	21,24,32	7:27	28	40–48	30–32,41,120,
22:30	21	12:10	28		213,241,244,
23:1–4	22	12:12	28		255,264–265
23:1–6	165	16	250	40:46	150
23:5	130–131,195,	17	29	43:19	150
	217,251	17:1–4	25	44	43
		17:1–10	25	44:3	30

44:6–31	43	5:1	17–18,20,242	3:8	53–55,59–60,
44:15–16	140,150	5:1ff	24		130–131,251
44:23–24	30	5:2	18	3:8–10	56
45:7	30	5:3	17	3:10	157
45:8–9	30,163	5:4a	18	4:1–6a	60
45:16–17	30			4:2–3	60
45:22	30	*Habakkuk*		4:6b–10a	56–58,60
46:2	30	3:13	25	4:7	57
46:4	30			4:10	82
46:8	30	*Haggai*	72,91,111,120,	4:10b–14	60
46:10	30		214,266	4:14	60,99
46:12–15	30	1:1	46,51,105	6:9–14	57
46:16ff	31–32	1:3	51	6:9–15	56
46:18	30	1:8b	49,51	6:11	56,58
47:13	163	1:12	46,51	6:11–14	58
47:21–22	163	1:13a	51	6:12	53–55,58,130–
48:11	150	1:14	46,51		131,251
48:21–22	30	1:15	51	6:12–13	55,60
		2:1	51	6:12b–13a	58
Hosea	91	2:2	46,51,105	6:13	59–60
2:2	17	2:4	51	6:13b	59
3:4–5	17,24,33	2:5	49	6:14	58
3:5	18,27,33,66,175	2:6–8	49	7:1–8:23	56
		2:6–9	70	8:2–8	55
Joel	63	2:10	51	8:15	55
3–4	66	2:20	51	9–11	113
		2:20–23	45–53,58	9–14	66,113–114,
Amos		2:21–22	70		123–125
1:2	62	2:21–23	51	9:9	125
5:3	121	2:21a	51	10:2–3	125
8:5	64	2:21b–22	46–49,51	11	113
9:11	62,194–195,197,	2:21b–23	46	11:4–17	125
	212	2:22	51	11:11	113
9:11–12	61–62	2:23	46–51,148	12	43,66,105–107,
9:11–15	61–63,66–67,	2:23a	51		113
	197,266			12–14	113,123,125
9:11a	195–196,268	*Zechariah*	9,72,91,120	12:1	113
9:13–15	62	1–8	51,52–60,82,	12:1ff	120
			111,113,213,	12:2–3	116
Obadiah	63		266	12:2–13:1	67,112–126,
		1:1–6	56		266–267
Micah	91	1:7–6:15	56	12:2–13:6	113–115,123
		1:14–17	55	12:2–14:21	113
3:1–5	17	1:14b–17	56	12:2b	114,116
4–5	197	2:4–5	55	12:3	114–115
4:1–3	47	2:7	55	12:3b	114,116
4:4	157	2:10–12	55	12:4	115–116
4:13	242	2:10–17	56	12:4a	114
4:14–5:3	27	3:4–7	59	12:4aα	116
4:14–5:4a	17	3:5	55	12:4bα	114
4:14	17	3:7	55	12:4bβ	114

12:5	114,116	18:44	40	122:5	183
12:6	114–116	18:44–45	39	132	15,22–25,97–98,
12:6a	114	18:44–50	39		263
12:7	115,125	18:50	39	132:7	53
12:7–8	114,116	21:4	143	132:8–10	97
12:8	115,119,121,125	45:6	16	132:10	16,97–98
12:8–9	114	45:15	250	132:11	147
12:9	115,117	46:9–10	47	132:11–12	16
12:9f	114	48:2–9	47	132:12	16
12:10	115,125	50:1–6	47	132:13	48
12:10ff	122	72:1–4	16	132:17	16,55,130–131,
12:10aα	117	72:3	16		145
12:10aβ–14	117	72:7	16	135:4	48
12:10b–11	117	72:8	16	136	148
12:11	115	72:8–11	164	148.14	145
12:12	119–120	72:12–14	16		
12:12–14	119	72:16	16	*Job*	
12:12b–14	117	78:67–72	29	31:36	58
12:14	119	78:68–72	16		
13:1	115,117,122	78:70	47	*Proverbs*	
13:2	114–115	89	13,18,24–25,39–	16:10	21
13:2–6	115,117,123		40,49,147,214,	20:8	21
13:2a	115		266	20:26	21
13:2b–6	115	89:2–5	39,253	20:28	21
13:4	115	89:3–4	160,174	25:5	21
13:7–9	113–114	89:4	160,185	29:4	21
14	116,125,197	89:4–5	15,187	29:14	21
14:1–21	113–114	89:5	160	31:4–5	21
14:2	125	89:18	145		
14:11a	125	89:19–37	160	*Ruth*	
14:11b	125	89:19–51	48	4:17	222–223
14:12–13	125	89:20	15		
14:14	125	89:20–38	15,39,187	*Ecclesiastes*	
14:14a	116	89:21–26	15	1:13	175
14:20–21	125	89:25	39		
		89:27	164	*Lamentations*	
Malachi	66	89:27–28	15	4:20	25
3:20	130–131	89:28–37	174		
3:21	61	89:29–30	15	*Daniel*	169
3:23	27	89:30	15	2	262
		89:31–36	15	7	218,221,250
Psalms		89:35–38	253	9:3	176
1	191	89:36–37	96	9:3–19	176
2	16,24–25,47,	89:37–38	15	9:17	176
	163,191	89:38	45	9:25	208
2:1–2	195	89:39–52	15	9:26	208
2:7	16,19	105:8	96	11–12	211
2:8–9	16	106:28–31	139	12:1–3	197
2:9	47,163	110	16,47		
2:12	47	110:3	47		
15:51	25	110:5f	47		

Ezra–Nehemiah
52,70–74,76–82,
103,109,151

Ezra   78,80,90
1:1   103
1:1–3a   79,103
1:5   119
1:8   32,241
3   72
3:2   46
3:8   46
4:3   119
5:2   46
8:1   119
8:2–3   106
8:2b   85,88,124,126
8:2b–3a   85,87,107
8:16   122
9:6–15   176
10:23   122
10:33   122
10:38   122
10:39   122

Nehemiah   78
3:10   85
3:23   87
5:1–13   120
7:61   119
7:61ff   119
9:6–37   176–179
9:7–25   177
9:25   177
9:26–30   177
9:31   177
9:32   177
9:32–37   177
9:34–37   72
10:4   85
11:32   87
12:1   46
12:2   85
12:10–11   140–141
12:11   82
13:15–16   64
13:15–18   65
13:15–22   64
13:18   65
13:26   79
13:29   185

1–2 Chronicles
5,9,52,69–111,
151,227,245,
266–267

1 Chronicles
1–9   72,80–81,83–84,
      110
2:10–17   105
2:22   88
3:1–9   104
3:1–24   104
3:5   122
3:10–14   84,104–105
3:10–24   107
3:15–16   104–105
3:15–24   104
3:16   84
3:16–19   46,50
3:17ff   81
3:17–21a   86
3:17–24   81,83,85,88,
          104–109,120,
          124,126,266
3:18   32
3:19   46,66,105,266
3:19–24   87
3:20–24   87
3:21   83–85
3:21a   83–85,87
3:21b   83–84,86–87,
        105–107
3:21bff   83
3:22   22,83,85,87
3:22–24   86–87
3:22b   83
3:24   87–88,105
5:27–29   140
6:26   122
6:34–38   140
9:2–32   103
9:2–34   107
10–2 Chr 34   74
10–2 Chr 36   74
11:3   224
16:15   96
17:10–15   224
17:10b–14   88–89
17:12   89,96
17:13   94
17:14   89,94,96

17:17   96
17:22   96
17:24   96,118
17:27   96
22:6–16   90
22:8–10   89
22:10   89,96,225
22:13   90
28:1–10   90
28:4   47,96
28:5   48
28:5–6   90
28:6   48
28:7   90,92,94,96,147
28:7–9   92
28:9   147
28:10   48
28:20   94
29:7   82

2 Chronicles
      73
6:15   93
6:16   90,92–93
6:41   98
6:41–42   97–98
6:42   97–98
7:17–18   92
7:19   92
8:3f   82
10:15   94
10:29   93
11:17   94
13:4–12   99
13:5   99–100,102
13:8a   99
16:9   82
17:17–18   90
21:7   94,100,102,118
23:3   100,102
30:6–9   100
32:16   48
35   78
35:25   103
36:10   104
36:12   103
36:21   103
36:22   103
36:22–23   79,103,111,257
36:23   228

SEPTUAGINT

1–4 Kingdoms
129

2 Kingdoms
7:12–16   129

1 Paralipomenon
6:18–32   137

NEW TESTAMENT

Matthew
1:1–17   4
2   190
9:27   4
15:22   4
21:5   125
21:9   4
21:15   4

Mark
10:47–48 4

Luke
1:32   4
1:32–33   233
2:4   4
3:23–38   4

John
12:15   125
19:12–15 190
19:37   125

Acts
13:22–23 4

Romans
1:3–4   4

1 Peter
1:19   250

Revelation 251
5   250
5:5   4
12–14   251
22:16   4

APOCRYPHA/
PSEUDEPIGRAPHA

Additions to Esther
14:1–19   176

Baruch
2:6–3:8   176

1 Esdras   74,78,80
1   109,151
3–7   52
5:5   50
8:29   85

4Ezra/2 Esdras
              3,9,127,216–
              222,228,263,270
7:1–5   137
7:5   137
7:26ff   217
7:28–29   219
7:29   220
7:45–74   220
11–12   218–219,221
11:1–12:3   216
11:37   216
11:40–43   216
11:44   217
11:45–46   216
12   218–219,269
12:1–3   216
12:4–9   216
12:10–34   216
12:31   218
12:32   216–221,269
12:32–34   217
12:34   217
13   218,269
13:5   218
13:8   218
13:14–20   218
13:21–53   218
13:26a   219
13:37–40a   219

Judith
9   176

1 Maccabees
              9,127,153–159,
              166,176
2:49–68   156
2:51   156
2:51–60   156
2:54   154,185
2:57   152–159,172,
              173,267
2:61   156
2:64   156
4:30   157
5:55–62   153
5:61–62   153
6:15   49
6:24   152
13:36–14:15   155
14:4–15   157
14:41   153,157
14:41–49   153
14:47   153

2 Maccabees
              176

3 Maccabees
2:1–20   176
6:1–15   176

Prayer of Azariah
              176

Sirach   5,9,127,228,267
Prol 14   134
30:26a   136
36:1–17   151,176
44:1–50:24   132
44:14–45:26   135
44:17–45:26   142
45:6–22   141
45:7   145
45:12   143
45:22   136
45:23–26   139
45:23a   140
45:23b   140
45:24   139,145
45:24c   138
45:24d   138
45:25   132–144,149,
               215,267

45:25a–b	133,136
45:25a–d	139
45:25c	133,136–137
45:25c–d	133
45:25d	137–138
45:25e–26d	139–140
45:26b	139
45:26d	140
46:1–49:13	142
47	132
47:1–11	142
47:1–22	144
47:5	145
47:7	145
47:8–10	109,151,245
47:11	132,140,144, 180,185,267
47:12–18	146
47:12–22	142
47:13	145
47:19–21	146
47:22	132,144–146, 149,180,267
47:23	146–147
48:17–25	142
49:4–5	144–147,267
49:4a	136
49:5	145,254
49:11	149
49:11–12	52,148
50:1–4	142
50:1–24	142,168
50:22–24	140
50:24	140
51:12	132
51:12(8)	148–150,267
51:12(9)	148–150,267

2 Apocalypse of Baruch
29–30	197
36–40	205

Assumption of Moses
9:4	156

1 Enoch 127
10:10	96
10:14–11:2	197
83–90	169
85–90	211
90:13–19	211

90:28–39	197
90:37	255

2 Enoch 220

Jubilees 181
31:11–20	249

Psalms of Solomon
	6,9,127,159–169,191
2	161
4	161
8	161
17	5–6,159–170, 210,214–216, 221,246,263, 267,270
17:1–3	160
17:4	160,174
17:4–20	160
17:4b	253
17:5–6	161
17:5–7	165
17:5–17	169
17:5–20	169
17:7–10	161
17:11–15	161
17:16	168
17:16–18a	161
17:18–20	169
17:18b–20	161
17:21	162
17:21–43	160
17:22–24	163
17:22–25	162
17:24	163
17:24–25	250
17:24b	168
17:25	163
17:25–44	160
17:26–27	168
17:26–28	163
17:26–42	163
17:27a	163
17:28b	163
17:29	164,168
17:29–32	164
17:30–31	163
17:30a	164
17:30b	164

17:31	164
17:32	164
17:32–43	164
17:32a	164
17:33	162
17:33–34a	164
17:34b	163,165
17:35	162,168
17:35b	165
17:36	168,250
17:36a	165
17:36b	162
17:37	164,168
17:37a	165
17:37b	164–165
17:38	164
17:38b	165
17:39	164
17:40a	165
17:40b	165
17:40d	165
17:41a	165
17:41b–c	165
17:42	168
17:43	162,168
17:43c	165
17:44	160
17:44–46	160
17:45–46	160
18	170

Sibylline Oracles
3	255–258,264
3:191–194	257
3:193	257
3:286–287	256–257
3:318	257
3:608	257
3:635–651	256
3:652–656	256–257

Testaments of the Twelve Patriarchs 9,246–255

Testament of Benjamin
9:1–3	254

Testament of Dan
5:4	249
5:10	249
5:10f	254

Testament of Gad
8:1   249

Testament of Issachar
5:7–8   248

Testament of Joseph
19:8   250
19:8–12   249–250
19:11   250–251
19:12   251,254

Testament of Judah
             246
1:6   252
12:6   252
15:1–3   252
17:5–6   249,252
21:1–2   252
21:1–22:3   249,252–253
21:6–22:1   252
22:2–3   252–255
22:2a   254
22:2b   253–254
22:2b–3   253
22:3a   254
22:3b   253–254
23:5–24:6   254
24:1–4   252
24:1–6   249,251–252
24:4   251
24:4–6   251–252,254–
             255
24:5   251
24:5–6   252
24:6   251–252

Testament of Levi   242
2:11   249
8:14   249
18   242
18:3   242
18:7   242,253

Testament of Naphali
4:4–5   254
5:1–7   249
8:2   248–249

Testament of Reuben
6:11–12   249

Testament of Simeon
6:3   189
7:1–2   249

Testament of Zebulon
9:8   254

QUMRAN LITERATURE

CD   195,234,237–
             239,243,245
5:5   244
5:19   196
6:7   195
7:16–18   195
7:18   195,239
7:19–20   239
7:20   201,239
12:23–13:1   201,237–238
13:1   185
14:19   237–238
19:10–11   237–238
19:21–20:1   237–238
20:1   201

1QapGen   181

1QH   240

1QM   185,204,209–
             211,239–240,
             243,245,269
1   211
1:3   198,211
1:5   184
1:6   190
2–9   211,240
4:1   185
4:2   185
5:1   244
5:1–2   210,239
5:3   185
5:10   190
6:8   185
7:8ff   209
10:2   209
10:4   196
10:7–8   196
11:1–3   196,244
11:3   196
11:7ff   196

11:16   201f
12:4   185
12:9–15   204
13:2–17   203
14:4ff   204
15–19   204,211
15:2   190,207
15:4ff   209
16:8   209
16:11ff   209
17:7–8   184
17:8   184,187
18:2–3   190
18:5–6   209
18:7–19:8   204
19:11–13   209
19:13   209

1QpHab   182,240

1QS   202,238–240,
             243
2:21   185
9:9b–11   238

1QSa   238–239,243
1:2   202
2:1–17   213
2:11b–22   238
2:17–21   213

1QSb   204,213,239–
             240,242–244
3:7   185
5:20–21   240
5:20–29   208,240–242
5:21–22   240
5:22   250
5:23   240
5:24–26   240

4Q171   208

4QDibHam^a
             171–180,212,
             268
Frgs. 1/2:
recto 7:4   172
4:2–10   178
4:2–5:18   177–178
4:4–5   175,178

4:4–14	177	4:1	188	*4QpsDan^d*	232–233	
4:5–8	173	4:1–3	188			
4:6–7	174,178	4:3	181	*4QSerek HaMilhamah*		
4:6–8	172–180	4:5	181		171,173,190,	
4:7–8	172	5:1	186		195,198–199,	
4:8	175	5:1–7	180–191,217		203–212,233,	
4:8–10	178	5:3	184,187		243,245,269–	
4:8–12	179	5:3–4	208		270	
4:8–13	178	5:4	187	1	204–205,209	
4:10	175	5:5	187	2/7	203	
4:12–13	179	5:6	187	3	203	
4:14	178			4/6	203,206,210	
4:15–21	178	*4QpGen^b*	180,181	4:2–6	206	
5:1–6	178	1:3	181	4:6	207	
5:6–8	178	1:4–5	180	4:10	207	
5:6–14	178			5	203–212	
5:10–11	178	*4QpGen^c*	180	5:1–6	203–212	
5:15–18	178	1:3–4	180	5:1	205	
Frag.3		15:2	181	5:2	205	
2:5	172			5:3	201,205–208	
		4QpIsa^a	171,173,195,	5:4	206–209,243	
4QFlor	171,173,182,		197–207,212–	5:5	209	
	201,206,212,		213,233,242–	5:6	209	
	233,268,270		243,250,270	6:1–2	206	
1–3	192	1:3	198	6:2	207	
1:1–6	192–193	2–4:4	198	8	203	
1:1–11	187	5–6:2–3	198	10	203	
1:7–9	192–193	5–6:3	201,206,243			
1:10–13	191–197,202	5–6:5–13	201	*4QTest*	245	
1:11	194–195,209	5–6:10	199			
1:11–12	195	8–10	204,209	*4QTLevi^a*	248	
1:12	193–195	8–10:1–9	199,201	1:14	242	
1:13	196	8–10:2–9	199			
1:14–17	193	8–10:3	202,205,209	*11QBer*	204	
1:15	205	8–10:8	206			
1:18ff	195	8–10:11–16	199	*11QMelch*	182,208,220	
1:18–19	196	8–10:11–24	197–203,243,			
1:18–2:4	193		269	*11QPs^a*	171,245	
6–7	195	8–10:17	201,206	27:2–11	109,151,171,245	
		8–10:17–21	199			
4QM^c	240	8–10:18	201	*11QTemple*	232,234–237,	
		8–10:19	201		244,264,271	
4QMMT	167,244–245	8–10:20	201	15:15–16	141	
		8–10:21	202,206	56:12–59:21	234	
4QpGen^a	171,173,180–	8–10:21–22	199	56:13–14	235	
	191,201,206–	8–10:21–23	202	56:13–18	236	
	207,212,233,	8–10:23–24	199	56:13–21	236	
	268,270	8–10:24	202,209	56:14f	236	
2:4	181			56:14–15	235	
2:5–6	180	*4QpIsa^c*	182	56:15	236	
3:2	182			56:18–20	235	

56:20–21   235
57:4   185
58:4   185

JOSEPHUS

The Antiquities
            222–229,270
1.14   227
2.6   190
5.336   222
5.337   222
6.165   223
7.53   224
7.93–95   224
7.337   225
7.373   224
7.384–385   225
8.113   225
8.126–127   225
9.145   226
10.142   223
10.151   223
11.112   223
14.9   189
14.41   166
14.403–405 189
15.267   191
15.281   191
15.371   189
15.373–374 189
17.41–43   190
17.150   191
17.191   191
17.271–272 258
17.273–274 258
17.276   263
17.278   262
17.278–281 259
17.285   259
17.304–310 191
17.312–314 191

The Jewish War
            228
2.433   259
2.434   259
3.351–351   228
3.400–402   228
4.507–508   260
4.510   260

6.312–313   228,262
6.313   262
7.29   260
7.153–155   260

RABBINIC LITERATURE

Eighteen Benedictions
            6–7,150
Ben 14   7
Ben 15   7

Mishnah   4–5
Taanith 2:4–5
            176

Babylonian Talmud
            4

Mekilta
Ex 17:16   189

Targums   4,116,181
Deut 28:57 185

Fragmentary Targum
            186
Gen 49:1   183
Num 24:20   189

Targum Neophiti
            186

Targum Onqelos
            186

Targum Ps. Jonathan
            186
Gen 49:1   182f
Gen 49:10   162,210

EARLY CHRISTIAN
LITERATURE

Barn. 12:9 189

Hippolytus, Ref. omn.
haer. 9:30   4

Just. Dial. 49:7f
            189